Dr Richard Shannon, who was born in the Fiji Islands, was formerly Senior Lecturer at the University of Auckland, New Zealand and Reader in History at the University of East Anglia. He is currently Professor of Modern History at the University College of Swansea. Besides articles for historical journals and reviews, he is the author of *Gladstone and the Bulgarian Agitation 1876*.

RICHARD SHANNON

The Crisis of Imperialism 1865–1915

Granada Publishing

Paladin Books
Granada Publishing Ltd
8 Grafton Street, London W1X 3LA

Published by Paladin Books 1976
Reprinted 1979, 1984

First published in Great Britain by
Hart-Davis, MacGibbon Ltd 1974

Copyright © Richard Shannon 1974

ISBN 0-586-08249-2

Printed and bound in Great Britain by
Hazell Watson & Viney Limited,
Aylesbury, Bucks

Set in Monotype Ehrhardt

THE PALADIN HISTORY OF ENGLAND

General Editor : Robert Blake

Other titles in this series will be:

In Memoriam
Isabella Shannon
Née Sutherland
1874–1967

Grateful acknowledgements are due to the help of Lord Blake and Dr Cameron Hazlehurst in bringing this book into being. Mr Robert Woodings has performed editorial duties of an exemplary nature. I owe much to the comments and conversation of Professor Malcolm Bradbury, Mr Peter Conradi, Mr Jonathan Cook, Mr Anthony Dyson, Mr Simon Edwards, Dr G. S. R. Kitson Clark, Mr Timothy McFarland, Professor Sheldon Rothblatt, Dr Michael Sanderson, Dr Barry Smith and Professor Ian Watt.

FOREWORD

by Robert Blake

History does not consist of a body of received opinion handed down by authority from the historiographical equivalent of the heights of Mount Sinai. It is a subject full of vigour, controversy, life – and sometimes strife. One of the purposes of the Paladin History of England is to convey not only what the authors believe to have happened but also why; to discuss evidence as well as facts; to give an idea and an evaluation of the controversies which surround so many episodes and interpretations of the past.

The last twenty years have seen important changes in the approach to history and to historical questions. There has also been much painstaking research which throws new light on old problems and brings new problems into the field of discussion. Little of all this has so far got through to the general reader because it has been, naturally, confined to specialist journals and monographs. A real need exists for a series of volumes to inform the wide public interested in the history of England, and this is what the Paladin volumes are intended to meet.

All history is in one sense contemporary history. These volumes inevitably and rightly reflect to some extent the outlook of those who, whatever their own age, are writing in the 1970s. But there are in any decade a wide variety of attitudes and schools of thought. The authors of this series are not chosen to represent a particular body of doctrine; conservative, liberal, Marxist – or whatever. They are scholars who are deeply involved in the historical questions of their particular fields, and who believe that it is possible to put across something of the challenges, puzzles and excitements of their theme to a large audience in a form which is readable, intelligible and concise.

All historical writing must in some measure be arbitrary as to dates and selective as to area. The dates chosen in this series do not depart far from convention but perhaps just enough to encourage both author and reader to take a fresh view. The decision to make this a history of England, rather than Britain, is quite deliberate. It does not mean omission of the important repercussions of events in Scotland, Ireland, Wales or the countries which later constituted the Empire and the Commonwealth; rather a recognition that, whether for good or ill, the English have been the dominant nation in what Tennyson called 'our rough island-story', and that a widening of the scope would lead to diffuseness and confusion.

Historical writing also has to be selective as to themes. Each author uses his own judgement here, but, although politics, ideas, art and literature must always be central features in any work of general history, economic background, social structure, demography, scientific and technical developments are no less important and must be given proper weight.

All sorts of reasons can be given for reading history, but the best of them has always seemed to me sheer pleasure. It is my hope as editor of this series that this enjoyment will be communicated to a large number of people who might otherwise perhaps have never experienced it.

CONTENTS

CONTENTS

INTRODUCTION

The years between the 1860s and the First World War transformed Britain more swiftly and more profoundly than any other comparable era. British society became urbanized and suburbanized, secularized, democratized; general assumptions about social relationships and politically legitimate behaviour shifted from the basis of vertical hierarchic community groupings to stratified classes: in a word, it became 'modern'.

A person born in the eighteenth century and formed within its characteristic attitudes would have found the Britain of 1865 still a society whose structures and institutions were tolerably familiar and understandable. He would have observed a political system founded on the strength of an agricultural ruling class. Industrialism would have meant to him only more of what he already knew about. The great revolution in transportation, especially the railways, certainly would have astonished him. But otherwise familiarities predominated over novelties. The London of Dickens and Thackeray, of the 1840s to the 1860s, was not radically changed from the London of the Regent. The great traditional establishments were still intact and generally popular: Court, Lords, Commons, Church. Adjustments had been made. Protestant Dissenters and Roman Catholics no longer laboured under severe civil disabilities. Agricultural protection – the notorious 'Corn Law' of 1815 – had been repealed in 1846. Adjustments in the parliamentary representation had been made by the famous Reform Act of 1832. Municipal government, state policy towards public health and pauperism, and many other aspects of public life had been altered or reformed. Constitutional shifts were perhaps significant, but it was rather too early to be sure. A monarch had failed to install the minister he desired in 1834, and his successor had been obliged to accept a minister (the same man) she did not desire in 1841. But on the other hand the monarchy had been the vital factor in the formation of the coalition of 1853. In any case all these things had been done within the framework of debate appropriate to the early and middle nineteenth century, which was not deliberately attempting – a point too often overlooked – to transform itself into the later nineteenth century.

Conversely, a person born in the middle of the twentieth century would have found the Britain of 1915 equipped with the features and institutions which he would regard as characteristic of 'normal' modern society. The formative styles of life and modes of consciousness reflected a culture of great cities, of commerce and industry, of 'mass'. The new signs and symbols, the multiple shops, the cinemas, the motor vehicles, electrical power, proclaimed the triumph of the second industrial revolution, the flowering of tertiary industries, services, mass-production techniques, orientations to a consumer society. He would find himself at home in the prevalent styles of politics on the eve of the era of Lloyd George.

Compared with the speed of this process the transformation known as the first industrial revolution developed at a very much slower rate. The alteration of the character and substance of the major institutions was immensely more radical than in either the religious revolution of the sixteenth century or the political revolution of the seventeenth century. The developments of the pre-nuclear, pre-automated twentieth century have been essentially a working-out, a fulfilment of the themes which first began to assert themselves significantly in the 1870s, 80s and 90s. There has been no alteration of crucial importance in the system of politics then established, culminating in 1918 with universal adult male suffrage (with a large element of female suffrage), one man one vote, and equal electoral districts. The class structure, characterized by working-class consciousness on the one hand and a symbiotic relationship of new middle class and old aristocracy on the other, is still substantially intact. The characteristic 'Englishness' of English culture was made then very much what it is now. The quip that all the oldest English traditions were invented in the last quarter of the nineteenth century has great point.

The technology of the late nineteenth century and early twentieth century which refined and sophisticated the crude steam power of early industrialism is still at the basis of high twentieth-century Britain. Even chronic economic problems have their origin there: Britain by 1914 was a net importer of the products of the second industrial revolution. The pressures compromising British independence and freedom of action as a great power in the world were clearly in evidence before the turn of the century. The end of 'splendid isolation' was the beginning of the process which led to Britain's sheltering under the umbrella of NATO.

The problems of 'culture' and 'civilization' assumed their places in the modern intellectual debate of the 1870s and 80s. George Gissing and Henry James in their different ways both had at the centre of their concerns the function of the alienated artist in a mass industrial society fed by the 'best-seller' industry. The Whistler *versus* Ruskin trial of 1878 opened up the issues of aestheticism, announcing the invasion of 'French principles' in culture as subversive as the earlier challenge of 'French principles' in politics.

Contemporaries sensed the speed of the process. Some were exhilarated. The later nineteenth century was the greatest age of utopias. Sophisticated technology made possible the idea of scientific predictability. The steadily rising standard of living of the mass of the people, the sheer improvement in material conditions, seemed to many to be the best evidence for the reality of progress, one of the classical Victorian claims. Many were anxious. The central preoccupations of Matthew Arnold or John Stuart Mill or William Morris or Henry James, however much they may have quarrelled among themselves, however much they might have been off the track in particular diagnoses, are still central. Kipling, so often miscast as a hearty optimist, well represented the anxiety about the present and the future which was at the heart of imperialism. C. F. G. Masterman's sombre exposition of the 'reality' of British life in 1909, *The Condition of England*, is in essence a version of Arnold's *Culture and Anarchy* of 1869 transformed in the light of the immense social revolution in the years between. By the beginning of the twentieth century the High Victorian synthesis of nature, art, society and morality had irretrievably broken down. In *Locksley Hall Sixty Years After*, in 1886, Tennyson uttered a cry of pain at the agony of the Victorian disintegration. The elements of the coming pattern of external conflict were already shaping themselves. Bismarck, taken in old age to Hamburg to see the great modern city, murmured, 'It is a new age, a new world.' The aged Gladstone, taken to Kiel to see the new German navy, muttered, 'This means war.'

The elements of the physical and material basis of this transformation are as easy to state as they are difficult to interpret. Growth of population is the obvious starting point. The population of England and Wales was just over 20 million in 1861, and by 1911 had increased to just over 36 million. Scotland in the same period increased from 3 million to somewhat under 5 million, and Ireland continued the decline set off by the catastrophe of 1846 by dropping from just under 6 million to somewhat over 4 million. In the larger perspective, a population which had doubled itself between 1801 and 1851 doubled itself again between 1851 and 1911. Rates of increase or decrease – an equation of birth rates, death rates, and migration rates – reveal that the English and Welsh population increased almost as fast in the decade 1871–81, as it had in 1831–41, and tailed off to its slowest rate of increase in the decade 1901–11. The Scottish pattern was the same, except that the rate of decrease was faster. In Ireland, the decade 1881–91 showed the fastest rate of decrease since the decade of the great famine; but by 1901–11 the rate was easing off to the point of equilibrium.

Movements of population are just as significant as the gross figures. Emigration was an important factor throughout the nineteenth century. Between 1861 and 1901, over 4 million English and Welsh emigrated, 795,000 Scots and more than 2,600,000 Irish. But internal migration was an even more important factor. Between 1841 and 1901, 3 million people migrated to cities and more than half a million to colliery districts. Rural areas lost more than 4 million. In 1851, agriculture employed one quarter of all males aged twenty and over; by 1901 less than 10 per cent. Agricultural wage rates never averaged more than 55 per cent of industrial wage rates between 1867 and 1914. In 1851, 50 per cent of the population of England and Wales lived in urban areas. The census of 1861 revealed for the first time an excess of urban as against rural population. By 1901, the figure for urban dwellers was 75 per cent, and by 1911 it was just under 80 per cent. This was the human material which formed the half dozen great conurbations of modern Britain – Greater Manchester, Merseyside, Clydeside, Tyneside, West Yorkshire, West Midlands and Greater London; and of these London was the monster, Megalopolis. Central London, nearly 3 million in 1861, was over 4½ million by 1911. But Greater London was the scene of the really spectacular growth. The distinction between Central and Greater London in 1861 was hardly apparent, a mere 400,000 or so. Greater London had a population of nearly 3·3 million in 1861 and 6·6 million by 1901. By 1911 Megalopolis was well beyond the 7 million mark. The decade of peak rate of increase was 1891–1901. This was the measure of suburbia.

The material occupation of this expanding and urbanizing population resulted in a growth of gross national production which expanded noticeably faster (in Great Britain). Calculations taking a constant price rate into account give a figure of £565 million in 1861, increasing to £1,948 million by 1901. But the figures per head tell the real story: £24·4 in 1861 becomes £52·5 in 1901, giving some indication of the dimensions of the new capacity for mass consumption of goods and services.[1]

These were the blind forces at work, unconscious and un-directed. Conscious or directed aspects of the social system – broadly, 'politics' – did not relate to these blind forces in a neat one-to-one ratio. Very often indeed the relationship was at best tangential. Very few people, if canvassed in 1865, would positively have chosen the end result in the early 1900s as the best of all possible worlds. Indeed, so far as conscious effort and desire is concerned, it would be justifiable to assert that quite the con-trary was the case. The literary aspect of the national culture, especially the various modes of 'modernism', lamented the loss of the moral order of nature and rejected the world of great cities and industry. The picture as a whole is not that of a society moving surely and confidently in self-possession of its destiny. Rather, it is the story of a society at odds with itself, the blind forces working very often at cross-purposes with the conscious wishes and efforts of those who felt it their task to define the ends, the purposes, to which the 'movement' would best be directed.

These conscious or political aspects expressed themselves within two major themes. There was a domestic theme in which the central ambition was to adapt changing society to the imperatives of public policy but in which, in hard fact, the central necessity was to adapt public policy to the demands of changing society, to cope with it by equipping it with institutions, services, structures of administration, necessary to enable it to function adequately as a society. And here 'adequately' meant a modest and negative achievement: avoiding such a breakdown or dislocation as would discredit the otherwise largely unchallenged ascendancy of the ruling class.

Secondly, there was the external theme of Britain as a power in the world. Again, ambition and necessity were at cross purposes. British interests required a world at peace, in which her great and vulnerable economic and commercial network around the globe based on free trade could be as secure as it was beneficent and profitable. The necessities of the case were of much the same kind as in the domestic sphere, but of a more dangerous and compromising degree. There was a third theme, which kept intruding, neither domestic nor entirely external, but something awkwardly in between: the seemingly insoluble problem of Ireland.

During the fifty years before the outbreak of the First World War in 1914, the forces of conscious purpose and design in Britain struggled to avert the threats of the blind, largely uncontrollable internal forces and of the dangerously uncontrolled external forces. Their failure or success measured the capacity of Britain as a society and a power in the twentieth-century world.

PART I

The Years of Readjustment: The Search for a New Victorian Equilibrium
1865—74

Chapter One

POST-PALMERSTON

I

In 1865 died both Lord Palmerston and Richard Cobden, the two greatest political men of their time. Their deaths had a symbolic quality which contemporaries recognized. Palmerston had lived long (he was born in 1784) and had become identified with the established forces of society, the ruling class of the Regency still exercising its authority, still confident in its capacities. The Whig Reform Act of 1832 had consolidated it, as Palmerston insisted it would; the repeal of the Corn Laws had extricated it in time from an unnecessary identification with narrow class interest; it had lived down the scandals of the Crimea and had presided for over a decade over an economic boom which added buoyancy to the *status quo*. Cobden, conversely, had died before his time, retired to Sussex as 'one of the agricultural interest', aware that the great Radical hopes that had been pinned on him had not been fulfilled; aware, indeed, that the more visionary quality of his Radicalism compared with his partner Bright's made it likely that he never would live to see their fulfilment. The immediate future lay with what was to emerge in the dealings between the ruling-class heirs of Palmerston and the slowly gathering, rather disparate and not always mutually amenable popular forces which looked to John Bright for leadership.

Palmerston's death did not release an irresistible Radical flood, contrary to what some hoped and others feared. There was, certainly, a considerable amount of aspiration and indignation outside the established order of political society, mainly from the leaders of the more skilled and confident sectors of the urban working classes. The religious Dissenters, or Nonconformists as they were now generally called, identified their grievances against the Established Church with much of the secular griev- ance being expressed against the established political order. And there were many people watching for opportunities created by a new situation, particularly two of the most prominent and 'coming' among the ruling-class heirs of Palmerston – Disraeli and Gladstone. The Radical movement was quite certainly resistible; the question was whether resistance was necessary or expedient.

To the extent that Palmerston performed a unique political function, his departure inevitably meant that adjustments, re- alignments, disturbances, would ensue. Palmerston had been prime minister virtually for a decade not because he embodied any major idea or interest: the secret of his success had been in fact that he had concentrated on the relatively easy and rewarding external sphere while leaving Russell and Peel to discredit them- selves in the difficult and ungrateful domestic scene. Then, with the Crimean War as his vehicle, he had stepped in and enjoyed the fruits of their labours. He was never a dominant force, and his parliamentary majority was always fragile. He succeeded in being tolerated because he divided politics least. A Canningite Tory in origin, he was a Whig by convenience and a Liberal by cour- tesy. Many Conservatives had been much more enthusiastic for his policies, or lack of them, than many Liberals and Radicals on the benches behind him. Many Radicals who disliked him for his domestic inertia and for his hostility to Lincoln and the Northern cause in the American Civil War were obliged to love him for the enemies he had made in Europe, Metternich and the Czar, all oppressors of freedom and freedom-loving peoples.

Palmerston acted as checkmate. His position on the political board was such that so long as he remained a force no other forces were either strong enough or sufficiently motivated to free the board for manoeuvres. The existing parliament truly represented the narrow constituency of 1832 in which one out of five or six adult males possessed the franchise. Although it had often talked in favour of reform of the franchise, it had no strong desire to do anything about the question, particularly as there had been no impressive demand from the country, at least until 1864. But in any case it wanted politics to be based firmly and unequivocally on property, and especially landed property. It was essential for this purpose that Liberalism be contained. For the political traditionalists of the earlier nineteenth century were well aware of the identity of their most dangerous enemies. These were not the working classes. Shrewd traditionalists knew quite well that had manhood suffrage been conceded in 1832 the results would hardly have differed from the £10 household franchise. The important question was always not who had votes, but how these votes were cast; under what influences and pressures. Liberalism was dangerous because it sought to remove all illegitimate pressures and influences over men which compromised their freedom to act disinterestedly as individuals; and Liberals regarded these traditional pressures and influences of landed magnates over the lesser people in their vicinity as highly illegitimate. If the Liberals could convince the unenfranchised masses that they were offering them 'freedom', that would indeed be a very dangerous proposition. Palmerston's death had the effect of opening up a debate between Liberals and traditionalists in which they asserted rival and conflicting views on the strength of their confidence that the masses agreed with their particular opinion about the moral and legitimate use of the franchise.

From the Palmerstonian point of view, granting that in any case the working classes as a whole had shown no impressively unified desire for the franchise, the way to prevent the debate opening up was to preserve a permanent parliamentary majority firmly against admitting the issue in any practical or serious form. One obvious way was a majority of Conservatives in the manner of 1841. Another way was a combined Whig and Tory gentry front (this was in fact often canvassed in 1866 and 1867). The Conservative solution was out of the question, for the party had never managed to recover from the catastrophe of 1846 and remained restricted to an amost purely agricultural basis in the counties. The other solution was perfectly feasible but undesirable because, like the Corn Laws themselves, it would have the effect of making the political system appear too openly the agency of an obvious and narrow 'interest'. In fact it was unnecessary because Palmerston enabled the parliament of the 1832 franchise to talk liberally without actually putting their opinions to the test.

This situation on the political board is the key to all the complicated manoeuvrings of 1866 and 1867. The keenness of the Liberals and the reluctance of the traditionalists to enter into debate in 1866 had little to do with a traditionalist sense of inferiority in terms of the merits of their case. It was because they were quite content with the *status quo*, and wanted to avoid unnecessary risks. As for merits, in the long run the traditionalists were no more in the wrong than the Liberals, and indeed in the end did rather better out of the business in ways quite unforeseen by either party in the 1860s.

That the issue of reform would come inevitably once Palmerston's death opened up the board was made quite clear in 1864 when Gladstone, acknowledged as the coming leader of the Liberal forces, threw in his lot with the leaders of the hitherto not very convincing reform agitation, Bright and the president of the Reform League, Edmond Beales and, on the intellectual wing, John Stuart Mill. Had Gladstone remained aloof, Bright and Mill would have been left stranded. With the added mobilization of the Nonconformists and the trade unions in support, Gladstone was becoming the centre of a very formidable collection of forces. The Whigs, correspondingly uneasy, began to worry how, with Palmerston gone, and Russell, his titular successor, old and feeble, and in any case obsessed with the idea of a new Reform Bill, they could hold the brakes of the Liberal wagon against this tractive impetus. The Whigs had more or less to stay in to act this part. This left the Conservatives under Derby and Disraeli, leaders of a minority party no longer able to shelter behind Palmerston, exposed and presented with the task of meeting the Liberal challenge.

The traditionalists had on their side the integral strength of the existing system, which was very impressive. Hippolyte Taine, a penetratingly intelligent French observer of the English scene in the 1860s, testified to the sinewy quality of English institutions; and his most abiding impression was of the animal, almost brutal, vigour of the English governing order. He could well understand the remark made to him by 'one of the greatest industrialists in England, a radical and a supporter of Mr Bright': 'It is not our aim to overthrow the aristocracy: we are ready to leave the government and high offices in their hands. For we believe, we men of the middle class, that the conduct of national business calls for special men, men born and bred to the work for generations, and who enjoy an independent and commanding situation.' Property, especially landed property, was indeed the backbone of the system, as an analysis very clearly demonstrates.

Membership of the House of Commons undoubtedly is the most revealing paradigm of the ruling class. In his contribution to the *Essays on Reform* of 1867, part of the propaganda of the 'advanced party' for a 'more national Parliament', the barrister Bernard Cracroft offered an analysis of M.P.s designed to expose the overwhelming over-representation of the 'territorial class' at the expense of others. He pointed out that it was quite misleading to assume that if the eleven million borough population had 396 M.P.s as against the 256 M.P.s for the eighteen million county population, that therefore 'population' was at an electoral advantage as against 'land'. He estimated that to the 256 country members whose representation of 'land', apart from three or four cases in industrialized counties, was unquestionable, must be added at least 246 of the 396 borough M.P.s as belonging to the 'territorial interest' as peers, or relatives of peers, or landowners or 'under landowners' influence', giving about 500 M.P.s as the 'territorialists' in a House of 658 members. This division, not 'Conservatives' versus 'Liberals', or 'Free Traders' versus 'Protectionists', was the real division of the House of Commons. Mercantile, manufacturing and shipping interests, including colliery owners, had between them only 122 members, four or five of them sitting for counties. There were 78 bankers and bank directors, but many of these were landowners or connected with peers or landowners.

Social cohesion was equally striking. Thirty-two per cent of the House had been at Eton, Harrow, Rugby, Westminster, Winchester or Shrewsbury – 'men who, in spite of even superficial political difference of opinions, belong, so to speak, to one vast cousinhood'. The cousinhood of the House included thirty-seven peers or elder sons of peers, sixty-four younger sons of peers, fifteen grandsons of peers, seventy-one baronets, eleven sons of baronets, nineteen younger sons of baronets and eight grandsons of baronets. Hereditary interrelationships were at the heart of the cousinhood. Seventy-nine M.P.s represented a relationship between a peer and another peer, fifty-three a peer and baronet relationship, twenty-three a baronet and baronet relationship. Cracroft cites one ex-governor of the Bank of England as saying that he was related to thirty other M.P.s all sitting at the time.

The writers of the *Essays on Reform* were in no doubt as to the 'efficient secret' (to use Bagehot's phrase) of the territorial grip on the House of Commons. From their (at present, at least) unassailable base in the agricultural counties, their bridgehead of aggression into politics was the vulnerable small county town constituencies. 'Whoever wishes well to the moral and social progress of the country,' wrote the Scottish journalist and barrister J. B. Kinnear in his essay on 'Redistribution of Seats', 'must earnestly urge the entire abrogation of the system of small constituencies. It is not that individuals in such constituencies are worse than their neighbours, but that they are placed in circumstances more trying to their intelligence and virtue.' Even were such constituencies not under 'external influence', they would still be undesirable because they are community constituencies, where communal, or internal, influences are strong enough also to compromise individuality. 'It is more concerned with its own circle than with the great men of the nation; more interested in some point of local improvements or taxation than with the affairs of the commonwealth.'

Further, Liberals had no difficulty in demonstrating on the basis of an assumption that one individual's vote should more or less be equal to another individual's vote that such constituencies, doomed one way or another to corruption, occupied a disproportionally large part of the political terrain. The 6,000 inhabitants of Bodmin had two members, just as had the 600,000 inhabitants of Tower Hamlets. 400,000 persons in Liverpool had the same representation as 4,000 persons in Thetford. Eleven boroughs with a total population of 44,000 had seventeen members: Wells,

Totnes, Thetford, Northallerton, Marlborough, Lyme Regis, Honiton, Evesham, Falmouth, Ashburton, Arundel. These boroughs exhibited, to Liberal eyes, the degradation of 'belonging' to various aristocratic and clerical patrons. Cracroft compared these degraded constituencies with Birmingham, Finsbury, Lambeth, Leeds, Liverpool, Manchester, Marylebone, Tower Hamlets and Westminster, with a population of 3,300,000, and only eighteen Members of Parliament.

The social character of the House of Commons of 1865 thus corresponded precisely to the ascendancy of the traditional ruling class. The classes enfranchised in 1832 had made no serious inroads into positions of place, power or influence. Cobden in 1859 confessed his astonishment that the 'people at large' were so 'tacit in their submission to the perpetuation of the feudal system in this country'. Mill's sarcasm of 1839 was as true as ever: 'At the head of the Privileged, or in other words, the satisfied classes, must be placed the landed interest. They have the strongest reason possible for being satisfied with the government; they *are* the government.' Nor was there much discernible alteration in the 1870s. An analysis of the 1879 edition of Bateman's *The Great Landowners of Great Britain and Ireland* reveals that of 2,500 or so heads of great agricultural families with annual rent rolls of £3,000 or above, 156 were M.P.s and 315 were former M.P.s. That is, nearly one-quarter of the House were heads of agricultural families, and nearly one-fifth of the heads of agricultural families had been in the House of Commons. And this calculation leaves out of account all cadet members of such families. Here was a distinct hereditary parliamentary class, the same family names recurring again and again in the lists of parliaments and parliamentary candidates. And the dominance of the territorial class is even more stark if cabinet membership is considered. Palmerston's cabinet in 1865 consisted of two dukes (Somerset and Argyll), one younger son of a duke who was also a peer in his own right (Russell), six other peers, (Palmerston,[1] Cranworth, Granville, Ripon, Clarendon, Stanley of Alderley), two baronets (Grey and Wood), one son of a peer who was also the brother of one of the peers in the cabinet (Villiers, whose brother was Clarendon) and only three 'new men' (Gladstone, Cardwell and

Milner-Gibson, though even here Gladstone was the son of a baronet).

Justification of territorial ascendancy was an integral part of the received political folklore of the land. Burke had enshrined it for his own era, and his doctrines of prescription became the clichés of uncountable numbers of later speeches and tracts. Coleridge imported German philosophy further to underpin and justify the landed dispensation. Bagehot, writing his *English Constitution* in 1865, had translated the almost mystical celebrations of Burke and Coleridge into inspired commonplaceness. His argument that cabinet government was only possible in deferential nations because that alone allows excellence in government was a utilitarian defence of élites; which, in the English context, was an argument justifying deference to the historic territorial class and its dependencies. A deferential society, Bagehot pointed out, cannot be created. 'Respect is traditional; it is given not to what is proved to be good, but what is known to be old.' The county constituencies constituted most conspicuously just such a web of 'old deference and inveterate homage' relationships, nexuses, locality-oriented, community-structured styles of life and behaviour which the Liberal writers of the *Essays on Reform* so deeply deplored not merely because they served the purposes of reaction but because in themselves they were a primitive form of human organization. They were tribal and hierarchical, whereas the course of human progress seemed to the Liberals to move clearly along the line of the emancipation of the autonomous individual.

But the immediate issue of reform in politics in the middle 1860s revolved about a more restricted aspect of the question of what was legitimate behaviour in politics. The claim for the legitimacy of the local influence of the landowner derived from the same argument at bottom as the new challenge to it: the argument of the independent man. Only large acres guaranteed a man independence to defy alike despots and mobs. Hence land was the bulwark of the liberties of the nation. Therefore the only class that can be truly independent is justified in assuming the direction of the commonwealth, justified in maintaining its ascendancy through its social and economic influence and justified in resisting any measures designed to undermine that ascendancy. That had been the purpose of the Whigs in 1832 and it was to be the purpose of their heirs in 1866 and 1867.

The contrary argument insisted on the possibility and desirability of independent men outside communities, landed or otherwise. Most Liberals accepted the traditional justification of land as applying to the past; but they agreed that the progress of society was such that primitive assumptions about how people behave must be replaced by enlightened ones approximating to what Gladstone called in his *Chapter of Autobiography* of 1868 the 'movement of the public mind'. The question was to decide where lay the point which divided the populace whose enfranchisement was a negotiable issue – on the grounds of their now being capable of enlightened individualism – from the unenfranchisable 'residue' still in a condition of degradation.

The debate of the middle sixties was essentially unaffected by arguments advocating a social democratic structure of society and politics. The Chartist tradition was still strong in a few places, mainly in London, and could still give life to self-consciously proletarian movements like the Land and Labour League of 1869. But these had relatively little weight. The obscure socialist emigré Karl Marx produced the first volume of *Das Kapital* in 1867 but he never succeeded in becoming the centre of an influential circle in England. The trade union chiefs who formed the 'Junta' of the 'New Model' unionism – Robert Applegarth, Alexander MacDonald, George Odger and George Howell – guided the general outlook of working-class public activity essentially within the framework of bourgeois Radicalism. Their maxim was 'defence not defiance'. Marx had an uphill battle trying to instil some serious socialism into the International Workingman's Association set up in London in 1864.

Even among bourgeois Liberals and Radicals there were important differences of attitude about the legitimate expectations even of the middle class. The more aggressive of them, represented by John Bright, held that they had been 'defrauded' of the inheritance due to them following their victories in 1832 and 1846 by aristocratic chicanery, especially by the unfair distribution of constituencies. They calculated that a sufficient extension of the franchise – Bright had in mind something between 200,000 and 400,000 – and a just redistribution as managed by a parliament elected under an extended franchise would provide them with the means necessary to redeem their defrauded inheritance and establish an enlightened directorate of the commonwealth, free of the political vices and corruptions endemic in the 'class' politics either of aristocracy or 'mere' democracy. The struggle, in John Morley's words in his review of *Essays on Reform*, was between 'brain and numbers on the one side and wealth, vested interest, rank and possessions on the other.'

Other Liberals had more modest expectations. Cracroft, for example, did not imagine, nor desire, that the extended franchise he advocated would be a vehicle by which a new ruling class could be translated to power. He assumed that very much the same people would be elected to parliament as under the old dispensation. But he expected also that the enlarged new constituencies would oblige them to consider social and political problems which they had hitherto been able to ignore. Leslie Stephen stressed the same point with an eloquent, almost Bagehotian, admission of the 'occult and unacknowledged forces' which made England fundamentally an aristocratic country, the 'instinctive liking for the established order of things' which made the whole upper and middle and a great part of the lower classes combine to defer spontaneously to it. The significant assumption is that there is a 'duty' to do obvious and necessary things to forward the cause of progress. It is some measure of the extent to which the future did not answer to their expectations that many of the contributors to the *Essays on Reform* ended up as supporters of the administration of Lord Salisbury, who, as Lord Robert Cecil and then Lord Cranborne, had been one of the most convinced opponents of Reform in 1866 and 1867.

II

Debate about reform took place in the setting of a prosperous society. This prosperity not only made the debate possible, it also determined its character. Prosperity provided the basis of the claim for reform by creating in the 1850s a post-Chartism class of ambitious skilled and semi-skilled workers large enough to make a serious political force in conjunction with sympathetic middle-class patronage. Prosperity was the foundation for the New Model trade unionism which concentrated on extracting the maximum benefits from the existing economic system rather than on ambitious schemes for social transformation. For the skilled craftsmen this policy brought convincing results. The old Chartist Thomas Cooper recorded his disgust at the decline of working-class militancy in 1870: 'well-dressed working men talking, as they walk with their hands in their pockets, of "Co-ops" (Co-operative Stores), and their shares in them, or in Building Societies. And you will see others, like idiots, leading small greyhound dogs, covered with cloth, in a string!' Unskilled workers who were not getting proportionally so big a cut of the cake were as yet almost wholly unorganized. Prosperity provided also the basis of confidence within the social and political establishment which made an aristocratic and middle-class symbiosis mutually advantageous and made reform negotiable.

Although a relatively declining sector of the national economy, agriculture still grew in absolute terms and in the 1860s still represented one-third of the value of the total national capital. By 1885 it would be less than one-fifth. But the climate of the sixties was still that of the 'golden age'. A total agricultural income estimated at £118·8 million in 1861 increased to £130·4 million in 1871, which would, in fact, be its peak.[2]

In almost every other respect, the sixties seemed either to confirm assumptions of prosperity based on the boom of the fifties or to promise expectations of increased prosperity for the future. Exports reached their peak relatively in the early seventies, when they accounted for 23 per cent of the national income. The net balance of payments surplus for the decade of 1850–60 set the pattern for the era of large surpluses which characterized the later nineteenth century. Between 1851 and 1871 income from investments abroad nearly quadrupled. In the same period wages and salaries in Britain from manufacturing, mining and building about doubled. Those of trade and transportation more than doubled. The growth rate of the real product of the economy accelerated markedly in the sixties; by this time the value of industrial production was running at a level six times greater than in the first decade of the century, and did not begin to slacken markedly until the later seventies and early eighties. Total gross investment in terms of annual rate of capital formation rose to a peak in the late sixties and early seventies; a peak which was not to be exceeded until the decade immediately prior to the War. From a contemporary viewpoint none of the great staple industries seemed to give serious cause for anxiety. The traditional prime staple, cotton, was at its peak in terms of value of the final product in the years 1869–71. Coal was at the end of its 'golden age' of growth in the 1860s: between 1830 and 1865 the industry increased four and a half times; in the next twenty-five years it would merely double. The iron industry's share of the British national product attained its maximum point in 1871. British pig iron was still more than half the total world production (it would fall to 20 per cent by 1900). 1873 would be the peak year for blast furnaces in operation. All this attracted an accelerated flow of new capital into iron and steel, marked especially in the decade 1865–75. Railways and shipping both expanded vigorously in the 1860s. Railways indeed reached almost twice the level of average net output of the previous decade.

Prosperity also made for significant shifts in the structure of distribution of national income. R. D. Baxter, in *National Income* (1868), estimated that the lower-skilled working class had become the single greatest component both in numbers and income: 1,610,000 lower-skilled working-class families took in a marginally higher income than the 4,500 families with incomes of £5,000 and above.[3] Despite the enormous relative factor, it was a portentous fact that agriculture and unskilled labour had ceased to be the numerically greatest category: this was the first time it had happened in any country in the world. Higher- and lower-skilled working-class families together accounted for over a quarter of the total national income. General income distribution of course still reflected the vast disparities and disproportions of a transitional traditional community society on the brink of becoming a primitive but substantially 'modern' class society. With only 1,576,000 families, the upper and middle classes took in 60·9 per cent of the national income, and with 4,588,000 families the manual worker classes took in 39·1 per cent. This, in time, would be the occasion of an increasing and formidable amount of working-class agitation; but in the context of the 1860s it was the fundamental means of a social and political viability: never before in Europe had so many poor people been absolutely so well off; and never before, arguably, had consciousness of this been more pervasively a part of folklore. From the early 1860s real wages began to increase markedly. By 1865 they were 20 per cent improved on the 1850 level. By 1875 they had increased by a third. The *per capita* consumption of commodities such as tea, coffee, sugar and tobacco told the same story. In the music halls of 1866 the beneficiaries of this prosperity joined in the chorus of 'Don't Stop, Let "Progress" be the Word':

> For no matter how good the time that has come
> We mean to have a better time still.

Working-class memories in the 1860s naturally referred to the recent past of the Hungry Forties and the triumphs of free trade. Moreover, the spirit of accommodation represented by the New Model trade unionism was reflected in a reciprocal phenomenon of 'New Model employers': industrialists like the Basses, Lord Elcho, Brassey, Samuel Morley, Alfred Illingworth and Titus Salt, believers in the economy of high wages and in working together with trade unions. The Liberal politician A. J. Mundella made a point of cultivating the newly founded Trades Union Congress. There was in all this acknowledgement of the reality of potential working-class strength; but there was also an increasingly confident assumption, central to Liberalism, of the reconcilability of competing interests by means of rational good will.

III

Thus the years of the Palmerston era were important from the point of view of the economic basis of society. But economic developments did not define its passing. And though the Palmerston era defines itself in political terms, its ending did not involve a sharp political break with the past, nor did the immediate consequence of its ending, the Reform Act of 1867. Rather, the 1860s were marked most significantly by manifestations in the intellectual dimension of public life and in external developments with important implications within that dimension.

The traditional structure of intellectual debate evolved in the early decades of the century was still intact. Mill, in two famous essays on Bentham and Coleridge in 1838 and 1840, had interpreted plausibly for the first time the contrasted intellectual ingredients of the debate between the essential liberal and conservative minds of the English culture. He expounded the view that between them, Coleridge and Bentham had provided philosophical methods and foundations of knowledge – intuitive on the one hand and empirical on the other – necessary to equip English society with the means to understand itself and to organize its thinking about the ends to which it should be addressing itself through the means of politics. Mill's interpretation stood the test of time; it became something more than plausible. Carlyle found to his indignation that in conformity to this scheme he was placed in the public view as a rather eccentric outrider of the Coleridgean tradition. Marx found to his even greater indignation that such a scheme accurately corresponded to a culture almost wholly impervious to his doctrine.

By the 1860s the tradition of Bentham was represented by Mill himself. More inspiringly than anyone else of his generation Mill represented the quest to establish a science of society that would provide guarantees of legitimacy for the new progressive politics of the future. He had offered a credo as a guideline for public policy in On Liberty in 1859. Here he tried to found on the surest foundations of utility the tolerable limits of interference by the state or society at large in the life of the individual. Liberty, especially liberty of opinion, was for Mill the key to progress; for Mill believed that in a fair intellectual fight good opinions would defeat bad opinions, and that progress could be defined as the elimination of controversy about important issues. He wanted to establish this clearly in the public consciousness because he feared that the coming democracy might spoil the chances of progress by being intolerant, and so waste the great chance for humanity offered in the nineteenth century by the crumbling of the traditional dispensation of society and politics.

Mill then moved on to practical political applications of his doctrine, most notably in *Considerations on Representative Government* of 1861, in public advocacy of reform, and in election for the Westminster constituency in 1865. Mill looked forward to a new kind of society, democratic yet sensible of the claims of intellect, 'free' in the sense of establishing the utmost possible degree of individual rights as against the State, pacific, beneficent in its attitude to the world outside, representing a new dispensation of middle-class political morality triumphant over the old aristocratic ruling class and finding in the emerging lower orders of society grateful pupils and emulators. In the economic sphere he had by the 1860s moved far to the 'left' of his *Principles of Political Economy* of 1849, stressing the distributionist aspects of that work in a socialist direction. Mill thus saw himself as the representative of forces subversive of the social and political establishment.

For the Coleridgean tradition the authentic representative in the 1860s was, equally as appropriately, Matthew Arnold. Arnold agreed with Mill that the fundamental social transformation of the nineteenth century was the ending of the traditional sources of authority in Church and State: religion was wounded mortally by science; aristocracy by democracy. But Arnold disagreed with Mill's supposing that this transformation was necessarily, by virtue of rationalist historicism, all to the good. Provoked by the agitation for reform in 1866 and 1867 in which Mill took a prominent part, Arnold in *Culture and Anarchy* attempted to provide a fresh intellectual basis for tradition as the ruling social idea. Arnold had jettisoned certain things from the inheritance of his father Thomas Arnold and the Broad 'national' Church School, most conspicuously, even such orthodox religious faith as his father had possessed; and literary culture had come for him to occupy a position of centrality to which even Carlyle would have hesitated to endow it. Culture in fact replaced religion. And just as Thomas Arnold, J. R. Seeley and others had hoped to Christianize the nation by nationalizing Christianity, so Matthew Arnold offered a notion of cultivating the nation by nationalizing culture. The agent of this nationalization was to be established by the state of an intuited 'right reason', a kind of historically derived 'intelligence'. As Arnold defined culture as the best that has been known and said transmitted from the past and thus made available by tradition, so 'right reason' was the historically conditioned intuition of the bearers of tradition in society, the ruling class. Arnold's defence of culture was, in political terms, the defence of an idea of a clerisy which had the capacity and the confidence and, most important of all, the legitimacy of traditionally derived right reason, to decide for society as a whole what is good and what is bad.

Arnold's loyalties and sympathies in the era of the reform debate were as clear as Mill's. But their confrontation was not direct. Possibly this reflected Arnold's appreciation that, in reality, Mill's brand of élitism was not so much removed from his own as far as practical effect was concerned. Moreover their debate was internal to Liberalism, to which Arnold had as much claim as Mill. The Tory party was 'stupid' for Arnold as for Mill. It had nothing to offer Arnold in the way of intellectual stimulus.

The major distinction between them was that Mill's concern with reform was much more immediate than Arnold's, and indeed his involvement is rather more appropriate to a later consideration of the politics of reform itself. Arnold's immediate concern with the issue in 1866 and 1867 is not particularly important or illuminating, except in as much as it reveals the extent to which even so urbane a sensibility could lose its poise in rather unworthy panic. The provocation offered by the rioting crowds in the genteel preserve of Hyde Park revealed Arnold's weakness just as Mill's successful mediation between the rioters and the Government revealed his strength. Arnold's strength would be in the relatively long term, which would reveal, conversely, Mill's weakness. *Culture and Anarchy* was the prime social text of the new English ruling class of the later nineteenth century, for it provided more persuasively than anything else the intellectual basis upon which aristocracy and bourgeoisie could adopt a common style. To this extent Arnold did in fact secure the nationalizing of culture. The authority of the one and the discipline of the other would be transmuted via a national culture into a very tough, resilient, self-confident and persistent new model ruling class.

Significantly the 'interest' which Arnold most delighted to make his enemy was Nonconformity. The religious dissenters were the most formidable obstacle to any concept of a state establishment of culture. They were the head and front of the anarchic philistine forces of provincialism, of every man for himself in politics, economics and religion, with no thought of a higher national ideal. Nonconformity was precisely the interest which Gladstone was soon to hail as the 'backbone of Liberalism' and whose famous 'conscience' was to sustain most powerfully the causes dearest to the heart of Mill and his disciples.

But reform was only one of the issues over which the dualistic intellectual inheritance renewed and recharged itself in the sixties. There was also the issue of foreign policy. And linking the two was the issue of the Jamaica affair, the public agitation in 1865-6 provoked by allegations that the British authorities in Jamaica, and particularly the Governor, Eyre, had behaved illegally and brutally towards legitimate Negro protest.

Foreign policy was a much less obviously prominent issue in the 1860s, and, though its significance emerged more clearly later, in many ways it played a more interesting part, since the issue of democracy did not long retain its panic-inspiring reputation of 1866. Indeed, foreign policy gave much better grounds for panic in the 1860s than the British public realized. Democracy was to remain comparatively a subterranean theme, only occasionally building up enough pressure to open a fault-line on the surface, whereas the problem of British external relations gradually came from the 1870s especially to form the most consistent single element in the equation of national debate. More than anything else, the issue of British external problems preserved the integrity of the inherited dualistic intellectual structure. Debate about how Britain should relate to the external world – including Ireland – became significant to a degree that debate about such things as the role of the State did not, for divisions about the first were more urgent in the sense of what was at stake than divisions about the latter. Moreover, debate about external problems was more open than debate about internal problems; there was a greater area of freedom of choice. Domestic debate ceased comparatively to be free as the blind forces moving society imposed irresistible pressures. British society was not free to decide whether or not to make what would later be known as the foundations of the 'welfare state' in the same sense as it was free to decide whether to go to war in South Africa in 1899 or with Germany in 1914.

IV

While both these greater themes were in their different ways in a formative stage in 1865, the Jamaica issue served in a way to represent both: domestically, it raised the issues of freedom and authority; for the external sphere, it opened up problems of the morality of policy which link both back to Don Pacifico in 1850 the Bulgarian agitation in 1876. And in its immediate context it served to underline the issues raised in Britain by the Civil War in the United States.

Debate in Britain over the merits of the war had quite clearly divided on the fundamental domestic fault-lines. The establishment – the Clubs, Society, *The Times* of Delane, *Punch*, Palmerston himself at the head of the Gentlemen of England – had made no secret of their sympathy for the cause of the Gentlemen of the South, of their contempt for Lincoln and the Northern cause. Conversely, the British 'advanced party' were eager to accept the implications drawn by their enemies. A triumph for Lincoln and the Union would be a triumph for the popular cause against such enemies; not merely a defeat for Negro slavery but a defeat almost as direct for the English Cousinhood.

John Stuart Mill was in his element here. He relates in his *Autobiography* how his 'strongest feelings were engaged in this struggle', which, he felt from the beginning, 'was destined to be a turning point, for good or evil, of the course of human affairs for an indefinite duration'. A Confederate victory would be 'a victory of the powers of evil which would give courage to the enemies of progress and damp the spirit of its friends all over the civilized world . . . and, by destroying for a long time the prestige of the great democratic republic, would give to all the privileged classes of Europe a false confidence, probably only to be extinguished in blood.' Together with Mill were Cobden and Bright, Thomas Hughes, Thorold Rogers and the young T. H. Green, Goldwin

Smith, who would soon resign his Oxford Chair and emigrate to the democratic New World, John Morley of the *Fortnightly Review*, the newly founded organ of the 'advanced party', the Nonconformist Conscience, most significant of all, incipiently, hintingly, Gladstone. Here were the forming elements of a party of politics and ideas which was to become one of the most important influences in the general national debate. The Jamaica case, which followed on the Civil War question almost immediately, had the effect of transferring the same issues to a colonial area for which Britain was directly responsible. Relatively minor in itself, Jamaica was the preliminary exercise for the three great issues which were to punctuate the period up to the First World War, which tested the validity and relevance of the national political and intellectual equipment: Bulgaria and the Eastern Question in the 1870s; Irish Home Rule in the 1880s; and 'imperialism' and South Africa particularly in the 1890s. 1914 itself could, in this perspective, indeed be interpreted as the culmination of the train of issues of which Jamaica was the prologue.

Again, with Jamaica, Mill was the inevitable leader. A disturbance among the Negro ex-slaves – a legitimate political protest or a premeditated rebellion – had been suppressed by Governor Eyre with atrocious severity or with promptitude and firmness. The case became a *cause célèbre*. Immediately British society divided once more down its natural fault-line, with memories of the Indian Mutiny jostling with recent remembrances of the American War. 'The question', as defined by Mill, was, 'whether the British dependencies, and eventually, perhaps, Great Britain itself, were to be under the government of law, or of military licence; whether the lives and persons of British subjects are at the mercy of any two or three officers however raw and inexperienced or reckless and brutal, whom a panic stricken Governor, or other functionary, may assume the right to constitute into a so-called Court-martial'.

Mill became chairman of the Jamaica Committee set up to prosecute Eyre in a criminal court. For two years he led the attack, ultimately unsuccessfully as far as the criminal prosecution was concerned, for two sturdy English juries proved themselves to be of much the stuff that the 'national' cause was made of. Mill regarded his speech in the House of Commons on Jamaica in 1866 as his finest parliamentary effort. Behind him were mobilized the forces of moral protest and conscience in politics, inheritors of earlier traditions of evangelical godly public activity, of agitations against slavery and corn laws.

Huxley, Darwin's public spokesman and tireless exponent of his evolutionary theory and the claims of science generally in modern society, is interesting as one who took the trouble to make it clear that men took sides on the Jamaica question according to their 'deepest political convictions'. He rebuked Kingsley for putting himself at the head of the Carlylean defenders of Eyre, 'the hero-worshippers who believe that the world is to be governed by its great men, who are to lead the little ones, justly if they can; but if not, unjustly drive or kick them the right way'. Huxley denounced the 'idolatry' of hero-worship and the essential immorality of the attitude of mind of the hero-worshipper. He insisted that it was 'better for a man to go wrong in freedom than to go right in chains'; and he looked upon the 'observance of inflexible justice as between man and man as of far greater importance than even the preservation of social order'. The 'Jamaica business' did indeed mark the opening of a fault-line in the structure of intellectual Liberalism.

These issues of order and freedom indicated the nature of the ultimate split among Liberal intellectuals in the 1870s and 1880s. That many of them waited until 1876 to come down decisively against the Liberalism of Mill and Gladstone was a measure of their unwillingness to accept at this stage that the cause in which they had been reared and which they regarded as their natural and inevitable political home had reached a level of fundamental inadequacy to requirements as measured by 'national' criteria. That bitter analysis would come later.

Goldwin Smith, the arch-individualist, the arch-representative of 'Little England', did later point to the larger significance of the Jamaica case in relation to 1876. In his view the failure to convict and break Eyre represented a larger failure of the 'two great Liberal sentiments – the love of justice and the love of humanity' – to assert themselves as the guiding elements of national life.

1865 was the turning point on the way to defeat. 1876, in his view, was confirmation of this.

But the two larger issues which Jamaica links in 1865 and 1866, the problem of British external relations and the problem of 'democracy', specifically the issue of reform, must now be considered.

Chapter Two

RECOIL FROM EUROPE
1865–74

I

1864 had been a year of humiliation for British foreign policy. Palmerston and Russell challenged Bismarck in the matter of the 'Danish Duchies' of Schleswig and Holstein; and when Bismarck called their bluff, they collapsed ignominiously. No event in living memory had so compromised the international reputation and prestige of Britain. And this, moreover, on top of the notorious blundering insolence displayed by these two 'dreadful old men', as the Queen called them, over the matter of Russian treatment of Poland in 1863. Palmerston's death in 1865 might have been thought an appropriate occasion to mark a new departure in Britain's conduct of her external affairs. The Cobdenites – the 'Manchester School' – indeed assumed that the collapse of Palmerston's policy and then Palmerston's death opened the way at last for them. The public, they assumed, would make the necessary deductions, and conclude that they had been cheated since the Crimean War and earlier by letting themselves become the dupes of meddlesome truculence cloaked under the guise of the patriotic 'national' policy. Now they would appreciate the wisdom of Cobden's and Bright's recommendations of non-intervention and reliance upon the ameliorative effects of free trade.

Certainly, historians in the main share these assumptions in seeing a decisive turning point in the years around 1870. This interpretation sees a distinctly post-Palmerstonian situation, with Gladstone on the one hand representing a new Liberal initiative of internationalism and Disraeli on the other a new Conservative initiative of 'imperialism'.

Yet on a closer examination there seems as little reason to

interpret 1864-5 as the period of reappraisal in foreign affairs. Gladstone indeed thought of himself as the exponent of a policy not only distinctly post-Palmerston but essentially anti-Palmerston in character; but the reasons for his attitudes were inherited from the past. The same is equally true of Disraeli. Claims on his behalf as the pioneer exponent of 'imperialism' in any sense of an original response on the basis of an original analysis and appreciation of the British international predicament do not withstand critical investigation. In fact it was to take the best part of twenty years before either the internal or the external spheres were subjected to fundamental revision. Thus an analysis of British foreign policy between 1865 and 1885 reveals essentially the persistence of received traditions and attitudes, attempts to reassert policies based on assumptions inherited from the past. The phase from Palmerston's death to Disraeli's taking office in 1874 was distinctly one of suspended animation. The shock of the events of 1864 induced a kind of paralysis of will, an unwillingness to commit British policy in any positive direction for fear of further failures and humiliations. Hence there was a well-defined period of recoil from Europe. But this was an isolation not, as the Cobdenites congratulated themselves it was, of calculation, but of bewilderment, of an inability to understand why policies which had hitherto appeared to answer requirements with complete satisfaction had suddenly ceased to carry conviction and credibility.

There was no lack of criticism and demands for new attitudes in 1864 and afterwards. Salisbury, perhaps the most virulently effective of all the critics of Palmerston and Russell, launched as early as April 1864 a caustic general assault on the character and quality of their policy, a 'policy of cowardice', of 'bluster', a 'portentous mixture of bounce and baseness', 'dauntless to the weak, timid and cringing to the strong'. He believed that the old high-spirited policy of aristocracy, of Pitt and Grenville and Castlereagh, had been replaced by a policy tailored to the demands of the middle class, a muddled mixture of blundering assertiveness and sentimental morality.

Another significant critic was Matthew Arnold. *Friendship's Garland* of 1871 was in effect the external aspect of his critique of the domestic scene in *Culture and Anarchy*. In both cases the villain was the philistine middle class, 'testy, absolute, ill-acquainted with foreign matters, a little ignoble, very dull to perceive when it is making itself ridiculous'.

> The foreigners, indeed, are in no doubt as to the real authors of the policy of modern England; they know that ours is no longer a policy of Pitts and aristocracies . . . they know that our policy is now dictated by the strong middle part of England . . . It was not the aristocracy which made the Crimean War; it was the strong middle part – the constituencies . . . It was the strong middle part which, by the voice of its favourite newspapers, kept threatening Germany, after she had snapped her fingers at us, with a future chastisement from France, just as a smarting schoolboy threatens his bully with a drubbing to come from some big boy in the background.

Very different from these stings and barbs was the critique of a professional diplomatist, Robert Morier, then a secretary in Berlin. 'Our foreign policy,' he wrote on 15 March 1864, '. . . requires immediate and radical reform.' It was of 'immediate and paramount necessity', he argued, that reconsideration of 'first principles' should be undertaken; intellectual toughness, 'correctness of vision', was essential if foreign policy was to be emancipated from 'the public opinion of which that policy is but the echo'. The ignorant moral indignation of public opinion and 'our hack statesmen' have combined to reduce Britain to the 'inglorious pass' of Schleswig–Holstein.

Two general criticisms are central to these three: first, the theme of the irremediable bankruptcy of Palmerstonism; second, the theme of an ignorant public opinion imposing itself against the claims of instructed intelligence. Morier specifically represented the outrage of the professional expert. For whereas Salisbury and Arnold thought in terms of the aristocracy abdicating in favour of middle-class values, he saw an older generation obstinately hanging on and keeping a more informed and expert younger generation (represented by himself) out of positions of decisive influence. Morier hoped to become permanent under-secretary at the Foreign Office on Hammond's retirement; but when his chance came in 1873 the post went to Tenterden and the embassy at St Petersburg never really compensated Morier for this failure to attain the strategic post where his 'first principles' might have been put to some effect. Morier's prickly earnestness reflected two strains of importance for the future. First, as a disciple of Jowett at Balliol he represented with fidelity the kind of mandarian élitism which was to become so markedly associated with Jowett's influence and which relates him, through Jowett's continued mentorship, to the developing criticism within Liberalism of Gladstone's inadequate handling of affairs. Second, and more specifically, his Foreign Office professionalism and his impatience with the politicians – especially Gladstonian politicians – marked him as the precursor of the 'Hardinge crowd' whose incursion in the Foreign Office in 1905 inaugurated the most formidable challenge offered by 'instructed intelligence' to the normal political process.

Meanwhile, the inherited traditions were still free to work themselves out. Essentially, these traditions derived from the 1830s and 1840s: rival claims to manifest British moral leadership of Europe.

A Conservative version held that British moral leadership remained essentially as Castlereagh had envisaged it in 1814: Britain giving unobtrusive guidance to the concert of the powers from a position of advantage, achievement and obligation, better able than any other power to trim the balance on the continent, combining with the inert weight of Austria to adjust and contain the dynamic potentialities of France and Russia. Implicit in this version was the assumption of conservative ideological identification, the idea of British Conservatism relating to a general conservative cause in Europe against the aspirations of Jacobinism and popular sovereignty. The Peelite conscience expressed the moral sense of the Conservative version most appropriately; and Aberdeen's disciple, the young Gladstone, most conspicuously.

The 'Manchester School' of Cobden and Bright was the central focus of an international Radical version. Free trade naturally was the essence of their claims to British moral leadership. They renounced, however, all obligations to any form of active diplomatic participation in a concert of the powers and subscribed firmly to principles of non-intervention in the affairs of other countries. They offered no guidance, only example. They calculated that, since free trade was the fundamental truth at the bottom of all social and political progress, its irresistible future triumph would in any case remove the necessity for diplomacy as the peoples, liberated from feudal ruling classes, came together freely.

One thing united the Conservatives and the Cobdenites: their common detestation of the third version in the field. This was a combination of Whig, Canningite, Liberal and Radical strains, finding in Palmerston its foremost exponent. Britain's role of active leadership was here explicit to the point, if necessary, of assertiveness. It was the right and duty of Britain to encourage conformable developments among the European peoples, with the aim of establishing under British auspices a concert of powers sharing a common liberal ideology. Thus Palmerston's assumption of the direction of the general liberal movement unavoidably meant incessant friction with the conservative ruling forces of Europe. He was attacked by the Conservatives because he encouraged subversion; by the Cobdenites because he meddled; by both because of his presumption.

Palmerstonism convinced the larger part of the public mind of Britain, and became the 'national' foreign policy, expressing the patriotic consensus. The Conservative version had long lost this status. The Cobdenites disdained to compete for it. Palmerston provoked both the Peelite conscience and the Manchester conscience by the shameless arrogance of Britain's bullying of Greece over the affair of Don Pacifico in 1850. His successful resistance to their combined assault registered his supremacy. The Crimean War and the 'Crimean System' confirmed it. Thereafter he faced no serious challenges until Poland in 1863 and the Danish Duchies in 1864.

The latter of these occasions signified the collapse of the western aspect of Palmerston's European system. He had attempted to repeat his success of the 1830s over Belgium in European conditions which no longer permitted him the necessary resources. His basic resource had always been his ability to manipulate a European concert. But 1864 revealed that 'Europe' in the old sense no longer existed. France, Austria and Russia refused to cooperate, the Russians in particular directing their diplomatic energies almost exclusively towards relieving the pressures and burdens imposed upon them under Palmerston's leadership in the Black Sea and Poland.

This indeed was the tragic irony of Palmerston's policy. Continued success in its western aspect depended in the last analysis on the cooperation of the villain and victim of its eastern aspect. Worse: failure in the west meant the end of the concert as the true working system of Europe, and this meant the end of any effective British leadership in Europe, for this in turn depended upon British capacity to manoeuvre and manipulate. Bismarck's success in 1864 depended upon a paralysed concert. His further successes against Austria in 1866 and France in 1870 meant that the concert was permanently paralysed, and would in fact be replaced as the working arrangement of Europe by an alliance system which the British were to find impossible to relate to in any advantageous way.

The concert was in fact dead, though no one really realized it at the time, certainly not the British, who assumed it as part of the normal equipment appropriate to the enlightened nineteenth century. One is concerned then in these years from 1865 to 1874 with observing the British response to the consequences of the western collapse – broadly, the emergence of a hegemonic Prussia–Germany at the expense of Austria and France – and the British response to the strains being imposed increasingly on the Crimean System in the prelude before the great Near Eastern crisis starting in 1875 brought it also to collapse.

II

Liberal governments were in power in this period except for the Derby and Disraeli ministries from June 1866 to December 1868. When Russell succeeded Palmerston, Clarendon went to the Foreign Office, to which he returned in 1868 when Gladstone formed his first cabinet. Stanley was foreign secretary for his father, Derby, and Disraeli. They were very different in approach but they illustrate the difficulties at this time of an effective foreign initiative for Britain. Clarendon was an old Whig firmly hostile to Bismarck but unable to hit upon a means of putting his hostility to effect. He could no more pay Louis Napoleon's price than could Palmerston. Stanley was virtually a Cobdenite in sympathy and devoted all his energies to avoiding all commitments and positive decisions. It was his misfortune to have to cope with the consequences of the Prussian victory over Austria in 1866, principally Louis Napoleon's frantic efforts to secure 'compensation'. Stanley nerved himself to an initiative of good offices over the Luxembourg crisis of 1867, following Bismarck's veto of the proposed sale of the grand duchy to France by the bankrupt King of the Netherlands. A compromise was patched up which did not conceal Louis Napoleon's bitter humiliation. His consequent thrashing about for alliances with Austria and Italy, his clumsy designs on Belgium, his military augmentations and rearmament frightened the British much more than Bismarck.

In the eastern aspect the Crimean System was commencing visibly to crumble. The Treaty of Paris of 1856 guaranteeing the integrity and independence of the Ottoman Empire was still part of the public law of Europe. The Russian flag of war was still interdicted from the Black Sea. The Tripartite Treaty of Guarantee between Britain, France and Austria directed against any Russian effort to subvert the Treaty of Paris was still technically operative. But the Russian campaign to convince Europe that a great mistake had been made in 1856 had the advantage of being better in phase than the Crimean System with the facts of the Near East. Gorchakov's famous Circular pointing out to Europe the delinquencies of the Turks, especially in Bosnia and Bulgaria, read even more aptly in 1876 than it did when it was issued in 1860. The *coup d'état* in Romania in 1866 seriously compromised the credit of the Treaty of Paris. Then the Cretan revolt of 1866–8 against the Turks added to the load of embarrassment bearing on the British. The pattern of 1857–8 over the Danubian Principalities attempting to make themselves into Romania was repeated: Britain aligned with Turkey attempted to stand in the way of emancipation patronized by France and Russia. One particular incident, of Cretan refugees being refused asylum on British warships, caused a public stir which gave the first hint of the public capacity to react critically against the assumptions of the Crimean System and the 'national' policy that was to make the year 1876 so memorable.

But these events and these responses were of relatively little consequence. Britain was trying to get away with having as little foreign policy as was decently possible for a Great Power. What was important at this phase was the readjustment of attitudes to foreign affairs in relation to the general political realignments consequent upon Palmerston's death and the coming into the leadership of the Liberal and Conservative parties of Gladstone and Disraeli.

When Gladstone succeeded Russell in the leadership of the Liberal party in 1867 he certainly did not regard the Palmerstonian 'national' policy as a part of the heritage of Liberalism to which he wished to lay claim. As a Peelite and as a Liberal Gladstone had distinguished himself as an opponent of Palmerston. They agreed on only one thing, the cause of Italian emancipation. Together with free trade that had been enough to secure Gladstone's allegiance to the Liberal party in 1859. But clearly Gladstone had developed his own version of a properly Liberal foreign policy, and it was that version which he intended the new and improved Liberal party of the future should make manifest to the world. In essence, Gladstone fused his Peelite inheritance from Aberdeen with the Manchester lessons he had been taught by Cobden. From the pious Aberdeen – the man, as Gladstone said, he most loved – he derived the ideal of a creative and constructive British role in the concert of Europe. Palmerston had based his claims to British prerogatives on British achievements. Aberdeen and Gladstone offered their services on the basis of obligation. To the extent that Britain enjoyed peculiar advantages denied to less fortunate continental nations, to the extent that her relative security from disturbance had granted her opportunities for greater social and political progress and consequent moral superiority, Britain owed in conscience extraordinary duties of service to Europe. Like Aberdeen, Gladstone renounced Palmerston's assertive style. Britain would offer a leadership of guidance rather than coercion, the exponent preeminently of good offices, of reconciliation, of diplomatic emollience. Moreover, Gladstone always emphasized – for the benefit of the Cobdenites – the advantages of selective intervention. That is, not a policy of incessant activity, but one of hoarding good will and waiting for the right moment to invest it to maximum profit. As Gladstone remarked in 1869, Britain's 'credit and power form a fund, which in order that they may be made the most of, should be thriftily used'.

Though Gladstone always repudiated the isolationism of Cobden and his followers as a 'noble error', it was the Manchester School more than any other influence which created the climate of public attitudes and assumptions in which Gladstone was to operate most sympathetically in the decades to come. In particular, as the contingency of intervention in Europe became in any case increasingly remote, the anti-imperialist ideology over which Gladstone was to preside found in Cobden its richest single source of inspiration.

Thus by the early 1860s Gladstone had come to embody a fusion of the two traditions which had challenged Palmerston in 1850. With Palmerston and Russell out of the way, and despite Whig grumblings and with his pliant protégé Granville replacing the deceased Clarendon at the Foreign Office in June 1870, Gladstone was set fair to inaugurate a distinctly new era of Liberal achievement in the external sphere.

Disraeli's situation was quite otherwise. The Conservative party had lost the 'national' status for its foreign policy which it had held in the days of Castlereagh. The revolutions of 1848 had made nonsense of Aberdeen's conscientious efforts to relate Britain usefully to the Europe of Metternich and Nicholas I. Moreover, the break-up of the party over the issue of protection in 1846 had robbed it of the chance of a parliamentary majority ever since. With the Peelites hopelessly estranged, the rump under Derby and Disraeli could make no effective challenge to Palmerston's 'national' version.

Two factors provided Disraeli with the means of making a new departure advantageous both to the party and to himself. The first was that with the passing of the 1860s old European ideological issues of 'liberalism' *versus* 'conservatism' had faded and largely ceased to be materials for party disputes in Britain. Italy was 'free', Hungary was 'free'. Germany was being united under the leadership of Protestant and enlightened Prussia. Alexander II's emancipation of the Russian serfs in 1861 had removed a great liberal grievance; and though the Polish insurrection of 1863 had revived old 'Crimean' sentiments, the days were long past when the Turks could be seriously regarded as fit representatives of the European liberal cause. Even the Liberal Empire in France seemed to fulfil the liberal prophecies. All this relieved the Conservatives from the thankless task henceforth of defending lost causes.

Secondly, Gladstone's renunciation on behalf of the Liberal party of the Palmerstonian 'national' heritage left an obvious opening for Disraeli. He was in the position of a sharp political dealer able to pick up bankrupt stock at a cheap rate with an eye to future appreciation. Disraeli had spent his public life denouncing all the works of Palmerston. And indeed, during the months of Derby's and his own ministries in 1866-8, Disraeli devoted most of his energies to competing with Gladstone for the merit of domestic retrenchment, and left Stanley largely to his own neurotically timid diplomatic devices. But given a new relaxed European ideological situation, there was no serious impediment to snapping up bargains in the emporium of politics spurned by Gladstone, provided that it was not done too obviously and too openly in disregard of consistency. There was, however, a very distinct element of consistency involved in Disraeli's manoeuvres. Although the Conservatives had lost the 'national' status for their external policy to Palmerston, they never accepted this as permanent, and never renounced their claim to be historically the natural 'national' party. Palmerston, after all, had been a Canningite in origin. It was not going to be too difficult for Disraeli to develop a general theory of Conservatism and the nineteenth century which would integrally incorporate a plausible explanation of failure in the external aspect. The essence of the opportunity was that a national party defrauded of its rightful policy was matched providentially with a national policy deprived of its party.

III

Meanwhile Gladstone, back in power as prime minister at the end of 1868, had his hands too full of domestic problems to be able to devote much time or energy to external matters. Like Disraeli, he too had to move fairly cautiously. The larger part of his own party, all the Whigs and most of the 'moderate men', hankered, and continued to hanker, after the golden days of Palmerston, and did not relish the idea of the party being remoulded on the pattern of shopkeeping Cobdenites and priggish Peelites. There was no question of simply disowning the Palmerstonian inheritance outright.

It was Gladstone's misfortune to find himself entangled in a major European crisis before he had time to prepare the ground for a new departure. In the summer of 1870 Bismarck managed to goad the French into war. There was absolutely nothing the British could do. Louis Napoleon was just as much a prisoner of his Bonapartist heritage in 1870 as he was in 1864 and his price was just as inhibitive. Belgium obsessed the British in 1870 much as Venetia had obsessed Louis Napoleon in 1866. Britain could come to the aid of France only after a French disaster; which, as it happened, came soon enough, despite assumptions again as in 1866 that the more seasoned, experienced army would triumph. Even then, Gladstone could not get his cabinet to agree to a protest in the name of Europe's right to be consulted against the German annexation of Alsace-Lorraine. He had to content himself with an anonymous article in the *Edinburgh Review*. It was a by-product of the French disaster, however, which caused Gladstone most trouble.

Gorchakov had dedicated Russian policy to the task of persuading Europe to reverse its judgement of 1856, as symbolized most conspicuously and humiliatingly by the neutralization of the Black Sea. He had already received Prussian support. Prussia was not a party to the Tripartite Treaty of Guarantee, and Bismarck had every interest in keeping his line to St Petersburg in good repair while he completed his dealings with Austria and France. To Bismarck, these two powers were elements of the old concert and barriers to Prussian hegemony in Germany; to Gorchakov they were two elements of the 'Crimean Coalition' and two of the parties to the Tripartite Treaty. Clearly, a revived Crimean Coalition would depend for its effective strength on the French. The British were even more militarily negligible than they had been in 1854. The British fleet and the Turkish army would not make a formidable combination. Thus the French disaster in

1870 gave the Russians a safe opportunity for unilateral repudiation of the Black Sea clause of the Treaty of Paris. This was only second best for them: what they really wanted was a voluntary apology from the concert of Europe. Their moral position was good, especially after the Romanian breach of the Treaty in 1866, but their patience had worn thin, and the opportunity of 1870 was irresistible. Gorchakov took it on 31 October 1870.

Only a month before this Gladstone had spoken of an 'eventual settlement of the Eastern question'. Clearly he anticipated the possibility of future initiatives in terms of his general definition of Britain's international role: seeking tô 'develop, and mature the action of a common, or public, or European opinion, as the best standing bulwark against wrong', but taking care to avoid 'seeming to lay down the law of that opinion by her own authority', thus running the risk 'of setting against her, and against right and justice, that general sentiment which ought to be, and generally would be, arrayed in their favour'. Certainly Gladstone was by no means identified with the career hitherto of the Crimean System. He had resigned from Palmerston's cabinet in 1855. Equally, he had not distinguished himself, apart from the cases of Romania in 1857-8 and the Ionian Islands in 1859, for promise as a critic of the system when there was no lack of opportunities to do so: Syria, Serbia, Bosnia, Crete. In any case, he was given no time, and was forced by the joint pressures of Gorchakov and the aroused 'national' public opinion of Britain to adopt a much more rigid attitude than was natural to him. His concert principles obliged him to be stiff in defence of the integrity of the public law. But in the end, at the conference arranged in London in 1871 at Bismarck's officious instance on behalf of the Russians, Gladstone found himself in the position of presiding over a refurbishing of the Treaty of Paris less the Black Sea clause, together with the absurdity of the continuation of the now totally discredited Tripartite Treaty. This was a highly dubious price to pay for the assertion of the principle of European consent.

Gladstone was thus caught off balance, and he never thereafter recovered it during the period of his ministry as far as his public reputation in relation to the external sphere was concerned. His one positive exploit, the *Alabama* arbitration, offended not only

Palmerstonian 'national' opinion for its lack of 'patriotism' and its truckling to the insolent Yankees; it offended the opinion of 'instructed intelligence' for its apparent truckling to the Cobdenites, the Peace Society, and the advocates of international arbitration. Gladstone could with entire credit have continued the policy of previous governments by offering the United States a joint commission to settle the matter of the American claims against Britain for the depredations of the British-built Confederate privateer. But to Gladstone this would have been like two European powers settling an important issue between them without consideration for and consultation with a wider European opinion. Gladstone had been unsuccessful in convincing his cabinet that this was an appropriate attitude to take over Alsace-Lorraine. Now he insisted in 1872 on getting his own way, and putting the issue on the equivalent of a 'concert' basis, in the form of an international tribunal in Geneva. The tribunal awarded the United States £3,250,000 damages against Britain. Gladstone thought this award 'harsh in its extent, and unjust in its basis'; but he insisted on regarding the damages as but 'dust in the balance' compared with the 'moral value of the example set' by two great nations equally jealous of their honour going in peace and concord before a judicial tribunal instead of resorting to war.

IV

The cue for Disraeli by this time was indeed obvious. For him the most significant manifestation was the surge of bellicose 'national' public opinion against the Russians in 1870. This made it clear that Palmerstonian attitudes were still in fact truly 'national'. Disraeli's task was to manoeuvre the Conservative party into the posture of natural and legitimate exponent of the 'national' policy. There would, of course, be votes in this. But there would also, for Disraeli, be a grand redressing of historic wrong. But for Peel and Aberdeen and Gladstone and their ilk, in his view, Conservatism need never have been deprived of its 'national' status. Hence, for Disraeli, Palmerston, the renegade Canningite, was merely the *tertium gaudens*, the fortunate exploiter of the misfortunes of others. And hence, for Disraeli there was justice as well as expediency in ignoring Palmerston in his bid to establish Conservatism as the legitimate 'national' party.

This bid was made in two important speeches in the spring of 1872. The first, in Manchester, specifically attacked Gladstone for the weakness of his external policy. He denounced the 'incompetence' of Gladstone's handling of the Black Sea affair, and predicted that there was 'every chance that that incompetence' would be 'sealed' in the *Alabama* negotiations with the United States. On the issue of the Crimean War he was able to make the best of both words: to the extent that it was rather flyblown as an achievement of British policy it was safe to reassert the consistent Conservative line that it 'need never have occurred'; but at the same time he could emphasize the 'national' nature of his Conservative criticism by underlining the point that it was a policy of weakness and 'drift' which led to the war. The second speech, at the Crystal Palace at Sydenham a little later, laid down authoritatively the 'national' theory of nineteenth-century Conservatism. No less than five times Disraeli asserted the 'cosmopolitan' character of Liberalism in contrast to the natural patriotic party. In place of the Crimea Disraeli offered the Empire: it amounted practically to much the same thing, a specific focus for a public sense of British power and achievement – for a public, moreover, bewildered and very eager to respond to such offers as much because of their implications of reassuring normality as for their invitation to what would soon be known as 'Jingoism'.

Thus, beneath the surface of a general retraction of diplomatic initiative following the Danish fiasco, the phase from 1865 to 1874 is characterized in fact by a great deal of manoeuvring and regrouping of political forces as if in preparation for a new trial of strength. The victorious forces of 1850 were now equipped with a restored confidence. The two defeated forces of 1850, no longer rivals, were fused in a new Gladstonian matrix and in a much stronger position to make a decisive bid for the allegiance of the public mind of Britain. One of the largest themes of the next decade was to be this trial of strength.

Chapter Three

THE
POLITICS
OF REFORM
1866—8

I

Gladstone's decisive conjunction with the movement of reform 'out of doors' gives the whole period from 1865 to the beginning of the decline of his first ministry in 1872–3 a general unity of character. But it divides itself naturally into two phases: the first concerned with the business at the head of the national agenda, the franchise; and the second with the great series of measures after the Liberal electoral success in 1868 beginning with Irish Church disestablishment.

Alone of all the great political leaders of the nineteenth century, Gladstone was offered at the optimum moment opportunities and potentialities for positive and creative statesmanship which he was fully prepared to accept and exploit. Gladstone was at his prime physically and mentally and the 'movement of the public mind' had reached a point of critical mass.

It was not in the nature of things in the 1860s that the established political order which had confronted and outfaced the assault led by the Chartists could withstand much longer the demands of a revised 'New Model' popular movement which asked essentially to cooperate with rather than replace the established order. That was the basic operative fact at the bottom of the reform question. It was Gladstone's genius to embody the positive aspect of the ruling class response to it. He discerned that because reform had become safe it also became inevitable; and that therefore to attempt to block it would be very much more dangerous than resistance to the more extreme movement of the 1840s had been. Once launched in parliament, the mode of and extent of reform would depend on the distribution of opinion in the Commons and upon the tactical line Derby and Disraeli would take. But Gladstone made it inconceivable that a second Reform Act would not eventually emerge from the 1865 parliament.

For Gladstone alone had the capacity and desire to bridge the great gulf in British society between the traditional political class and the masses 'out of doors'. Undoubtedly this was his single most important contribution towards the Victorian dispensation which had the effect of leaving the *optimates* largely in control of the political process and at the same time leaving the *populares* more or less reconciled to that fact. Gladstone insisted that politics would have to respond to the ideals and aspirations of an age characterized by the movement, for the first time in history, of large bodies of people from levels of subsistence and (in Marx's phrase) 'idiocy' to awareness of the reality and relevance to them of ideals such as 'progress' and 'freedom'. This response would involve transferring political debate out of categories of 'interest' and into categories of 'morality'. The politics of 'morality' would be concerned centrally with the realization for the emerging masses of the promise of the new enlightenment. They, in their turn, would, in this view, accept that 'good government' meant government for the 'whole community' and not one selfish class interest, upper or lower; and that commercial and economic growth with its attendant social elevation would best be promoted by moral qualities of thrift, independence, private philanthropy, enterprise and devotion to the principles of free trade. In making this shift of the basis of politics the essential task of the Liberal party Gladstone made it into a vehicle of political moralism. 'Please to recollect,' he admonished his wife's indignant brother-in-law Lord Lyttelton, 'that we have got to govern millions of hard hands; that it must be done by force, fraud or good will; that the latter has been tried and is answering; that none have profited more by this change of system since the corn law and the Six Acts, than those who complain of it.'

Gladstone's pilgrimage from Toryism through Peelitism towards what Morley called 'light and freedom' coincided with the formation of the critical mass of the 'movement'. They came together and became mutually aware of the intoxicating charges of attractive power surging between them when Gladstone made his famous northern tour in 1862. Always half a Peelite, Gladstone was alarmed: he sensed the possibilities of addiction. But the very Peelite qualities of rigorous devotion to ideals of service, of manifest moral earnestness which were so attractive to the crowds, the congregations of back street chapels, undermined his resistance. He was simply not capable of declining such an appeal because it was at bottom a moral appeal and it hit him at the most vulnerable point of his ruling-class armour. The rapport he sensed half elatedly, half uneasily in Manchester and Newcastle became the central axis about which his politics revolved.

Gladstone's surrender was finally signalled in two public confessions in 1864 and 1865. First he announced, or rather disclosed in passing, that he had come to the conclusion that society would benefit by a 'reasonable extension' of the parliamentary franchise, admitting within 'the pale of the constitution' carefully 'selected' classes of men at a 'fitting time' on the basis of a presumption as to their not being so 'morally incapacitated' as to be likely to abuse the privilege of their suffrage; and provided always that such an extension would not constitute a sudden, or violent, or excessive, or intoxicating change. It is the best measure of Gladstone's new portentous reputation that so guarded, qualified, even embarrassed a disclosure should have provoked a furore. To the reformers it was the signal they had anxiously awaited, for without it they could not seriously contemplate a successful campaign. On the other hand the Whigs and 'moderate men', as well as the Conservatives, realized that this meant the end of stalling and prevarication, for they could not hope to shelter behind the aged Palmerston's throne much longer. Then in 1865 Gladstone disclosed an even more embarrassing confession, which caused him later to write an elaborate autobiographical justification: he, an old, even bigoted High Churchman and champion of the Church Establishment, indicated that he was no longer able to defend the establishment of the Anglican Church of Ireland.

These two events set the scene for the immediate future with precision. One was about the moral capacity of a new electorate to raise the character of the nation's conduct of its affairs; the other was about exactly the kind of issue of principle and morality which such an electorate would expect an appropriately oriented government to resolve.

Irish Church disestablishment especially meant for Gladstone a break with his beloved constituency, the University of Oxford, for that indignant Anglican body would not tolerate such apostasy at a time when the disestablishment campaign of English Non-conformity was growing alarmingly. Retreating to a hard-fought South Lancashire constituency after he had been unseated in the 1865 elections, he pointedly distinguished between the two ways of life:

> I come into South Lancashire, and find . . . the development of industry. I find the growth of enterprise. I find the progress of social philanthropy. I find the prevalence of toleration. I find an ardent desire for freedom. If there be one duty more than another incumbent upon the public men of England, it is to establish and maintain harmony between the past of our glorious history and the future that is still in store for her.

Here Gladstone specifically saw himself as the bridge between the traditional past of the political class and what he conceived to be the future of a society reconciled to itself and exalted through moral commitment.

Naturally Gladstone, like Mill, Bright and all the other leaders of the 'movement', assumed that he represented the future. He and they supposed that their assumption would be substantiated by the very fact of a Reform Act itself, by the very fact of a new Liberal government which would set in train so many and long desired acts of progress and enlightenment. Mill and Bright are more important here, for Gladstone was a newcomer, indeed, as he himself saw it, a pupil. Though different from one another in many ways, as indeed Gladstone was different from them both, they yet agreed fundamentally that the great requirement of politics was to set it on a 'natural' basis. Bright tended to see this in historical terms. He looked back to a time when the Puritans of the seventeenth century had restored the medieval liberties and 'happy unity of social intent' of England; and he wanted to see the end of the rule of aristocracies and bishops which the Tudors and then the Restoration and Whig Revolution had foisted on the country. He wanted, he said in 1866, 'to restore the British constitution in all its freedom to the British people'. And it was as a mill owner with labour relations very much on his mind that he thought that a 'happy unity of social intent' could be restored by the enfranchisement of between 200,000 and 400,000 new voters with appropriate redistribution of electorates to ensure that traditional influence could be reduced to a minimum. Bright was convinced of the right of the middle classes to leadership.

Mill is more interesting, though by no means more representative, because his theory of 'natural' political society was more fully developed. He was clear that achievement of the desired 'natural state of society' would require a decisive element of leadership. Mill saw as the obstacles to this quest the 'selfish interests of aristocrats, or priests, or lawyers, or some other species of imposter'. It was the imposter element which gave offence, not the idea of leadership in society itself. Mill defined the 'natural state of society' as that 'in which the opinions and feelings of the people are, with their voluntary acquiescence, formed for them'. The more intelligent and educated they were the more likely they would be to 'defer' to people more intelligent than they. Mill's aim was to make such guidance and leadership natural and moral, just as aristocratic leadership was unnatural and immoral. Mill indeed thought of the group or community as 'natural' and as a guarantee of public morality, and he actually opposed one of the standard Radical planks, the ballot, on these grounds. Most Radicals thought of the ballot as the small man's means of escaping from the big man's influence. But Mill saw open voting, under the critical eye of the community, as a means towards the legitimate moral shaming of voters who tried to use their votes in an illegitimate way. Thus Mill aimed at a society of intelligent individuals who would yet, through their very intelligence, see the necessity of deferring to what amounted to an élite of the most intelligent. Hence the question is really as much about deference as about rational individualism. Mill always coupled proposals for a democratic franchise with schemes to give plurality of voting to intelligence and knowledge as opposed to property. Mill in fact foresaw the need for establishing a 'systematic National Education by which the various grades of politically valuable acquirement might be accurately defined and authenticated' for this purpose. Thus 'property' and 'numbers' were both illegitimate; and for Mill 'the reform process reflected the effort to maximize legitimate political behaviour'.[1]

In this general way, Mill's outlook did represent that of the leaders of the reform movement as a whole. And this consideration underlines the point that the 1860s were not consciously straining to make themselves the 1890s. The debate of 1866 and 1867 looked back rather than forward. One must be above all careful to avoid teleological assumptions about the nineteenth century despite the relative speed of social change. It is obvious, looking back from the twentieth century, that the blind forces at work in the nineteenth century inevitably caused profound changes in political behaviour. As the mass of people came to live in cities, to have a higher standard of living, to be literate, to think less in terms of groups and communities and allegiances to traditional institutions like church and chapel and more in terms of stratified class allegiances, necessarily the political process would reflect such changes and pressures. But this was not at all the context of consciousness in which the debate of 1866-7 took place. And hence it is quite mistaken to think of the Act of 1867 as an 'instalment' towards paying up fully a general nineteenth-century political account. 1867 was not a promise to the future that happened; it was an attempt in one sense to settle problems left over from the past, and a promise in another sense to a future that aborted, that never happened. It did not look forward to a declared goal of universal suffrage, one-man-one-vote, equal electoral districts and strict limits on electoral expenditure which have in the twentieth century become regarded as the 'normal' and inevitable mode of operating politics.

Nor can 1867, any more than 1832, be looked at in terms purely of the extent to which the concessions necessary to this march of political progress were wrung out of a frightened and reluctant ruling class. If members of the ruling class were frightened and reluctant in 1867 and 1832 it was for reasons basically concerned with what they thought of as 'natural'. It was a matter of dispute about the definability of what was and was not morally legitimate in politics; and both Radicals and traditionalists in

1867 would be equally horrified at the twentieth-century assumption that it is 'natural' and legitimate and indeed integral to politics that classes may be bribed though individuals may not. That is, class-based parties compete to win the support of a majority of the electors by promising material benefits. This was regarded in the earlier nineteenth century as the ultimate in political immorality, and a great deal of the doubt in some minds in 1867 was the extent to which this kind of immorality might be encouraged by a too large enfranchisement of working-class voters necessarily obsessed with purely material interests.

The spokesmen and representatives of the working-class movement demanding an extended franchise in 1866-7 did not contradict these attitudes and assumptions. On the contrary: they were demanding admission to the club, not demanding that the club be demolished, or even that the rules be changed drastically. The first Trades Union Congress in 1868 – as an example of a characteristic new development of working-class self-expression – was an assertion of the idea of the legitimacy of a working-class contribution to the debate about a revised social and political settlement. Beales, the president of the Reform League, stressed that the working classes increasingly, as members of cooperatives, building and friendly societies, depositors in savings banks, were 'becoming themselves capitalists and landowners', 'deeply interested in the preservation of law and order of the rights of capital and property'. Extremist elements demanding manhood suffrage and one-man-one-vote and equal electoral districts were by no means the most considerable part of the general agitation. There was general agreement in the ranks of the Reform League as much as in the House of Commons about excluding the unworthy 'residuum'. The problem was in drawing the line. A great many working-class leaders as well as their middle-class sympathizers were painfully aware of the extent to which manhood suffrage was susceptible to the kind of manipulation and demagogy so apparent in France in 1848 and under the Second Empire. The vote-hungry working class were indignant at their continued exclusion on grounds of dignity as much as interest. They resented being told that they were untrustworthy or worse – venal and necessarily corrupt, since their depressed social circumstances made them incapable of conceiving politics in terms other than of material envy. Robert Lowe, the most brilliant debater in what is generally admitted to be the most brilliant series of debates to which the House of Commons ever rose, made allegations along these lines which did more than anything else to raise the temperature of the agitation and which were never forgiven. But undoubtedly the clearest evidence of working-class modesty – even humility – was their readiness to understand and forgive John Stuart Mill's forthright statement that the working classes, though ashamed of being so, were 'generally liars'.

Nor do the notorious riots in Hyde Park on 6 May 1866, when an application to hold a reform demonstration was refused by the authorities and a collision resulted between demonstrators and police, compromise this interpretation. To Matthew Arnold, watching from his balcony overlooking the park the railings being broken down and the flower beds trampled, the spectacle seemed a signal manifestation of the 'anarchy' he was devoted to opposing. There was certainly an element of provocation in the demand to hold a demonstration in the heart of the fashionable West End as there was a good deal of misjudgement and misunderstanding on the part of the authorities. Yet the provocation was deliberately aimed against exclusiveness; and the contrast between the government's stern resolution in April 1848 and its wavering irresolution in May 1866 was in itself a measure of the relaxation permitted by the new dispensation of things. As a recent authority on the reform period justly puts it, 'the Riots were a protest against class isolation, not a symptom of class war'.[2] George Howell, the secretary of the Reform League, insisted that he wanted 'neither aristocratic rule, nor the rule of the middle classes, nor the rule of the working classes'. He wanted 'a government of the entire people – where wealth and intellect will have its fair share of power – no more'.

The essence of the question of reform is thus to be seen in terms of debate about the justice and expediency or otherwise of making the existing system of politics more comprehensive and not in terms of setting the existing system on a prescribed path towards twentieth-century democracy. It was a problem of striking a settlement that would satisfy the country and provide the point of rest and stability for a reconstituted Victorian equilibrium.

II

When Gladstone heard of Palmerston's death he wrote to Russell: 'any government now to be formed cannot be wholly a continuation, it must be in some degree a new commencement'. Russell was in no mind to deny Gladstone's proposition that the function of Liberalism was now to fulfil promises implicitly made on its behalf by Gladstone as the pre-eminent representative of its new spirit. Russell, old and feeble, would succeed Palmerston as prime minister; but Gladstone was universally acknowledged as his heir apparent, and he was now Liberal leader of the House of Commons. Russell had long wanted a new Reform Act with which to round off his career which had begun so brilliantly with the first Reform Act. The Palmerstonians did their best to put the brakes on by suggesting a Royal Commission; but the impatient Radicals pressed successfully for an immediate measure.

In the session of 1866 Gladstone introduced in the Commons on behalf of Russell's ministry a bill designed to enfranchise 400,000 men, about half of them working-class, by lowering the 1832 £10 rental level to £7 and by various other concessions to lodgers and 'compounders' (occupiers who compounded with their landlords to pay the rates), by lowering the county occupation franchise, and by such things as allowing votes to men with deposits of £50 in savings banks. To the surprise of the ministry they found themselves in difficulties in the Commons, with thirty-five Palmerstonian Liberals voting in an important amendment alongside the Conservatives, and six more absenting themselves. The Conservatives initially proposed to help the Bill through in order to avoid the mistake of 1832 and to keep some control over its provisions. But Disraeli balked at this subordinate role. He was convinced that if the Conservatives boldly took advantage of Liberal dissensions they could wrest the initiative entirely from the hands of the government. Audaciously, Disraeli, to Derby's dismay, decided to ride the whirlwind and direct the storm. This meant in the first instance defeating rather than assisting the government.

The defecting Liberals were led by Lowe, who had distinguished himself by oratory designed to establish a case against further enfranchisement on the basis of utility: that is, assessing its merits on the grounds of its probable consequences rather than on grounds of 'natural right' or 'social justice'. In this he was strongly supported by another utilitarian, the Conservative Lord Robert Cecil, from 1865 Lord Cranborne and from 1868 third Marquis of Salisbury. Their argument was that the best possible political results were already attainable with the existing franchise. Further enfranchisement would upset the balance of the classes by giving preponderant weight to a class presumably actuated by ignorance and venality. Disraeli, for the Conservative party, accused Gladstone of wanting an 'American constitution' with Parliament reflecting mere numbers. Eventually ministers were defeated by 304 to 315 votes on an amendment. Gladstone, in the hour of defeat, replied defiantly in terms which well illustrate his sense of what it was he represented:

> You may bury the Bill that we have introduced but . . . [you] cannot fight against the future. Time is on our side. The great social forces which move onwards in their might and majesty . . . those great social forces are against you; they are marshalled on our side; and the banner which we now carry in this fight, though perhaps at some moment it may droop over our sinking heads, yet it soon again will float in the eye of heaven and it will be borne by the firm hand of a united people . . . perhaps not to an easy, but to a certain and to a not distant victory.

Disconcerted by this setback, the ministry could not make up its mind to any positive response; and rather feebly decided to resign. Derby took office for the third time as prime minister of a minority ministry in June 1866. Disraeli replaced Gladstone at the Exchequer and as leader of the House. Cranborne entered his first cabinet as secretary for India. Derby was in no mind to act yet again as a mere caretaker, filling in such time as Liberals chose to quarrel among themselves. Like Russell, he too wanted to round off a career which had started with support for the Act of 1832 with a stroke of great national policy. In the circumstances it was natural for him to think of reviving an earlier Conservative reform proposal of the 1850s, which could be used to re-establish Conservative political credibility, give reasonable satisfaction to the country on the issue of some extension of the franchise, and allay ruling class anxiety by emphasizing, through plural voting systems, that property would be in no danger. He hoped at first to broaden his parliamentary support by securing the allegiance of dissident Liberals to pass such a 'safe' Reform Bill. But the 'Cave of Adullam', as Bright called Lowe and his friends,[3] were interested in blocking any Reform Bill, not in assisting a Conservative one. Disraeli now seized the opportunity to try to get a Conservative Bill through against both the erstwhile Liberal government and their Adullamite enemies by striking a reasonable bargain with the Liberal centre. By 1867 most members of the House were anxious to get some sort of Bill through and settle the issue. Undoubtedly also the unrest expressed in the Hyde Park riots and the widespread indignation provoked by Lowe's counter-productive insults and a series of massive demonstrations in the major cities throughout 1866–7 added weight to the argument that expediency pointed to a prompt settlement. To this the Queen added arguments about the desirability of clearing away domestic distractions in the face of the tense international situation as Prussia allied with Italy moved to the brink of war with Austria.

Thus Palmerston's last parliament, elected in 1865, performed deeds which it would have been astounded to have heard predicted of it. The child of an aristocratic dispensation, it yet found itself marching and countermarching behind rival banners of reform. The child of caution and common sense, it yet found itself lost and dispersed amid what Disraeli aptly quoted as the 'Serbonian Bogs' of franchise-mongering politics. And at the behest of ministers who had opposed a first bill as too advanced, it eventually launched itself on the celebrated 'leap in the dark' of household suffrage which almost doubled the electorate from about 1,430,000 to 2,470,000 voters, probably about a third of the adult male population, making the artisan class the largest body of the borough electorate, which was increased by nearly 140 per cent.

Yet there is no paradox in the passing of a Reform Act by the 1865 parliament. True, a majority of its members were reluctant to do so. This was only to be expected since for one reason or another they were quite content with the *status quo*. The issue of redistributing constituencies naturally reinforced this inertia. But once it became clear that reform could no longer be evaded and had become an immediate and practical issue the parliament did its duty as it saw it to the country and attempted to give it substantial satisfaction. If each M.P. had been left simply to his own personal devices, no act would have been passed.

But the leadership was very prepared to coerce the members. In this situation Disraeli had the advantage over Gladstone and that is why the act was eventually passed under Disraeli's auspices. For whereas there was a substantial body of Liberals who were ready to defy Gladstone to the point of effective veto, there was no parallel Conservative group prepared to defy Disraeli. Most Conservatives were willing in the last resort to accept the proposition of their leadership that a settlement was necessary in the public interest and that their leadership was best placed to decide when and how that interest would best be served. In any case, Tory fears about the size of the dangerous social 'residuum' lessened as they sensed the nearness of parliamentary victory; while Bright and many Radicals grew increasingly worried in 1867 about the dangers of a too large enfranchisement and its possible consequences, such as an agitation to repeal the New Poor Law. Thus in the end Disraeli, who had started off under Derby's initiative with a bill rather less adventurous than Gladstone's, ended up with one very much more adventurous, to Gladstone's indignation but to the tacit approval of Gladstone's most eager supporters.

Disraeli's motives were short-term and his outlook was as essentially backward-looking as Mill's. He wanted a parliamentary triumph for himself and a victory for the Conservative party. So long as he got a bill through and could take credit for the settlement almost anything short of manhood suffrage was expedient. His tactical strength was that he realized what Gladstone did not, that 'household suffrage' was a solid-sounding thing which could give a national satisfaction that no combination of what Bright called 'fancy franchises' designed to give extra weight to property could.

Derby and Disraeli, leaders of a minority party, had been left by Palmerston's death in the exposed position of having to cope, on behalf of the traditional ruling class as a whole, with Gladstone's offensive. 'Coping' did not necessarily mean blocking or thwarting; it meant ensuring that the mistake of 1832 would not be repeated. That mistake had been to let what should have been a 'national' settlement pass into the hands of one political faction. Blocking the Liberal bill of 1866 was easy, for it was simply a matter of deploying the Conservative party in the posture the party was most content to be deployed in. The redeployment of 1867 was a perfectly logical consequence of 1866. If the Conservatives could pass a 'better' bill, more accurately attuned to the requirements of natural and legitimate political behaviour as they defined it, they could re-establish their prestige and perhaps attract across from the Liberals important elements of Whiggish and 'moderate' opinion being worried at the prospect of a party led by Gladstone and his friends. That in the event Disraeli, rather to Derby's misgivings and the indignant resignations of Cranborne, Carnarvon and General Peel from the cabinet, threw all the original Conservative safeguards to the Radical wolves and thus let a 'worse' bill through is explicable because Disraeli, besides realizing that Conservative 'fancy franchises' were no more plausible than Liberal ones, was convinced that household suffrage would be no threat to the Conservative party. True, it was not likely to be much advantage in the borough constituencies themselves; but on the other hand neither was a more restricted enfranchisement on the lines of 1866. And since the boroughs were largely Liberal in any case, Conservatism would not thereby actually lose seats. Moreover, the new householders in the counties were likely to be Conservative. Having nothing to lose one way or the other on the actual extent of enfranchisement, Disraeli's calculations logically centred on immediate parliamentary advantage. Moreover, he liked making dramatic gestures calculated to strike the public imagination. And he was careful to try to see to it that the Redistribution bill complementing reform should reinforce the strength of the landed interest in the country and county towns. Bright and his friends accepted this rather than cause any more delay: the new parliament would do the job properly. Derby loyally followed through and gave the House of Lords its marching orders in Wellingtonian style. Indeed, the only 'fancy franchise' to survive was at the Lords' insistence: a system of constituencies was established in six large cities and six counties designed to protect minority rights by having three members and giving each elector only two votes (four members and three votes in the City of London).

Above all, what 1866 and 1867 most clearly reveals from the angle of Conservatism is that it was Disraeli who was being 'educated'. Circumstances obliged him to accept the inevitability of household suffrage. Converting necessity into virtue followed naturally.

The received Disraeli myth is that he was educating his party to become the mass popular party of the 1870s and 1880s on the doctrinal foundations of the Young England movement. In practice there is no evidence that Disraeli anticipated that the future of Conservatism would be based upon a 'national' working-class electorate. He never troubled himself seriously to cultivate artisan votes. Rather it is clear that Disraeli could not imagine a Conservative party other than as established on an agricultural basis. To that extent he always remained faithful to the picturesque principles of the 1830s and 1840s. Disraeli simply could not accept the possibility that the permanently dominant political force in England could really be the alliance of the 'Hudibrastic crew' of Liberal manufacturers, dissenting shopkeepers and utilitarian intellectuals. At bottom his was an aesthetic politics like Matthew Arnold's. His major concern with redistribution had been to shield the agricultural constituencies from urban contamination. So far from thinking in terms of the 'Conservative working man', Disraeli was not even thinking in terms of that truly richly rewarding source of Conservative strength in the future, suburbia.

Disraeli's hopes for a revived Conservatism therefore depended on the party's gaining a sufficient majority on a traditional basis. It would certainly be a 'national' basis, but defined in terms of Palmerstonism rather than Young England: the domestic counterpart, in other words, to the bid for the 'national' stakes in the external sphere. Like Palmerston, Disraeli wanted to be able to call on the support of many interests as a means of preserving the one great interest, 'the national interest', which he identified centrally with land.

Disraeli had made his name on the strength of his being the most vitriolic and brilliant denouncer of Peel's bad faith to the Tory party. He had made his career since then on the strength of his being the only man left on the Conservative benches in the Commons who could give as good as he got from the heavy guns on the other side, Whigs, Liberals and Peelites; and especially his duels with Gladstone became in the 1850s and early 1860s one of the established parliamentary features. They were two men so obviously made to be good enemies. Disraeli however also had good enemies in his own party. He had never been popular and only his indispensable talents had saved him from being dropped on several occasions. His efforts to re-establish the fortunes of the Conservative party were therefore intimately bound up with his need to secure his own position. When Derby retired at the beginning of 1868 Disraeli contrived to secure the succession without open dispute on the grounds of the personal prestige he had achieved in outmanoeuvring Gladstone in 1867 and in giving Conservative M.P.s the rare sensation of success. But even so his position was vulnerable.

Certainly, Disraeli failed conspicuously to display throughout the crisis any large outlook of creative imagination. If there is a paradox to be resolved about 1867 it is perhaps this, for Disraeli's general reputation is founded upon his alleged forte for just such a quality. The curious contrast is pointed to[4] between Disraeli the alleged adventurer stolidly pinning his hopes to an agricultural future while Salisbury the notorious reactionary argued that Conservatism must seek salvation by gaining a foothold in the great urban constituencies, for the counties and small county boroughs would be too narrow a basis for convincing national political strength. The resolution suggests itself that fear is a very good spur to creative imagination. Salisbury, a calculating utilitarian, was frightened enough of democracy to do some new thinking. He deduced that class – the 'masses' versus the 'classes' – would be the sovereign factor in future politics. Conservatism would essentially be about building up an aristocratic-bourgeois combination against the democracy to defend property against confiscation. Disraeli's imperturbable confidence allowed him to nurse complacent fantasies that Palmerstonism had not been replaced but put on a new and firmer footing and blinded him to possibilities offered to Conservatism by social change.

Traditional interpretation attributed the Conservative revival in the later nineteenth century to the Disraelian genius of 'Tory Democracy'. Later interpretations have swung towards the view that it was in truth a thoroughgoing Peelite procedure concealed by a smokescreen of Disraelian myth.[5] By 'Peelite' is meant that, as Peel between the Tamworth Manifesto of 1834 and the electoral victory of 1841 had adopted a negative posture of waiting for support to come over from discomfited and anxious moderates frightened by Radical excesses, so the real strength of Conservatism between 1868 and 1874 came from the same migration of moderate men frightened by the excesses of Gladstone. 1874 undoubtedly is to be so explained; but the assumption that if Disraeli cannot be given credit for genuine Tory Democracy he must be given credit for ingenious crypto-Peelism does not necessarily follow. In fact, Disraeli deserved as little credit for the villa vote as he did for Tory Democracy. This again is to confuse what actually happened with what was expected to happen. Obviously, it can be seen that the optimum advantage to be gained by Disraeli in the circumstances of 1867 was to combine the credit for establishing Conservatism as a great popular party with the credit for providing a refuge for the bourgeoisie anxious about that very same popular element in politics: in other words, to transform a situation of contraction into one of double advantage. In the long run this can certainly be accepted as Disraeli's legacy to his party; but it was a legacy Disraeli was not intending to pass on.

III

Unlike Disraeli at this time, Gladstone was excited by large ideas of imaginative creativity. The fact that circumstances made him play but a sorry role in the actual matter of the reform issue in 1866 and 1867 did nothing to dampen this excitement. Rather, his indignation made him all the more determined to scotch Disraeli, and eventually earned him the awed tribute that he was 'terrible on the rebound'. But his pilgrimage towards 'light and freedom' requires to be examined with care and reservations. Gladstone used language in a manner peculiar to his time which requires to be decoded to avoid confusion. When Gladstone used words like 'future', 'time is on our side', 'great social forces', 'firm hands of a united people', 'certain and not distant victory', they have no necessary objective validity. In fact in practically every respect Gladstone's assumptions about the shape of the future were belied by events, just as were Disraeli's assumptions about the possibilities of perpetuating a traditional Palmerstonian past. In what amounts to a contest in misapprehension between these two great national leaders in the coming decades Gladstone, as it happens, came off rather the worse through no great fault of his own and no great merit in Disraeli. But for purposes of immediate analysis it must be stressed that the day-to-day range of Gladstone's imagination did not reach significantly beyond the boundaries of Liberalism as variously defined by Mill, Bright and others. He would never go with Mill in the direction of socialistic 'constructionism'; he would never go with Bright against the Church and into a diplomacy of isolationism.

In practical terms, Gladstone's Liberalism was pretty accurately reflected in the hedging qualifications with which he almost smothered his 'pale of the constitution' statement. And the central motive of his political actions was always the design to create the kind of community in which the kind of élite most consistently depicted in Mill's theory would flourish, though always with a good deal more of the nobility, a good deal more of the Church, and a good deal more of Oxford than Mill would relish. Again, as with the 'pale of the constitution' furore, the important extra factor which made all the difference was a climate of expectation, a mobilizing of millions of individual aspirations and moral attitudes which found their natural focus in himself. There was always the likelihood, therefore, with Gladstone, that expectation would outrun achievement; that high hopes would end up with disappointment; and this indeed was to be the pattern of his administrations.

Near the end of his life, Gladstone looked back over his career and tried to analyse what it was about his approach to politics that most distinguished him. His analysis, in a memorandum of about 1896, is worthy of careful attention because of its extraordinary penetration in a general way and because of its particular value as evidence on specific points of later controversies. If, he wrote, providence had endowed him with anything that could be called a 'striking gift' it was that he had the power of divining at 'certain political junctures' 'what may be termed appreciation of the general situation and its result'. By this Gladstone was careful to insist that he did not mean a mere opportunism, 'a simple acceptance of public opinion, founded upon the discernment that it has risen to a certain height needful for a given work, like a tide'. On the contrary, it was something much more positive, exalted and creative: 'It is an insight into the facts of particular eras, and their relations one to another, which generates in the mind a conviction that the materials exist for forming a public opinion, and for directing it to a particular end.' Gladstone considered that there were four such crucial occasions in his career: the renewal of the income tax in 1853; the 'proposal of religious equality for Ireland' in 1868; Home Rule for Ireland in 1886; and his attempt to get his last cabinet to agree in 1894 to a confrontation with the House of Lords.

Thus, the key fact about 1868 is this claim to 'insight' that the materials existed to be manipulated for a great work, and that great work was to be the Irish Church, to which complementary issues of Irish land and Irish higher education were by now attached. What needs to be stressed here most decisively is what might well be termed the Olympian aspect of intervention from on high of all this: it marches well with Mill's élitism. What is conspicuously absent is any sense of a theory of democratic action. To Gladstone the masses were 'materials' in a manner not so far removed from Lenin's theory of revolution. Certainly there is little indication with Gladstone of any feeling of closeness or identification or partnership with popular moods and attitudes. And yet there was undoubtedly some sense of a kind of epic poetry of politics: the political possibility of moral action on a grand scale, even if many of its 'materials', such as Nonconformity, were hardly poetic in themselves and exhibited enough prosaic narrowness almost to justify Arnold's sardonic gibes.

Gladstone's analysis of 'insight' does not exclude another interpretive framework in which 1868 may with advantage be placed, that of 'mission'. Gladstone was in no doubt that Ireland so qualified in 1868. One of the classic Gladstonian moments was after the 1868 elections when Gladstone, tree-felling at Harwarden, received news of a summons from the Queen. 'Very significant', he remarked to Evelyn Ashley,[6] who was in attendance holding his coat; and then, 'with deep earnestness in his voice and with great intensity in his face', 'My mission is to pacify Ireland.' The two succeeding 'missions' which relate back to 1868 and to one another to form the moral spine of his career were the destruction of 'Beaconsfieldism' from 1876 to 1880 and Home Rule for Ireland in 1868 and after (to which the House of Lords issue is integrally connected).

Ireland in the early and late phases was therefore the area in which both the 'insight' and 'mission' analyses coincided. This is as good an indication as any of the stature it was to take as a problem of statesmanship, and specifically of Liberal statesmanship, in the Gladstone years. Already the dim outlines of a new phase of Irish insurgency were becoming discernible. The ultimate consequences of the British failure either to leave the Irish essentially alone or to transform them basically from their aboriginal Irishness were about to begin revealing themselves. The thin layer of the Anglo-Irish Ascendancy was beginning to crack. Something would have to be done about religion, something about land. Certainly, on a strictly practical level in the later 1860s, its urgency as a problem was underlined by the provocations of an organization know as the Fenian Brotherhood. Founded in New York among the Irish émigrés in 1858, Fenianism aimed at overthrowing English rule in Ireland by force. Fenian gunrunners had been arrested in 1865. There had been an 'invasion' of Canada in 1866. *Habeas corpus* had to be suspended in Ireland in 1866 and a general Irish insurrection was planned for 1867. At the end of 1867 an attempt to free some Fenian prisoners at Clerkenwell caused twelve deaths and many injuries. These outrages did not force Gladstone's arm on Ireland any more than the Hyde Park riots forced the Reform Act. But, like the riots, they manifested a depth of feeling which politicians would be foolish to ignore. For Gladstone, the public shock at the outrages was indeed one of his 'materials'.

The elections of 1868 themselves were little more than a formality. The conditions which since 1847 had made a Conservative majority virtually impossible still obtained. The cry of 'the Church in danger' did not help the Conservatives much, since the Irish Church was not a popular cause. Impregnable as ever in the counties, Conservatives had little hope of significant inroads into the new urban electorate. The issue was how large the Liberal majority would be. In 1865 it had been about 70; in 1868 it proved to be about 110; with gains mainly in Scotland, Wales and Ireland. The most notable change made by the 1867 Reform Act was to heighten political interest and consequently more seats were regarded as worth contesting. Even so, only about half the seats in 1868 were contested by both parties. Conservatives did well in Lancashire, an area in which they were traditionally strong, on a basis of Liverpool mercantilism which shared little of the Liberal fervour of Manchester's causes, on anti-Irish and anti-Catholic sentiment, and on Stanley influence. In 1865 they had held fourteen out of thirty-two seats; in 1868 twenty-four out of thirty-eight seats. So long as Lancashire voters held their allegiance to religious rather than to class lines Toryism would retain its ascendancy. Gladstone himself, whose mode of election for South Lancashire in 1865 by no means corresponded to the exalted rhetoric of his addresses, had to retreat once more, to Greenwich. In Westminster Mill was unseated by W. H. Smith, the newsagent, a circumstance that developed a retrospective significance as Smith came to symbolize a new class of urban or suburban voter passing from Liberalism to Conservatism, and often, as in Smith's own case, on the basis of a conversion from Nonconformity to Anglicanism. He described himself in 1868 as an 'Independent Liberal Conservative', a nicely transitional label. Lord George Hamilton's success in Middlesex over the Radical Henry Labouchere was also a significant pointer to growing

Conservative strength in middle-class constituencies. The 'minority clause' of the 1867 Act probably gave the Liberals three extra seats in 1868 by stimulating electoral organization, most notably in Birmingham, where by careful allocation Liberals were able to secure all three seats. This was the germ of Birmingham Radicalism's efforts over the next two decades, under the leadership of Joseph Chamberlain, to become the directive impulse of 'advanced' Liberalism.

Apart from this organizational aspect, undoubtedly the most significant feature of the election results was the formidable corps of Nonconformists entering the House of Commons for the first time. Guttsman estimates ninety-five 'anti-State Church' M.P.s in 1868, of whom sixty-three were Dissenters.[7] This was almost double the previous Nonconformist parliamentary body. Although not liking the alliance of Roman Catholicism on the Irish disestablishment issue, they thought the principle and its prospects in England compensated for such discomfort. Many Wesleyans were beginning to feel a solidarity with the older dissenting denominations and began voting Liberal. Although by no means representative of a monolithic 'interest', Nonconformity yet registered in 1868 its arrival at a new and enhanced status in political and national life.

On the whole, the elections of 1868 are not to be regarded as in any decisive way 'modern'. The fact that Disraeli created a constitutional precedent by immediate resignation rather than waiting for a formal vote at the beginning of the next session of parliament was not intended to signify a procedure appropriate to a new political era. Rather it reflected Disraeli's awareness of his false position as the head of a government filling in the interim while the new electoral rolls necessitated by the Reform Act were being prepared. Already Gladstone had reunited the Liberals and defeated the government with resolutions to disestablish and disendow the Church of Ireland.

What was new and important was undoubtedly Gladstone's personal situation and the manner of his becoming the focus of national attention. His 'stump' in South-West Lancashire adumbrated the great Midlothian campaigns of 1879 and 1880. As with Midlothian, Gladstone in 1868 composed a series of addresses together making up a coherent programme directed ostensibly to the local constituency but in reality to the national constituency. The kernel of the programme was a moral appeal against an institution representing generalized political evil – in this case the Irish establishment – and the consequent obligation of men of good will to rally to Liberalism as the means of eradicating it and re-establishing politics on a basis of virtue and the general good as against the selfish interests of class or 'monopoly'. In his *A Chapter of Autobiography*, published in November 1868 and virtually an election pamphlet, Gladstone did much more than explain his change of attitude on Irish Church disestablishment. He introduced an element of demagogic personality into politics much greater than anything of the kind hitherto. Gladstone had become a 'leader' in a sense that Peel or Russell or Palmerston had never been.

Chapter Four

LIBERAL INITIATIVES: GLADSTONE'S MINISTRY 1868—74

I

The second stage of the Liberal effort to establish a new Victorian equilibrium in the Liberal image fulfilled itself in the great programme of reforms between 1869 and 1873. Their overall design was to maximize opportunities for and to minimize obstacles to the attainment of a natural and legitimate political society as broadly defined within the Liberal tradition. Always there was the aim of reducing the financial burden of government. It was a tremendous political achievement, not matched in scope and importance until the second and final Liberal effort before the 1914 war and the Labour programme after the Second World War. Gladstone entered upon it in an appropriate spirit. He wrote at the end of 1868: 'The Almighty seems to sustain me for some purpose of his own, deeply unworthy as I know myself to be. Glory be to His name.'

All this ended in 1874 with the first Conservative electoral majority since 1841, and a bigger one at that. Gladstone suffered the personal humiliation of being relegated to junior representative of Greenwich by a Conservative distiller. He took his dismissal hard. At the beginning of 1875 he abdicated the leadership of the Liberal party.

Two obvious general explanations of this train of events immediately suggest themselves. Either the Liberals had fundamentally miscalculated about their definitions of naturalness and legitimacy, or the country had somehow allowed itself to be diverted into paths of unnaturalness and illegitimacy.

Liberals tended of course to the latter explanation; and it

became a recurrent theme in their interpretations of political development. Masterman, for example, would later account for the failure of the country to respond properly to the opportunities offered in the early 1880s in terms of the seduction and perversion of an unnatural and illegitimate influence summed up in 'imperialism'. In the 1870s this diagnosis had not been hit upon by Liberals: 'imperialism' in any case was not yet launched on its astonishing semantic career and still meant simply adherence to the cause of an emperor. The classical Liberal explanation for 1874 is to see the effect of a series of untoward and unfortunate events which in their cumulative pressure diverted the country away from a true relationship between national need and political response into a course which was *a fortiori* false.

II

In the meantime, however, as Gladstone uttered his praise of the Almighty, the Liberal tide ran with every appearance of an irresistible force. He had assembled a formidable administration. Bright was induced to take the Board of Trade. He was the first Nonconformist in a cabinet. He had neither the taste nor the talent to manage a great department, but his sheer presence until the collapse of his health in 1870 added great weight to the government. Lowe, considered by Gladstone as likely to be more dangerous outside than inside the cabinet, was given the Exchequer. This turned out not to be a lucky appointment. There was an imposing array of Whigs: Ripon, Kimberley, Clarendon, Granville, Argyll (Hartington was added in 1871). Cardwell, a former Peelite, went to the War Office. The Education Office (not in the cabinet) was entrusted to W. E. Forster, who, as an ex-Quaker and Matthew Arnold's brother-in-law, had a foot in both camps of the delicate schools question. The session of 1869 was to be devoted principally to Irish disestablishment. Gladstone proposed to take personal charge of this legislation, and so for the Irish Secretaryship chose Chichester Fortescue, a relative lightweight who could be closely supervised.

The circumstance of a church established and endowed in a state where the ratio of adherents to dissenters (in this case both

Roman Catholic and Protestant) was about one to nine[1] had increasingly come to be regarded as anomalous. Having failed in its missionary endeavours, the Irish Church had relapsed into blatant religious reflection of the political Ascendancy. Some Whigs, Russell among them, had advocated disestablishment and disendowment since the 1830s. Then even modest Whig efforts to make the system less intolerable to the Roman Catholic majority had largely provoked the Anglican reaction in England known as the Oxford Movement. By the 1860s, however, many English Churchmen had come to regard the Irish establishment as more a hindrance than a help to the establishment cause in England. Nonconformists were in two minds: on the one hand they naturally welcomed the destruction of any kind of state establishment of religion; but on the other they were reluctant to contribute to a policy which would inescapably represent a triumph for Roman Catholicism rather than Protestantism. The balance of advantages for Nonconformity, however, seemed to fall on the side of conceding an advantage to Romanism in the lesser sphere of Ireland in return for the prospect opened up of using the precedent of Irish disestablishment for the campaign against English establishment, the primary enemy. In sum the Church of Ireland was the most conspicuous institutionalization of alien privilege on the political scene, and comparatively few felt able to defend it without serious reservations.

The logic of disestablishment was thus irresistible to the moral sense of the Liberal movement in Britain. And even if the Conservatives found its blatancy quite endurable they did not find it altogether expedient or politic. Consequently the Conservatives put up no desperate opposition in 1869. Disraeli did not fight it seriously in the Commons. The Lords mounted a rearguard action to save as much as possible of the endowment, but Gladstone was implacable, and forced them to disgorge.

Gladstone well understood that his mission of pacifying Ireland could not be accomplished by disestablishment alone. More than any other leading British statesman he had the capacity to see Ireland in perspective: historical and European. He hoped to settle the chronic land problem, the consequence of centuries of confiscation and of absentee and irresponsibly avaricious landlordism, and he hoped to equip Roman Catholics with a system of higher education on a par with the Anglican establishment of Trinity College, Dublin. A rural proletariat would be transformed into a contented tenantry; and the Catholic gentry, equipped with the equivalent of Oxford and Cambridge, would train themselves like their English counterparts to the role of a native ruling class of selfless guardians imbued with moral ideals of service and professionalism. In a word, Gladstone wanted to legitimize the government of Ireland in terms of the assumptions of the Liberal tradition. He assumed a community of interests between the legitimate and natural ruling classes of Britain and Ireland which would in turn legitimize the Union. Any idea of a repeal of the Union was therefore ruled out for Gladstone, for in effect it would represent the failure of a central Liberal ideal of legitimacy. It would take nearly twenty years for Gladstone to reconcile himself to the inadequacy of his assumptions of 1868.

For there was all the difference in the world between pushing over the tottering fabric of the Irish establishment and creating the social foundations for a regenerated and reconciled people. Gladstone, above all, had to cope with the consequences of the famine and the collapse of O'Connell's political movement. O'Connells were indeed precisely what Gladstone needed: gentlemen of rather conservative disposition, landowners, lawyers, inheritors of the traditions of Grattan, who yet enjoyed the trust and loyalty of the Irish masses. But they did not exist in meaningful numbers in the 1860s and later. Rather, outside Ulster, there was a nationalized and radicalized and half-starved proletariat which wanted to become landowning peasantry, through a policy of confiscation of the confiscators, led by a Roman Catholic priesthood eager to make Ireland a shining example of a nation regenerated through and by devotion to Holy Mother Church. All that was lacking was a political leadership able to combine these two (often conflicting) nationalist forces effectively and apply the necessary pressure at Westminster. That would take a decade. In the meantime Gladstone went through the performance, with intense solicitude and devoted good will, of trying to build the edifice of Irish national content with the straw bricks of his Liberal assumptions.

It was not a totally thankless task, for he did get a Land Act through in 1870, though the ultimate failure of his Irish University Act in 1873 broke his morale and that of his government. On the land question Gladstone wanted to alleviate the major grievances of the tenants: to give them more security in their tenancy, to give them fair rents, and to give them some compensation for improvements of their holding in the event of the ending or renewal of their tenancy. The question was complicated by conflicting cultural attitudes: on the one hand 'Norman' ideas of property in land; on the other, 'Celtic' ideas of traditional tenant-right. In the end Gladstone had to compromise between those Liberals, led by Bright and supported by Mill, who wanted a system of buying out landlords and converting tenants into a peasantry, and on the other side the Whigs, many of them Irish landlords, who shared fully the prejudices of the landed order generally and who were apprehensive that Irish land reform might be a precedent for English land reform, much as Nonconformists saw Irish disestablishment as a precedent for English disestablishment. They naturally raised the issue of the sanctity of property. Many Radicals of stiff principle simply did not see the creation of a peasantry – notoriously the most reactionary and backward-looking kind of community – as a natural and legitimate function of Liberalism. On the other hand there had been important precedents in India and Canada for government intervention on behalf of tenants in land tenure disputes. Indeed, Gladstone's appreciation that concessions to Irish ideas of tenant-right would be a necessary preliminary to achieving an ultimate 'natural' tenant-landlord relationship in Ireland owed much to recent Indian legislation.

Gladstone had a difficult time of it, but in the end achieved a bill which had the effect of making the life of the Irish tenant farmers more tolerable and which the Lords thought best to let through without serious resistance. If it did not penetrate deeply into the land problem in Ireland, it was a major positive legislative stroke of British good will towards Ireland and a token of a desire to make practical amends of a vicious inheritance.

But with the third leg of his Irish tripod Gladstone came badly to grief, for the Irish Catholic Hierarchy would not tolerate any scheme of higher education for Catholics which any Liberal government could realistically offer.

III

The Irish legislation demonstrated how much more at ease Liberalism was in dealing with an institutional problem like disestablishment than with a social problem like land. A similar pattern is discernible in Liberalism's domestic programme. With reform of the Civil Service, the Army and the universities, and with measures enabling or encouraging people to extend the boundaries of their moral activity, as with the secret ballot or with reduction of liquor licensing, Liberalism found itself on congenial ground and was able to give itself substantial satisfaction. This was not the case with the trade unions and elementary education.

The Order in Council of 1870 regulating entry into the Civil Service was the culmination of the first period of Civil Service reform inaugurated by the recommendations of the Northcote–Trevelyan Report of 1853. That had led to the establishment of a Civil Service Commission to examine all candidates for junior posts. Political nomination was not abolished. In 1859 the regulations were tightened by requiring a certificate from the Commission for all permanent posts in the Service. In 1860 it was recommended that nomination should be abolished and open competitive examinations of a high standard should replace pass examinations. The measures of 1870 put these recommendations into effect. Henceforth no candidate could be posted until he had satisfied the Commissioners in open competitive examination. Only the diplomatic service was exempted from this requirement. Thus the morality of merit was accorded signal recognition. Gladstone both as Peelite and Liberal had always been a keen advocate of open examination as against nomination, and his reasoning well expresses the spirit of the 'out-and-out inegalitarianism' informing his Liberalism. He was certain that reform would tend to 'strengthen and multiply the ties between the higher classes and the possession of administrative power'. He had looked forward 'eagerly', as an M.P. for Oxford University, to reform, for he had a 'strong impression' that 'the aristocracy of this country are even superior, in natural gifts, on the average, to the mass'; and that it was clear that with their 'acquired advantages, their *insensible education*, irrespective of book-learning, they have an immense superiority'.

Gladstone had since then ceased, to his intense grief, to represent Oxford University; but the connection in his mind between the University and 'administrative power' was equally as strong in 1871 when the University Tests Act abolished the religious subscriptions left by the legislation of 1854 and 1856, which in effect still restricted the government of the universities to Anglicans. True, Gladstone was reluctant to promote 'secularism' in this form – he was very sensitive to the bitter cry of people like Pusey that Oxford was thenceforth 'lost to the Church of England'. But just as Peelite notions of the morality of merit had overridden his scruples as a Churchman in the 1850s, so his Liberal notions about the morality of merit took priority in the 1870s. He was at one with the Liberal reformers in the universities as to their assumptions of the power of reformed universities to underwrite to a critical and decisive degree the Liberal achievement of a natural state of society. In particular Jowett at Oxford and Seeley at Cambridge thought in terms of a very deliberate and calculated teaching programme to prepare an intelligent ruling class for the tasks of government. Theirs was an educational theory of legitimacy and morality, merit and service, just as Gladstone's politics was a public theory of the same.

In many ways the various reforms of the British military system during Gladstone's first ministry exemplify as well as anything the interconnectedness for Liberals of principles of morality, efficiency and economy. Again the direction of vision is backward rather than forward, an implementation of the consensus of Liberal debate over the period since the Crimean War. The basic aim of the Liberal military policy was to shift Britain from what may be termed a 'Wellingtonian' posture to a posture characterizable as being on unmistakably Liberal principles. In other words, again, from a system fundamentally unnatural and illegitimate to one natural and legitimate.

Of the influences at work the most important were the 'objective' considerations: on the immediate level, a chronic shortfall of recruitment, aggravated by the depopulating effects of the famine in Ireland, traditionally a rich source of enlistment in the British service; and, on a larger view, recognition that the fundamental lesson of the Crimean War was not so much its misconduct as that it registered the end of Wellingtonian or Peninsular assumptions that Britain could be a military power on a par with the continental Great Powers. This appreciation was underlined with dramatic emphasis in 1866; at the battle of Königgrätz or Sadowa in northern Bohemia, the greatest battle fought in Europe before the mass collisions of the First World War, almost half a million men faced one another along a front of nearly ten miles. The magnitude of the elements involved startled the world: 672 Austrian guns fired 46,535 shots in the engagement, failing to win the battle for the Kaiser, but arousing, as one modern historian puts it, 'the respect of a materialistic generation'.[2] Likewise, the great cavalry actions at the end of the battle were of equally startling magnitude, never again, as it happened, to be surpassed. These were dimensions of war beyond the capacity of the British military apparatus to contemplate. Moreover, the surprising Prussian success led the European powers to move towards various versions of the Prussian universal conscriptive system. Armies of up to a million on a war footing became the general rule. The British establishment after the Army Estimates of 1869 was 89,000 based in the United Kingdom and 91,000 based abroad, mainly in India; with auxiliary militia, yeomanry and volunteers totalling theoretically over 300,000. The non-European Indian Army was something of the order of 120,000. The regulars were long-service professionals: conscription was out of the question in Britain.

Though in sum the British figures looked respectable enough, the bulk of effective British military power was stationed in India. In fact, India was a great barracks whose taxpayers supported up to a half of the British regular Army. The part of the regular Army based in the United Kingdom was dispersed as necessity demanded. Ireland of course required a constant garrison, as did the major strategic fortresses, Halifax, Gibraltar,

Bermuda and Malta, and other strategic points like Capetown. Expeditions in Canada, wars in New Zealand, punitive measures in China, absorbed men and money constantly. Until the Liberals set about a new system in their own image, British military policy thus reflected a strategic dispersal though with a 'Crimean' eye to Europe as where the application of power mattered most in the long run, with a special Indian garrison to secure against internal disruption or possible Russian pressure in Central Asia, the market for 20 per cent of British exports and 20 per cent of British overseas investments, and as a convenient base of operations in the Middle and Far East.

The Liberal aim, in essence, was to leave the Indian situation more or less where it was as far as strength was concerned (there was no real alternative) but to bring home the bulk of the rest of the army, reduce it in numbers and expense and make it an efficient expeditionary army which could be dispatched where it was needed instead of being a dispersed aggregation of strategic garrisons. Any large scale European intervention was in effect ruled out.[3] Thus from being a colonial garrison army with a European interventionist frame of intention, it would become a home army with a colonial or expeditionary frame of intention. The recruitment problem would be solved by improving conditions of service and above all by reducing the term of service from twelve years to six years in the regular service followed by six years in the reserve. Thus a large reserve would theoretically be accumulated. The line regiments would be 'territorialized' to aid recruiting and establish links with the auxiliary formations. Cardwell put all these reforms into train with energy, as well as many others: the commander-in-chief, George, Duke of Cambridge, was subordinated to the War Office and had his traditional connections with his cousin the Queen severed. Most controversial of all, purchase of commissions was abolished, a stroke of the same morality of merit contemporaneously evident in Civil Service and university reform. Gladstone was obliged to resort to the prerogative to outflank the Lords' resistance on this point. The rationale of this resistance was the expediency of maintaining an integral relationship between the social and the military establishments, thus avoiding the risks of either a Bonaparte or of a Bazaine; but to Liberals the lessons of the great continental events of 1866 and 1870 pointed unmistakably to the need for a professional and intelligent officer corps.

In most of this Cardwell had the support of younger military men like Garnet Wolseley, who wanted above all an intelligent army adaptable to modern conditions. But the radical military views by no means corresponded in all respects to those of the majority of Liberals, and Gladstone especially. Gladstone's general idea about military reform was that he would accept immediate augmentations of expenditure demanded by the reforms in return for the early and considerable abatements calculated to be derived from the new system of relying considerably upon reserves. Gladstone in particular wanted to be able to draw on this reduction of expenditure account for the next election. Unfortunately he could not avoid his share of the numerous and expensive expeditions and punitive campaigns which occurred almost every year in the nineteenth century: as well as the 1870 Red River expedition in Canada, brilliantly conducted by Wolseley, and the Looshai expedition of 1871-2, there was the Ashanti War of 1873-4, again a Wolseley performance. In fact the reserve system never really worked, and the home army was always hard put to find sufficient drafts for overseas operations; it never existed as a potentially formidable expeditionary force in itself. Nor, in sum, did Liberal assumptions about the natural and legitimate relationship of military power to the responsible authorities of government allow much scope for the creation, for example, of an 'intelligent' general staff and war college such as the military radicals demanded.

However much the Cardwell reforms may have fallen short of military requirements, they constituted a decisive political achievement. The new system was distinctively expressive of Gladstonian Liberalism especially in its renunciation of military great power claims. In ideological terms the army of Toryism and privilege and power politics was made into the army of free trade and a world at peace through police supervision. The abolition of purchase gave particular satisfaction, chiming in well with the final passing of the Ballot Act of 1872.

IV

With the issue of elementary education Liberals found themselves much less satisfactorily placed. There was no question but that Liberals were in favour of as much of all levels of education as possible. Liberal notions of political naturalness and legitimacy postulated necessarily an educated general public. Ignorance, like superstition, obviously was a weapon of reaction, of priests and aristocrats. Statistics made it painfully clear, also, that of all the advanced western countries, England lagged conspicuously in its provision of education, especially elementary education. In 1851, it was estimated that only a half of all children in England and Wales of the 3–13 years age group attended school. The Newcastle Commission on elementary education reported in 1861, somewhat complacently it was felt, that about 70 per cent of children were getting some sort of schooling; but by 1870 less than 40 per cent of such children attended schools designated as 'efficient'. After the franchise extension of 1867 these figures began to alarm a generation increasingly prone to accept either the arguments of men like Matthew Arnold (an inspector of schools) that anarchy would prevail over culture unless the populace were brought under the disciplines of schooling, or those of men like John Stuart Mill, that liberty depended upon the greatest possible degree of diffused social intelligence. There were plausible arguments, moreover, which stressed the correlation between success in education and success in war: the victory of the North over the South in the American Civil War, the victory of Prussia over Austria in the German *Bruderkrieg*, were victories, it was alleged, founded on the labours of schoolmasters. The poor British showing at the Paris Exposition of 1867 alarmed observers like Lyon Playfair, who pointed especially to British backwardness in technological education.

England had been groping towards some kind of general provision of elementary education for the past forty years.[4] Like franchise reform, most people were in favour of it, more or less. A system of modest state financial aid to existing schools had been developed. The time was ripe for something much more comprehensive. Education generally had been the subject of much debate and attention. Oxford and Cambridge had been subjected to examination by Royal Commissions which reported in 1852 and which resulted in legislation in 1854 and 1856. The position of the older established and expensive public schools had been examined by a Royal Commission presided over by Lord Clarendon in 1862, which delivered its very conservative findings in 1864. Another commission headed by Lord Taunton was then instructed to examine the position of education between the nine old public schools and the elementary education level. They recommended in 1867 – in vain – that a comprehensive system of central and local authorities be set up to supervise secondary[5] education. The issue of elementary education followed logically.

In England and Wales elementary education was in the hands of 'voluntary' agencies. The greatest of these by far was the Church of England, directly or indirectly. The Church regarded this role as its by right, as the inheritor of the educational tradition of the pre-Reformation Church, and as the official guardian of the morals of society. It accepted financial aid from its partner, the State, as a matter of course, and looked forward to receiving more help to carry on the good work. It was obvious that much needed to be done. In 1869 about 1,300,000 children were at schools aided by Treasury grants. These were predominantly schools in which the formularies and doctrines of the Church of England were part of the curriculum. They were inspected by the State, and were generally efficient. Another one million children were at schools not in receipt of grants, not inspected, and not very efficient. About two million children, mostly in the slums of the industrial conurbations, were not at school at all.

The close Church–State relationship in education reflected long-standing and intimate links which were an integral part of the historical fabric of England. Although the removal of political restrictions on Dissenters, Roman Catholics and Jews, and relaxation of discrimination against non-Anglicans at the universities had broken the formal Anglican monopoly of public affairs and public institutions, and despite the traditional erastianism of the Whigs, the position of the Church remained immensely strong. Moreover, to the extent that the Church's relation to the State was in effect a sympathetic partnership, Nonconformity persisted in being correspondingly extreme in its traditional distrust of the State.

It was precisely this State–Church–Dissent relationship which exposed Liberalism to its major dilemma. Almost all Dissenters were Liberals; but not all Liberals were Dissenters. Most Liberals, like Mill, distrusted the idea of State compulsory education, such as Arnold was advocating with authoritarian zeal. Many Liberals, like John Morley, were 'secularists', who wished to wrench the dead hand of superstition from control of the education of the people. Some Liberals, like Gladstone, were zealous and devoted Churchmen who wanted to uphold and even extend the role of religion in education. All Dissenters agreed with this in principle but in the last resort feared the Church more than the State. Not all Liberals agreed with the young Radical T. H. Green that 'it was certainly within the province of the State to prevent children growing up in that kind of ignorance which practically excludes them from a free career in life', and that elementary education thus should be a means to a positive democratic idea of transforming the social foundations of politics. Green was a supporter of the National Education League, set up in 1868 principally at the instigation of the Unitarian Birmingham screw manufacturer Joseph Chamberlain, dedicated to converting the Liberal party to the idea of free, secular and compulsory elementary education, with the 'common school' of the United States as the model. Nor, in any case, was the movement for universal elementary education by any means a monopoly of Liberalism: there was a long tradition of Tory educational philanthropy which had done more than anything else to reduce the peak illiteracy rates of the 1820s.

Out of this muddle Gladstone's government had to formulate an Elementary Education Bill and get it passed. Given general agreement that public money should be appropriated on a large scale for the purposes of elementary education, two contrasted solutions proposed themselves. The first was to supplement existing resources: to give public money to the various voluntary agencies and thus necessarily mainly to the Church of England to enable it to fill the gaps in its provision of schools. This was known as 'putting Church schools on the rates'. The second was to set up a complete system of secular or state provision of elementary education which would absorb the existing voluntary schools. The first alternative would obviously please the Church of England, the Roman Catholics and, to a great extent, the Methodists; would get Conservative support; and above all, would be cheap, because it would leave the voluntary agencies to find a lot of, perhaps most of, the necessary money. On the other hand the second alternative would please all who favoured the separation of Church and State, and of education and denominational religion, and the secularist Radicals who would make a virtue of what to Dissenters was merely a necessity. In the Education League these groups had a formidable engine of pressure politics.

Nonconformity, though still very much on its dignity as a voluntary second-class citizenry for conscience' sake, was beginning to take the offensive against the Church. In the 1840s a movement to disestablish the Church of England got under way, led by Edward Miall, the great Congregationalist and editor of *The Nonconformist*. This new Nonconformist aggressiveness reflected a new confidence, and a corresponding weakening of old assumptions about the State as merely the secular arm of the religious enemy. One ideal aimed at was now a purely secular state, such as that of the United States. And with the new developments in Liberalism following Palmerston's death Nonconformists saw the beginning of a great new era of hope. They responded eagerly to Gladstone as a man who spoke their kind of language, who shared as they imagined their kind of thinking. The first really formidable body of Nonconformist M.P.s assembled in 1868 at Westminster reflected a general Nonconformist feeling that they were now in a position to turn the tables against the Church. By campaigning for a national system of elementary education which would be secular and, if possible, compulsory and free, they would make the State a weapon against the Church, and by depriving it of its schooling system deal it a deadly blow which, together with Irish disestablishment, would herald the coming of disestablishment in England.

The Church party, naturally, was in no mood to sit back and allow all these dreams to come to pass. It patronized a counter-agitation against 'Godless schools' which depended, negatively, on the inertia which would preserve its parliamentary ascendancy over the Nonconformists, and positively, on the very telling argument that it is good policy to reinforce success: Church education was a going concern, and the easiest solution would be for the State to give it extra money to enable it to fill in the gaps. This was very much Gladstone's personal predilection.

The result was an impasse: the Liberal party got stuck between the two alternatives, unable to give decisive support to either. Forster's first bill in 1870 was indeed very much what the Church desired, putting its schools 'on the rates'. Gladstone, however, did not push for it, and such was the storm of outrage from the Education League lobby and the Nonconformists generally that Forster replaced it with a 'compromise' version. In this, voluntary schools were not to be put on the rates, but were to be given increased central state money, and the principle was adhered to that non-voluntary rate-based schools were only to be established where it was clear that voluntary provision was impossible. This caused almost as much outrage from the Leaguers; but the only further major concession they got was the 'Cowper–Temple' amendment, which stipulated that there should be strictly non-denominational religious teaching in rate-aided schools. These schools were to be administered by School Boards elected by ratepayers; the Boards were forbidden to help voluntary schools with rate money; and they could, if they wished, make elementary education in their district free and compulsory. The Leaguers bitterly denounced Forster as a renegade and the government achieved its Education Act of 1870 only by the grace of support from the Conservatives, who rejoiced for the sake of the Church and at the discomfiture of Liberalism.

The Church's victory, however, as it proved, was Pyrrhic. The failure to 'get on the rates' was in the end decisive. The Act of 1870 envisaged 'Board schools' as merely filling the gaps; in fact, by the end of the century, the Board School system had, by virtue of the local financial resources it could tap, established itself as a parallel and equal educational system. Board Schools became one of the great shaping factors of later nineteenth-century English society. The School Boards themselves were in many ways perhaps even more important. They were a kind of participatory democracy, and they trained a new generation of local activists, including women. Elementary education was made compulsory in 1880 and Board School education free in 1891. This tended to put an unsupportable financial burden on the voluntary schools, even when shored up with extra doses of State money by anxious Conservative governments. By the end of the century nearly 6,000 Board Schools educated over two million children; while over 14,000 voluntary schools educated two and a half million children.[6] The next major conflict in elementary education would be provoked by the Church's desperate need of more public money; and by the determination of a Conservative government, in 1902, to put Church schools back where Forster originally intended them to be in 1870, 'on the rates'.

V

The Education League and the Nonconformists generally were grievously disappointed in the failure of the Liberal government to come up to their expectations. To a great extent this reflected a false estimation as to what they legitimately might expect. Gladstone certainly never supposed that his government was under a special obligation to Nonconformity as an interest. Nor did he envisage Liberalism as an agency of positive or 'constructive' social policy, deliberately aiming to change by legislative means the balance of power between classes and interests. For this reason Gladstone and his government were unsympathetic to recommendations from various Royal Commisions that British technological and scientific weaknesses should be countered by the creation of a Ministry of Science. They were uncomfortable with so direct a concept of governmental response. Thus for Gladstone and most Liberals of his time, Liberalism was a mediating force, a broker, between classes and interests, not in some constructive sense the political essence of 'the people'. Lowe's celebrated *mot* after 1867, 'We must compel our masters to learn their letters', was not at all the kind of motivation that lay behind Liberal agitation for an elementary education at least for every child in England; it never crossed Gladstone's mind that the products of elementary education ever would or could become 'masters'.

The same disinclination to 'constructivism' – a derogatory word Gladstone was to use often later – disappointed the trade unionists, now emerging as a significant interest putting in claims to attention. It was precisely characteristic of the Liberal government's behaviour under Gladstone's direction that a sharp distinction was made between settling the dubious legal standing of the trade unions – the 'moral' side of the issue – and refusing to concede the union desire to legalize peaceful picketing, which was the practical nub of the matter as far as the trade unions were concerned. Here, as with Irish land, Liberal attitudes about legitimacy in general were susceptible to classical doctrines of political economy as reinforced by the prestige of free trade which stressed the desirability of the freest possible play of market forces. The result was much the same as with the Nonconformists, though on a much smaller and less important scale. George Howell, the secretary of the parliamentary committee of the T.U.C., found his task of lobbying the Liberals entirely frustrating. He was bitter about the Liberals, as he admonished Goldwin Smith, not only because they did not help, but even more because they actively obstructed. There were of course 'noble exceptions' – Radicals like Mundella – but Howell insisted that his accusation was broadly true. Liberals discouraged all his attempts to bring the unions into a more active role in politics because they feared, Howell alleged, that they would exact a return for their aid. But, Howell demanded indignantly, did not the Nonconformists do this? Liberals thus encouraged unhealthy class antagonisms. The Tories, warned Howell, were doing their best to conciliate the artisan class, and this would be repaid with gratitude, while the Liberal leaders shut their eyes.

The Liberal political troubles began to assemble in battalions. Bruce, the home secretary, through incaution, and Gladstone, through lack of interest, had allowed the government to become committed in 1871 to an impractical and unpopular Licensing Bill which gave mortal offence to the Trade. This offence was not exorcized by the much milder Act of 1872. Then general offence was given to the 'national' public by the government's conciliatory policy to the United States over the *Alabama* affair. Comparatively few people shared Gladstone's opinion in the *Alabama* claims that the $15,500,000 awarded to the United States by the Geneva Tribunal was but 'dust in the balance' as against the precedent set and the example offered to the nations for the peaceful settlement of international disputes. Robert Lowe at the Exchequer had no luck: his sensible proposal for a tax on matches was frustrated by a strike of Bryant and May's match girls, whose pathos caught the public imagination; and then financial irregularities under his responsibility in 1873 led to his being shunted to replace Bruce at the Home Office.

On the Irish University Bill in the 1873 session the Liberal ministry over-extended itself and suffered a damaging parliamentary defeat. The Irish Hierarchy would not accept as sufficient the limit Gladstone could offer them in the way of financing an institution in which the Catholic youth of Ireland could be protected from 'liberalism' in the dangerous fields of philosophy, modern history, zoology and geology. Moreover, a good deal of Liberal and Protestant sentiment was outraged at the extent to which Gladstone was prepared to go to mollify the 'Roman bishops'. Deserted by most of his Irish *corps d'armée*, Gladstone was left exposed to a united Conservative party under Disraeli who had nothing whatever to gain by assisting the government in its distress as they had in the case of the Elementary Education Bill. The government, and Gladstone in particular, suffered a severe impairment of their 'moral power'. Disraeli caught the mood perfectly in his celebrated description of the Liberal front bench as a 'range of exhausted volcanoes'.

Gladstone, whose health was under severe strain, now looked forward with increasing eagerness to the release of retirement from the leadership of the party. Resignation of the government was more convenient from his point of view than dissolution of the House and new elections; and the cabinet agreed. Disraeli, however, declined to form yet another Conservative minority government. He felt that the Conservative position was at last strong enough to justify an all or nothing bid. Grumbling and reluctant, Gladstone was obliged to resume office. Probably he would have done better to accept electoral battle, for the last months of the ministry increasingly exposed the impairment of its prestige and credit. The one final achievement of 1873 was the Judicature Act which reorganized the law courts and set up a court of appeal. In February 1874, after a conflict with the War Office and the Admiralty over unforthcoming financial abatements, Gladstone decided to dissolve the House and appeal to the electorate for a renewal of their confidence.

VI

Disraeli had lain low during 1869, 1870 and 1871. He had no real choice in the matter. There was little he could do to hinder the Liberals without at the same time damaging his own interests. It was much better to let through a compromise and moderate Irish Land Bill, for example, than provoke a major and unnecessary political and constitutional crisis by trying to block it. Moreover, the essence of his Palmerstonian strategy was to wait until the election issues of 1868 were largely out of the way and then concentrate on broader political themes designed to wrest the intellectual initiative from the Liberals and legitimize Conservatism as the historic 'national' party. Further, it was not too difficult to calculate that the longer Gladstone was allowed to go on the more enmeshed he would get in difficulty and unpopularity.

The decision to launch the Conservative bid early in 1872 was well timed, and particularly so for Disraeli personally, for there was increasing criticism of his leadership from within the party. Disraeli made his two famous sorties shortly after, the first at Manchester, in the centre of the area in which the Conservatives had done best in 1868, in April, and the second at the Crystal Palace at Sydenham in June 1872.

The essential element in the Conservative 'programme' as presented by Disraeli represented the ideological aspect of the match between the partyless Palmerstonian heritage and the disinherited Conservative party. The central message, the maintenance of the constitution and the great historic institutions of England, was common to both. Disraeli added two conspicuous things: one, the improvement of the conditions of the people through a comprehensive programme of social reform, derived from the Young England rhetoric; the other, the 'national' bid, with its heavy emphasis on foreign affairs, derived from the Palmerstonian substance. Just as important, however, was a rather inconspicuous point: Disraeli made it clear that a future Conservative government would accept fully the orthodoxy of established political economy. The 'great problem', as Disraeli put it in his Crystal Palace speech on 'Conservative and Liberal Principles' on 24 June, was how to elevate the condition of the people 'without violating those principles of economic truth upon which the prosperity of all states depends'.

The theme of disinheritance was basic for Disraeli. His thesis was that the Conservative party had suffered in the early part of the century a great, and largely deserved, overthrow. Its fault had been to lose touch with the instincts of the people; and this fault had been exploited by the conspiratorial purveyors of 'cosmopolitan' doctrines imported from the continent, passed off on the innocent British public under the plausible guise of 'Liberalism'. Having seized power from the demoralized Tories, the so-called 'Liberals' introduced a 'new system' and endeavoured to 'substitute cosmopolitan for national principles'. But the instincts of a fundamentally patriotic people were reasserting themselves, and the Conservative party, recovering its morale, was preparing to restore to the British people the historic national heritage from which the 'Liberals' had attempted to defraud them. This 'national' claim was the *leitmotiv* of the Crystal Palace speech; at Manchester Disraeli had been more specifically 'national' on the foreign policy issue. He denounced Gladstone for both the Black Sea and the *Alabama* settlements. While disavowing all ambitions to conduct a 'turbulent and oppressive' diplomacy, Disraeli made it clear that Britain had not been fulfilling under Gladstone the European function to which she was entitled. But the nub of his message was to those 'mistaken statesmen who have intimated the decay of the power of England, and the decline of its resources', and it was simply Disraeli's 'confident conviction' that never was there 'a moment in our history when the power of England was so great and her resources so vast and inexhaustible'.

This was grateful language to the ears of the old 'national' public which had observed the vicissitudes of British policy since the fiasco of 1864 with bewilderment and resentment. After the caustic sermons of Salisbury and the irritating stings of Matthew Arnold, they wanted comfort and reassurance, and this Disraeli was anxious to give them.

Beyond this general level of denunciation on one hand and reassurance on the other Disraeli had no need to go; if the middle-class constituencies were going to swing against the Liberals this would be sufficient impulse. Anything more specific would do harm rather than good. Gladstone's situation was quite different. The Liberal party, distracted with disputes and divisions, defeated in 1873, needed to be pulled together by a reversion to an 1868 programme. Gladstone wanted, as he told John Bright, a '*positive* force to carry us onward as a body'. Yet this force eluded him. It was in fact the only election before 1914 in which Liberalism did not have such a positive claim. There would in future be 'Beaconsfieldism', Home Rule, Free Trade, Peers *versus* People. In 1874 Gladstone had no 'mission' claim; he had no 'insights' making him aware that 'materials' existed to be employed for a given work. In the end he relapsed into almost pure Peelite moralism and offered a repeal of the income tax. He had always regarded this tax as undesirable, and, as has been seen, elevated his reluctant renewal of it in 1853 to the status of a major crisis in his political career.

Joseph Chamberlain, by this time famous as an exponent of 'municipal socialism' as Lord Mayor of Birmingham and preparing to enter national politics on a Radical programme fuelled by the Nonconformist moral steam of the Education League, was perfectly correct from the 'constructivist' point of view to denounce Gladstone's appeal as unworthy of a great political party. Naturally he interpreted the heavy Liberal defeat in the elections as confirmation of his attitude. Yet there is little reason to suppose that had Gladstone made the sort of appeal Chamberlain desired, the party's fortunes would have been mended. The organizational weakness so apparent among the Liberals derived from Nonconformist disaffection more than anything else; and Nonconformity was much more preoccupied with its sectarian interests than with Radical programmes. Liberalism lost decisively in 1874 in areas largely unattracted by such programmes. Suburbia was passing over to Conservatism, now equipped, by J. E. Gorst, with an effective national organization. Significant shifts occurred all over the middle-class commuting constituencies of the Home Counties created by railway development, Middlesex, suburban Kent, Surrey and Essex, and the City itself, all of which had been overwhelmingly Liberal in the 1850s.

In all the government dropped 137 seats in the Commons. Eighty-three were lost to Conservatives. The balance of fifty-four, many of them former Liberals, formed a new Irish Home Rule party, marking the end of Liberalism as a major political force in Ireland and the beginning of a three-party system. Soon to join the new Irish nationalist members was Charles Stewart Parnell, who would replace the moderate Isaac Butt as leader and inaugurate a new and more critical phase of the Anglo-Irish relationship.

There was no lack among Liberals of explanations of particular points of weakness: Gladstone himself made up a list of them – Nonconformist resentment at the Education Act, too many 'independent Liberals' and consequent lack of cohesion in the parliamentary party, Roman Catholic sectarianism, Protestant sectarianism. But Liberals would not be content to explain so fundamental a reversal of their assumptions merely by adding together such symptomatic items. Many Liberals pinned the blame on material prosperity as having dulled the political sensibility and social conscience of the country. Green himself was clear on this point. He saw the country as passing through a phase of 'sudden and unexampled commercial prosperity' causing a 'general riot of luxury in which nearly all classes had their share' and in which 'money and beer flowed freely'. Political enthusiasm in these degenerate circumstances naturally fell away. The election found the Liberal party disorganized and demoralized, though of course the 'vested interests' which it had rightly harassed were 'alive and vindictive'.

Equally revealing is the case of John Morley. Mill had died in 1873, and Morley set out to establish himself as Mill's successor as pre-eminent Liberal intellectual guide and to defend Mill's reputation against the assaults of enemies like James Fitzjames

Stephen. *On Compromise*, published in 1874, was Morley's first bid for this pre-eminence. In essence this was a call to Liberalism to pull itself together, to regain its political and intellectual nerve by a harsh cure to strip off all flabbiness of thinking and action and restore the needed implacability and fitness to resume its proper role of fulfilment of the laws of social development. Morley analysed a great many inimical interests and influences: there were the debilitating 'French examples', by which he meant the discrediting of 'abstract theory and general reasoning among us' by the unfortunate events in France, compounding which was the successful fraudulence of the Second Empire in perverting the natural instincts of the people by means of demagogy, militarism and materialism; there was the new vogue for the 'historical method', with its morally subversive relativity and its implied justification of the *status quo*; there were the new corruptions of the popular press; there were reactionary institutions like the State Church, for indeed Morley, together with Chamberlain, thought of disestablishment as the central feature of the future Radical programme. But all these found their opportunity in a time of decline in the 'sincerity of spiritual interest' consequent upon material prosperity, the 'most penetrating of all the influences impairing the moral and intellectual nerve of our generation'. Morley was clear that the electoral expectations of the contributors to the *Essays on Reform* had remained unfulfilled.

Undoubtedly *On Compromise* is the cardinal document of disillusion at the expectations and assumptions, 'the whole-hearted assurance of better times', prevalent among advanced Liberals in the middle and later 1860s. The quantity of 'vivid belief in the possibility of certain broad general theories being true and right' had dramatically declined. The old causes at home and abroad had largely been fulfilled, and now seemed prosaic. Nor had new causes risen to replace the old. Morley's call for a new 'realistic' approach, an awareness of the difficulties to be surmounted, of the formidable enemies yet to be overcome, fittingly closed an era informed more than anything else by Liberal confidence that the future was theirs.

PART II

The Failure of the New Victorian Equilibrium
1874—85

Chapter Five

THE CONSERVATIVE VERSION: DISRAELI'S DOMESTIC BID 1874—80

The essence of the conduct of affairs in the decade 1874–85 was the effort of both Conservative and Liberal governments to operate on the basis of a desired and assumed Victorian equilibrium. Conservatives interpreted this equilibrium to mean a return to 'normal' procedures as defined in Palmerstonian pre-1867 terms. That is, the country having been given the satisfaction it was legitimately entitled to demand in 1867, things could be allowed to settle down after the unfortunate Liberal interlude of disturbing activity. 'We came in,' as Disraeli put it, 'on the principle of not harassing the country.' Liberals of most strains interpreted the equilibrium in terms of a revised dispensation required by the country to fulfil the purpose of 1867 provided by Liberalism but unaccountably mishandled, thus allowing the Conservatives to take an untoward advantage.

Disraeli's task as the head of the first Conservative government with a parliamentary majority since 1846 was to provide the repose and tranquillity expected of him in the domestic sphere and to revive the 'national' foreign policy. He was not expected, nor did he intend, to adventure beyond safe limits. He quickly disillusioned eager Tory social reformers who read a great new positive era of legislative popular Toryism into his Crystal Palace speech. For Disraeli was now seventy, frail and bronchial. His wife, created Viscountess Beaconsfield in 1868, had died in 1872 – the last occasion of decent personal civilities with Gladstone – and this loss sapped inspiration and energy which his flirtations with elderly countesses and the 'Faery' Queen Victoria never replaced. Even the few minor scrapes he got into such as the

Public Worship Regulation Bill and the Royal Titles Bill were not of his doing, but pressed on him by the eager Queen. Nor did he anticipate high adventure in the foreign sphere. The alarms and excursions that did occur did not result intentionally from the renewal of 'national' Palmerstonism in itself; they resulted from the circumstance that 'national' Palmerstonism had not grown less bankrupt with the passage of ten years. As much as in the domestic sphere, Disraeli imagined that there was a 'normal' posture of things which could be got back to without too much trouble. The story of Disraeli's great ministry is how both kinds of normality evaded him, and especially how his failures to achieve it in foreign affairs compromised his domestic efforts and introduced a passion and bitterness unknown in public life for a generation.

Disraeli's cabinet was little altered in personnel from the one he had inherited from Derby in 1868. Two of the malcontents of 1867, Salisbury and Carnarvon, accepted the Indian and Colonial Offices respectively. The new Lord Derby went back to the Foreign Office, Cairns to the Woolsack; Stafford Northcote, Ward Hunt, Gathorne Hardy formed the core of experience behind Disraeli in the Commons. The one new name was that of Richard Cross, who was made home secretary. A Lancashire barrister, a protégé of Derby's, of 'no family',[1] Cross represented, along with W. H. Smith, who was appointed financial secretary to the Treasury, an attempt on Disraeli's part to make a profitable gesture to the Palmerstonian bourgeoisie. All the great Tory 'interests' were represented: Land by Richmond, Lancashire by Derby and Cross, the Church by the Evangelical Cairns and the High Church Salisbury.

An ironic element in the situation is often alleged: 'The great Conservative champion of social reform and the reconciliation of classes came into office in 1874 without a single concrete proposal in his head ... Not only was Disraeli without a definite policy in 1874, he was virtually incapable of constructing one.'[2] Yet there is little evidence in the 1870s of a widespread working-class interest in social reform legislation and state intervention.[3] The skilled 'artisan' class felt no great need of it, and tended to share traditional middle-class suspicion of it as a legacy of the old aristocratic dispensation of State and Church. These artisans formed the rank and file of the trade unions. They certainly wanted legislation for the benefit of trade unionism, but their 'social' demand was essentially for a greater degree of prosperity rather than for interventionist State activity. The mass of the lower orders had hardly any consciousness of the issue beyond a general dislike of intrusiveness and coercion from above. The great desire was to be left alone: not to be conscripted, not to be taxed, not to be 'improved'. For them the most familiar institution of State intervention was the hated workhouse. There was much popular resentment at such things as compulsory vaccination against the smallpox. The Public Health Act and the Artisans' Dwelling Act of 1875, two cornerstones of the Disraelian social reform edifice, express in their very titles upper-class concerns with which the poor shared little or nothing: cleanliness. The Artisans' Dwelling Act in any case owed less to the government's solicitude than to the energy and initiative of Canon Samuel Barnett, one of the many Churchmen who carried on the work of F. D. Maurice and the Christian Socialists into the new generation. In much the same way the Merchant Shipping Act of 1876, which for the first time gave seamen some protection against unscrupulous shipowners, was forced on a reluctant government by Samuel Plimsoll.

In the days before the unionization of unskilled labour the lower orders lacked any effective institutional means of translating social demands into effective pressure on the political process. Religion, for example, could not serve this purpose. Doctrinal religious confession was overwhelmingly a middle-class and artisan preoccupation, as was the secularist infidelity of such Radicals as George Holyoake and Charles Bradlaugh. On occasion, as with particular homogeneous working-class interest groups such as agricultural labourers and miners, Primitive Methodism could become the agency of a significant degree of political Radicalism. But in general the lower orders distrusted Church or Chapel as much as State. And for the populace, enfranchised as well as the unenfranchised, politics was less a matter of issues and policies than of personalities, of spectacle, pageant, a kind of grand secularized miracle play. Palmerston, likewise, appealed by his 'moral' belligerence; and Disraeli was to arouse far more popular support through his neo-Palmerstonism abroad than through his programme of social reform at home. To an extent impossible for many of the upper classes to comprehend, lower-class politics was generally indifferent to material ambition. Lowe's misguided fears of 1866 were the consequence of applying middle-class intellectual calculations to working-class circumstances. By the 1870s only a relatively small number of trade unionists were starting to do this. In any case there was certainly not the popular demand for social legislation in the 1870s that there was for franchise reform in the 1860s.

It is extremely doubtful whether Conservative opinion would have supported Disraeli in any thorough-going legislative programme of social Toryism; and criticism of Disraeli's alleged 'neglect' to go beyond the satisfying of particular pressure groups depends upon assumptions much more appropriate to the circumstances of the later 1880s and beyond than to those of the 1870s. By the 1880s the idea of social legislative programmes was beginning to make political sense, but it remained distinctly a minority taste as far as the working classes were concerned right up to the First World War. Nor did Disraeli in any sense 'betray' the promise of Young England. Certainly Disraeli hoped for, and expected, a 'reconciliation of classes'; but he did not suppose, either in the 1840s or the 1870s, that reform legislation as such was essential to this. He thought that popular confidence in the capacity and good will of the natural ruling class would suffice. That confidence was fundamental to a Tory theory of a natural state of society, and did not depend on legislation. Such dependence would in effect reduce politics to a condition appropriate to utilitarianism. For Conservatives confidence was historic and based on custom. Legislation would neither make it nor unmake it.

Therefore such legislation as Disraeli offered would be a legislation essentially of gesture to this general view of what was desirable and possible. What this amounted to as a whole was a series of reassurances to the commonalty that there was once more in power a government which understood them and was understood by them. These elements – confidence, gesture, reassurance –

explain what otherwise has been accounted the almost inexplicably ludicrous bathos of Disraeli's own confidence that he had 'solved' fundamental social problems. He wrote, for example, to one of his countesses, Lady Bradford, after the second reading in 1875 of the bill to give the trade unions the legal protection denied them by Gladstone: 'I cannot express to you the importance of last night. It is one of those measures, that root and consolidate a party. We have settled the long and vexatious contest between capital and labor.' The Trade Union Congress which in October 1875 carried a motion of gratitude for the government's efforts was under no such illusion, but it did have much to be thankful for: apart from useful sanitary, food and drug, and housing measures, the Employers and Workmen Act of 1875 which replaced the old law of masters and servants (the change in nomenclature was in itself a good example of gesture) paired well with the trade union legislation. But by 1879 the Trade Union Congress was singing a quite different political tune.

The same point can be made with respect to Disraeli's so-called 'imperial' lead. In his attacks on the alleged Liberal determination to dissolve the British Empire, Disraeli had appeared to advocate a large policy of imperial consolidation, and had even adumbrated the principle of imperial tariff preference. Ever since that moment Disraeli has been credited as the prophet and genius of British imperialism, the original inspiration for the policies of Joseph Chamberlain at the end of the century. Strokes such as the purchase of the bankrupt Khedive of Egypt's shares in the Suez Canal Company in 1875 and the proclamation of the Queen as Empress of India in the Durbar of 1877 added verisimilitude to appearances. Yet, 'ironically', in office Disraeli made no effort to translate his attacks on Liberal anti-imperialism into practical effect. The irony is indeed compound. Gladstone interpreted the Suez shares purchase quite incorrectly as a manifestation of the new political immorality of imperialism. And in fact the true imperialists of the day, such as Edward Dicey and the *Spectator*, were urging Disraeli to do the obvious imperial thing and occupy Egypt. Yet Disraeli had not the slightest intention of operating upon any basis but that of the received Palmerstonian policy of indirect control of places such as Egypt. For Disraeli, occupying Egypt would have been as desperate an expedient as introducing unemployment benefits or the eight hour day. Suez and the Durbar were pure gestures, symbolic actions which altered nothing. And there was conspicuously no more serious effort of fulfilment of the 'imperial' implications of Crystal Palace than of the social reform implications. There was, certainly, a 'forward' policy in southern Africa and Afghanistan, but that is rather a different matter, and in neither case did the motivation reflect any radical departures from attitudes and assumptions inherited from the past.

The fact is that in no respect was Disraeli's 'imperialism' prophetic of a large, new future. As much as his view of the domestic basis of Conservative politics, his imperial attitudes were strictly in conformity with Palmerstonian assessments and requirements. A close reading of what Disraeli actually said at the Crystal Palace makes it clear that he never intended to do anything serious. He regarded the issues involved as 'closed' in the same way as he regarded free trade as no longer a question of controversy. When he talked of an 'Imperial tariff', and the institution of 'some representative council in the metropolis', and a 'code' to expedite military cooperation (these were all the kind of ideas being currently aired by the Imperial Federation League), he was careful to use a kind of past conditional mood. *When* responsible government had been granted to colonies *then* it would have been correct national policy to have imposed conditions in terms of a coherent imperial concept. The Liberal fault had been to allow such opportunities to pass, never to return, for clearly there was no question of imposing such conditions for colonial independence now or in the future.

Thus, far from giving a lead to imperial policy for the future, Disraeli, as far as the colonies of settlement were concerned, virtually announced that the question was closed. The parallel with the issue of social reform is revealing. The programme wanted by the Conservative social reform group, Gorst and Sandon and Sclater-Booth and Selwin-Ibbetson and their friends, corresponded to the kind of imperial policy advocated by the Imperial Federation League. The kind of 'gesture' social reform actually provided by Disraeli corresponded to the symbolic events of Suez and the Durbar. Equally, the ludicrous bathos of Disraeli's confidences to Lady Bradford over the trade union gesture corresponds appositely to Disraeli's 'ridiculous hyperbole' as to what ownership of nearly half the Canal Company's shares actually signified. Certainly the chances of mobilizing colonial support for federation were as dubious as those of inspiring a positive response both from the party and the country to a programme of social Toryism. Noises in favour of federation from the colonies, as a generation of Liberal colonial administrators knew full well, meant in fact that colonies wanted British men and money and a voice in British foreign policy in return for cheap concessions. In any event, it was clearly not a practical prospect in the 1870s, and Disraeli was perfectly correct to recognize this.

Nor is there any evidence of a Disraelian imperial lead in the tropic zone. It so happened that from 1874 British involvement was intensified in various ways in the Gold Coast, the Malay States and the Fiji Islands, and these are traditionally cited as examples of a new 'forward' policy in action. Yet a close examination of these cases results in precisely the opposite conclusion. All the preparatory decisions in every case had been recommended by Kimberley and accepted by Gladstone's cabinet. Again, the issues were inherited and 'traditional': the problem as to whether further intervention should follow on existing involvement in unsettled 'frontier' areas. It was only the fall of Gladstone's government early in 1874 which put these decisions into the hands of Disraeli's cabinet.

On the other hand there is no question but that Disraeli's imperial symbolism did come to have, in a manner he possibly dimly foresaw, a posthumous importance as a source of propaganda and myth – two, after all, of the most important constituents of politics. The word 'imperialism' was by now beginning to develop its modern sense. Carnarvon, Disraeli's Colonial Secretary, remarked in 1878 that 'We have been of late much perplexed by a new word, "Imperialism", which has crept in amongst us.' Here again 'Imperialism' corresponds to social reform. They became the two ambrosial secretions with which Conservatism nourished itself into the twentieth century, and which provide the spurious justification for looking back on Disraeli as the founder of modern Conservatism. This is the true irony of Disraeli's career. He founded his bid to restore Conservatism to its proper 'national' role in the restored Victorian equilibrium upon a rejection of what were to prove the two great sources of Conservative strength in the 'modern' post-Victorian equilibrium era. This allowed the Conservative party to be the vehicle of the 'genuine' imperialism of the early 'modern' era, which was, as a matter of fact, the creation of a dissident Liberal diagnosis of a British political performance in which Disraeli and Gladstone were judged equally inadequate. Thus Joseph Chamberlain, as different from Disraeli as chalk from cheese, in no sense inherited a Conservative mission. He was a positive, creative statesman in precisely those areas where Disraeli made what were in effect his two great renunciations.

These renunciations do not necessitate a negative judgement on Disraeli's achievement. In the first place, the issues they involved were not 'realistic' politics in the 1870s, and would have done enormous damage to the Conservative party. In the second place, they were not within his frame of intention. He intended to operate within a tradition and a consensus which he understood better than any other statesman of the time. His successes in 1867 and 1874 prove this. His failure in 1880 was not a consequence of these renunciations. It was a consequence of the fact that the restored Victorian equilibrium which encompassed his frame of intention became so compromised both in the domestic and external spheres by obtrusive and unaccommodating circumstances as to be reduced to a state of disequilibrium.

In the first place, defeat had a sobering effect on the Liberals, and helped to close ranks. Education remained rather a sore point with the Nonconformists, but Conservative licensing legislation in the interests of the 'trade' in 1874 redressing the iniquities of the Liberal Act of 1872 raised Liberal moral hackles and did Liberal morale a lot of good. Then the Public Worship Regulation Act brought the bees buzzing out of the ecclesiastical hive. This was a measure devised by Archibald Campbell Tait, the ex-presbyterian Archbishop of Canterbury, to suppress 'Ritualism', the ceremonial innovations of the extreme Anglo-Catholic wing of the

High Church. The Queen herself, an ardent Protestant, espoused the measure fervently and Disraeli, whose Anglicanism was Protestant to the extent that it was anything in particular, was obliged to push it through. Suppression of the 'mass in masquerade' was generally popular in the country, but highly unpopular in important sections of the Conservative party. The Royal Titles Act of 1876, again pressed by the Queen, had much the same effect. It added the style 'Empress of India', which Disraeli rather enjoyed for it went well with the strain of oriental fantasy never far from the surface of his sensibility, but it deeply offended the mass of old-fashioned opinion inside as well as outside the Conservative party, which resented 'un-English' associations with discredited and dubious imperial régimes in France and Mexico.

But much more important compromising developments were occurring subterraneously. The shine was going off the boom economy which had provided the climate of confidence in which the political equilibrium of the 1850s and 1860s had been established. Disraeli's expectations of a return to 'normality' depended absolutely on the assumption of a 'normal' prosperity such as had come to be taken for granted since the 1850s. The economy thus tended to be looked upon as a fixed entity, sanctified by Free Trade and expressive of the genius of the greatest industrial society in the world. In the 1860s this confidence was still wholly intact, and every major economic sector seemed secure. By the later 1870s confidence had been shaken.

The phenomenon which came to be called the 'Great Depression', dated usually from 1873, was a collection of surface symptoms – a kind of economic syndrome – of shifts and changes in the economic substructure of society. They signalled (though of course it was extremely difficult for contemporaries to read these signals correctly) that new kinds of activities, usually summed up as the 'second industrial revolution', involving more refined and consumer-oriented techniques than the original crude production of earlier industrialism, were expanding, and old kinds of activities inherited from early industrialism, which had gathered patina and prestige as 'staples', were contracting. Coal, iron, cotton and – of particular consequence for Conservatism – cereal farming, were beginning to falter. As time went by it seemed to be coming clearer that the booming heights achieved in these traditional sectors in the 1860s and early 1870s were in fact peaks from which significantly steady declines had set in.

The 'myth of the Great Depression'[4] arose out of contemporary obsession with these disturbing symptoms. The fact that they were symptomatic in the long term not of 'depression' in any orthodox sense but rather of the socio-economic manifestations of the transformation called 'modernism' did not make the circumstances of the later 1870s any more comfortable. Unemployment rose sharply in 1879; distress was widespread and vocal. Estimated value of the gross product of the iron and steel industry had increased enormously in the boom years, from £65·02 million in 1865–9 to £113·51 million in 1870–74; in 1875–9 it slid back to £102·44 million. The production value of the prime staple, cotton, slid from its 1869–71 peak of £104·9 to £101·6 million in 1874–6 and down to £94·5 million in 1879–81. Unprecedented slides of this kind dragged down banks which had incautiously over-extended themselves in the boom years. The City of Glasgow Bank failed spectacularly in 1878 amidst a welter of bankruptcies.

But it was agriculture, especially wheat, barley and wool, that suffered the sharpest pains. Two heavy blows fell simultaneously. The first was a series of bad seasons. These had been threatening, like the potato blight of the 1840s or cholera, for some time from the east. In 1875 Bosnian peasants were unable to satisfy exigent Ottoman tax farmers; from 1876 to 1879 four consecutive bad seasons hit Britain. By 1878 Irish tenants were unable to satisfy exigent English landlords; and by 1880 there were registered 2,500 agrarian 'outrages', the murder of Lord Leitrim, and more than 2,000 evictions for failure to pay rent. This would be the basis of the 'New Departure' under Parnell.

On top of this, the opening of the American prairies by new mechanized techniques of harvesting and the development of railway networks with special grain freights led to a flood of cheap imports. In 1874, 47·6 per cent of wheat available for consumption was imported;[5] in 1875 imports accounted for 60·7 per cent;

by 1879, 76·7 per cent. After a slight recovery in 1878 wheat prices started on their steady decline, almost uninterrupted, to the nadir of 1894, dragging down with them over many parts of the country incomes from rents. The Agricultural Labourers' Union, founded by Joseph Arch in 1873 in the face of much hostility from the farmers, shared in this collapse: in 1874 it had 86,000 members; by 1880 it was down to 20,000. The ominous fact, obvious before 1880, was that with free trade the cheap imports were going to be a constant factor in the future. By 1879, as a Liberal critic of the government put it, the 'Agricultural Depression had become a political as well as a social fact'.[6]

Disraeli's response to all this could only be stoic passivity. He had in any case grown increasingly remote from domestic affairs, immersed in the 'Great Game' of foreign policy. At the end of the parliamentary session in the summer of 1876 he took a peerage, and went to the House of Lords as first and only Earl of Beaconsfield (the title Burke would have assumed). His health was no longer equal to the assiduous attendance at the Commons for which he was famed. He supposed that Gladstone had indeed abdicated and no longer needed to be taken into account as a first-class threat. On the whole, until the onset of the 'bad times', he could regard the domestic policy of his ministry with satisfaction. His appointments, except in the case of Adderley at the Board of Trade, had worked well, and some of them had been notable successes. Cross had gained the confidence of both the House and his cabinet colleagues. When Ward Hunt died in 1877 Disraeli promoted the popular W. H. Smith to the Admiralty. But it needed more than good appointments to restore a golden age.

Bad times undoubtedly compromised the prestige of the ministry. Could ministers have reacted more positively against them? Gorst and others certainly thought so. It was only too obvious that the Liberals were making immense electoral capital out of distress, though it was equally obvious that a Liberal government in office would have done as little as the Conservatives. The Liberal explanation of why times were abnormally bad amounted to little more than the proposition that since Conservatism was a conspiracy against the people, the hardness of the times simply reflected the success of the conspiracy. Budget deficits ascribed to expensive external adventures were the core of this Liberal accusation, especially formidable in Gladstone's hands.

A convinced and coherent remedial policy in 1878 and after was no more within the bounds of feasibility than had been the thoroughgoing programme of social reform dreamed of by the proto-Tory Democrats of 1874. Again, the element of irony is there to be pointed to. Of all men, Disraeli, the apostle of Young England, might have been thought of as equipped, if not to legislate prosperity, at least to remedy distress; of all men Disraeli might have been thought of as providentially destined to restore to agriculture the defences it was deprived of in 1846. Yet these cancelled one another out. The Palmerstonians would not countenance the 'socialism' of the first; the democratic Tories and the trade union leadership would not swallow the dear bread of the second. But in any case Disraeli's whole programme of 'normality' presupposed definitions derived from the success of the Victorian equilibrium of the 1850s and the 1860s. It was quite out of the question for him to throw these aside and expect widespread support for experiments and adventures on the strength of analogies with the Hungry Forties. In sum, the advantages which Disraeli had coined from the existing system of politics committed him to acceptance of the validity of the currency. He firmly declined to consider the possibility of 'remedial measures' to alleviate the extensive distress that prevailed in December 1878 on the grounds that there were 'symptoms of amelioration and general amendment which must in time – and perhaps sooner than the country is prepared for – bring about those advantageous results which, after periods of suffering, we have before experienced'. This was as clear a statement as could possibly be made of a complete identification with the received wisdom of post-1850 Victorianism; a decisive confession that in fact Disraeli had no distinctly 'Conservative' solution to the 'great problem' he had alluded to at the Crystal Palace in 1872 of reconciling popular aspirations for social justice with respect for the immutable 'principles of economic truth'.

It would have been no consolation to Disraeli and the mass of

Conservatives to learn in 1879 that their problems were misconceived: the Great Depression was neither great nor a depression. Either way it meant the passing of conditions which sustained the only kind of politics they knew about and wanted to know about.

Chapter Six

THE CONSERVATIVE VERSION: DISRAELI'S EXTERNAL BID 1874–80

I

Of his foreign policy Disraeli wrote in 1874: 'I believe since Palmerston we have never been so energetic, and in a year's time we shall be more.' But there is nothing to suggest that he anticipated that his aim of restoring Britain to her rightful place among the powers of Europe would mean extraordinary difficulties or extraordinary efforts. As in the domestic sphere, he was thinking in terms essentially of an underlying normality and naturalness of things. Thus when, in May 1876, he vetoed an initiative by the Three Emperors' League called the 'Berlin Memorandum', he signalled this as a restoration of the 'natural' order of Europe in exactly the same manner and almost exactly the same terms as he had signalled the end of the war between capital and labour in 1875. His conduct with respect to external problems repeats very much the same pattern as with domestic problems: in the face of unforeseen difficulties he displayed very little resource and clung as long as possible to orthodox doctrines.

Orthodoxy led to the 'renunciations' which have been analysed of social reform and empire. Undoubtedly they – especially the first – saved him much more trouble than he would have got into otherwise. The central point about his orthodoxy in foreign policy was that it produced the contrary effect: renunciation of the 'national' bid undoubtedly would have avoided a great deal of difficulty, but the logic of his position made this as impossible as it made the others necessary. Palmerstonism in every sense, both in terms of doctrine and votes, made renunciation of thoroughgoing social reform and empire-building imperative; but it made implementation of the 'national' policy equally as imperative. Hence this is the area of policy in which Disraeli was most positive and active during the years of his ministry, quite apart from his personal predilection for international *haute politique* and resounding dealings with the chancelleries of Europe.

In many ways Derby, the foreign secretary, exhibits better than Disraeli the difference between the old pre-Palmerstonian Conservatism of the early 1860s and the Disraelian 'national' Conservatism, since his eccentric Cobdenite leanings[1] make for greater contrast. Salisbury, an eccentrically pessimistic utilitarian, can serve for much the same purpose; but it was Derby (then Lord Stanley) who made in 1864 the notorious speech on the imminent and much-to-be-desired break-up of the Ottoman Empire. The independence and integrity of the Ottoman Empire had been elevated to the status of a capital British interest by Palmerston in the 1830s; it was the very essence of the Treaty of Paris and the Crimean System. To question it was to question everything. The Turks, Derby said, had 'had their day'; and Derby did 'not understand, except it be from the influence of old diplomatic traditions, the determination of the elder statesmen to stand by the Turkish rule, whether right or wrong'. Derby was clear that as the Turkish régime's incapacity to reform itself meant the necessary emancipation of the Christian subject peoples, so this Palmerstonism was making for Britain 'enemies of races which will very soon become in Eastern Europe dominant races', and that Britain was keeping back countries by whose improvement 'we, as the great traders of the world, should be the great gainers; and that we are doing this for no earthly advantage, either present or prospective'.[2]

Derby in fact contradicted this argument as early as 1866–8, over the Cretan question, so quickly did the 'diplomatic traditions' of the 'elder statesmen' impose themselves on a government which, under Disraeli, was only too willing to be thus imposed upon. By 1874 Derby was thoroughly conditioned, and it took just over four years of the implementation of the 'national' policy to de-condition him. He consummated his eccentricity by joining Gladstone's second cabinet in 1882. A great part of Derby's problem was his personal closeness to Disraeli, which made resistance more difficult, so that the pattern of Derby's relationship was one of increasingly grudging consent broken sharply by resignation. Salisbury, on the other hand, who disliked and distrusted Disraeli and was disliked and distrusted in return, and who needed no instruction in the criticism of Palmerstonian traditions, could relate much more effectively; he could argue against Disraeli when Derby was silent and yet could replace Derby at the Foreign Office in 1878 and accompany Disraeli to Berlin on a healthy basis of mutual forbearance derived from hostility and acknowledged differences of opinion.

II

Disraeli's immediate sense of how to set about a 'national' policy naturally derived from study of how Palmerston had operated. Disraeli could never project plausibly the element of Liberal moralism in Palmerston's policy. He could merely insist that Europe could not be securely at peace without full British participation in its affairs. He understood clearly that the secret of Palmerston's success had been his ability to manipulate the concert of Europe. Equally naturally he looked back to Palmerston's most brilliant exercise in concert leadership, in the later 1830s. He wrote to Derby in 1875: 'My own impression is that we should construct some concerted movement to preserve the peace of Europe like Pam did when he baffled France and expelled the Egyptians from Syria. There might be an alliance between Russia and ourself for this special purpose; and other powers, as Austria and perhaps Italy might be invited to accede . . .'. The occasion of these rambling thoughts, and the reference to 'the peace of Europe', arose out of the so-called 'war scare' of 1875 when it appeared that Bismarck contemplated a preventive war in view of the unexpectedly swift recovery of the French from their military prostration of 1871. Disraeli was eager to join the Russians in a joint policy of remonstrance. For Britain it was a minor and subordinate part, which Derby entered on with characteristic reluctance; but it was a start. Then the Suez Canal Company share purchase looked well as a supporting feature. It was a gesture clearly signalling a revival of confidence.

The Queen indeed interpreted it as 'a blow at Bismarck' and his 'insolent declarations that England had ceased to be a political power'.

Working with the Russians naturally raised memories of the 1830s and Palmerston's great triumph of the Treaty of London of 1840 and the Straits Convention. Unfortunately, a consistent policy of cooperation with the Russians would require either that the Russians renounce their hostility to the Crimean System, or that the British renounce the System itself. The first was just as impossible as it had been in the 1860s, despite the ending of the Black Sea issue, because too much Russian capital was still invested in it: the humiliation of the ceded Bessarabian lands still rankled; Orthodox sentiment against the Turks had grown; pan-Slav sentiment in favour of liberating the oppressed brethren of the Balkans and recovering Tsargrad[3] had become a force to be reckoned with in Russian public opinion. The second was impossible because the British also had invested too much capital in the System. It was the core of the 'national' policy. Gladstone in 1870–71 had been obliged to reaffirm it against all his better instincts. Specifically, Disraeli and the Conservative party had recently invested a large part of their political future in it, and there was now no chance of a Conservative dismantling of it in terms of Derby's 1864 speech.

A Palmerstonian concert policy on the 1830s model such as Disraeli envisaged would have in fact no serious future. Bismarck certainly was not going to challenge Europe alone as Thiers had done. His entire career was dedicated to making sure that his enemies were isolated and that he was not, and he receded very swiftly in 1875. The French were no longer available for a Palmerstonian concert policy against the Russians, their necessary patrons against Bismarck. The Austrians were no more willing to risk a great war in Poland than they had been in the 1850s. Thus Russia could not again be a European target. Hence, given that the Crimean policy was indispensable and a concert policy was impossible, and given also that he had to go 'forward', Disraeli had no options, no room for manoeuvre. He had to follow where the logic of things led. That this should have led him into patronage of Turkish imbecility was unfortunate but unavoidable. He did not intend it as such. Until startled by the Turkish bankruptcy he had no conception that a major crisis was brewing in the Near East. His first thoughts were that 'the Eastern question that has haunted Europe for a century, and which I thought the Crimean War had adjourned for half another,' would fall to his lot to 'encounter – dare I say, to settle?' There is indeed nothing to suggest that he had ever given the fundamental assumptions or likely prospects of the Crimean policy any serious critical thought. Certain essential prerequisites to criticism would certainly have been difficult for him to adjust to. He despised Balkan national-ism. Insurgent peasantries against aristocratic landowners held no attractions to such a celebrator of the territorial dispensation of England. Indeed, he was very quick to sense the unwelcome analogies between Bosnia and Ireland. On the other hand, there was no firm intellectual substance to his philo-Turkism. At mo-ments of frustration and impatience he talked quite readily of partition. But always the inescapable logic of his situation pulled him back on to the Palmerstonian rails.

It was Disraeli's misfortune to take up the Palmerstonian Crimean inheritance at a time when all the returns from it as an investment had come in and it had started on its downward trend. The essential point that Disraeli needed to understand, but did not, was that the Crimean System had been fundamentally out of phase with the realities of the Near East at the time of its formu-lation and had got increasingly out of phase ever since. It was based centrally on the proposition that the Ottoman Empire made a third with Poland and Hungary as representatives of the cause of the liberties of Europe against Russian ambitions of aggrandizement and dominance. The Crimean War was fought in terms of European themes; and the Treaty of Paris assumed that a reformed Ottoman Empire could take its place in a Euro-pean liberal system.

The realities of the Near East had to do with the complete impossibility of this. The Ottoman Empire, a system of military and religious encampment over subject peoples, was not sus-ceptible to the developments normal even to a primitive kind of state in the modern sense. If the Ottoman system could not maintain its traditional forms of authority it would inevitably collapse and be replaced by a series of nationality-based states, of which Turkey itself would be one. The situation by the 1870s was that the traditional forms of Ottoman authority were starting to collapse seriously. The Sultan's bankruptcy in 1875 (which dragged the Khedive of Egypt down with him and forced the Canal Company shares sale) was merely the most obvious manifestation of decadence.

Then, in the summer of 1875, the pace of dissolution accelerated. Serb peasants in the Herzegovina and Bosnia took arms against the Ottoman authorities. The Turkish military were unable to suppress the insurgents. As the affair dragged on through the autumn, neighbouring Serbs in the autonomous principality, in Montenegro and in the Austrian lands of Slavonia and Dalmatia, began stirring in sympathy. Pan-Slav emotion grew in Russia.

Foreign Office opinion, the wish being father to the thought, was that the insurrection, though 'unexpectedly prolonged', would fade out. When a proposal was made on Austrian initiative in consultation with Berlin and St Petersburg for a delegation of the consuls of the powers at Sarajevo to the insurgents, the British reaction was cold. Derby, in the purest accents of Palmerstonian orthodoxy, instructed the British consul in effect to sabotage the operations of the delegation.

This was accomplished successfully and the Turks, encouraged, did nothing to come to terms. Then the Austro-Hungarian foreign minister, Count Andrassy, in concert with Berlin and St Petersburg, again proposed an initiative on behalf of the Three Emperors' League. Vienna was worried about repercussions among the neighbouring Serb peoples; conservative St Petersburg deprecated pan-Slav enthusiasm; Bismarck was anxious above all to remove any possible source of friction between Austria and Russia; all were agreed that a quick solution was desirable before things got out of hand generally in the region, and all were agreed that, as in fact the consuls over British protest had recommended, the Turks should make the concessions – security of property and person, religious freedom, taxation, limited autonomy – demanded by the insurgents. The Andrassy Note of December 1875 recommended this procedure to the Turks.

The Note was adhered to cordially by the French and Italian governments. Disraeli and Derby wanted to reject it. To the Foreign Office it was another insidious Gorchakov Circular, worse to the extent that it was treacherously promoted by a party to the Tripartite Treaty. Disraeli was especially hostile. In the first place Disraeli resented the Note because it infringed the Treaty of Paris and thereby called into question the validity of the Crimean System. He resented its Irish implications with 'home rule' and tenant right. He resented it because it expressed the European leadership of the Three Emperors' League, and thus represented a fundamental obstacle to the restoration of a Palmerstonian concert of Europe, with Britain manipulating the balance of forces. Disraeli put the matter succinctly: 'There is no balance, and unless we go out of our way to act with the three Northern Powers, they can act without us, wh. is not agreeable for a State like England.'

Given his assumptions about the naturalness and normality of what he was trying to achieve, Disraeli of course regarded the Three Emperors' League as an 'unnatural alliance'. It was 'unnatural' because it existed merely as a consequence of the failure of Britain to assert her 'just position' in Europe. Gladstone's cosmopolitan feebleness had abdicated Britain's due authority and prerogatives, and encouraged the imperial powers under Bismarck's guidance to imagine that, with France lying low, they henceforth called the tune.

However, in the end, Disraeli and Derby grudgingly and reluctantly acceded to the Note, and there the matter rested as the insurrection dragged on into 1876. By the spring of that year the situation had become extremely critical. The Serbs in the autonomous principality and in Montenegro could not much longer be restrained from going to war with the Turks. The Bulgarians, emboldened by the examples of Bosnia and the Herzegovina, were likely to follow suit. Muslims grew correspondingly fanatical: in May the French and German consuls in Salonika were murdered, and in Constantinople itself the throne of the discredited Sultan Abdul Aziz tottered.

Again, in May, Andrassy and Gorchakov in Berlin conferred with Bismarck and agreed on a second initiative. Known as the

'Berlin Memorandum', it recommended to the Turks in very decisive terms the expediency of reaching a solution before matters got completely out of hand. Again the French and Italian governments concurred. This time there was a clear threat to the Turks that they would, if necessary, be coerced.

Thus far the public response in Britain to these developments was restrained. Gladstone, who had been querulous and captious about the Canal Company shares purchase, warrantably critical of the financial arrangements and unwarrantably suspicious of ulterior expansive motives on Disraeli's part to found a 'North African Empire', welcomed the government's adherence to the Andrassy Note. He offered his congratulations on the strength of his assumption that Disraeli's government was asserting its non-'national' solidarity with the concert of Europe, and that a new era for the European ideal was thereby inaugurated. In Gladstone's view, Europe, having guaranteed Turkey, was clearly under an obligation to assume responsibility for ensuring that the Turks fulfilled their undertakings of 1856 to their subject peoples; and as a member of Aberdeen's cabinet in 1854 he felt a special 'historical' personal responsibility. Gladstone's congratulations were particularly ironic since in offering them he deliberately cut across some criticisms that Hartington and other Palmerstonians in his own party were making of the government's improper departure from Crimean orthodoxy. Disraeli was a little embarrassed to find himself in this false position; but his opportunity to make clear his true position had now arrived.

All Derby's and Disraeli's objections to the Andrassy Note were now renewed in much stronger form. The extra objection to the threat of coercion by the imperial powers was decisive. The British government declined to adhere to the Memorandum and offered the Turks their full diplomatic support. To underline the point, Disraeli arranged for a squadron to sail to Besika Bay outside the Dardanelles, ostensibly in case of disorders in Constantinople and threats to British life and property. The message both to the Turks and to 'Europe' was unmistakable: Palmerston had sent the fleet to Besika Bay in 1849 at the time of the Austrian and Russian ultimatum over the Hungarian refugees; and it was largely at his instance that it had returned there in 1853 to make British support for the Turks manifest at the commencement of the Crimean War. Decazes, the French foreign minister, had diagnosed Disraeli as 'dreaming of Palmerstonian glories'; now he had painful evidence of it, and addressed more than one 'pressing appeal' to Derby to reconsider the 'regrettable' action of the British government, pointing out correctly that it was virtually a veto, since the Turks would certainly ignore the advice of the other powers if they were sure of British support. Disraeli and Derby were unmoved, merely reiterating their 'deprecation' of the 'diplomatic action of the other Powers in the affairs of the Ottoman Empire'.

To add to the embarrassment of the five powers, the Turks staged a 'liberal' revolution, deposed the Sultan and proclaimed an enlightened programme which would reform and regenerate the Empire. In these combined circumstances the Berlin Memorandum faded miserably away.

By now, British public opinion was more alert. There was some uneasiness at the possible rashness of standing aside from Europe in such conspicuous isolation. The Queen, for example, was a little worried that the dispatch of the fleet in particular might encourage the Turks to dangerous over-confidence. Gladstone and the enthusiasts for a concert policy were of course outraged. Gladstone was particularly offended because the hopes he had nursed in February about the Andrassy Note were clearly deluded. He accused Disraeli of unworthy distrust of the good faith of the powers acting on behalf of a European conscience in relation to the subject peoples of Turkey.

In general, however, the response was favourable. The Palmerstonians, anxious and puzzled in February, were now reassured. The Whig duumvirate of Granville in the Lords and Hartington in the Commons who had succeeded Gladstone as leaders of the Liberal party praised Disraeli with the faintest of damns. The discomfiture of the European powers was distinctly relished: the 'national' public applauded an assertion of British authority such as had not been seen since the days of Palmerston. Disraeli had made his great stroke against the hegemony of the 'unnatural alliance' of the Three Emperors, which he now judged to be at an end. 'I think not only peace will be maintained,' he wrote, 'but that Her Majesty will be restored to her due and natural influence in the government of the world.' By July he was remarking that 'something like the old days of our authority appear to have returned'.

Even assuming that Britain had thus resumed her 'just position' in the councils of Europe, there was a great difference between a successful thwarting of a European initiative and a moral leadership of the European concert as in Palmerston's day. This was not a problem which worried the inert Derby. But for Disraeli it was the whole point of operation. Clearly he was at a loss as to how to set about effectively achieving this end. He could get no sympathetic response from any of the other powers, who remained convinced that he had ruined the last chance to hold the situation. In June Serbia and Montenegro declared war on the Turks. All Disraeli could do was renew his rather ineffectual approaches to the Russians as in the 'war scare' phase. He was on occasion notably conciliatory in tone towards Russia at this time. But in any case he had no opportunity of even trying to complete the edifice of his restored Palmerstonian ascendancy. His position was soon hopelessly compromised by news from Bulgaria.

Encouraged by the successes of the Serbs in Bosnia, Bulgarian patriots in the spring of 1876 attempted to overthrow Turkish rule in the area mainly near Philippopolis.[4] The Bulgarians were neither so efficient as the Bosnians nor were they favoured so much by the terrain. Apart from such regular soldiery as could be dispatched from Adrianople or Constantinople, settlements of Circassians, Muslim refugees from Russian penetration in the Caucasus who had been 'planted' among the Bulgarians, were set upon the Christian population. These formed the core of the Turkish irregular bands – the *bashi bazouks* – who were to become so notorious. The insurrection itself was never very formidable, but the suppression of it was very formidable indeed. Something between 12,000 and 15,000 Bulgarians, mostly unarmed and incapable of resistance, were massacred.

In the Near Eastern perspective, and in particular in the historical perspective of atrocious massacre as an endemic feature of Ottoman misrule, the Bulgarian episode of 1876 was by no means remarkable. This fact was pointed out quite correctly by Elliot, the British ambassador, indignant at charges of some kind of moral complicity. In words which became classic to the 'atrocitarians' as the most shameless revelation of the moral bankruptcy of Palmerstonism, Elliot protested that while indignation must be felt at the 'needless and monstrous severity' with which the Bulgarian insurrection was put down, nevertheless 'the necessity which exists for England to prevent changes occurring here which would be most detrimental to ourselves, is not affected by the question whether it was 10,000 or 20,000 persons who perished in the suppression'. There had been before and were to be after much greater massacres. Nor is there any reason to suppose that the Bulgarian instance was somehow uniquely atrocious in its character. Yet it provoked in England between July and September 1876 a public outburst of moral outrage spilling over into political dissent from the Palmerstonian premises of British policy unsurpassed in intensity. Disraeli's government was so damaged by the force of this indignant protest that it never thereafter quite recovered its full confidence and composure. Certainly Disraeli lost in the late summer and autumn of 1876 any chance he ever had of establishing a truly national consensus behind a revived 'national' policy.

Thus Disraeli was so unfortunate as to run into two intractable difficulties at once: there was the 'objective' difficulty of a European situation quite unamenable to his efforts to restore a Palmerstonian British authority; and there was the 'subjective' difficulty of a large part of domestic public sentiment so susceptible to feelings of moral complicity in the indirect consequences of their government's policy as to be impervious to 'national' arguments of *raison d'état* and the priority of the greater good urged in defence of the Palmerstonian policy. It is this second difficulty for Disraeli, the phenomenon of a new public dissent, that must now be noticed, both for itself and for the relationship which Gladstone came to have to it.

III

The 'Bulgarian atrocities agitation' was the greatest public incursion into the official conduct of foreign affairs in British history. Hundreds of meetings denounced the government's pro-Turkish policy and demanded that it be reversed in the direction of Christian and national emancipation. By 22 August, Derby warned Elliot in Constantinople that the 'universal feeling of indignation' had reached such a pitch that in the extreme case of Russia declaring war on the Turks the British government would find it 'practically impossible to interfere'. The Bulgarian issue was a seismic shock which opened the national fault-lines. The Conservative party was affected least of all. Apart from a few renegade High Churchmen there was no move of revolt or dissent. The Liberal party was much more vulnerable to the tremors. By and large the party went with the agitation, though the movement always remained essentially an 'out of doors' phenomenon, leading the politicians rather than being led by them. The Whigs generally were aloof and loyal to their Palmerstonian heritage. Radicals tended to lukewarmness or coolness: traditional hostility to Russia on the one side, a Cobdenite sense of the interventionist implications of the agitation on the other.

The agitation was undoubtedly the vehicle of a great deal of politics, secular and religious. Joseph Chamberlain, the emerging leader of the Radicals, cared little for the Bulgarians but a great deal for the chances of Gladstone's return to the leadership at the expense of the Whigs. But beyond this level of concern lay the true significance of the agitation. It manifested on the largest scale a public conscience stricken with a sense of complicity in political transactions of the utmost immorality. Public capacity for moral dissent was at this time at its maximum in terms both of volume and refinement of sensibility. It was maximum in volume in that two lines of political development converged in the 1870s: the 'moral' constituent in political attitudes had emancipated itself to the greatest extent it was ever going to achieve from the traditional thraldom of 'interest'; and this coincided with the existence of a political constituency popular enough to represent itself plausibly as a new and therefore authentic public mind, and yet not sufficiently democratic to dilute the colour and flavour of its essentially bourgeois definitions of morality. It was maximum in terms of refinement of sensibility in that it inherited the accumulated fund of the tradition of the politics of conscience going back to anti-slavery and anti-corn laws. The agitation seemed to many to confirm that the sensitivity manifested on a relatively small scale in the Jamaica case of 1866 had fulfilled its promise, and that henceforth politics would increasingly be informed by a consistent and ineluctable moral imperative.

The fault line of 1876 indeed repeated the essential patterns of that of 1866. Dissent dissented, and the Church rallied to the State. Mill had died in 1873, but his heirs and successors faithfully executed his legacy. The major inconsistency was Carlyle, who in 1876 made famous the 'unspeakable Turk' phrase. But Carlyle had been an old anti-Turk since Crimean days; and his own internal consistency was absolute. It was simply that instead of equating Eyre and the Turks, as the mass of atrocitarians did, he equated Eyre with the Russians as instruments of divine retribution upon the transgressor of the moral law: he equated the Turks with the Negro rebels of 1866 as such transgressors. But much more significant was the impact of the issue raised by Bulgaria in 1876 on the wavering Liberals of 1866, Arnold, Fitzjames Stephen, Bagehot. Now they were linked with Liberals like Jowett and J. R. Seeley and Edward Dicey and Henry Maine. The hostility of this group to the agitation and what it represented was indeed a crucial point of development within the Liberal intellectual tradition, marking in fact the inauguration of the movement later to be known as Liberal imperialism. In most respects 1876 marked the culmination of developments: never again would Nonconformity or the political tradition of John Stuart Mill look quite so confident and impressive, and never again would 'national' Palmerstonism ever be quite the same. The one important new development from 1876 was precisely the germ of a Liberal critique of British policy which repudiated the claims equally of Gladstone and Disraeli as being inadequate to national requirements on the grounds essentially that they were neither instructed nor intelligent. 'The intelligent part of the nation', as Jowett put it in October 1876, was beginning to feel itself 'humiliated' by the rival nonsenses of Disraeli and Gladstone. This will be a theme of growing importance from now on.

IV

Disraeli and Gladstone shared one initial misconception about the movement of public protest aroused by the Bulgarian case. They both assumed that the agitation would fade away after the ending of the parliamentary session early in August. Pressures had started building up against Disraeli from the first major *Daily News* report on 23 June. On the basis of advice supplied officially by the Foreign Office he contradicted the reports. The Foreign Office was in fact the victim of its own unwillingness to recognize that the orthodox Crimean policy failed increasingly to correspond to reality. In the debate on 31 July Disraeli came out with his famous sneer at 'coffee-house babble'. But within a week he was aware that he had allowed himself to be seriously misguided. However, he was in no mood to compromise the credit and *éclat* of the Berlin Memorandum stroke by admitting to certain unfortunate occurrences which, however deplorable in themselves, were not of material significance in relation to the necessities of high policy. The government's paramount duty, he announced on 11 August, was to maintain 'the empire of England'.

That was Disraeli's last speech of the session. He was confident that there would not be 'much further trouble on the subject'. It was also his last speech in the Commons. It was announced the following day that he was to go to the Lords as Earl of Beaconsfield.

Gladstone had no intention of challenging the government on the issue of the atrocities in Bulgaria. His highest hope was that they should not be allowed to be forgotten during the recess so that the issues involved in them could be raised again at the beginning of the next session of parliament. There is every indication, in fact, that Gladstone was extremely reluctant about the whole question. Moreover, he emphasized that he was 'not ashamed' to assert that he believed that the territorial integrity of the Ottoman Empire should continue to be the guideline of British policy. He thought an independent Slav state too dangerous to be contemplated. Earlier, at the time of the Turkish bankruptcy, he had expressed his confidence that Disraeli would handle the crisis 'rationally'. He had gone out of his way to congratulate Disraeli over the Andrassy Note. Gladstone, in fact, was trying his best to preserve the integrity of his status as abdicated leader of the Liberal party and not to get at all deeply involved. He was not waiting for opportunities to pounce on Disraeli. Certainly, he had been quite active in the Commons since his abdication at the beginning of 1875. But he consistently drew a sharp distinction between abdication and retirement. He wanted to be free to preserve his personal and religious interests – Homer, attacks on Vatican policy, defence of religious belief – free of burdensome official responsibilities. Abdication allowed him the luxury of choosing his own time and his own themes. He had attacked Disraeli often enough: the Canal Shares purchase, the Empress of India title, the Public Worship Regulation bill, had all aroused his intense indignation. Yet on the one large issue where he might have done Disraeli mortal damage he was almost totally insensible. He was obsessed as it happened at this moment with the theological problem of Future Retribution. The leaders of the agitation building up in the country, people like Freeman, Liddon and Stead, were beside themselves with frustration at Gladstone's failure to recognize his duty to the popular agitation and to the country at large.

Gladstone's eventual intervention of 6 September 1876 – the famous pamphlet *Bulgarian Horrors and the Question of the East* – was one of the most dramatic acts of his enormous career. Overnight it made him the leader and public spokesman of the agitation against Disraeli's eastern policy. Belatedly he had come to realize that the 'masses', so inert in 1874, had recovered their moral sense. As he put it: 'the game was afoot and the question yet alive'.

V

Thus Gladstone's intervention of 1876 had nothing in common with the series of instances of his 'striking gift' of divining at 'certain political junctures', 'appreciation of the general situation and its result', of creative 'insight into the facts of particular eras, and their relation one to another, which generates in the mind a conviction that the materials exist for forming a public opinion and for directing it to a particular end'. Rather, 1876 was only too painfully a case of mere opportunism, a simple 'acceptance of public opinion, founded upon the discernment that it has risen to a certain height needful for a given work, like a tide'. Far from forming a public opinion, Gladstone became only belatedly aware that a public opinion had already been formed. It was the shock of this awareness that set him off on the path to intervention. He realized that the issue of the atrocities was alive in the popular constituencies quite regardless of whether parliament was in session or recess. In 1868 Gladstone had been 'watching the sky with a strong sense of the obligation to act with the first break of dawn'. Now the dawn for Gladstone was to break again, though he had not been watching for it. Gladstone's reading of the significance of the agitation was that it expressed the true popular political genius which he feared had been smothered by the Tory reaction of 1874, by the demoralizing materialism of the times. He had failed in 1874 to 'reanimate' that 'sentiment' in favour of Liberalism which had carried it 'in a manner so remarkable through the election of 1868'. Abdication was for Gladstone a logical consequence of that failure. He could not conceive a satisfying and fulfilling political future on a conventional or traditional basis. There had to be at the foundations of politics the bedrock of what Gladstone described as popular 'mental integrity', greater than that of the 'classes' since the masses were morally shielded by 'the comparative absence of the more subtle agencies of temptation'. The whole point of the Liberal franchise programme of 1866 had been precisely to allow and encourage the effective reality of such a popular mental integrity. For Gladstone the atrocities agitation of 1876 bore witness to it as having, after all, survived. The 'noble support' of Nonconformity for his campaign impressed him deeply as the largest and most telling symptom of the general moral rehabilitation of the popular constituencies. That, rather than the atrocities themselves, was what excited Gladstone: 'it was far less a case of Gladstone exciting popular passion than of popular passion exciting Gladstone'. He wrote to Granville: 'Good ends can rarely be attained in politics without passion: and there is now, the first time for a good many years, a virtuous passion.'

Bulgarian Horrors and the Question of the East was thus for Gladstone the celebration of the restoration of his rapport with the masses 'out of doors'. It was a tremendous success more for its fiery rhetoric than for its specific proposals, which in fact advanced little beyond his cautious position of 31 July. He did not immediately press home the attack against Beaconsfield because of the awkwardness of his position as abdicated leader. He spent a fruitless month trying to persuade the government on the one hand to recede from its stiffly Turcophile position and on the other trying to persuade Granville and Hartington to give a lead to the Liberal party in a pro-agitation sense. He failed in both cases. The party leaders, Hartington especially, were too Palmerstonian. And they did not, in the words of a Whig chief at the time, like to 'force the Executive in Foreign Policy'. Almost all the Whigs and most of the 'moderate men' agreed with them, as Gladstone found to his dismay when Parliament reassembled in February 1877. As for the government, if Beaconsfield had felt any temptation to ingratiate himself with the agitation, Gladstone's incursion abruptly ended it. Beaconsfield counter-attacked vigorously on 20 September in a speech abusing Gladstone as being worse than any Bulgarian atrocity and blaming everything on Slavonic Secret Societies. This latter point has been a stumbling block to his admirers ever since, though in fact a conspiracy theory had always been a feature of the official British diagnosis of Turkish problems at least since Sir Henry Bulwer's public relations exercise of 1860 to rebut the Gorchakov Circular.[5]

Beaconsfield had been under some pressures recommending a more conciliatory attitude from within his own cabinet. Carnarvon advocated some 'decided action' to reassure the public. Stafford Northcote urged similar advice. More weighty than both these was Salisbury. He wrote to Beaconsfield: 'it is clear enough that the traditional Palmerstonian policy is at an end'. He advocated a comprehensive project of reforms to be forced on the Turks under supervision of the concert. But Beaconsfield and Derby refused to budge. Derby insisted, 'We have nothing to unsay or undo, and we must not make things look as if we had.' Beaconsfield insisted that any appearance by the government of truckling to a mob of dissenters and ritualists would make it look contemptible; and he assured Salisbury that a 'great reaction' against the agitation would soon set in.

A 'national' reaction did indeed set in in the autumn as the Palmerstonian forces began to recover some of their poise and nerve. Anti-Russian sentiment recovered ground. Russian volunteers flocked to aid the Serbs. In spite of this – or perhaps because of it – the Serbs were defeated soundly by the Turks. This boosted both 'national' emotion in Britain and pan-Slav excitement in Russia. Gladstone, who had wasted a month in his fruitless efforts with the Whig leaders and the government, now found that the steam had gone out of the public movement. One last great effort was made in the National Conference on the Eastern Question in St James's Hall in December 1876. This, modelled on anti-slavery and anti-corn laws precedents, was designed to establish a truly popular consensus in favour of a concert policy of co-operation with the European powers and especially Russia to oblige the Turks to undertake supervised reforms; and to offer advice and encouragement to Salisbury, who had been chosen by Beaconsfield to be plenipotentiary to a Conference of the Powers at Constantinople to try to settle the whole problem of the relations between the Sultan and his Christian subject peoples.

In this phase Beaconsfield revealed very clearly the straits he was in, trying to reconcile his European ambitions with his 'Crimean' intransigence. His acceptance of the project of the Conference showed him swinging towards a European attitude. But at another moment, as in his notorious Guildhall speech of November, he was truculent and bellicose to the Russians. Again, Beaconsfield talked of the necessity of coming to an understanding with some European power – Germany, Austria, perhaps France. On the other hand, he behaved with respect to the question of the armistice between the defeated Serbs and the victorious Turks exactly in the spirit of his spoiling policy to the Berlin Memorandum. This was not, as it is usually interpreted, feckless 'opportunism'.[6] It was rather the futile thrashings of a policy of reconciling the irreconcilable.

Thus Salisbury was sent as plenipotentiary to Constantinople having already had his own comprehensive scheme of reforms to be imposed on the Turks rejected by Beaconsfield and Derby. Derby's official instructions ostensibly left Salisbury considerable freedom of manoeuvre of which he took full advantage, brushing aside contemptuously the Palmerstonian hindrances offered by the ambassador, Elliot. Had matters been left to Salisbury in January 1877 there would have been agreement and that agreement would have been imposed on the Turks. Salisbury was quite ready to call the fleet to the Bosphorus if necessary. But Beaconsfield and Derby blocked him at every turn. The Turks, as at the time of the Berlin Memorandum, did their liberal turn, and proclaimed a brand new enlightened constitution just at the moment the Conference of Powers opened. This, however, failed to put the Conference off its stroke. The Russians were desperately eager for a European agreement, since under the pressures of pan-Slav excitement they had virtually committed themselves to enforce terms on the Turks unilaterally if Europe would not bring them to terms by peaceful persuasion.

Beaconsfield and Derby repudiated Salisbury and sabotaged the Conference. They were convinced the Russians were bluffing and would not seriously contemplate war. Indeed, the Russians were not prepared and took an agonizing time to nerve themselves to it. But eventually in April 1877 they declared war as executors of a European will. Had the campaign been short they might well have enforced a peace in those terms, which would have left Britain completely isolated and discredited. But the campaign was long and bitter. The British 'national' public was now fully in the ascendant; the term 'jingo' came into currency to signify a belligerent nationalism.[7] Russian pan-Slav emotion was equally aroused, making it impossible for the Russian government to settle with the Turks on a moderate 'European' basis. The Russians finally broke down Turkish resistance at the beginning of 1878. The Turks desperately asked for help. Beaconsfield was ready with schemes, but Derby at last was starting to revolt. As the Russians approached Constantinople Beaconsfield dispatched the fleet through the Straits. Carnarvon, Salisbury's most intimate collaborator, resigned. Derby, having swallowed so much, finally choked, and resigned also. He consented to return after reassurances, but his nerve was gone, and he left for good shortly afterwards when the reserves were called out and Cyprus occupied. He was replaced by Salisbury, who patiently hung on to wait his chances.

These came when the Russians, in March 1878, imposed at San Stefano not 'European' terms on the Turks but pan-Slav terms. This was the temptation they did not have the strength left to resist. By the same token they did not have the strength left to defend it against 'Europe'. They created a 'big Bulgaria' which virtually abolished Turkey-in-Europe. This had the effect of rescuing Beaconsfield from his European–Palmerstonian contradiction. At last he got his European ally. Austria would not tolerate San Stefano for very good Hapsburg reasons: Russia would have a client state sprawling across the Balkans. Beaconsfield and Andrassy finally had a clear basis for an agreed policy of opposition to the Russians. Andrassy insisted on a Congress of the Powers to revise the Treaty of San Stefano. Bismarck, embarrassed at the breakdown of his Three Emperors' arrangement, offered himself as 'honest broker'. The Russians, furious, had to accept in the face of Anglo–Austrian solidarity.

From the Berlin Congress in 1878 Beaconsfield and Salisbury returned, bearing, as Beaconsfield claimed, 'peace with honour'. They both got the Order of the Garter. The essential issues of the Congress were of the simplest. Bismarck staged a face-saving operation for the Russians whereby he cajoled them into replacing San Stefano with a 'European' settlement. 'Big Bulgaria' was trisected and Turkey-in-Europe re-emerged. The largest part was restored to direct Turkish rule. The rest was divided between an autonomous Eastern Roumelia and a tributary state of Bulgaria proper. The Austrians were invited to occupy Bosnia on behalf of the Porte with a specific motive of preventing the Serbs from trying to get it. The British were allowed to occupy Cyprus to balance Russian acquisitions in the Caucasus. Salisbury also announced a British reinterpretation of the Straits Convention, which in effect asserted that Britain could legitimately force the Straits if there was a reasonable presumption that the Sultan was subservient to Russian designs. The Russians got back their corner of Bessarabia lost in 1856. Serbia and Romania became independent. The French were promised Tunis. The Italians, who wanted a great deal, got nothing; Bismarck, who had done his best for the Russians, got their bitter reproaches.

Thus Beaconsfield was rescued from the consequences of his persistent application of bankrupt policy by the brokerage of Bismarck rescuing the Russians from the consequences of succumbing to their pan-Slav temptations. Beaconsfield achieved nothing serious personally at the Congress except to be the gratified recipient of Bismarck's heavy flattery. There was really nothing for him to do. The logic of the situation was quite clear and everything depended on Bismarck's seeing it through. Salisbury admirably sustained Beaconsfield in this hollow role, much as Shuvalov on the other side sustained the senile Gorchakov. Salisbury had abated nothing of his original conviction that the Palmerstonian policy was clearly at an end; but he was, after all, a comparatively young man, and could afford to wait. Beaconsfield's empty role at Berlin aptly symbolized the speciousness of his ultimate achievement in foreign affairs. Turkey-in-Europe was saved; but more of it could have been saved at the Constantinople Conference at the beginning of 1877, and more of it still at the time of the Berlin Memorandum. The division of the two Bulgarias in any case lasted only until 1884. Otherwise, nothing substantial was achieved except perhaps to please the 'national' public. Above all, the re-imposition of a Palmerstonian European credit was not attained. Berlin, far from inaugurating a new era of concert politics, in fact inaugurated, in 1879, the first of the alliances – the Austro-German alliance – which indicated definitively the direction in which the post-concert system of Europe would henceforth find its logical expression. But it would be Salisbury's task to cope with that situation, not Beaconsfield's.

VI

Beaconsfield's great external adventure in the Near East thus has this negative significance: it represented the last great effort and ultimate bankruptcy of Palmerstonian assumptions as to what was possible. It also, in conjunction with the lesser external problems of the Transvaal and Afghanistan, provided Gladstone with a potent source of propaganda for his own alternative solution as offered in the two Midlothian campaigns of 1879 and 1880. Gladstone's response to Disraeli's claim of 'peace with honour' was to accuse him of operating a sinister Tory foreign policy deliberately designed to stifle liberty and progress; the diplomacy of Metternich, in short. Just as Disraeli in 1872 and after had made a bid for a Tory inheritance of the 'national' Palmerstonism by not mentioning Palmerston, so Gladstone now turned his own claims against him by insisting on a libertarian British tradition of foreign policy before 1874, linking his own performance back to Canning, Russell and Palmerston; and by studiously not mentioning the Near Eastern aspect of Palmerstonism which circumstances had obliged Disraeli to cope with. 'In the foreign policy of this country,' as Gladstone cunningly put it, 'the name of Canning ever will be honoured. The name of Russell ever will be honoured. The name of Palmerston ever will be honoured by those who recollect the erection of the Kingdom of Belgium, and the union of the disjoined provinces of Italy.'

Beaconsfield was hardly in a good position to complain at this kind of deliberate evasiveness. In any case his luck in having Bismarck to turn the Russian mistakes to his account kept his credit buoyant with the 'national' public. Gladstone's accusations of Metternichism did Beaconsfield little damage. Much more damaging was the unfortunate turn of events in the South African and central Asian spheres, coinciding with the domestic bad times. These had little to do either with old Palmerstonism or any alleged new imperial forwardness; but by seizing the opportunity to link them together with Bulgaria and the Berlin Congress and make a plausible charge that they constituted a revealing pattern of conscious design, Gladstone seriously began to penetrate Beaconsfield's defences and compromise his credit.

Southern Africa and Afghanistan were cases of chronic 'frontier' problems, much like the tropical instances of West Africa, Malaya and Fiji. Ever since the Great Trek of the Afrikaner 'Boers' out of the Cape Colony British policy had oscillated between the argument that the best security for the strategically vital Cape was to ignore the hinterland and the argument that security at the Cape demanded that the hinterland be secured. By the later 1870s the pendulum had swung to the latter argument.

The existence of the two Afrikaner republics of the Transvaal and the Orange Free State relentlessly expanding at the expense of the Matabele, Basuto, Swazi and Zulu peoples, increasingly imposed upon the British authorities in the Colonial Office the realization that instability in the interior inevitably had repercussions at the Cape. The great diamond finds at Kimberley in 1871 made the interior economically significant. The grant of responsible government to the Cape in 1872 only added another element of uncertainty. Kimberley had tried federation, mooted regularly since the 1850s as a solution. He failed to secure acceptance: as with larger schemes of imperial federation, colonists expected Britain to bear the burdens and the costs. Disraeli's colonial secretary, Carnarvon, was determined to impose a scheme of federation on the grounds that the right policy would justify itself and be accepted eventually. In 1877 the Transvaal was annexed as a crown colony. This secured in fact the worst of all worlds: the Transvaal was saved from financial collapse and from being overrun by the African tribes they were dispossessing; yet the British gained no gratitude, only bitter resentment among the Afrikaners; and this resentment developed among the Dutch majority in the Cape Colony.[8'] Moreover, the British now had to cope with native wars: the Kaffir War of 1877–8, then the Zulu War in 1879. The Zulu success at Insandhlwana caused pained shock in Britain. Then the young Prince Napoleon, 'Napoleon IV', a volunteer in the British service, was killed in a skirmish; and as he was a sentimental favourite of the public, Beaconsfield was in more trouble. Wolseley was rushed out with reinforcements, the Zulus defeated under Cetawayo, and the situation saved, but the expense contributed heavily to a financial deficit which Gladstone exploited to the hilt.

Very much the same pattern of events repeated itself in the case of Afghanistan. An attempt by the British to stabilize instability led to increasing involvement and expense. The Russians increased tension by sending a mission to Kabul in 1878 as a gesture of response to Beaconsfield's sending of Indian troops to Malta. The Afghans were in an impossible position and fell back upon procrastination. British impatience led to the Second Afghan war of 1878–9. Afghan resistance was subdued and Afghanistan was reduced to the status virtually of a British protectorate. Then the British commissioner, Sir Louis Cavagnari, and his staff were massacred. A second punitive expedition was sent, in which Major-General Frederick Roberts made his name. In the end the results for the British were much better than in South Africa since the problem was fundamentally much less complicated than South Africa with its humanitarian, racial and economic considerations on top of the fundamental imperial strategic factor. Beaconsfield deserved as little credit for the success of the one as discredit for the failure of the other. But this made no difference; all was grist to Gladstone's moral mill.

Gladstone held the initiative now. His abdicated status was little more than a fiction. As in the middle 1860s he was becoming the focus of a huge mass of excited moral sentiment. Once more he was the most important single factor in the political equation. Clearly the elements of a mission had assembled themselves. He had been 'called' away from Future Retribution to write on the Bulgarian case; by now there was no question of not seeing the great issue through to the end, which would be in his eyes the extirpation of a pathological political condition which he generalized as 'Beaconsfieldism'. This was a compound of delinquency having as its central purpose a deliberate corruption of the quality of public life by appeal to debased and unworthy emotions: lust for glory, aggressiveness, expansion, chauvinism, all at the expense of the freedom of small peoples and at the sacrifice of the well-being and progress of the British people. The bad times, the increased taxation,[9] Gladstone denounced not so much as being in themselves heinous, but as being revealing consequent symptoms of a fundamental moral malaise. It was not likely, therefore, that ideas of a more positive attitude to social conditions would play any part in Gladstone's thinking. His assumptions of the 1860s were still intact and under no pressures. The new difficulties the government was experiencing bore, for Gladstone, testimony to the validity of his assumptions. Thus, paradoxically, social distress did nothing to make Gladstone question or revise those assumptions in a social welfare direction.

In this respect Gladstone was not so far removed from the body of his party. The Radical wing were not pushing anything more at this time than an extension of the borough franchise to the counties, a proposal Gladstonian Liberals were having less and less difficulty responding to sympathetically since it corresponded well enough to their desire to provide more people with more opportunities to practise morality in politics. For Chamberlain, increasingly emerging as the leading Radical force of the future, with Morley of the *Fortnightly Review* as his propaganda collaborator, disestablishment of the Church of England was still at the top of the Radical agenda; but this underlined even more emphatically the distance between even the Radical wing of Liberalism from a social reform programme in 1880. The National Liberal Federation, inaugurated at Birmingham in 1877 mainly at Chamberlain's instigation, challenged Gorst's earlier National Union of Conservative Associations as a means to more effective electoral organization. It was intended also as a Radical weapon against the Whigs, by making the party more responsive to elected constituency representatives. But it was based on the Nonconformist Education League; and it derived its motive power from the moral dissent of the Bulgarian atrocities agitation. Although the Whigs were rightly suspicious of Chamberlain's motives, Gladstone was perfectly ready to lend his patronage to the organization as yet another manifestation of a popular will to atone for 1874.

The Conservative position by 1879–80 was one purely of defence. Beaconsfield had shot all the bolts he had to shoot. Conservatives could only hope that sufficient of the elements making for success in 1874 would remain intact in spite of Gladstone's mounting offensive. It is possible that had he dissolved in 1879 Beaconsfield might have scraped home with a small majority. But he hung on, hoping for a turn in the economic tide. In 1879, spurred by rumours of a dissolution, Gladstone signalled his full commitment to finishing the task he had set his hand to in 1876 by announcing that he would abandon Greenwich and become a candidate for Midlothian county (also called Edinburghshire). His motives for selecting this constituency were that it was held by a Conservative member, the Earl of Dalkeith, heir to the dukedom of Buccleuch, and that careful canvasses indicated that a Liberal could win it.[10] This point was essential for

Gladstone if he wished to give a lead to the country by exploiting the maximum dramatic effect of a conspicuous electoral challenge. He was taking a calculated risk, but the chances were distinctly in his favour. His two 'pilgrimages of passion' (to use Beaconsfield's sarcastic phrase) in Midlothian in 1879 and 1880 were by far the greatest political events of those years apart from the fall of the government itself in 1880.

In a carefully planned series of speeches Gladstone elaborated his indictment of the Conservative administration. The demagogic technique hinted at in Lancashire in 1868 was now in full maturity. Traditionalists in both parties were disturbed in varying degrees by this tendency to shift the central focus of the political process from the chamber of the House to excited and roaring mass demonstrations. Not that Midlothian was a mass constituency: in 1868 the victorious Liberal Maitland had won 1,146 votes (at an expenditure of £1,089 10s. 10d.) against Dalkeith's 905 votes (at an expenditure of £4,477 1s. 5d.). More ironically, perhaps, the contest was anything but a model designed by the authors of *Essays on Reform* to demonstrate the new Liberalism as it ought to be: the hard facts of the voting had to do with the Buccleuch influence behind Dalkeith and the Dalmeny influence of the young Lord Rosebery behind Gladstone in the most old-fashioned manner. Gladstone won in 1880 with 1,579 against Dalkeith's 1,368, out of a total population of 78,000. Undoubtedly the larger number of voters in 1880 is to be accounted for more by a higher turn-out than by natural increase; and this appears to be the general pattern of the election throughout the country. Liberalism secured the margins necessary to win over 100 seats from Conservatives by getting out its voting strength – something it had failed to do in 1874, particularly with offended Nonconformists.

Gladstone made of Midlothian a holy drama of politics, in which a small minority of those with the franchise acted as supers on the stage dominated by the protagonist, playing to an audience of the vast unenfranchised. Midlothian had more in common with a morality play, an Oberammergau Passion, than with a modern election. Being in Scotland, where constituencies were smaller, rather heightened this effect, already charged with associations of

Sir Walter Scott. But the smallness of the constituency involved for Gladstone no inconsistency. He was appealing over the head of the classes to the virtuous masses; and his demand was essentially that the classes voting in Midlothian should vote in this sense as moral proxies to a higher electorate. The message of the morality play was of the 'evil instinct' which 'guided' the Conservatives in the 'choosing' of demoralizing policies. Most emphasis was placed on foreign affairs. Gladstone summed up his message in 'six right principles' of foreign policy which would constitute the guidelines for Britain's international mission in the future: to foster the strength of the Empire by 'just legislation and economy at home' and to 'reserve the expenditure of that strength for great and worthy occasions abroad'; to defend the cause of peace; to strive to cultivate and maintain the concert of Europe; to 'avoid needless and entangling engagements' (this, with the emphasis on selective intervention, for Cobdenite consumption); to acknowledge the equal rights of all nations; and to ensure that the foreign policy of England should be inspired always 'by the love of freedom'.

Holding the initiative, Gladstone successfully imposed his priorities of debate and the general style of a sort of 'state trial' on the election campaign. Beaconsfield disdained to compete on Gladstone's terms, though being a peer he was in any case by convention debarred from active participation as were most of his ablest lieutenants. He attempted to steer debate in the directions of 1872. 'The power of England and the peace of Europe will largely depend on the verdict of the country . . . Peace rests on the presence, not to say the ascendancy, of England in the councils of Europe.' Liberal plots to abandon the Empire were also alleged once more. Beaconsfield's one new contribution was to attempt to inject Ireland into the debate. The Irish Home Rule movement, he alleged, 'challenged the expediency of the imperial character of this realm', and was a threat 'scarcely less disastrous than pestilence and famine'. Gladstone brushed this aside as illegitimate and evasive irrelevance. Ireland, like everything else, would respond naturally and revert to 'normality', or at least to the new conditions making normality possible there, by the very existence of a Liberal government. The 'true supporters of the

Union,' Gladstone insisted, were those who firmly upheld the supreme authority of Parliament, but who exercised that authority to 'bind the three nations by the indissoluble tie of liberal and equal laws'. There was indeed no pressing need for Liberals to feel that Ireland contradicted the plausibility of their general interpretation and diagnosis. Parnellite Home Rulers, it is true, gained ground at the expense of the 'Whig' Home Rulers; but Parnell as yet was unknown and unregarded in England. Nor had the evictions as yet forced Davitt's Land League on the attention of Westminster.

For their part the Conservatives were equally confident in the plausibility of their general interpretation and diagnosis. Gorst had resigned from the Central Office in disgust in 1877 at the party's neglect; but later by-elections seemed to indicate that the government was holding its ground. Beaconsfield dissolved in March 1880 confident that the situation was in hand. But the Liberal enthusiasm focused on Gladstone compromised the Conservative position in sufficient constituencies to restore the Liberals and reduce the Conservatives to the situation of 1868. John Morley could rejoice that he had not written *On Compromise* in vain: he claimed for the 1880 election that it was 'the first occasion on which, after a long campaign in one great pitched battle, the party of justice, moderation, and peace, have routed the party of aggression, intrigue, and lawless national vanity'. Gladstone was justified in writing to Rosebery: 'The romance of politics which befell my old age in Scotland, has spread over the whole land.' Again, as in 1868, Gladstone ruminated 'on the great hand of God, so evidently displayed'.

Chapter Seven

THE LIBERAL VERSION: GLADSTONE'S EXTERNAL BID
1880−85

I

There was no real doubt that Gladstone would be prime minister. He had accepted this rather awkward consequence quite firmly in 1879. He felt a slight embarrassment at supplanting Granville and Hartington, but much less than he had felt at the initial stages of his return to commitment in 1876 and 1877. He had urged the party leaders constantly to follow the people's lead and had got little response. So they had forfeited the right to complain in 1880. The Queen did enough complaining for them in any case. Beaconsfield suited her in every way, politically and personally, and the election had come as a most unpleasant shock. She had never found Gladstone sympathetic; and her sentiments of mild antipathy had turned to violent animosity since the Bulgarian agitation in 1876. But she had no recourse but to summon the Ogre to kiss hands. Beaconsfield immediately resigned without waiting to meet Parliament. Like Gladstone in 1874, his action expressed a sense of surprise at the unexpected turn of events in relation to the assumptions of normality and legitimacy with which he, just as much as Gladstone in 1868, had taken office in 1874. Thus, rather than representing the beginning of 'modern' constitutional procedures, these two resignations of 1874 and 1880 reflected attitudes integral to the backward-looking expectations with which the generation of the 1860s to the 1880s endowed politics in the last era of generally shared confidence in the natural directive capacities of the inherited political system.[1]

Gladstone accepted the commission to form a government in April 1880 not at all in the spirit of repudiating his abdication of

1875; rather he looked upon his return to office as a temporary interlude, a duty imposed upon him, imperative and unavoidable, but strictly defined and demarcated within obligations to restore the natural and legitimate pre-1874 order but not obliging him to stay on after this had been achieved. He regarded the 'special commission' of the new government as 'the foreign policy of the country, the whole spirit and effect of which we were to reconstruct'.

Gladstone's problem in the external sphere was to match the opportunities seemingly offered by a Liberal majority and a Liberal government with those seemingly offered by the European situation in order to liquidate the legacy of Beaconsfieldism and realize for the first time the potential of a Liberal new order in international policy. Ripon, the new viceroy of India, set out with the same idea of a Liberal mission to legitimize British rule through conciliatory reforms and 'cutting down the swagger' of Lytton. Although Gladstone saw his position as clear and his task essentially a straightforward one, he was aware that a good deal of careful manoeuvring would be necessary.

In the first place, there was the cabinet. Whigs, naturally, predominated. They had most of the administrative weight and experience; and in any case Gladstone was predisposed to them increasingly, notwithstanding their general coolness to his crusade since 1876. Gladstone was quite well aware that Radicals like Chamberlain had jumped on to his Bulgarian bandwagon because of its tractive effect on the party as a whole, and because of their calculation that it could be exploited for their benefit and correspondingly at the expense of the Whigs. Gladstone had no intention of allowing this to happen. For him Liberalism was still, just as much as in 1865, the fundamental means of establishing and maintaining a 'harmony between the past of our glorious history and the future that is still in store for her'. The louder the Radicals talked and threatened of 'their' future, the more Gladstone trimmed towards glorious history, which meant, in practice, the Whigs. Granville, back at the Foreign Office, was once more well under Gladstone's wing, and the focus of Whig loyalties was pre-eminently Hartington. The Whigs were able to cooperate with Gladstone against Beaconsfield by agreeing with Gladstone that Beaconsfield represented a sinister throwback to reactionary Toryism – 'the worst minister since Castlereagh', as Gladstone put it. This was a fragile and artificial basis of agreement, operable only in a situation of opposition.

Support for Gladstone's alternative was weakest in cabinet, stronger in the parliamentary party, strongest in the party 'out of doors'. John Bright was trundled into office once more, like a great totem-figure of 'moral force', Gladstone's effort at a makeweight focus of loyalty to counteract Hartington. But in fact Bright would be as dubious an ally for Gladstone as any Whig. He had been notoriously cool towards the crusade of 1876 because of its European 'concert' implications; he was and remained a bigoted isolationist. In cabinet Gladstone might reasonably expect support more or less in Cobdenite terms from Bright, Harcourt and the one new Radical who had forced his way in, Joseph Chamberlain. Yet the strongest influence on Chamberlain at this time was the other luminary of the new Radicalism, Dilke, as yet not in the cabinet,[2] but who was the foremost political exponent of the Liberal imperialism for which the events of 1876 had been a baptism of fire. Chamberlain would, during the course of this ministry, leave the fold of his Birmingham colleague Bright and enter that in which not only Dilke but the brilliant young Rosebery would find more plausible explanations of how Britain might relate most advantageously to the external world. Already the intellectual foundations of the new imperialism were being laid: the deductions drawn by Seeley from the events of 1876–8, dismissive equally of the claims of Beaconsfield and Gladstone, were being delivered as lecture courses at Cambridge, and would be published in 1883 as *The Expansion of England*.

Thus Gladstone had to face not only the sullen resistance of the Palmerstonian Whigs and the obstinate negations of the Cobdenites. For just as Salisbury had argued that the old Palmerstonian policy was bankrupt, so Dilke, Chamberlain and Rosebery would increasingly question the validity and efficaciousness of the assumptions which Gladstone tried to translate into the new foreign policy of Britain. At the highest decision-making level Gladstone was usually blocked. Indeed, after a while he avoided holding cabinet meetings if at all possible, conducting a curious and exhausting kind of personal government, which, given the concatenation of problems and crises, he was unable to discharge adequately. When he did hold cabinets he tended to 'count heads' too often and allowed himself to be overruled; but since there was hardly ever a clear majority for positive action this usually resulted in procrastination. He had only the amiable Granville in support as a rule of positive 'Gladstonian' measures. Otherwise there was impasse. There was indeed the likelihood of a working agreement between the Palmerstonians and the imperialists.

An imperialist could be defined variously: one who had become intellectually convinced of the inadequacy to national interests of both Gladstone and Beaconsfield; or one who, in the practical terms of the first major crisis arising which forced the issues to the front, had come to the conclusion that Britain's security as a power in the world had become compromised to the point where the luxury of not occupying Egypt could no longer be afforded. A Palmerstonian of the stamp of Hartington or Kimberley or Northbrook or Spencer, faced with the final shipwreck of the Crimean system in 1880–82, would come naturally to the latter conclusion, simply as a matter of empirical expediency. If not Constantinople on the cheap, then by all means Cairo on the dear. From this angle, the eventual presence of the Whig chief Hartington and the Radical chief Chamberlain in the third cabinet of Lord Salisbury had about it none of the atmosphere of paradox with which it is usually invested.

Gladstone was strongest where it was least practical use. The 'people' might win elections for him, but they could not win him cabinet votes. The great Liberal public shared with Gladstone the assumption that what had happened in 1876, the healthy irruption into corrupt policy of the forces of public morality, would remain a permanent and decisive influence in the national and international scene. It was taken for granted that the electoral triumph of the anti-'national' Liberal conscience in Britain would somehow be translated into beneficial consequences for Europe. For part of the Liberal conception of 'normality' was of course the supposition that a 'normal' Europe depended upon a 'normal' Britain; and that logically the former would therefore result from

145

the latter, just as the unnaturalness of Beaconsfieldian Britain had necessarily resulted in a contamination of Europe. This was the meaning of 'moral leadership' in Gladstonian terms.

These were the views held more or less by the wide Liberal public, the Claydens, the Freemans, the followers at first or second or third hand of Cobden, Mill, Spencer, Morley, among the established guides, of William Morris, T. H. Green among the newer names. Unfortunately, while there was indeed much to be said for the proposition that a 'normal' Britain was indispensable for a 'normal' Europe, a Europe already deprived of its character of normality would not necessarily respond to the overtures of the newly reconstituted Liberal Britain. Gladstone, though in every respect hostile to the policy of Beaconsfield, nevertheless shared with Beaconsfield the fundamental requirement of having to establish a relationship of leadership within the European system. The irony of Gladstone's crusade against Beaconsfield was precisely that the conditions making Europe amenable to Palmerstonian styles of leadership were the same conditions making it amenable to Cobdenite–Peelite styles of leadership.

Europe was, in fact, amenable to neither of the styles offered from Britain, and had been so ever since 1864. Bismarck's achievement was to preserve the Europe whose paralysis had enabled him to launch the Prussian bid for hegemony. He did this in many ways: the Three Emperors' League of 1872; threats against the French in 1875; 'honest brokerage' in 1878; alliance with Austria in 1879 against Russia; the renewed Three Emperors' League in 1881; alliance with Italy to make the Dual into the Triple Alliance of 1882; vigilant and unrelenting determination, in short, to thwart any attempt from any quarter to re-establish a pre-1864 'concert' Europe. Since this was Gladstone's central aim, it became Bismarck's business to see that he did not succeed.

Gladstone anticipated that he could restore the concert on the foundations of a liberal relationship with the Third French Republic as a joint representative of parliamentary values and a liberationist relationship with the Russians as emancipators of the Slav Christians. He had no hopes whatever from the heirs of Metternich in Vienna, but he calculated that Austria would in any case have to conform to any European consensus. As for

Germany, Gladstone seems to have assumed that with careful yet firm pressure combined with resolute expectations of reciprocal goodwill, Bismarck could be managed. After all, Gladstone equated his cause, as the authentic accredited representative of the most advanced and successful European society, with the cause of progressive civilization, which manifestly was the spiritual expression of the Europe of emancipated nationalities, of developing constitutional values, of immense material construction. Bismarck, even entrenched behind the new protectionist conservative political cartel and the Austrian alliance of 1879, could not long stand against the irresistible current of the times. Apart from momentary bursts of irritation, Gladstone's attitude to Bismarck was enigmatic. Obviously, he did not think of Bismarck as the criminal who had killed the concert of Europe, since for Gladstone it was still alive. But Bismarck had thrown over the German Liberals and free trade, and had worked all too well with 'the old Jew', Beaconsfield. Bismarck, on the other hand, made no secret of his hostility to Gladstone. He aimed to maintain the hegemony of Germany and he aimed to reconcile both the French and the Russians to that hegemony as he had already reconciled the Austrians; and he aimed at preventing a liberal 'Gladstone cabinet' from taking power in Berlin. Bismarck's frankness reflected, no doubt, a difference of personality; but it reflected also the possibility that whereas Gladstone had an imperfect understanding of what Bismarck was about, Bismarck had an excellent understanding of what Gladstone was about.

Even with the French and the Russians prospects were not especially promising for Gladstone. Certainly the republican régime welcomed the opportunities offered by the 'liberal alliance' to play a larger European role and escape from the isolation imposed by Bismarck. On the other hand, however, whereas the British were ready to offer them nothing but moral uplift, Bismarck was very ready to encourage them to take any amount of 'imperial' consolation for Alsace-Lorraine. Bismarck even launched out on a German policy of colonial acquisition largely for the purpose of picking quarrels with the British and posing in ostentatious solidarity with the French. Specifically, in 1881, the French occupied Tunis, which Bismarck had been dangling before them since 1878. For their part, the Russians were almost as furious with 'Europe' for Berlin in 1878 as they had been for Paris in 1856. The new tsar, Alexander III, was to repudiate both his father's liberal projects inside Russia and his cosmopolitan sympathies outside, and conduct Russian policy on a narrow basis of national interest.

Moreover, Gladstone soon discovered that he would have much more difficulty than he anticipated in disengaging Britain from Beaconsfield's 'forward' positions in the Near East, Central Asia and South Africa. He had repudiated the annexation of the Transvaal, the Cyprus Convention, and the Afghan war. But it was one thing to disavow policies in opposition and quite another to extricate oneself from them and their consequences when in office. To his dismay, Gladstone found that he was the inheritor of a secret agreement negotiated by Salisbury with the French in 1879 to maintain Egypt exclusively as an Anglo-French preserve. To denounce this would do the 'liberal alliance' no good. These matters began to get entangled with his larger concert policy in Europe. On top of it all, the Irish question, which he had brushed aside as an irrelevance in 1880, mounted suddenly to a dangerous crisis and established itself formidably as yet another problem area for the British government to cope with, involving not only all the ingredients of a social revolution but compounding also aspects of frontier, colony and empire.

II

For most of the period from taking office to the end of 1880 Gladstone had a fairly free hand to concentrate on the 'reconstruction' of the 'whole spirit and effect' of British foreign policy. The one 'forward' area he successfully extricated himself from was Afghanistan. Beaconsfield's government had in fact already decided to evacuate the far northern area of conquest. Lytton wanted to keep a garrison in Kandahar. Gladstone's ministry decided to enlarge the area of withdrawal, giving up Kandahar but keeping Quetta. This was finally decided in January 1881, much to the disgust of 'national' opinion. In the meantime, after a series of reverses leading to the British garrison in Kandahar being besieged, Roberts's famous forced march to its relief in August 1880 restored the credit of British arms and made withdrawal on essentially the same terms as 1879 – a virtual British control of Afghan foreign policy – both possible and expedient. This brilliant feat of arms made Roberts the candidate of the Indian Army to match against the reputation of the Home Army's Garnet Wolseley, 'the very model of a modern major-general'.[3] Henceforth the issues of military debate tended to polarize around these two magnetic forces. Wolseley himself had recently restored the military situation in South Africa; he left behind on his departure in June 1880 the most promising young disciple in the 'Wolseley Ring', Major-General Sir George Colley, who was destined not to be so fortunate as Roberts.

However, in the larger European scene events promised fair for Gladstone. As early as May 1880 Saburov, the Russian ambassador in Berlin, could remark only half-ironically: 'Behold at long last, the realization of the philosophers' dream. The concert of Europe is established.' The occasion of this desirable circumstance was the attitude of the powers towards Turkish evasion of certain clauses of the Treaty of Berlin obliging the Sultan to make boundary 'rectifications' in favour of the Greeks and Montenegrins. Gladstone particularly took up these issues because he wanted deliberately to focus the energies of the concert on matters of established public law, which moreover enabled him to claim 'continuity' of policy with the preceding ministry. Gladstone and Granville successfully ushered into being a conference of ambassadors in Berlin in June 1880. They also succeeded, very much in terms of Gladstone's principle that the concert was the means of 'fettering' and mollifying the selfish temptations and ambitions of individual powers, in actually getting the powers to agree to a self-denying ordinance in the matter of Turkish boundary disputes in September 1880. Gladstone in fact was far more belligerent than anyone else against the Turks; in his hands the concert, ostensibly designed to avoid war, became an instrument of threatening it.

However, as it proved, the successful conclusion of the Greek and Montenegrin issues was to be the first and last triumph Gladstone's concert would secure. His schemes to apply concert pressure to obtain reforms in Armenia came to nothing. Gladstone also found Cyprus left rather embarrassingly on his hands. He would have preferred to hand it over to the Greeks in the spirit of his recommendations as high commissioner in the Ionian Islands in 1859. But this would have been contrary to the Public Law, since the Sultan was the legal sovereign and Abdul Hamid had no reason whatever for being agreeable to so virulent an enemy of his people or his House as Gladstone. Gladstone toyed with ideas of making it a bargaining counter with the Turks in various contingencies; but in any case events so overtook him elsewhere at the end of 1880 and the beginning of 1881 that all affairs concerning the legacy of the Berlin Congress were permanently overshadowed.

Between December 1880 and February 1881 three signal events took place which substantially set the pattern for the succeeding years of Gladstone's ministry. First, the Transvaal Afrikaners, saved by the defeat of Cetawayo and then freed by the departure of the British regiments, broke out in revolt and proclaimed the Republic of South Africa. Then a bill in the Commons to restore the system of legal coercion in Ireland was passed after unprecedented scenes of obstruction and by an unprecedented stretching of the powers of the Speaker of the House. And a rising of Egyptian army officers, disgusted with the subservience of the Khedive's régime to the interests of European bondholders, threatened the stability of Egypt.

Of these the first was the most obviously and immediately significant; the others were ominous of future significance.

The Afrikaners in the Transvaal and the Orange Free State had welcomed the news of the election results in Britain in April 1880 as tidings of deliverance quite in the spirit of the Children of Israel learning of the end of their pharaonic bondage: if their Jehovah was Gladstone, their Moses was Paul Kruger, and their oppressors were the overbearing high commissioner at the Cape, Bartle Frere, and, not least, meddling humanitarians and missionaries. Gladstone had promised that the injustice of 1877 would be undone; but as with Cyprus, office revealed difficulties. Frere, indeed, was recalled in August 1880, the Liberal public enjoying immensely the spectacle of a Beaconsfieldian head rolling in the dust. Perhaps the evidence suggested after all that annexation would be the best thing for all concerned in the long run?

While Gladstone pondered, chastising the Turks, the Afrikaners grew impatient. In December they proclaimed the Republic; in February 1881 they annihilated a small British force led rashly and fatally by Wolseley's disciple Colley at Majuba Hill, just inside the Transvaal near the junction of the Natal, Orange Free State and Transvaal borders. The 'national' public, which had shared fully Frere's humiliation and which still smarted under the decision to evacuate Kandahar, loudly demanded condign chastisement of the insolent Boers. Gladstone had in any case come to the conclusion that first thoughts were best, and that substantial independence should be conceded. He was faced now with the prospect of cancelling this conclusion in order to punish a people for their impatience at his not arriving earlier at the conclusion he had given them every ground for anticipating. On top of this, the Cape Dutch, who were a majority of the white population in the Colony, gave increasing indications of a dangerous nationalist identification with their 'oppressed' *trekker* brethren beyond the Vaal. Gladstone decided to brave the 'national' public and proceed as if nothing had happened. In April 1881 by the Treaty of Pretoria a convention conceded independence to the two Afrikaner republics subject to something called the 'suzerainty' of the British Crown. Each party had its own interpretation of what this meant, and these interpretations differed widely. For the time being, however, the situation was restored to something like stability.

Negotiations at Pretoria were hurried through because Gladstone belatedly realized that he had on his hands an Irish crisis of alarming dimensions. Ireland was in the throes of profound social and political turmoil. Unlike Britain, land was the crucial issue. Although there was considerable migration to the larger cities – at the beginning of the century Dublin had been an English city in the same way that Prague had been German, but by now was essentially Irish – Ireland never became urban and industrial. The vast majority of the Irish remained on the land, and were now beginning to claim it back from English landlords as a national inheritance of which they had been unjustly deprived. The effects of the medieval Pale and the Cromwellian settlement would soon be destroyed; and only the Elizabethan and Jacobean settlement in Ulster would remain intact. Such were the general dimensions of the problem that now confronted Gladstone.

One of the first acts of his Irish secretary, Forster, had been to announce, in May 1880, the end of coercion in Ireland at the expiry of the Coercion Act of 1875. This was very much in the style of the principles of the Midlothian gospel. But in that same month of May, Davitt, the genius of the Irish Land League founded in 1879 to challenge the mounting incidence of evictions, left for the United States to raise funds for his campaign. In July 1880 an attempt by Gladstone's government to alleviate the distress caused by the evictions – over 10,000 people were evicted in that year – in the form of a Compensation for Disturbance bill was defeated in the Lords. In September 1880 Parnell challenged the government on the issue of the evictions and recommended public protest against landowners and their agents which soon added the word 'boycott' to the language.[4]

This provoked the authorities to prosecute Parnell and the Land League executive for seditious conspiracy. The trial dragged on from December 1880 to January 1881 in an atmosphere of mounting excitement. In the end the Dublin jury failed to agree and the prosecution lapsed. Meanwhile Forster had become converted to a renewal of coercion, and its opponents in cabinet, Gladstone, Bright and Chamberlain, reluctantly conceded. Parnell's triumph in Dublin almost coincided with Forster's forcing through of his Coercion bill in January. What shocked Gladstone about the whole matter was Parnell's deliberate neglect to behave like O'Connell, to denounce violence and illegality. He still assumed that Ireland could be ruled by a native ruling class of the O'Connell stamp. In fact, Parnell saw himself resisting a British suzerainty in much the same terms as Kruger in the Transvaal and the Egyptian nationalists.

To the extent that Gladstone came to admit a national factor and the necessity of governmental institutions based on that factor as central to the problem, he implicitly accepted a kind of analogy, however limited and qualified, between the cases of Ireland, Egypt and the Transvaal. Indeed at times, to Liberal ministers, the Fenians of the Transvaal and the Boers of Ireland seemed indistinguishable in their implacability and efforts at intimidation.

Gladstone could not contemplate a negative policy of coercion alone; he concluded that the basis of a 'national content' had not in fact been sufficiently provided by his legislation of 1869 and 1870. In April 1881 he brought in another Land bill to do the things the Act of 1870 had left undone. This provided for courts to fix 'fair' rents and gave tenants considerable concessions on fixity of tenure and the right to sell their interest in their holding to the highest bidder. That he got it through the Lords in August more or less intact was a measure both of his own commanding statesmanship and widespread public recognition of the extraordinary requirements of the crisis. In short, a different attitude to property in land as between Ireland and Britain was legislatively recognized. It was in principle a form of dual ownership. But this led to the resignation from the cabinet of the Duke of Argyll. The Whigs were starting now to secede in considerable numbers, and the loyalty of those who remained with Hartington would not survive another such test.

The Land Act was Gladstone's equivalent to the Pretoria Convention: a policy of magnanimity, appeasement and reconciliation. It failed, however, to get from Parnell even such grumbling and devious acquiescence as 'suzerainty' had got from Kruger. Privately, Parnell could recognize that it conceded the major practical demands of the Irish tenantry. But publicly he could not afford to admit this. He had a difficult struggle to maintain his ascendancy against the fanaticism of Davitt and his friends and to keep up his advantageous relationship with the Irish Hierarchy on the other side, most of whom looked upon the anti-clerical Davitt and his more extreme leaguers with increasing distaste. Parnell seized upon the fact that the Land Act did nothing about the question of the vast amounts of arrears of rent still owing to repudiate it publicly while assisting its practical operation privately. Gladstone was more shocked than ever. The more Parnell was appeased the less like O'Connell he behaved.

As Gladstone, in September 1881, warned Parnell that the 'resources of civilization' were not exhausted, a second revolt of nationalist army officers took place in Egypt, directed against both Turks and Franks.⁵ The French, who had the larger financial stake in Egypt, started getting restless. The Suez Canal was their achievement and their pride. Gladstone and Granville were unresponsive to French suggestions of some major demonstration to frighten the rebels and bolster the Khedive. Their view was that the official suzerain, the Sultan, should do it. Abdul Hamid was in no mood to assert his suzerainty for the benefit of Gladstone who had threatened him at Smyrna or of the French who had robbed him of Tunis. The French in any case did not want Turkish interference. While Gambetta in Paris dreamt of great strokes in the Levant which would smash the threatening resurgence of anti-western Islamic sentiment already worrying the French in Tunisia and Algeria, Gladstone's attention was devoted to arranging for the arrest and imprisonment of the contumacious Parnell and two of his lieutenants under the powers conferred by the Coercion Act. The Land League was suppressed at the same time. Imprisonment made Parnell the 'uncrowned king of Ireland'. Incidence of acts of terrorist subversion accelerated markedly.

In Egypt during the early months of 1882 the situation, from the point of view of Paris and London, deteriorated badly. In January Gambetta, with the 1879 agreement as his lever, persuaded Gladstone and Granville to launch jointly a bold policy of intervention to support the Khedive against the Army. Granville proposed, as with Montenegro and Greece, a conference of ambassadors to agree on an efficacious means whereby Europe could sustain the Khedive's authority. But in February the Khedive was obliged to accept a nationalist ministry with Arabi, the rebel leader, as war minister. Gladstone disliked intensely the idea of entanglement in Egyptian affairs. He had committed himself as forthrightly on this issue of a 'North African Empire' as he had on any other. He ran the risk of damaging the concert, for Bismarck succeeded in uniting Austria, Russia and Italy with Germany in opposing any Anglo-French action over the head of the Sultan without Europe's approval. Moreover, while it was one thing to find extrication from Beaconsfield's forward positions difficult, it was quite another to push forward to where Beaconsfield himself had never actually been. That would be the supremely ironic comment on Midlothian. Yet before the end of 1882 a British fleet had bombarded Alexandria and a British army under Wolseley had smashed the Egyptian forces and occupied the country. The great Liberal public of 1876 and 1880 was appalled. John Bright, the symbol of Liberal moral integrity, resigned in disgust, denouncing the occupation as worse than anything Beaconsfield had ever done. Gladstone never fully recovered his credit with his most fervent supporters. Egypt for him in 1882 was what Bulgaria had been for Beaconsfield in 1876: it compromised fatally a bid to reassert a British moral leadership of Europe.

Gladstone was apprehensive as early as the joint intervention of January 1882 that a conflict between the Anglo-French financial condominium and 'any sentiment truly national' would end with Britain coming 'to grief in it'. He was clear that 'respect' was due to the fact of Egyptian national sentiment, and was appalled by the lack of any true liberal feeling in Gambetta's attitude to the Egyptians. In the event Gladstone blamed the French and the Egyptian nationalists for the 'grief' he had got himself into.

The question in all this is why did not Gladstone operate in Egypt a policy analogous to that he had operated in the Transvaal and was soon to operate in Ireland, a policy of direct appeasement of domestic nationalist sentiment on the basis of magnanimity and Liberal principles? Why was not Colonel Arabi groomed as another Parnell or even as another Kruger? The answer, in the last analysis, is precisely that Arabi could not be so groomed because Kruger already had been and Parnell was about to be. The political situation of the times was such that Gladstone did not have the capacity to carry his government and his party and his country in a policy of triple appeasement. Moreover, in Ireland and the Transvaal there was no question of the jurisdiction of the concert of Europe. Thus there was not something 'higher' that the interests of either the Irish or Afrikaners could be sacrificed to with a good conscience. The Egyptians were fated to be such a sacrifice to Gladstone's concert ideal.

Majuba still rankled, even with many Liberals of 1876. But that, as Gladstone assumed, was over and done with. Gladstone had also asked the 'national' public to swallow Kandahar and the Irish Land Act. He well knew that Whig loyalties were strained dangerously. He had been obliged to give up, in these circumstances, all ideas of relinquishing Cyprus. Appeasement could not go on indefinitely. Gladstone had to make a decision as to what further concessions could be most advantageously made. It was a version in unwelcome circumstances of selectivity of intervention and the hoarding of moral resources. Obviously, Irish concessions would have priority. Officially, Ireland was a domestic problem. Its scandals and atrocities were therefore more immediately painful, exposing Britain to more obloquy and embarrassment than any other issue. Gladstone's pretensions to international moral leadership were increasingly embarrassed. Gladstone calculated in April and May 1882 that a supreme effort to solve the Irish problem could be made, and that the necessary price to be paid would be to run the risk of letting the logic of the Egyptian problem lead where it would.

The essence of the opportunity as discerned by Gladstone was that at last Parnell had started to behave like O'Connell. He let it be known, from Kilmainham gaol, that he was ready to deal with Gladstone. Imprisonment and martyrdom had in fact saved Parnell from the embarrassing consequences of Gladstone's appeasement with the Land Act; but now he wanted to get out. Martyrdom was uncomfortable, and he was in love with Mrs Kitty O'Shea, who was about to bear his child. Her husband, Captain O'Shea, eager to exploit this relationship to further his political ambitions, negotiated with Chamberlain, whom he saw as the 'coming man' in British politics. Mrs O'Shea dealt with Gladstone and Grosvenor, the Liberal whip. By the so-called 'Kilmainham treaty' Parnell undertook to support publicly the execution of the Land Act if Gladstone would concede the matter of the arrears of rent. A tacit understanding was arrived at on this basis over the protests of Forster, who resigned, and Parnell was released from Kilmainham on 2 May 1882.

Also on 2 May 1882, the Khedive of Egypt appealed for the intervention of Europe to save him from his nationalist ministry.

Clearly, the Egyptian pot was beginning to boil. Gladstone had no particularly clear ideas as to what to do about it. He had never really tried to get a firm grip on the problem, hoping that it would eventually settle down of its own accord. But Gladstone had no time to spare for Egypt at this most critical juncture in trying to coax Parnell and his more moderate following on the one side and the Liberal party on the other into positions of potential cooperation. Parnell was exposing himself to attack from behind as a traitor to the Irish cause; many Liberals were restive and aroused in hostility to rebellious Irish nationalism. Forster had resigned on the point of principle of the appeasement of rebellion, and there were many who sympathized with him. Cowper, the Whig lord lieutenant, had resigned also. But worse was soon to come.

Gladstone appointed as Forster's successor as Irish chief secretary Lord Frederick Cavendish, Hartington's younger brother and Gladstone's nephew-in-law and family favourite. Cavendish was to be a token both of Whig loyalty to Gladstonian policy and Gladstonian good will to Ireland. To underline the point Davitt was to be released from prison on 6 May. On that same day, walking in Phoenix Park outside Dublin Castle, the seat of the Irish administration, Cavendish met Burke, the permanent under-secretary. Burke was the intended victim of a group of Fenian terrorists, called the Invincibles, armed with surgical knives. Cavendish, who was unknown to the assassins, shared Burke's fate.

The atrocity of Phoenix Park robbed Gladstone of any immediate chance of exploiting the potential seemingly promised by the Kilmainham treaty. Thus, against a background of tragedy, failure, hysteria and uncertainty, Gladstone was obliged to cope with the Egyptian problem. His problem, as events developed, was to reconcile on the one hand conditions making impossible a continuation of the *status quo* with conditions making impossible British non-involvement; and on the other hand to reconcile his desire that any settlement should be negotiated by the concert of Europe with his desire to maintain a 'liberal alliance' with the French as special partners in Egypt inside a wider European concert when the French themselves wanted to use the special partnership with Britain for the benefit of their grandiose projects for a restored 'Roman' empire on the southern littoral of the Mediterranean and without regard for the higher interests of Europe on one side or the suffering people of Egypt on the other. The affair was in fact a tissue of contradictions, and what Gladstone needed to do essentially was boldly to cut through them and decide either to endorse Egyptian nationalism and use British power to protect the nationalists from France, or to adopt a view that British interests demanded absolutely the security of the Suez Canal and British physical control, one way or another, over it. But the mirage of Europe inhibited Gladstone in both cases. In the end he founded a British empire in North Africa in spite of himself, and covered the nakedness of empire with the fig leaf of Europe: Britain, he later asserted, executed a 'task' in Egypt 'not alone on our own behalf, but on behalf . . . of civilized mankind. We undertook it with the approval of the Powers of Europe, the highest and most authentic organ of modern Christian civilization . . .'

With the collapse of the Khedivate the old conditions making a Palmerstonian policy possible – the 'imperialism of free trade'[6] – had gone for good. Moreover, British non-involvement was henceforth impossible. The Suez Canal had become a vital link in the strategy of the British world commercial-financial-economic-military and naval system. Britain accounted for 80 per cent of its traffic. Given that Gladstone's accession to power meant the final end of the Palmerstonian alliance with the Turks, Egypt became more exposed from the point of view of British interests at the same time as Egyptian capacity to maintain itself as a stable self-governing entity began to weaken dangerously. When he disavowed the traditional Turkish alliance Gladstone supposed that it would be replaced by the European concert and in particular by the 'liberal alliance' with France. Yet since the French consistently sabotaged chances of a real concert, and since, ironically, the only manifestation of a 'concert' that ever emerged was maliciously manufactured by Bismarck in support of the legal suzerain, the Sultan, Gladstone, like Egypt, was dangerously exposed. And since the domestic situation in Britain ruled out a surrender of British strategic interests either to the French or to

'Europe', and since Gladstone would not go against Europe either in favour of Arabi or straightforward British 'imperial' occupation, Gladstone was obliged to trail along behind the French and convince himself that this represented somehow a concert posture.

On 25 May a joint ultimatum forced the resignation of the nationalist ministry; but by 28 May the Khedive was obliged to recall it. Anti-European riots broke out in Alexandria with some deaths and much damage to property. British and French squadrons prepared to bombard. At the very last moment the French suddenly took fright at Bismarck's version of the concert, decided they could not challenge the rest of Europe with only British backing, and scuttled out. Thus, absurdly, Gladstone found himself sole master of Egypt. The British squadron bombarded the forts of Alexandria on 11 July. By 13 September Wolseley defeated Arabi's army at Tel-el-Kebir and occupied Cairo.

For the next two and half years of his second ministry Gladstone regularly announced that Britain was in Egypt for the good of the Egyptians and as the executor of a European will, and would withdraw, in the words of the famous Granville Circular to the Great Powers of January 1885, 'as soon as the state of the country and the organization of proper means for the maintenance of the Khedivial authority will admit of it'. But since the British presence was necessary to preserve the Khedivial authority in the first place, the maintenance of that authority would depend upon a continued British occupation. Gladstone and the Liberals never managed to evade that simple logic. British forces occupied the Suez Canal Zone until 1953.

In reality the two factors that counted were the necessity of replacing the Palmerstonian policy with something which would answer adequately to British requirements, and the determination of powerful political interests in Britain to achieve this one way or another. In the deteriorating situation of 1882 Egypt and the Canal were, after all, much more precarious and vulnerable from the point of view of the British world system than either the Transvaal or Ireland. The generally shared British assumption was that sooner or later the Afrikaner republics in South

Africa would inevitably return to the orbit of the richer, more advanced and civilized Cape and Natal. The British revenge for Majuba would take the form of the insensible conquests of railways, trade, culture, education. The activities of the young and energetic Mr Cecil Rhodes, who was devoting his huge fortune from Kimberley diamonds to the construction of a great British South African entity, seemed a convincing portent of this. As for Ireland, painful political embarrassment though it might be, it hardly constituted as yet a strategic danger. But Egypt was one of the great cross-roads of the world. For the British, the creators of the only world-system in existence at that time, the fundamental decisive geographical fact of the world was getting around Africa. There was no passage around the top of Asia or the top of America, and the long Cape Horn route was uneconomic except for special cargoes. These fundamental geographical facts determined the crucial importance for Britain of the Mediterranean and the Cape, and the vital necessity of securing her routes of communication via both. The Mediterranean and overland route had traditionally been the quickest passage to India, but the Cape naturally carried the bulk of heavy trade until the Suez Canal route became well established. As late as 1878 the Cape was still the more important: it carried British trade to the value of £91·3 million compared with the £65·6 million of the Canal.[7] Dilke, in *Problems of Greater Britain* (1868), summed up the significance of the Cape: 'The Cape is our half-way house, the loss of which would be almost fatal to our Indian Empire and our China trade.' Again it was Dilke, in 1882, who emphasized the growing importance of the Canal, now the principal highway to India, Ceylon, Malaya and British Burma, to China, and increasingly also to Australia and New Zealand.

Dilke, one of the first and foremost of the new imperialist school of statesmanship, foreign under-secretary since 1880 and a member of a cabinet since December 1882, represented obviously a section of British opinion determined to make sure that the collapse of the Palmerstonian *status quo* in the Near East would not result in a situation compromising to the security of British interests. The imperialists, however, were a minority group both in the Liberal party and the Liberal cabinet. Joseph

Chamberlain and Rosebery had not, as yet, defined their positions, and the main strength of the movement for the securing of British interests in Egypt came from the ex-Palmerstonians of the party, led by Hartington. If not occupying Egypt was a luxury Britain could no longer afford, they were prepared to pay the price. Relentlessly, as Gladstone twisted and turned and threatened resignation, Hartington kept up the pressure for British intervention, preferably without the French. The decisive strength of the imperialists' position was that they knew clearly what they wanted. Gladstone himself persistently refused to see the strategic point urged by the advocates of occupation.

The fact that Gladstone was able to throw a cloak of moral righteousness over the operation was important politically because it preserved the unity of the Liberal party. Only nineteen Liberals voted against credits for the intervention, with the Conservative opposition in support 'in the national interest'. With the broader public at large there was considerable enthusiasm for an assertion of British power rather than a concession of British appeasement. Many Radicals denounced the enterprise as a conspiracy of bankers and bondholders, just as they had denounced Beaconsfield's Turkish enterprise: the beginnings of a fruitful interpretation of the capitalist roots of imperialism. But although the formal unity of the party was not broken, it never really recovered its morale after the shock of 1882. The great promise seemingly offered by the wonderful events of 1876 and 1880, the golden visions of a new foreign policy based on truth, humanity and justice, seemed somehow to run to waste in the sands of Egypt.

III

While Hartington and Chamberlain cooperated over Egypt they remained at daggers drawn over Ireland. Chamberlain wanted the Irish Office in 1882; but Gladstone, unwilling as in 1868 to entrust Ireland to a strong hand other than his own, appointed a comparative nonentity, G. O. Trevelyan. After Phoenix Park Gladstone and his supporters, of whom Chamberlain was one of the more prominent, could not resist demands for a further turn of the coercion screw. But they still argued, against the bitter opposition of Hartington and the hardliners, for the expediency of continuing to offer concessions in such matters as arrears of rents. Parnell, though he disavowed the Phoenix Park murders, was saved from the dangerous prospect of reaching an O'Connell-like agreement with Gladstone by the fresh measures of coercion which followed them. Under his auspices the illegal Land League was revived in October 1882 as the Irish National League. Ireland remained in 1883 and 1884 agonizingly poised between the evenly balanced forces of subversion and coercion. Trevelyan could make little impression. All Gladstone's earlier efforts had been wasted. In order to break the deadlock he would now have to raise his bid far beyond the level of the Land Act of 1881 plus offers on the matter of arrears. The debate among Liberals would be in terms of what logically next proposed itself: degrees of governmental autonomy for Ireland.

Chamberlain led the way in this direction. He was sure that only something very big in the way of local government would suffice. Gladstone's mind was moving in the same direction. This policy in fact represented the tactic of trying to separate Parnell from the Irish masses. Chamberlain linked this with the current domestic debate on the question of a further extension of the franchise. Chamberlain calculated that Parnell would not be able to control and organize a mass Irish electorate. In this way the Home Rule agitation could be headed off. It was the same factor essentially as the Land Act of 1881. Gladstone, however, would in the end go beyond it to offer Parnell what Chamberlain's policy centrally aimed at denying him. With the issue of Home Rule, and its profound efforts on the general structure of British politics, the case of Ireland enters into a distinct new phase.

South Africa and Egypt, however, continued to cause the British Government anxiety and concern more or less within the original terms of reference, though increasingly subject to the influence and repercussions of Bismarck's diplomatic system and its new colonial sideline.

The Transvaal had throughout the early 1880s played a kind of *obligato* to the Irish theme. In the perspective of the frontier problems of the British world system there were many remarkable similarities between the challenges to Britain of Irish and Afrikaners nationalism. Indeed, it has been persuasively argued that the British obsession with the Irish analogy in South Africa blinded them to the truth that, whereas a relatively united Irish nationalism was undoubtedly a reality, Afrikaner nationalism, the assumed unity of the Transvaal, Free State and Cape Dutch, was not.[8] It existed in special circumstances in 1877-81, but thereafter was more a figment of nationalist propaganda and British fears than a fact to be treated with the respect it was given by Gladstone and his successors.

The great difference between Ireland and the Transvaal was that the latter already had 'home rule'. Kruger as President of the 'Transvaal State' was thus in the position Parnell would have been in if, after 1886, he were premier of an 'Irish State' disputing with the Westminster government to test its will to resist a bid to assert a substantial independence against rather than within the wider interests of British paramountcy. But whereas Parnell was enigmatic about his ultimate aims, no one was in any doubt that Kruger and the Afrikaners in the Transvaal wanted in effect absolute independence from any kind of British control or interference; and further, that they envisaged a future South Africa in which the Transvaal would be the paramount power. They would achieve this by peeling away British paramountcy like the leaves of an artichoke. They would seep down around the flanks of the Cape Colony and Natal, blocking the route to the interior for the Cape in the West, through Bechuanaland, and reaching the sea in the east, between Natal and Portuguese Delagoa Bay. With the whole wide interior under their control, with useful arrangements with the sympathetic Germans in South West Africa, with unchallenged and unchallengeable powers to deal with the native peoples as they wished, and with more than half the white population of the Cape of kindred stock, the Transvaal Afrikaners would indeed subvert the British position at the Cape, already dependent on good relations with the responsible ministry there, which meant, in practical effect, that Britain could not expect the Cape government to exert itself for purely British interests.

The need for the British to maintain their supremacy at the

Cape, and therefore in South Africa, remained as imperative as ever. Although the Suez route to India and beyond was quicker, it was more vulnerable. Therefore the Cape still remained the best military route. Gladstone, and those like minds with him in the Liberal government such as Kimberley the colonial secretary, Granville and Derby, who succeeded Kimberley at the Colonial Office at the end of 1882, were well aware of these facts. None of them ever considered the feasibility or the possibility of a British abdication. Gladstone made no attempt to dismiss the strategic factor at the Cape as merely an excuse for greater military establishments or for empty 'prestige' as he did in the case of Egypt. The issues were whether it would be better to contain the Afrikaners by *douce violence* or by hitting them on the head.

Given that the Pretoria convention of 1881 was unworkable because the Transvaal Afrikaners did not want it to work, given that the Afrikaners were demanding further concessions, and given that a policy of force which presumably, as in 1877, would reunite the Transvaal, Free State and Cape Dutch and turn South Africa into another Ireland was highly inexpedient, the problem for Gladstone was to strike the right balance between conceding things to the Afrikaners which would not compromise the reality and security of the British paramountcy. The greatest strength that Gladstone felt he had was time: he assumed that the long-term forces, the influences of nineteenth-century progressive civilization, would eventually tame the Transvaalers. A convention agreed on in London in February 1884 replaced the Pretoria convention of 1881. The Afrikaners again accepted a British 'suzerainty', so long as the actual word was not used. The British position consistently was that though the word 'suzerainty' itself had been dropped the fact of a British veto over the external relations of the Republic remained. Gladstone did not object to the German penetration in South-West Africa or St Lucia Bay in the East so much in itself – in fact he shrewdly guessed it would have a salutary effect on the Cape government – as in its potential for mischief in connection with Transvaal aspirations. In the event, in 1884 and 1885, both possible points of German–Transvaal contact were blocked by British annexations of St Lucia Bay and Bechuanaland.

Bechuanaland became in fact the key to the London negotiations. It was the Cape's route to the hinterland, the 'Suez Canal of the interior' as Rhodes called it. The Transvaal Afrikaners very much wanted it, and were in the process of taking it over by means of freebooters. Rhodes in 1883 saw that the struggle for these lands meant the struggle for both the control of the interior, and for the 'ultimate supremacy in Southern Africa'. The weakness of the Gladstone–Kimberley–Derby policy was that they might have traded it away to Kruger for concessions in other matters. The turning point came when the combined forces of the humanitarians, Robinson the British high commissioner at the Cape, Rhodes the leading Cape advocate of the drive into the interior and above all the Cape government, agreed that it must not go. So the negotiations turned rather on the compensations the Transvaal Afrikaners might receive for renouncing their western ambitions in Bechuanaland. The Transvaal government sulkily ratified the London Convention and Gladstone hoped that at last a point of equilibrium had been found which, by neutralizing the Transvaal, would tranquilize the Cape Colony; and that British interests could rest securely on this dual foundation.

In fact, the London Convention proved as little successful as its Pretoria predecessor; but in this case the failure resulted in the long run in the South African War. For after these two Gladstonian exercises in conciliation and 'Home Rule' it appeared to British governments that nothing remained but a struggle for the fundamental prize in South Africa, Afrikaner paramountcy or British paramountcy.

Thus Gladstone had gained nothing but time; and as things turned out, time, after all, seemed not to be on the side of British paramountcy, for the opening of the Witwatersrand gold reef in 1886 transformed the Transvaal quickly into the dominant economic power of South Africa and Rhodes's efforts at a counterpoise in the north – 'Rhodesia' – proved not to have sufficient weight. But the most immediate and significant consequence of Kruger's blatant contumaciousness in 1885 in infiltrating Bechuanaland was that it provoked Chamberlain into strong recommendations that the South African Republic be obliged, by force if necessary, to respect the terms of the London Convention. He became very firm, also, on the matter of resisting German efforts to lodge themselves as a factor in South Africa. Chamberlain had passed from his pacific and anti-expansionist position of 1883 to a 'forward' and 'imperial' position in 1885: the first step, in fact, to the consummation of 1899. Thus Chamberlain exhibits the process of the making of an imperialist. Henceforth he would follow where the logic led him, appreciating that both Beaconsfieldian federation and Gladstonian home rule seemed incapable of securing the vital British interests at the Cape.

The London Convention of early 1884 was in fact Gladstone's last bid to solve a major external problem within the Midlothian mandate. The remainder of his office in 1884 and 1885 was spent in coping with the various symptoms of the failure and inadequacy of the assumptions of 1880. Ireland in this respect was a special case. Gladstone had not even included it in his original terms of reference, and his supreme bid for a solution was yet to come.

Possibly the most telling instance of the increasing debility and incoherence of the Liberal cabinet was the decision it made in January 1884 to send Major General 'Chinese' Gordon to supervise the Egyptian evacuation of the Sudan. The occasion of this had arisen out of the successes of a certain Mohammed Achmed of Dongola who set up as a prophet or 'Mahdi' of a puritanical Muslim sect with the aim of clearing the Egyptian presence from the upper Nile as a prelude to yet greater things. The last Egyptian effort to reassert control had ended in a catastrophe in November 1883 when the army of Hicks Pasha was annihilated at El Obeid. The British were by this time securely in the saddle in Cairo. Evelyn Baring had been set up in 1883 as resident and consul-general, and was to remain the strong man of Egypt until 1907 behind a façade of nominal rule by the Khedive and various advisory bodies. Hicks had been dispatched against the Mahdi before Baring's arrival. Granville characteristically evaded responsibility for or against the expedition. But once the disaster occurred Granville and Gladstone were adamant that losses must be cut. They had no more desire to extend British responsibilities on the upper Nile than they had to annex Bechuanaland. In the latter case they reluctantly allowed their hand to be forced. But nothing could force their hand in the Sudan. The Egyptians were bullied into compliance. The choice of Gordon to supervise the evacuation was a bizarre aberration on the part of a distracted and harrassed cabinet. In the midst of preparations to appease Kruger it was tempting to throw a sop to the restless and hungry public. Gordon was a popular hero: his appointment, like the bombardment of Alexandria, was one of the few acts of Gladstone's government received with any enthusiasm. Conversely, the farcical tragedy of his death in Khartoum in January 1885 reacted damagingly against the government. Substantially, the issue was quite unimportant. Anyone who knew Gordon knew that he was entirely unfitted for discharging the task. A mystical fanatic, he disregarded his instructions and attempted to restore the situation through sheer personal magnetism. What had impressed the Chinese, however, failed to impress the Dervishes. By the time Gladstone and Granville realized that Gordon had duped them and was daring them not to abandon the Sudan and that they would have to send an expedition to rescue the besieged hero it was too late. Wolseley arrived a few days after the fall of Khartoum.

It was in its way suitably ironic that the case of Gordon's death, quite insignificant in terms of the issues of Egypt and the Sudan, should have caused a greater public outcry than Majuba and Phoenix Park together. Gladstone resolutely ignored the recriminations and carried on the policy of withdrawal from the Sudan. As with Majuba, he was not going to be deflected into a futile policy of punitive revenge. Besides, he had bigger fish to fry than the outraged Queen or howling jingo mobs. The British dispensations in Egypt involved negotiations with Europe, which meant, in the circumstances, negotiations with Bismarck.

As Gladstone insisted that Britain was in Egypt as executor of the concert of Europe he unavoidably handicapped the execution of British policy. No other power took at all seriously his claims to be providing Europe with an example of moral leadership. The French resented the abolition of the dual control. Both the French and the Russians suspected that the British had stolen a march on them and secured the British share of the much-canvassed partition of the Ottoman Empire while they were as far off as ever from their designated spheres. Accordingly, they pressed strongly for British withdrawal. This pressure tended, however, to have a contrary effect. The more the French and the Russians advised the Sultan not to cooperate with the British in the matter of guarantees in the event of a British withdrawal, the more the British felt it necessary to sit tight. This situation suited Bismarck's book admirably. He did not especially rejoice at the collapse of the 'liberal alliance'. For all its not very effective ideological challenge to his leadership, it had the practical effect of tending to keep the French and the Russians apart. But, since it had collapsed, he set about making such profit as he could from it; and this naturally took the form of cultivating the French assiduously. In the various international conferences in 1884 and 1885 to settle the Egyptian financial situation Bismarck worked closely with Jules Ferry to frustrate British proposals and to secure the retention of as much international control as possible. This was achieved substantially at the Paris conference of March 1885. Britain would need to have a majority of the votes of the powers. Since the French and the Russians could usually be relied upon to cast their votes to impede British desires, the British depended on the good will of Bismarck and his allies. Thus a policy of polite blackmail became the rule.

Further, Bismarck improved the shining hour of his *rapprochement* with the French by launching a colonial policy. This enabled him to pick quarrels with the bewildered British at convenience. Ferry was the greatest French exponent of imperial expansion as a means to restore French confidence and greatness. Bismarck genuinely hoped that thereby the French would be reconciled to the loss of Alsace-Lorraine and that France would become a willing collaborator in his European system. In fact, there was no future for this policy. Restored French confidence and greatness would inevitably focus eventually on Alsace-Lorraine. Compared with this fundamental quarrel, the French quarrel over Egypt with the British was noisy but secondary.

German penetrations and grievances in South-West Africa, the Cameroons, Togoland, Tanganyika and New Guinea were continued largely with a view to impressing the French with the possibilities of a continental league against the British. A conference in Berlin was arranged to organize the final carve-up of Africa. This was the avalanche set off by the pebble of the British occupation of Egypt in 1882. Bismarck got in fact little return for his investment. The French concentrated on grabbing everything they could get and Gladstone blandly welcomed German co-operation in the great tasks of spreading civilization and Christianity. Bismarck's project of a maritime league 'à la 1780' against the British certainly contributed to the naval scare in Britain in September 1884, when the inadequacies of the British fleet became the subject of intense public concern; but since for the British the Mediterranean was at this time the key area of naval strength, the upshot of the crisis was in fact the 1887 'Mediterranean agreement' of Britain, Austria and Italy directed against France and Russia. Bismarck's problem was that if the French needed an ally against the British, Russia was far better for their purposes than Germany. Thus the more Bismarck encouraged the French in an anti-British direction the more he put at risk the integrity of Russia's participation in the Three Emperors' League as a means of keeping France isolated from Russia.

This point was not lost on the Russians when they had their quarrel with the British in April 1885 over Afghanistan. The merits of the Penjdeh incident are of little account. The Russians were probing and the British reaction was all the more violent since Gladstone took the opportunity to recover some of the political credit he had lost with the Khartoum fiasco. Troops were ostentatiously mobilized and credits were ostentatiously voted. Eventually a compromise settlement was arrived at, to Gladstone's gratification, by arbitration. But the point was that if Russia and Britain had gone to war, the vital area of conflict would have been the Straits. The Russians feared above all a British penetration into the Black Sea, with or without the Sultan's consent; and for the Russians a French fleet was of far greater consequence than Bismarck's diplomatic organization of a continental league, especially since, with good reason, they did not trust the Austrians. Moreover, if the French were to fight a war with the British they would do so for French colonial interests, not for the benefit of a Bismarckian continental *bloc*. But in any case the French would not push their colonial disputes with Britain to the point of war. Unlike the British, the French did not depend for their greatness and their independence on their world system. The British would fight to stay in Egypt or to preserve their position in South Africa: the French would not in the last resort fight to get them out of either. The only war they would wage in fact was a war against Germany for Alsace-Lorraine.

Gladstone's failure to achieve his external aims, in fact, was more profound than Beaconsfield's failure. Beaconsfield did not get what he wanted; Gladstone ended by getting precisely what he did not want. The concert idea was in hopeless ruins, the 'liberal alliance' shattered. A North African empire had been founded on the ruins of the liberties of a small people. By 1885 Granville, caught between Gladstone's demands on the one hand and an unyielding international situation on the other, was in a state of collapse. In this he well reflected the fate of the Liberal expectations of 1880. True, Gladstone had to contend with distracting troubles in Ireland, South Africa and Egypt which had not been so acute in Beaconsfield's time. But it is clear enough that even without these troubles Gladstone still would not have succeeded. Nor is this to be explained simply in terms of the adequacies of Bismarck's *Realpolitik* as against the inadequacies of Liberal idealism.

Certainly Bismarck missed no tricks in exploiting the possibilities of the situation for his advantage and Gladstone's disadvantage; after all, what did Gladstone have materially to offer? The British fleet was useless to the French and both useless and dangerous to the Russians. He would support the French against German pressure but would not help the French to put pressure on the Germans. He would not offer the Russians guarantees against Austria in the Balkans: indeed Gladstone and the Liberals rejoiced when the Bulgarians broke away from Russian tutelage in 1885. It had always been the Liberal thesis that the 'breasts of free men' would be a better barrier than the decrepit Turkish empire to Russian efforts at aggrandizement. Nor would Gladstone offer the Russians further security at the Straits than British goodwill. But even had the 'Gladstone cabinet' of the Crown Prince Frederick which Bismarck so feared replaced him in

Berlin, the situation could not have substantially changed. The Austrians and the Russians would not thereby have been reconciled in the Balkans and the Straits; and the more 'liberal' the régime in Berlin the more it would have been committed to the popular 'national' German cause, the alliance with Austria. Nor would a 'liberal' régime in Berlin have surrendered Alsace-Lorraine to the French. These were the determinant factors. Bismarck, in 1864, 1866 and 1870, exploited the circumstances that made them determinant. His achievement up to 1890 was to stem the logical flow of their consequences. But his presence or his absence in the 1880s did not make any difference as to their existence. And it was their existence that baffled Gladstone.

Chapter Eight

THE LIBERAL VERSION: GLADSTONE'S DOMESTIC BID 1880—85

I

Although Midlothian had been essentially about the external sphere of British responsibility, the Liberal assumptions of 'normality' applied equally to the domestic sphere. But the practical directions and requirements in terms of domestic responsibilities were unclear. In 1880 there was no 'programme' beyond the negative definitions by Gladstone of the morality of financial retrenchment and the lowering of taxes. A vociferous Radical wing, with Chamberlain and Morley in the lead, were busy trying to provide guidelines for the party as a whole. But they found it extremely difficult to hit upon anything both large and convincing and designed to serve this purpose. Even before 1880 they were frightening off the more anxious bourgeoisie.

Yet positive reform was still what the great majority of Liberals in the country assumed the Liberal party was about. Apart from the Whigs, who though large in the cabinet were small in the constituencies, Liberals could not rest content with the achievements of 1868–74. Nor was there any lack of sectional efforts to put particular crotchets at the head of the Liberal agenda. Nonconformists, naturally, interpreted the glorious transactions of 1876 and 1880 very much to their own sectional advantage, and prepared confidently for the final offensive which would bestow upon Anglicans the inestimable benefit of a Free Church in a Free State whether they liked it or not. The Temperance[1] party were equally assured that ultimate triumph against the evils of intoxicating liquor was at hand. Land reformers who ascribed all social ills to primogeniture and entail anticipated eagerly the day of reckoning with the monopolists. Those, like the former cabinet minister James Stansfeld and the women's rights campaigner Josephine Butler, who put the abolition of the Contagious Diseases Prevention Acts[2] as the most important duty of public life, looked with confidence to the new government to uphold the strictest moral standards of public purity. The supporters of the Tichborne Claimant[3] looked with equal confidence to the new government to vindicate the late Dr Kenealy and assert the rights of a poor man against the selfish exclusiveness of social caste, abetted by sinister Jesuits. The atheist propagandists Annie Besant and Charles Bradlaugh contemplated an auspicious era for the cause of secularism and 'free thought'. All these causes could, in anticipation, shelter together within the Liberal fold and march behind the banners proclaiming that the end of the unprosperous and warlike 'personal rule' of Lord Beaconsfield would bring about not only 'a foreign policy based on truth, humanity, and justice', but also 'honest and economical finance', and 'domestic legislation ruled by desire for the people's welfare'.[4]

Exactly what legislation was the problem. Obviously it is the Radicals who invite attention at this point, since they wished to go faster and further than the others in some direction or other. Also, though weaker than the Whigs in cabinet and the administration generally, they were much stronger in the constituencies. The Whigs had no desire for movement: by now they saw their domestic function almost exclusively as a brake against traction. Gladstone, by now very much the 'Grand Old Man' – Labouchere first coined the honorific in 1881 – assumed that his problem would generally be to use the Whig force of inertia against the Radicals. Instead, he found himself usually in need of Radical support against Whig pressure in cabinet on Ireland and the external sphere generally. Moreover, Gladstone both owed gratitude for Radical help against Beaconsfield's foreign policy and was committed to their central assumption: the 'vital principle' of Liberalism, like Greek art, was 'action'.

Morley, the ideologue, Chamberlain's 'spiritual adviser' and the prophet of Mill and Cobden for the Liberal faithful, is the most revealing case to observe. In 1874, he had, in On Compromise, deplored the prejudice in England against the intellectualization of political life. More than any other Liberal he wrestled with the problem of relating the intellectual dimension of Liberalism to practical Liberal politics. Morley wanted to hit upon a systematic politics in which this relationship would blend naturally, convincingly and irresistibly. By 1880 he had still not found it. Economic depression had not provided the anticipated congenial climate. Rather, it tended to intensify trade union sectionalism in the direction of ideas of 'working-class representation'. He feared that Liberalism would disperse its intellectual and political talents in a multitude of unconnected causes. Disestablishment seemed to propose itself plausibly as an essential Liberal task; yet Gladstone was a devoted Churchman. About disestablishment also there was by now something rather mean and spoiling. Once Nonconformity had emancipated itself from the old injustices of inequality its campaign against the Church began to look rather like a persecution. For Morley, even before 1880, disestablishment 'disappointed'. His central problem was to reconcile a Millian insistence on 'open-mindedness' with general agreement on a 'great principle' which would unite Liberals 'in a common project for pressing with systematic iteration for a complete set of organic changes'.[5]

By 1882 Morley was still disappointed. He hoped that the doctrines of Cobden – whose biography he published in 1879 – might provide the necessary centre of cohesion for a large and comprehensive political school. Cobden, clearly, 'fully possessed by the philosophic gift of feeling about society as a whole, and thinking about the problems of society in an ordered connexion with one another', had 'definite and systematic ideas of the way in which men ought now to travel in search of improvement' and 'attached new meaning and more comprehensive purpose to national life'. Yet Morley's hopes of the potentialities of Cobdenism for the circumstances of the 1880s were also disappointed: for one thing, old John Bright himself was still very much alive and full of suspicion at impious efforts to dilute the pure milk of Manchester doctrine with adjustments or expediencies, however well intended. Morley of course was not alone in attempting to provide Liberalism with intellectual equipment enabling it to respond adequately to the future without compromising the integrity of its fundamental principles: for example, T. H. Green's *Lectures on the Principles of Political Obligation* were published in 1883, and the doctrines Green expounded became very influential among those Liberals groping towards concepts of a 'positive' state creating the social conditions prerequisite to the achievement of realistic possibilities of freedom on a mass scale. Yet for Morley the influence of Green, with its implication of collectivism and enlarged State interference with individual liberties, appeared as yet another source of anxiety rather than confidence.

II

The sessions before 1883 were blighted by the Irish issue. Parnell and his party developed methods of parliamentary obstruction in their resistance to measures of coercion to such a pitch of effectiveness and uproar that business was paralysed and resort to counter-measures of *clôture* became necessary. On top of this came the time-wasting Bradlaugh imbroglio. Elected together with Henry Labouchere for Northampton as a Radical, Charles Bradlaugh was the most notorious and provocative propagandist for atheism at a time when such public profession could raise riots. Many atheists had entered Parliament before – John Stuart Mill for one – but Bradlaugh was the first to enter specifically on the 'free-thought' interest, and accordingly he requested that his oath as a Member of the Commons should be made by affirmation and not by the prescribed religious form. There was no official opposition to this ostentatious but harmless procedure. Unfortunately for Bradlaugh and for the smooth course of government business, Bradlaugh's case became entangled with the ambitions of a group of four Conservative M.P.s soon to become celebrated as 'The Fourth Party'.[6] The leading spirit in this group was the ambitious Lord Randolph Churchill, a younger son of the sixth Duke of Marlborough. The others were J. E. Gorst, still bitter at the party's neglect to come to terms with the new democratic age, Henry Drummond Wolff, and for a time, Salisbury's nephew Arthur Balfour. They were united initially by high spirits and then by cavalier disdain both for the

Hudibrastic Liberal ranks and for the dim front bench on their own side, where Stafford Northcote behaved as though he were still Gladstone's private secretary and relied mainly on the two Conservatives most offensive to aristocratic prejudice, Cross and W. H. Smith, or 'Marshall and Snelgrove', as they were contemptuously derided by the patrician Churchill.

The general line of Churchill and his friends was to claim the inheritance of Disraeli's doctrines of popular Toryism and to preserve them from the contamination of a narrow and timid unwillingness to 'trust the people'. Only by such confidence, they alleged, could Conservatism be redeemed from the disaster of 1880. They observed carefully Chamberlain's preparations for the coming Radical takeover of the Liberal party, and planned to emulate him by using the National Union of Conservative Associations against the Conservative Central Committee, the seat of power of the party establishment. Beaconsfield, having nothing to lose, himself encouraged them with faint admonition before he died in 1881. Bradlaugh was only incidentally their victim: their real target was Northcote and the official Conservative leadership, the 'Old Identity', as Gorst, probably the only one of the four wholly serious in his convictions, dubbed them. By brilliance and audacity they persuaded a majority of the House that Bradlaugh's reception among their number would be an intolerable offence to their Christian consciences; they ensured that the Bradlaugh affair remained a chronic scandal through the whole term of the parliament. As often as the offended Christian conscience of the House expelled him the resolutely Radical electors of Northampton sent him back. Eventually he was allowed to take his seat in peace in 1885 and relapsed into obscurity.

This was an absurd diversion, but it reflected accurately the collapsing morale of a political system in the last throes of trying to sustain the restored Victorian equilibrium of the 1860s. In its recklessness and irresponsibility the Fourth Party was just as apt a symptom of the consequences of the failure of the Conservative version, both external and internal, as the feebleness of the official leadership.

Liberal confidence, for all the encouragement of 1880, rested on just as rickety foundations as the Conservative confidence of 1874. The one positive achievement of the early sessions which related logically to considerations of advantage in terms of the attitudes of the 1870s was the Employers' Liability Act of 1880, an earnest attempt of Liberal willingness to repair its legislative reputation with trade unions. This was a measure giving workers a modest amount of compensation for injuries caused by negligence of their employers. So insignificant was it, indeed, as a retraction of Liberal *laissez-faire* purism that it failed even to provoke the indignation of so suspicious an observer of the Liberal betrayal of its heritage as Herbert Spencer, who produced his indictment *The Man versus the State* in 1884. The thesis he argued there was that 'most of those who now pass as Liberals, are Tories of a new type'. In fact, he found the Liberal record of the early 1880s relatively barren as a source of revealing signs of retrogression. This barrenness reflected in fact the paralysing combination of pressures upon Liberalism: subjectively, the difficulty of deciding in what direction and how far its domestic programme ought to go; and objectively, the difficulties opposed to freedom of choice and movement in any case by the Irish and other external impediments.

Extending the borough franchise of 1867 to the counties was for Liberalism as much an occasion of difficulty as an assertion of confidence. It meant the doubling of the existing county electorate and increasing the total electorate from about three millions to five millions. It would mean, in effect, because of the complications of qualification, that nearly 60 per cent of the adult male population would possess the franchise. Ostensibly, giving the vote to agricultural labourers in the time of Joseph Arch and to the miners in the time of Thomas Burt would be much the greatest stroke of Radical franchise politics in the nineteenth century. Yet, in the context of Liberal trouble, it came rather as an anti-climax.

For the mass of 'forward'-looking Liberals who identified themselves more or less with the view expressed by Chamberlain in January 1883 that Liberals were 'ripe for a new departure in constructive Radicalism' after the sterile futilities of the Irish diversion, the franchise extension of 1884 was to be the 'herald of far reaching changes in the elemental structure of society'.

> The work of the Liberal party in the State, maintained with un-altering persistence throughout half a century, had at length reached its consummation . . . With the machinery of legislation at length smoothly constructed and the government in the hands of the great masses of the population, careful observers, with satisfaction or foreboding, anticipated broad economic readjustments, designed to benefit the toiling multitudes of the common people.[7]

The new electorate would be the means to the end of what by 1885 was codified as the Radical Programme: better housing, heavier death duties on land, rating reform, payment of MPs, Church disestablishment, free elementary education, abolition of the laws of entail, allotments to farm labourers, restoration of illegally enclosed common land, a progressive income tax and a greater emphasis on direct taxes, reform of and greater powers for local government, a general reduction in the cost of government.

The chances for a Third Reform Act depended, however, on Gladstone's willingness to espouse it. Whatever Gladstone's motives might be for accepting the idea of a further extension of the franchise, they were not all those of a desire for 'far reaching changes in the elemental structure of society' on the basis of 'broad economic readjustments'. But Gladstone let events push him to it without resistance. For long he had intended to make his political jubilee of December 1882[8] the natural and appropriate point of resignation and retirement. It was a question as to whether or not he ought to stay on. Ireland rather than franchise was uppermost in his mind. He went to Cannes on the French Riviera in January 1883 and stayed, brooding, until March. He returned determined to see it through. In the circumstances a Reform bill in 1884 proposed itself as the primary practical objective; but his brooding concentrated on that 'perilous crisis which no man has as yet looked in the face; the crisis which will arise when a large and united majority of Irish members demand some fundamental change in the legislative relations of the two countries'.

Ireland did, indeed, give some pause. It was unthinkable for most Liberals that Ireland should not be treated with entire equality. But, as Whigs and Conservatives pointed out, there were disturbing implications. The Irish Reform Act of 1868 had been of little consequence in so thinly urbanized a country; so, correspondingly, enfranchisement of the rural proletariat would be of greater significance in Ireland than in Great Britain. In the end franchise reform imposed itself on the Liberal government insensibly by simply existing as an obvious and feasible large-scale potential public policy rather than by any compelling sense of necessity or design. It was not imposed upon a reluctant party leadership by Radical pressure, for the Radical forces were far too disorganized and incoherent to achieve any such feat. Though ostensibly a blow for the 'future', franchise reform exposed the weakness of the 'party of the future', for while Liberals could agree to do it, they could not agree what to do with it. In 1867 Conservatives had been persuaded to endorse reform on the grounds that Conservatism must establish its rightful role in the readjustment of the Victorian equilibrium; now, in 1884, with the failure of 1880 as a spur, Conservatives could be persuaded that Liberalism might be no more dangerous with the extended franchise than without so long as the issue of a thoroughgoing redistribution of constituencies, not involved in the 1867 settlement, were now turned to advantage wherever possible.

Reform thus filled a gap. Though it divided Liberals, it divided them less than almost anything else. And otherwise there was little enough to show on the domestic front. The expected return to 'normality' in Liberal definitions did not materialize after 1880. Pockets of economic distress remained chronic. The rate of unemployment – a word coming into general usage at this time – among trade unionists stood at 11·4 per cent in 1879; it dropped by 1883 to 2·6 per cent, but by 1884 it was up again to 8·1 per cent and by 1886 to 10·2 per cent, with consequent unrest and riots. The index of industrial production fell by 14·4 points between 1880 and 1886. Gladstone, personally taking charge of the Exchequer until 1882, had managed to get income tax down to 5*d* from 6*d* in 1881–2; but by 1882–3 his successor Childers was obliged to raise it to 6½*d*, higher than at any point in Beaconsfield's profligate reign. The Corrupt and Illegal Practices Act of 1883 restricting electoral expenditure was certainly a blow struck for the classic Liberal principle of curbing the illegitimate influence of both urban and rural magnates. The official returns of electoral expenditure in 1885 were three-quarters of the expenditure of 1880. But in view of the proposed vast increases of the electorate it was a blow struck rather late. Traditional modes of electoral spending would be ruinously prohibitive with a mass electorate. Party funds on a national basis were going to be more important in any case than local sources; and here the Liberals, with many of their richer supporters melting away, were to be in greater straits than the Conservatives.

There were, moreover, especially with Gladstone, tactical considerations. Reform was the obvious counterpoise to Whig aggressiveness in Ireland, Egypt and South Africa. Hartington would have to pay at home for his dividends abroad. And the more the problems of government got out of hand, the more Gladstone consoled himself with variations on the theme of the innate virtue of the masses. A third Reform Act would be his acknowledgement of what he interpreted to be their signal manifestation of that innate virtue between 1876 and 1880. He was not blind to Radical motives and designs. Indeed, he construed Chamberlain's programme in 1885 as having a 'far-sighted purpose which is ominous enough', part of which was a 'not improbable' 'plan or intention to break up the party'. Chamberlain had already, in 1883, caused a storm by his notorious assault on Salisbury as the spokesman of the class 'who toil not neither do they spin'. This resonant biblical phrase marked the emergence of Chamberlain as a first-class power on the platform. A little later Chamberlain crowned himself with John Bright's crown at Birmingham, claiming the inheritance of the Radical leadership in the new era of democracy. Even so, Gladstone refused to view the general prospect as critical. There was, certainly, 'a process of slow modification and development' mainly in directions which he viewed with 'misgiving': there was the 'demagogism' of Randolph Churchill's 'Tory democracy', which Gladstone saw merely as a continuation of illegitimate and deleterious Beaconsfieldism; there were the new tendencies within Liberalism, of which the 'pet idea' was 'constructionism – that is to say, taking into the hands of the state the business of the individual man'. But Gladstone's general conclusion was one of confidence:

> I have even the hope that while the coming change may give undue encouragement to 'construction', it will be favourable to the economic, pacific, law-regarding elements; and the sense of justice which abides tenaciously in the masses will never knowingly join hands with the fiend of Jingoism. On the whole, I do not abandon the hope that it may mitigate the chronic distemper, and have not the smallest fear of its bringing about an acute or convulsive action.

In truth Gladstone had virtually abandoned consideration of the 'chronic distemper' which made the relationship between Liberalism and the domestic scene so problematical. His thoughts were focused almost obsessively on Ireland; and the franchise issue for him had become integrally linked with Ireland. His hope was that, somehow, the latter problem would be resolved by the action of the former. Either, as most Liberals hoped and Parnell feared, a labourer franchise would be a useful 'counterpoise to the class of farmers who now have an inordinate and dangerous influence' on the Nationalist party; or it would prove conclusively the genuineness and unanswerable validity of Parnell's credentials as the true leader of Irish national opinion. After the failure of previous Liberal efforts at a settlement, some such decisive new development was the indispensable requisite to a further initiative in Liberal Irish policy. There was no other means of escape from the existing doldrums of distasteful and unrewarding coercion. Gladstone in fact was following the logic which Morley had been setting forth; and, given the strong probability that Parnell would not be swamped by the new Irish tenant electorate in prospect, Gladstone was heading straight towards Home Rule. But in the meantime he kept these thoughts to himself.

The Liberal party as a whole lacked this basis of purpose and intelligence. Consequently the debates about franchise reform in 1884 have about them a certain air of unreality. The only people inside the political system who seriously wanted reform and expected great things of it were the Liberal Radicals and the

Tory Democrats, the latter pushing it as part of their 'trust the people' gambit. But the eagerness of both these groups stemmed from weakness rather than strength. And in any case, the issue of redistribution of the constituencies became more important than franchise extension itself. Better than anything else this question illustrates the preliminary effects on politics of the fundamental social transition of 'modernism' which was eroding the foundations of traditional politics. Most of the Conservatives and the Whigs, as in 1866, had no desire for another Reform Act. Any departure from the *status quo* was risky. After all, despite the precedents, it was possible that, this time, Radical claims might be justified: a rural proletariat might join with an urban proletariat and be the means by which the Radicals might indeed finally extinguish the traditional social and political dispensation. Nevertheless, they concluded that the balance of advantages lay in not attempting to resist reform as such but in insisting as the price of their cooperation on thoroughgoing redistribution of the constituencies which had let in the Liberal majority of 1880 on a basis equitable to the two parties. The reform issue in itself was a poor substitute for Morley's great undiscovered 'unifying principle'.

On top of this, Liberalism was at a fundamental strategic disadvantage on both subjective and objective senses. Subjectively, Liberals were still confined by the obligation of assuming that they represented the future. Since redistribution or the principle of 'one vote one value' had in any case always been a classic Liberal demand – exculpation of the great sin of omission of 1867 – Liberals had to assume that naturally and inevitably it represented advantages for Liberalism. Therefore their capacity for manoeuvre was restricted compared with that of their enemies who were no longer in a condition to afford the luxury of old-established assumptions of confidence. The Whigs were desperately fighting for their survival: as drowning men they would clutch at the serpent of redistribution. Apart from the Tory Democrats, Conservatives since the catastrophe of 1880 generally saw themselves on the defensive, conducting a fighting retreat and looking out for occasions which could be turned to advantage to impede the avant-garde Radical pursuit. Naturally they too would try to squeeze any advantages they could out of a whole-sale redistribution of constituencies, most of which were at present held by Liberals in any case. The Irish aspect of course caused concern. Whig and Tory landlords had no illusions about what would happen there. It was clear there could be no reduction in Irish membership of the House of Commons commensurate with the decline of the Irish population since 1845, much as many Liberals desired it. The Liberals needed Irish votes to pass the Bill. And as far as the crucial British domestic area was concerned, Salisbury as early as 1882 had in fact put his finger on the key factor: 'I believe,' he told Northcote, 'there is a great deal of Villa Toryism which requires organization.'

Herein lay the objective Liberal strategic disadvantage. Certain important long-term social trends had begun to run against them. Liberalism was losing the allegiance of the middle class and above all many of the intellectuals. There were already evidences of this. The testimony in themselves of W. H. Smith and G. J. Goschen and their like was eloquent. Then there were the ten-dencies to what stern Liberals denounced as the social 'flunkey-ism' of suburbia. Class was beginning to be the determinant political factor in a situation where Liberalism was losing in the suburbs but not yet gaining in traditionally Tory working-class areas, such as Lancashire. Nonconformists noted with equal alarm the increasing manifestation of the parallel tendency for the younger moneyed generation to fall off from the faith, and send their children to Anglican public schools and universities. What redistribution essentially was about was precisely the electoral recognition of the overwhelmingly urban and suburban character of British society. Besides this decisive fact, the Reform Act of 1884 was indeed – apart from specific Irish applications – relatively insignificant, especially since the complicated and obstructive qualification system remained untouched.

Whig and Conservative determination to see what could be made of redistribution had nothing in common with Liberal principles of 'one vote one value'; yet the unavoidable irony for Liberalism was that practically it amounted to the same thing. Liberals were in the position of having to argue from dubious premises to ultimately non-productive results. The premises were the assumptions of the 1860s as revived in the later 1870s and triumphant yet again in the 1880s that the old politics of hierarchy, influence and 'interest' had been superseded by the new politics of principle and community consensus. The Radical Programme of 1885 proclaimed as its central assumption that, now that 'the people' had power, politics 'swayed by considerations of class interests' would be at an end. The realities of the new politics were that electoral reorganization responding to the changing face of social development would inevitably reflect the politics of class allegiance and class 'interest' in a new or 'modern' sense as yet generally unanticipated by Radicals but anticipated with varying degrees of distaste by most non-Radicals. Liberalism's next fundamental choice would be either to abandon the assumptions of 'principle' politics and conform to the new social dispensation of class politics, or to avoid making this 'surrender' of principle by hitting upon an issue involving centrally the 'moral' qualities of Liberalism which would thereby allow Liberals to avoid what Morley called the 'maelstrom' of social questions. 'Imperialism' was this kind of issue. For Liberals so inclined Home Rule for Ireland offered itself almost providentially. These were the essential elements of the crisis of 1885-6.

Meanwhile the issues of 1884 resolved themselves. Whigs and Conservatives, making use of the obstructive powers of the House of Lords, extracted from the Liberal government a pledge that equitable redistribution would follow in the next session. Each party had a compelling motive for compromise: the Liberals wanted a Reform Act more than they wanted a conflict with the Lords (though many were eager enough for that); Conservatives on the whole wanted a Reform Act with redistribution rather than provoke a Lords–Commons conflict. The Queen offered mediation to avoid such a dangerous outcome. Thus the Third Reform Act was allowed to pass and take its place as the crowning anti-climax of the second phase of the Liberal bid to impose permanently Liberal definitions of political legitimacy. Once more, as in the 1860s, exultant Radicals and despondent traditionalists deceivingly reassured one another.

Redistribution, as hammered out effectively by Salisbury, Gladstone and Dilke in a series of bargaining sessions, was a compromise between Radical views on the 'one vote one value' principle and traditional efforts to secure as distinct as possible a separation between rural and urban areas. It provided that henceforth most constituencies would be single member and as nearly as possible equal. Nearly 150 small borough seats, mainly in the south of England, were extinguished. The counties got ninety-seven new seats, the metropolitan area thirty-nine and the boroughs got thirty-seven. Only eighty-three seats were unaffected by the redistribution. The 'Celtic' fringe was treated with great tact and tenderness. The great cities were for the first time given their due electoral weight. Vast rings of suburban constituencies sprawled about the major conurbations. London spilled over the Home Counties. The modern pattern of politics was established.

Everybody was more or less satisfied. The Whigs had fought a good rearguard action. They had saved most of the two-member borough constituencies which had allowed Whigs to run in harness with Liberals or Radicals. Gladstone, with his drift towards the virtuous masses and his increasing softness on Irish coercion, was no longer the cohering pivot they needed him to be. But they were already packing their bags. The Radicals had got something that could plausibly be called a democratic electorate and electoral system. They looked forward to getting the kind of firm Liberal grip on politics which 1880 had failed to provide. As Chamberlain put it, 'The centre of power has been shifted, and the old order is giving place to the new.' Chamberlain in January 1885 launched his own personal 'unauthorized' Radical programme, in which the interests of the British electorate were given distinct priority over Irish demands. He advocated manhood suffrage and the end of plural voting, the direct representation of working men, payment of Members of Parliament, a smallholdings policy, free elementary education, an element of 'social' taxation, repeal of the Game Laws: a mixture of old and new, enlivened by the notorious demand as to 'what ransom will property pay for the security which it enjoys?' This shocked many Liberals as well as all traditionalists. It certainly marked Chamberlain's sense of a 'new departure'.

It marked the beginning of a final breach with Morley, for

whom Chamberlain was now emerging as a serious threat to fundamental Liberal values. More than anyone else, Chamberlain, with his demands for the primacy of Radical reform, stood between Home Rule and Liberalism, blocking them off from one another. For Morley, getting the two together had become the sacred duty of anyone who charged himself with the guardianship of the conscience and integrity of Liberalism. Morley interpreted Home Rule as the positive aspect of the anti-jingoism and anti-imperialism which he interpreted as the vital issue Liberalism must confront and defeat unless it were to betray both its own future and the cause of the future generations. More important, Gladstone, increasingly under the self-imposed pressure of his own decision to stay on, was very likely to be faced eventually with the prospect of making some sort of choice between the alternatives represented by Morley and Chamberlain.

The mass of Liberals straddled rather confusedly between Chamberlain and the Whigs. Gladstone himself, who would, so long as he remained in active political life, give the lead to most of them whichever way he went, had his eyes on Parnell. Parnell had his eyes on a new mass Irish electorate which he hoped would sweep away the rival 'Whig' Home Rulers, neutralize Davitt's rivalry, and deliver into his hands the undisputed tribuneship of a united Irish nation. With Irish representation left intact by redistribution, Parnell would have an aggravated weight as between the two major parties. There was always the possibility that, with eighty or so followers, he might hold the balance of power. In any case he made it clear that he was open to bids for his support in return for concessions on coercion and land purchase. Salisbury did not discourage him from hoping for concessions from a Conservative cabinet; and Parnell in fact, assuming along with Chamberlain and most Liberals that there would be inevitably a new Liberal majority, ordered his supporters in Britain to vote Conservative in 1885 as a means of punishing Gladstone for not abiding by Parnell's interpretation of the Kilmainham treaty and of helping to keep the Liberal majority as low as possible, thus allowing the Irish the chance to sell their support at the highest price.

Salisbury and the regular Conservatives pinned their faith on the villa votes, the reaction of anxiety provoked both by Chamberlain and Parnell. Salisbury, in his negative way, was weaning the party away from neo-Palmerstonian traditionalism just as effectively in the domestic as the external sphere. His primary allies and agents would be precisely those Conservatives or would-be Conservatives most closely identified with growth areas of Conservative strength, the Marshalls and the Snelgroves. Though Salisbury fully shared Randolph Churchill's patrician disdain for W. H. Smith and his fellows, he realized that here was a force not to be dismissed with Churchill's jeers at suburban 'pineries and vineries'. Moreover, the dramatic split in the Liberal intelligentsia indicated another growth area whose importance was quite out of proportion to the actual voting numbers directly involved. The strain in the 1860s of comprehending both Mill and Bagehot had been painful enough for Liberalism. Arnold in his way, Seeley in his, had made the strain even more painful. The lead given by Fitzjames Stephen in *Liberty, Equality, Fraternity* in the 1870s was being taken up by increasing numbers of Liberals anxious at the prospect of a political system presumably dominated by the vast mass of the uneducated and the unintelligent. There was grave disquiet at the pattern of Liberal appeasement of challenges to ruling authority: 'Socialism' at home; Afrikaners in the Transvaal; Parnellism in Ireland; the 'Ilbert Bill' giving way to nationalist agitation in India.[9] The revealing symptom of this anxiety in 1885 was Henry Maine's *Popular Government*, in which he argued that the assumption of progress integral to democratic idealism was 'not in harmony with the normal forces ruling human nature, and is apt therefore to lead to cruel disappointment and serious disaster'. In 1886 Tennyson set off a literary bombshell under Gladstone: *Locksley Hall Sixty Years After*, a document of intense disillusionment with Liberal claims and Liberal hopes. From Salisbury's point of view this sort of thing was all to the good.

In June 1885 a combination of Conservatives and Parnellites, as a kind of token of their new electoral understanding, defeated the staggering Liberal government on a question of increased duties on beer and spirits. Gladstone resigned and Salisbury formed a cabinet, with Randolph Churchill at the India Office and Churchill's enemy Stafford Northcote shunted up to the Lords as Earl of Iddesleigh. Parnell was repaid with an end to coercion and the important 'Ashbourne Act', giving £5 million to facilitate loans to Irish tenants to purchase land. The Conservative government dissolved parliament in November.

The election results in 1885 dissatisfied everyone, more or less. Two unprecedented developments indeed signalled a 'new departure'. The Liberals won a majority of English county seats; the Conservatives won a majority of the English boroughs. In Britain the Liberals gained a majority of eighty-six over the Conservatives. Their victory was substantial but not up to 1868 or 1880 levels: in 1880 they had enjoyed a lead of 10·62 per cent of votes cast; in 1885 the lead was 7·68 per cent. The Conservatives retained intact their Home Counties, metropolitan and Lancashire axis. But in Ireland all Liberals and moderate Home Rulers in Munster, Connaught and Ulster were defeated; and Parnell came through at the head of eighty-six Irish Home Rulers, thus depriving Gladstone of an overall majority.[10] Parnell nevertheless had miscalculated. He did not hold a decisive balance; merely the capacity to keep either party out but only to put the Liberals in. And the very fact of putting the Liberals in on his terms would in itself in all probability destroy their majority.

III

This was the situation faced by Gladstone who was in fact already a convert in principle to Irish Home Rule. A recent cruise in the fiords of Norway had impressed him with the merits of the Sweden–Norway relationship under the Swedish Crown.[11] Parnell's success in proving his tribuneship was the decisive last requirement completing the pattern of Gladstone's conversion and establishing the necessity of translating principle into practice. Gladstone hoped that the Salisbury–Parnell axis of 1885 could be preserved and encouraged to resolve the problem, with Liberal help if necessary. Gladstone supposed that Conservatives could be persuaded to accept the justice and expediency of conceding Home Rule much as they had accepted Reform in

1884; there would be negotiations, give and take, and Parnell would have to swallow what Liberals and Conservatives agreed to offer him. Further, this would be the best way of getting around the formidable obstacle of the House of Lords: Salisbury there would be as Wellington in 1846 and Derby in 1867. Undoubtedly, from everyone's point of view except Salisbury's and the Conservative party's and those who were opposed to Home Rule on principle, this would be the most convenient solution. But Salisbury was not prepared to accept analogies between franchise reform and Home Rule; and had no desire to repeat Peel's sacrifice of himself and his party. Peel believed in free trade; Salisbury did not believe in either the justice or the expediency of Home Rule and nor did the Conservative party. Moreover, Randolph Churchill, at the height of his campaign to use the Conservative Union as a weapon against the party establishment, was only too ready and eager to play the part of Disraeli to Salisbury's Peel.

Salisbury's flirtation with Parnell was purely an electoral calculation. Once it was clear that no advantage could come of it, Salisbury dropped it without compunction. This pushed the initiative back to Gladstone. He made one last effort in December 1885, with Salisbury's nephew Arthur Balfour as intermediary, to persuade the Conservatives that it was their duty to the highest and most solemn considerations of the national interest to swallow the bitter cup proffered to them by Gladstone. There was little chance of this appeal having effect; but in any case, through an indiscretion of his son Herbert, the public learned to its surprise or consternation that Gladstone was a convert to conceding Home Rule to Ireland. This 'Hawarden Kite' embarrassed Gladstone. He had concealed his conversion hitherto because he wanted to avoid any 'bidding' by the two parties for Parnell's support; and because he hoped to cajole and prod the Conservatives into putting Home Rule through. But now, with the Hawarden Kite revelation, all the virtues and benefits of reticence turned into evils and mischiefs. For the time Gladstone might have had but for his silence to 'educate' the Liberal party and convert it to Home Rule was now irretrievably lost; and Gladstone had to depend on the bewildered loyalty of a totally unprepared party in circumstances which gave colour to suppositions that his conversion had been sudden and opportunist.

Naturally, for Parnell the Hawarden Kite was like a comet of good omen in the sky. Moreover, it enabled him to do the only constructive thing it was possible for him to do – that is, put the Liberals in. Gladstone, reluctant but determined, decided to take office once more. A Liberal and Parnellite combination defeated the Conservative ministers in January 1886. Gladstone formed his third cabinet with the purpose of passing some measure of Home Rule. Hartington declined office, as did Bright, always one of the more virulent denouncers of Parnell as a disloyal incendiary. Harcourt, Rosebery, Granville, Spencer and Childers stayed on, and Chamberlain, in spite of every provocation offered by Gladstone to discourage him, insisted on coming in again to wait to see the nature of the final draft of the Home Rule measure to be proposed. Chamberlain wanted to give the Irish every reasonable satisfaction, but he wanted to stay with Liberalism, to ride out the Gladstonian convulsions, to hang on and wait to come into his post-Gladstone inheritance. John Morley, who had been elected to the Commons in 1883 and had never ceased to advocate substantial concessions to Ireland on Parnell's terms as the only policy both possible to and consistent with Liberalism, accepted the post of Irish chief secretary. Mainly with Morley's assistance, Gladstone produced a Home Rule bill in April 1886. It provided for an Irish parliament of two houses competent to enact legislation for all Irish affairs other than those relating to the Crown, foreign affairs, defence, trade and navigation, and certain other matters deemed to be of 'imperial' concern. Irish members were no longer to sit at Westminster. No provision was made to accommodate the Protestant minority in the north, who bitterly resented the idea of Catholic Dublin rule. Chamberlain, understandably incensed by Gladstone's deliberately cavalier treatment of him and convinced that Home Rule on this scale was both unnecessary in Ireland and fatal for Liberal hopes in the future, resigned from the cabinet; and he and John Bright and Hartington led ninety-three Radicals and Whigs into the lobby against the Liberal government and the

Parnellites, and together with the Conservatives defeated the bill by thirty votes in July.

Gladstone thereupon requested and obtained a dissolution, and another election was fought, this time explicitly on the issue of Home Rule. In the result the Gladstonian Liberals lost ground substantially, falling from 235 to 191. Chamberlain held fast to his Birmingham bailiwick, though he could not keep control of his 'caucus' handiwork, the National Liberal Federation, which soon fell into Gladstonian hands. The Conservatives gained correspondingly: from 251 to 316. Though not by any means discharged from the political bankruptcy registered in 1880 and 1885, they were already benefiting from several new sources of electoral credit. Randolph Churchill had emerged as a major platform force, providing Conservatism with a colour and dash it badly needed. He had used the Union very effectively against the Conservative Central Committee and appeared to be assuming a kind of co-regency with Salisbury. In 1885, he had dared to challenge Chamberlain on his own Birmingham ground, and indeed, deprived of his family seat of Woodstock by the Redistribution Act, actually disputed the new Birmingham Central constituency with John Bright. In 1886 he improved on his demagogy and 'played the Orange Card' against the 'G.O.M.' on Ireland: 'Ulster will fight and Ulster will be right.' Here Conservatives were tapping a rich vein of political ore. Moreover, all the gradations of suburbia were beginning to respond to such things as the Primrose League, founded in 1883 at Drummond Woolf's instigation in memory of Lord Beaconsfield, and already a promising means of rallying the country 'out of doors' to the Conservative cause.[12]

From Salisbury's point of view all this was gratifying; though the thought of the impossibility of keeping Churchill out of a new Conservative cabinet was not so alluring. The Unionist Liberals were somewhat reduced, to seventy-nine, but remained a coherent and formidable group. The Parnellites maintained their phalanx intact. Thus there was a decisive majority of 395 Conservatives and Liberal Unionists against the 275 Home Rule Liberals and Irish Nationalists. After having offered the leadership of a united Unionist government to Hartington, who declined, Salisbury formed his second Conservative cabinet as the head of a minority government but with the firm support of the dissident Unionist Liberals.

IV

The Liberal split over Home Rule registered the end of the old political era. Home Rule itself, however, was the occasion rather than the cause of this. Even had Gladstone resisted the logic which led him to acceptance of Parnell's claims, and kept the Liberals united, he would have been obliged to accept the logic implicit in that alternative: namely, that the role and function of Liberalism must be seen essentially in the kind of terms proposed by Chamberlain. His personal situation was that with the Reform Act behind him he had finally discharged all obligations directly or indirectly derived from 1880; and that he had the right to choose between definitive retirement and the conceivability that there might be one more great cause to justify his continued retention of the Liberal leadership. Home Rule alone, in the circumstances of the times, would have carried the potential of moral imperative sufficient to sway Gladstone in deciding for continuing in office and in fully committed political life.

There was thus not in practical terms a situation of Gladstone having to choose between Parnell and Chamberlain, as though they were political representatives of sacred and profane pleasures. Gladstone saw the alternatives both for himself and for Liberalism as being Parnell or nothing. Home Rule was not only good for Ireland; it was a good in itself, and by espousing it Liberalism would do itself good. Acceptance of Parnell's terms would allow the party to keep its integrity; by means of appeasement on principle he could avoid the surrender of principle. Parnell thus offered Gladstone the possibility of double advantages: on the one hand Home Rule and reconciliation with Ireland would be seen as the ultimate consummation of Gladstone's career and an inevitable fulfilment of the central point and purpose of Liberal politics; on the other hand Liberalism thereby would be saved from losing its soul to Chamberlain, the man

Gladstone had come to see rather as a potential second Beaconsfield, a power for political debauchery, instilling base passions of class jealousy.

For his part Chamberlain was convinced that Gladstone had deliberately manoeuvred him into a position where he had no option but to leave the party. All Chamberlain's proposals for substantial local autonomy for the Irish were bypassed. He blamed Morley bitterly also for abetting and encouraging Gladstone in this course.

For Gladstone Home Rule was inescapable on grounds both of virtue and necessity. But if he could have avoided making the decision, and if there had been the possibility of a future for Liberalism without his leadership but on his terms rather than Chamberlain's, would he have preferred to make a bid for reconciliation with the Irish on the basis of something less than Home Rule – something along the lines of Chamberlain's schemes for substantial local self-government? This hypothesis is worth raising, because it helps to clarify the situation Gladstone was in. The answer probably is that Gladstone's motives and decision were not determined by the Chamberlain aspect of things, though they were not independent of the leadership aspect as such. It is quite possible that if he thought Liberalism would solve the Irish question without him, he would have preferred to retire from the scene. But clearly he did not think so. He never, in any case, troubled to groom a successor. It is also quite probable that any ideas he may have nursed that Parnell could be bought off with substantial concessions short of Home Rule, or that Parnell could be separated from his mass following by such concessions, were finally jettisoned after the 1885 elections.

Gladstone was perfectly correct in his assumption that, given a decision to plump for Home Rule, he was the only, the indispensable leader. He had in effect made this decision inevitable during his withdrawal on the Riviera at the beginning of 1883 where he brooded on the significance of the implications of a further Reform Act with Ireland. Now, in the elections of 1885, the crisis he had foreseen in January 1883 had indeed arisen: 'when a large and united majority of Irish members demand some fundamental change in the legislative relations of the two countries'. In his view the kind of moral imperative involved in this situation, just as much as the menace to Liberalism represented by Chamberlain, made a necessity of virtue.

'The proposal of Home Rule for Ireland in 1886', it will be remembered, was one of the four critical occasions analysed by Gladstone in which his 'striking gift' of 'insight' manifested itself. He was perfectly aware that he was gambling on his ability to reconcile a public opinion at best largely indifferent to Irish claims and in good measure hostile to them with his insistence that those Irish claims must take precedence over claims directly relevant to that public. He was, as he put it later, going 'against nature'.

Whatever the precise motivating and directing influences on Gladstone, the fundamental point that emerges in 1886 is his insistence on committing Liberalism to a future within, and not beyond, the limits prescribed in the assumptions inherited from the formative years of the 1860s. 'Equal laws' may not have answered adequately to the Irish problem; yet Home Rule derived essentially from the same stock of attitudes. It was as logical an extension of the Liberal principles of Midlothian as the appeasement of Transvaal Afrikaners. Thus, by making Home Rule the primary political issue, Gladstone attempted to guarantee the continued relevance of Midlothian. Home Rule, in effect, would not only keep Liberalism trimmed and in balance to avoid being swamped in the 'jingo' and 'constructionist' tides; it would ensure also that the whole system of politics in Britain would be so ballasted.

This was Gladstone's bid to bind the future. It failed. Politics was not ballasted by Home Rule. Whatever its merits in itself as a policy – and plausibly it was the only possibility of reconciling enough Irish to the British connection to avert the eventual split and the founding of the Free State and then the Republic – it was not established as the central and guiding issue of the future. Although it determined a redeployment of political allegiances it did not accrue sufficient weight in the British constituencies to maintain its balancing function. Home Rule never retained the status of the 'great principle' of 'systematic politics', bringing a 'new meaning and a more comprehensive purpose to national life' which Morley had sought. After 1886, only twice did British governments attempt to deliver Home Rule to the Irish: both were Liberal governments dependent for their parliamentary majorities on Irish Nationalist votes. Thus, in the result, Gladstone ensured the worst of both worlds: he did not bind the future as a whole, but he hobbled the Liberal party. This is ultimately the measure of the inadequacy of the assumptions upon which Liberal politics had been based in the two great efforts since 1868 to establish Liberalism's claims to authority as the legitimate directive impulse of national life.

PART III

The Forming Elements of a Modern Society
1886–95

Chapter Nine

SOCIAL DYNAMICS
1886—95

I

Rather like dinosaurs at the onset of a new and uncongenial geological epoch, the generation at its prime in the 1860s, still at the head of affairs in the 1870s and 1880s, groped about in the wreckage of their familiar landscape, already being transformed and imposing new conditions of adaptation and survival. Gladstone's famous collision with Tennyson in 1887 over *Locksley Hall Sixty Years After* aptly illustrates this sense of lurching mastodonic creatures thrashing about in the shallows of a swamp inexorably drying up on them.

Tennyson was provoked into composing a sequel to his *Locksley Hall* of 1838 by indignation at the wickedness and decadence of the times. The first poem had been a statement of hope in the coming achievements of the 'wondrous mother-age' in lines that immediately took on the stature of classic expressions of Victorian confidence:

> For I dipt into the future, far as human eye could see;
> Saw the Vision of the world, and all the wonder that would be;
> . . . Yet I doubt not through the ages one increasing purpose runs,
> And the thoughts of men are widened with the process of the suns.

Now in 1886 Tennyson, the Laureate, shocked his immense Victorian public by revealing how insecure were the foundations of his confidence.

> 'Forward' rang the voices then, and of the many mine was one.
> Let us hush this cry of 'Forward' till ten thousand years have
>   gone.

And:

> When was age so cramm'd with menace? madness? written,
>   spoken lies?

The menaces were Demos, Socialism, the Russians, the Irish. The madness was the 'passions of the primal clan', mankind's refusal to turn the vision of the world into a reality of peace, harmony, goodwill, justice. The written lies were the

> Authors – essayist, atheist, novelist, realist, rhymester, play your
>   part,
> Paint the mortal shame of nature with the living hues of Art.
>
> Rip your brothers' vices open, strip your own foul passions bare;
> Down with Reticence, down with Reverence – forward – naked –
>   let them stare . . .
> Set the maiden fancies wallowing in the troughs of Zolaism –

Zola, the 'realist', pre-eminently represented to the respectable British literary public the very worst excesses of French immorality. (A bookseller, Vizetelly, was actually imprisoned for three months in 1889 for selling translations of Zola.) No nice distinctions were made between Zola's positivistic naturalism and the 'decadence' of the new aesthetic movement.

The spoken lies were those of the politicians, 'rivals of realm-ruining party', 'practised hustings-liars', the 'tonguesters' who would, if allowed to continue pandering to an ignorant democracy, demoralize the nation and betray its heritage of achievements.

It was this attack on the politicians which Gladstone felt it especially necessary to respond to publicly. To the extent that Liberalism had borne the burden of the young Tennyson's hysterical hopes it now bore the responsibility of the old Tennyson's even more hysterical disillusionment. Tennyson was by far the most famous and most influential poet in English literary history. In recognition of this fact Gladstone had honoured him with the unprecedented distinction of a peerage in 1884. His criticism was a much more hurtful blow to the Gladstonian cause than that of the 'intellectuals'.

Gladstone's vindication[1] took its bearings very reasonably on the proposition whether it was 'needful' of Tennyson 'to open so dark a prospect for the Future'; whether it was just 'to pronounce what seems to be a very decided censure on the immediate Past'. Present faults in society were not to be denied: festering slums, 'city children soaking in city slime', sweated labour, enforced prostitution. The great new fact was that people now found such evils intolerable whereas in earlier times they had accepted them as inescapable. Gladstone could point to the remedial efforts indicative of a new awareness, of heightened social conscience: Octavia Hill's and Lady Burdett-Coutts's work for better housing, Arnold Toynbee's work in bridging the gulf between rich and poor in his East End 'settlements', building on the basis of earlier efforts by philanthropic pioneers such as Edward Denison. And there was the great body of practical legislation testifying that the British people had laboured harder than any other to make 'popular government' work. 'Will it be too audacious to submit to the Prophet of the new *Locksley Hall* that the laws and works of the half-century he reviews are not bad but good?' Gladstone reeled off the catalogue of good works, from the abolition of slavery and the triumph of free trade to Post Office savings banks, cheap postage, cheap communications and cheap foreign holidays: 'Among the humanizing contrivances of the age, I think notice is due to the system founded by Mr. Cook, and now largely in use, under which numbers of persons, and indeed whole classes, have for the first time found easy access to foreign countries, and have acquired some of that familiarity with them, that breeds not contempt but kindness.' There was, moreover, the much improved new Poor Law. In sum, the general improvement of the conditions of the masses between the 1830s and the 1880s was, Gladstone affirmed, of the order of 50 per cent. The position of women was much improved, with new opportunities for 'public duties'. There were new evils and dangers, to be sure: there was more luxury and plutocracy, and there had been a great increase in government expenditure and a weakening of the position of the individual against the encroachments of the State; there was also less respect for 'ancient manners'. But 'upon the whole, and in a degree, men who lived fifty, sixty, seventy years back, and are living now, have lived into a gentler time', with a public conscience more tender and a far greater acceptance of the duties of wealth to poverty.

As a response to Tennyson Gladstone's vindication was often shrewd and in general extremely effective; as an analysis of the social movement and as a diagnosis of future problems and future policy it was as irrelevant as Tennyson's critique was hysterical.

II

Evidence of increasing national well-being was indeed impressive. With improving nutrition and sanitation, mortality rates declined steadily during the 1880s and 1890s, although infantile mortality did not begin to drop until after 1900. Cholera and typhus ceased to be endemic social threats. Male deaths per thousand stood at twenty-four in 1870 and fourteen in 1914; female deaths per thousand were twenty-one in 1870 and twelve in 1914. The fact that a higher proportion of the population now lived longer had the effect of making old age pensions into a major political issue, for it became evident that it was impossible for large sections of the working class to provide for old age either by savings from income or from subscriptions to benevolent societies. This situation in turn had the effect of softening and humanizing conditions in workhouses where old people in default of any alternative recourse had to go. In any case the numbers in receipt of Poor Law relief were falling: 0·77 per cent of the population received indoor relief in 1850, and 5 per cent received outdoor relief. By 1895 the figures were 0·69 per cent and 2 per cent respectively.

From the 1850s onwards, apart from brief interruptions in 1875-9, 1884-6, and 1900-1905, indexes of money wages increased steadily. Because of the tendency for prices to fall, real wages increased at a greater rate. Probably the gain in real wages for the average worker in the period 1860-1900 was about 60 per cent. There was much greater job mobility: it is estimated that half the rise in real earnings for wage earners between 1880-1910 came from movement into better paid jobs. Suburban railway expansion encouraged by Cheap Trains Acts to facilitate working-class commuting meant that workers no longer needed to live near their places of work. Moreover, wage-earners were getting a bigger share of the national income: wages as to profits were 52 per cent in 1870–74 and 62 per cent in 1890–94. The terms of international trade moved in favour of Britain as a purchaser of world commodities and so helped to stimulate the rise in standard of living. The most dramatic evidences of general prosperity are the figures for basic food consumption per head of population. These figures are startling even over a short twenty-five-year period: consumption per head of meats is estimated at 101·4 lb. in 1870 and 130·6 lb. in 1896. Between 1860 and 1900 consumption of tea per head more than doubled; sugar consumption per head nearly trebled. Between 1861–5 and 1906–10 imports per head of wheat and flour more than doubled; butter and margarine trebled. Imports of fresh meat during the same period underline even more the increasing dependence on the international market: from 0·1 lb. per head to 28·3 lb. Consumption of meat per head of the U.K. population rose as follows: 104·4 lb. (of which 10 lb. imported) in 1870; 114·1 lb. (of which 28 lb. imported) in 1880; 124·1 lb. (of which 32 lb. imported) in 1890; and 130·6 lb. (of which 37 lb. imported) in 1896. The new technique of refrigeration had opened up important new sources of cheap meat and dairy products abroad. The first refrigerated shipment left New Zealand for the U.K. market in 1882. Imported fruits were becoming for the first time common ingredients in the working-class diet.

The new social capacity for consumption was not restricted to foodstuffs. By 1891 there were more than 5,000 bicycle manufacturers in England providing a new kind of cheap transport. Print, paper, clothes, furniture, all testified to the immense growth of consumer power. Polytechnic Institutes, under the lead of the philanthropic sugar merchant Quintin Hogg, catered for a demand for further educational opportunities from 1882. In 1886 Hogg added organized holiday tours. Entertainment was by now a mass industry, with the beginning of the golden age of the music halls. The fastest-growing town in Britain in the 1890s was Blackpool, where shrewd entrepreneurship capitalized on the new demand for holidays and excursions.

Equally impressive were the evidences of entirely new patterns of distribution of consumer goods. The decline of British agriculture and the enormous increase in imported commodities made necessary new techniques of distributive trading with entirely new methods of sale and the development of new outlets. This was a consumer industrial revolution. Conspicuous examples of areas where old handicraft patterns of production were transformed by mass production techniques, with goods produced in anticipation of demand rather than in response to orders, were boots and shoes, men's clothing and food manufacturing. The agents of this distributive revolution were the great new retailing systems which began to dominate the scene in the late 1880s and early 1890s.

There were three major aspects of this new development. First, there were the retail societies or associations. The first of these, founded by Owenites in Rochdale in 1844 and with a working-class clientele, was the Co-operative Retail Society. After slow growth, the Co-operative by 1863 had 100,000 members (mainly in the North of England and Scotland) with a sales turnover of some £2½ million. Added sophistication (and a falling off in primitive idealism) came with the formation in the 1860s of the Co-operative Wholesale Societies in England and Scotland through which purchases could be centralized and large-scale buying increased. By 1881 there were 547,000 members with a £15 million turnover; by 1891 these figures had jumped to 1,707,000 and £50 million, and by 1914 there would be 3 million members and £77 million turnover. In 1862 there were 400 societies; by 1882, 1,043; by 1903, 1,445. In 1875 the Co-operatives are estimated to have accounted for between 2 and 3 per cent of total retail sales; by 1900 between 6 and 7½ per cent. The exclusively working-class membership of the Co-operative was reflected in the fact that foodstuffs were always the major items of the turnover. The Co-operative, moreover, was never simply a means of getting cheaper groceries. It was a moral cause, the idealism of cost price. It always had a strong missionary and popular intellectual improvement side to it: the Co-operative played a vital part in the later foundation of the Workers' Educational Association.

Upper-class retail associations which eschewed moral idealism and concentrated on the commercial shrewdness aspect also burgeoned in the 1880s and 1890s. Officers in the Civil Service began to get cheaper tea through bulk purchasing in the 1860s, and in 1866 the Civil Service Supply Stores got under way. Equally as appropriate, army officers in search of reasonably priced wine founded the Army and Navy Co-operative Society in 1871. The great Army and Navy Store built in Victoria Street, Westminster, in 1887 became a national institution, situated conveniently close to Victoria Station for the country trade and to the new St James's Park Station of the Metropolitan District Line (opened in 1884) for the metropolis.

The Army and Navy in fact had more in common with the second major aspect of the distributive revolution, the great new department stores, rather than with the original Co-operative Society. Usually old-established concerns, they capitalized on the advantages of offering a wide range of goods in a situation of free circulation and no obligation to buy. Harrods, originally a grocery, expanded in the later 1880s. Most of the great department stores specialized in clothing and footwear as the key areas. Three early foundations expanded in Oxford Street into famous names: Marshall and Snelgrove, Peter Robinson, and John Lewis. Harrods in Knightsbridge and Barkers in Kensington reflected the widening scope of West End shopping. Similar developments occurred in all the great conurbations. Such new shopping patterns reflected a new ease of transportation, with the development of suburban railways and tramways, and particularly in Greater London, the Metropolitan railway. Kensington and Earls Court were reached in the 1870s. North-western extensions reached West Hampstead in 1879 and Harrow by the end of 1880. Putney Bridge in the south-west was reached by 1880 and Hounslow by 1883. The inner circle was completed in 1884. Pinner was reached by 1887 and Chesham by 1889. The slogan of the Metropolitan Railway was 'Live in Metroland'. Schemes for cheap trains for workers, started by the Great Eastern Railway and taken up by the government, largely dictated the pattern of suburban working-class expansion in north-east London. By 1890 the techniques of tube construction and electrification permitted a higher intensity of service. The first electric tramway service in Britain commenced at Blackpool in 1885. Soon overhead trolley wires were in general operation. Advertising was an important implication, especially for newspapers. Harrod's took its first full page in the *Daily Telegraph* in 1894.

The third major aspect of the consumer revolution was the multiple shop firm. Home and Colonial Tea, Maypole Dairy, Liptons, Boots (Jesse Boot opened his first chemist shop in Nottingham in 1877) all had over 500 branches by 1914. Home and Colonial, founded in 1885, had 200 branches by 1895 and 400 branches by 1900. International Tea had nearly 100 branches by 1885, 200 branches by 1890. Freeman Hardy Willis footwear boasted nearly 500 branches by 1914. J. Lyons catering, Hepworth's tailoring, and International Stores, founded in 1880 by the future Lord Devonport, were three more typical concerns. But the giants were Eastman's and James Nelson's meat, Singer Sewing Machine and W. H. Smith's newsagents, each with over 1,000 branches by 1914. It is estimated conservatively that in 1880 there were 48 multiple firms of 10 or more branches with a total of 1,564 branches, of which 15 were firms of over 25 branches with a total of 1,090 branches. By 1895, 201 firms had a total of 6,017 branches. Like the Co-operatives, the multiples concentrated on the grocery and provision trades.

By 1900 large-scale retailing organizations were selling between 10 and 13·5 per cent of all commodities. These commodities in themselves were eloquent of a consumer revolution: Robertson, Hovis, Cadbury, Lipton, Pears, Players, Rowntree, Reckitt, Sunlight, Lifebuoy, Bovril, Beecham. They were staples of the enormously expanded advertising industry. Lord Randolph Churchill thought it worth remarking in one of his political orations: 'We live in an age of advertisement, the age of Holloway's pills, of Colman's mustard, and of Horniman's pure tea.'

Expansion of the multiples indicates the significance of the 1880s and 1890s as the period of maximum growth rate. Firms with ten or more branches in the period 1875–1915 achieved their maximum rate of expansion – 78 per cent of net increase – in the years 1881–5. The next two periods of highest net increase were 1886–90 (68 per cent) and 1891–5 (67 per cent). Rate of increase then slackened markedly, declining to 15 per cent in 1911–15. Of these, firms with twenty-five or more branches had their peak rate of increase in the years 1886–90 (80 per cent increase) with a 76 per cent net increase in 1881–5 and 74 per cent in 1891–5. Again the slackening was marked after 1896.

III

The rank and file who staffed these great new battalions of distributive commerce and the multifarious contingent services of the second industrial revolution – banking, insurance, transport, supply, communications, were the suburbanites, the dwellers in the expanding Metroland of the vast rings of socially demarcated suburbs, mainly on the less smoky western fringes of the conurbations. The great mass of them constituted the fastest-growing and most important social category of the time, the lower middle class. Estimated at about 20 per cent of families in the 1860s, they were over 40 per cent by the 1930s. Dynamic as an economic force, they were static as a social and political force: both a social cement and a social ballast, missionized by the middle-class virtues of conscientiousness, thrift, sobriety and by the middle-class vices of conformity, genteelism, banality. The rising newspaper magnate Alfred Harmsworth carefully tailored his *Daily Mail* in 1896 to cater for this socially mobile market. The *Daily Mail* offered itself as a penny paper selling for a half-penny: it was a popular paper designed to look like a 'quality' paper. Unlike the rather less important contemporary working-class movements, this suburban expansion went largely unnoticed; when noticed, it was generally for purposes of derision. Camberwell, a London suburb abounding in clerks, which had its maximum rate of expansion between 1871 and 1881, was used by Arnold in *Culture and Anarchy* and by his emulator Masterman in *The Condition of England* as a prime exhibit of dismal illiberalism, and by George Gissing, who responded to the phenomenon with more mixed and complicated emotions in *In the Year of the Jubilee* (1893), as a rich source of documentation of the habits of suburban man.

The classic contemporary document of this great social ballast was *The Diary of a Nobody* by George and Weedon Grossmith, first published in *Punch* in 1888. Charles Pooter, his wife Caroline, and their unsatisfactory son Lupin lived in The Laurels, Brickfield Terrace, Holloway, a semi-detached six-roomed residence 'with a front breakfast parlour', a little garden running down to the railway line and one female servant living in. A City clerk, honest Pooter does some modest social climbing, using Church attendance to this end, envying the people in 'those large houses in the Camden Road'. He is afflicted constantly by the problem of being a gentleman. Mrs Pooter, whose parentage is evidently suspect on the score of gentility, shops at Peter Robinson's. They go to Broadstairs for their holidays. They send out Christmas cards, dutifully keep up with the latest 'aesthetic' ideas on décor such as Oscar Wilde was propagating in *Woman's World* (1887–9), commenting on the 'ignorance of the lower classes in the matter of taste'. The Pooters were successful within the narrow limits of their ambitions; and their success story was a pattern of a great, possibly the greatest, Victorian phenomenon.

IV

Paradoxically, the 1880s and 1890s, swollen with such evidences of well-being, were noted for social restlessness rather than repose. It is a commonplace of historical analysis that revolutions are usually revolutions of rising expectations and that deprivation is usually a sense of relative deprivation. Compared with the generation of the 1850s and 1860s who were thankful enough for elementary levels of achievement in social well-being and harmony, the generation of the 1880s and 1890s were more conscious both of occasions of anxiety on the part of the comfortably circumstanced on the one hand and of resentment on the part of the uncomfortably circumstanced on the other. This was the essence of the 'social distemper' which so distressed Gladstone.

The great appeal Tennyson had in 1886 was almost exclusively this response of an anxious ruling class exasperated at a world growing increasingly unruly. They were irritated at the efforts of the spokesmen of Social Democracy to incite the masses to mutiny. They were indignant at the challenges to their moral conventions posed by the 'decadents'. They were outraged by the cultural manifestations of effeteness that were starting to be called 'fin de siècle'.

In another direction, a good deal of middle-class dissatisfaction arose out of the new tenderness of their own social conscience which Gladstone commented on as such a striking feature of the times. New charitable foundations multiplied: 136 were founded between 1880 and 1890. This was the secularized conscience of evangelicalism which would not allow the comfortably circumstanced to remain comfortable in the accusing presence of the children of the slums. Unemployment and distress at the end of the 1870s and the early 1880s had jolted many Liberals into a realization that fundamental rethinking was necessary. There was a feeling widespread among the possessing classes that remedial action was necessary to blunt the edge of socialist agitation. Some industrialists adopted schemes of enlightened paternalism. The soap magnate William Lever founded Port Sunlight in 1889 and started construction of a model workers' community. The Quaker chocolate magnate George Cadbury started his model village at Bournville in 1893. Among the religious denominations, anxiety at the steady erosion of the social authority of religion led to a feeling that religion would have to respond to the needs of a new era. A pamphlet about life in Bermondsey in 1883 by a Congregational minister, the Rev. Andrew Mearns, *The Bitter Cry of Outcast London*, was taken up in *The Review of Reviews* by W. T. Stead (who was running his own sensational campaign on prostitution, *The Maiden Tribute of Modern Babylon*), and set off a 'slumming' fashion. Within the Church also the same stirrings became evident: Henry Scott Holland, appointed to a canonry at St Paul's in 1884, was one of the founders of the Christian Social Union in 1890. This group fused the old Christian conscience with the new social conscience: among its members were Charles Gore (later first Bishop of Birmingham), G. K. Chesterton, Noel Buxton, G. P. Gooch and G. M. Trevelyan. The 'Salvation Army', founded in 1878 by 'General' William Booth, sometime apprentice to a Nottingham pawnbroker who set up as a religious revivalist, turned its attention primarily to social work. In his *Darkest England and the Way Out* (1890), Booth exploited the publicity value of the explorer H. M. Stanley's *In Darkest Africa* (1890) to delineate the plight of the 'submerged tenth', to which his Army brought colour, soup, soap and hope. Cardinal Manning, the head of the Catholic Hierarchy, extended his crusade against alcohol into sympathy with the cause of the unemployed.

New techniques of social analysis revealed the depth and extent of a great mass of ingrained and obstinate poverty. It was becoming increasingly recognized that traditional methods of charitable philanthropy were inadequate. Canon Samuel Barnett's renunciation of the Charity Organisation Society in 1886 was a symbolically decisive gesture. Arnold Toynbee, a disciple at Oxford of Ruskin and T. H. Green, gave the movement a sense of idealistic youthful crusade, attractive to young university men like Alfred Milner. Toynbee Hall in Whitechapel, founded in 1884 as a memorial on his early death, was to be a centre of contact between the upper classes and the poor and a source of information which would lead to effective remedial action on a large scale.

The young Beatrice Webb, *née* Potter, granddaughter of a cotton fortune and daughter of a Crimean War timber speculation fortune, brought up in an intellectual and political domestic ferment of which Herbert Spencer and Joseph Chamberlain were prominent ingredients, began her career of social investigation with Octavia Hill and the Charity Organisation Society in 1882. Soon dissatisfied with the likely efficacy of philanthropy, she turned in the direction of scientific method and socialism. Her cousin, Charles Booth, a wealthy Liverpool shipowner with a statistical turn of mind, provided scientific method in his great survey, *Life and Labour of the People of London*, issued in seventeen volumes from 1891. Booth's original motive was anti-socialist: to refute the claims of people like the Marxist Hyndman of the Social Democratic Federation that 25 per cent of wage-earners fell beneath an acceptable subsistence level of existence. Booth's own dismayed conclusion was that in fact Hyndman's estimate was too modest: 30 per cent would be more accurate. This impressive kind of finding stimulated intensely the ambitions of groups of progressively-minded young socialists with scientific pretensions of which the Fabian Society, founded in 1884, became the most famous. It helped stimulate also the founding of the London School of Economics and Political Science in 1895, intended as an institutional powerhouse of 'sociological investigation'.

Booth's revelations added the fuel of tender conscience to the existing flame of middle-class anxiety about the state of the economy. A good deal of bourgeois social conscience had gone into building up a critique of orthodox political economy with its emphasis on the freest possible market in labour. Mill himself had given a lead in this direction which was taken up by the younger generation of economists such as Alfred Marshall. Anglican clergymen of an economical turn of mind, usually of a Broad Church persuasion, were very prominent in this movement. Archdeacon Cunningham, a disciple of T. H. Green, argued historically the case for a managed rather than a *laissez-faire* economy. Toynbee himself had been important in helping to initiate in England a 'historical' as opposed to a deductive and *a priori* approach to economics, following the great German school of economic history.

The bad commercial patch in 1884-6, moreover, was marked by very serious riots of unemployed in the West End. The 'Great Depression' was a powerful myth and it shook a lot of inherited confidence. It shook the very pillars of the temple, Free Trade itself. As evidence of German and American progress and competition multiplied, protectionist sentiment revived. A Fair Trade League was founded in 1881 and in 1887 the annual Conservative Conference voted overwhelmingly in support of a protective tariff. Accumulating indications of a declining growth rate of industrial production disconcerted a generation bred up on expectations of inevitably accelerating expansion. The rate of growth of British industrial production was of the order of 20·8 per cent in the period 1870/79–1880/89; it slipped to 16·4 per cent and 17·4 per cent in the two following decades; made a recovery to 20·7 per cent in the 1885/94–1895/1904 decade but slipped again to 17·9 per cent in 1890/99–1900/1909. Britain had accounted for over 30 per cent of total world industrial output in 1850; by 1900 only 15 per cent. In 1883 Britain's share of world trade in manufactures was 37·1 per cent; by 1913 it was 25·4 per cent. The German share increased from 17·2 per cent to 23 per cent in the same period, and the United States from 3·4 per cent to 11 per cent. This was only to be expected; yet it could hardly be the basis of a reinvigorated confidence.

Closer to the bone were indications of a slipping relative financial position of the middle class. Calculations of the increase of real income in incomes over £150 (the exemption limit from income tax) show a boom period in the 1871–81 decade, with a 48 per cent growth rate, compared with 37·2 per cent in the previous decade. But 1881–91 reveals a drop to 33·8 per cent, with a further drop to 27·9 per cent in 1891–1901, and a fall again to 11·1 per cent in the 1901–11 decade. This slackening of the growth of middle-class purchasing power correlates with the decline in the numbers of domestic servants. It was a major factor in the marked slackening of the middle-class birth rate. There was a general decline in the national birth rate discernible from the 1880s concurrent with the decline in the mortality rate; but the decline in births was most notable in the upper social levels. The tendency of the better-off to have fewer children than the less well-off was one of the marked social facts of the later nineteenth century. Malthus had earlier advocated a prudential attitude among the working classes to help ease the burden of their poverty; now it seems the middle classes prudently took steps to ease the pains of a contracting growth of prosperity. Fertility among the upper and middle classes declined sharply; that of skilled working-class families slightly; while that of unskilled workers, miners, and agricultural labourers actually increased.

The motives and methods of this renunciation of fertility among the upper classes are not easily explained. Sophisticated birth control methods were not available. So it seems likely that there was a tendency towards a deliberate reduction of sexual intercourse. Some social developments have an obvious bearing on this. Women were emancipating themselves: the concept of the 'New Woman' would soon become a stock theme of social comment. They were demanding an equal share in family decisions whose burden they would have, literally, to bear. There were the new educational opportunities at the universities; the new industries and particularly the invention of the typewriter and the telephone offered them a wide range of jobs; the invention of the 'safety bicycle' with pneumatic tyres gave them important new freedom of mobility (the first lady bicyclist appeared in *Punch* in July 1894); the old rules of chaperonage inherited from the raffish Regency were in decay. It was natural for educated women to want to take advantage of opportunities for a life not circumscribed by continuous pregnancies.

There were, also, less obvious social developments which possibly have an equally important bearing on the question of fertility. The general decline of 'grossness' such as Gladstone celebrated had many manifestations. Typical educated Victorians of the mid-century had large families eating vast meals in rambling houses filled with massive furniture, all shrouded by heavy drapes in a permanently crepuscular gloom. The great movement of the later nineteenth century was towards lightness in every sense. New houses, such as those of the leafy Bedford Park estate designed by Norman Shaw in the first planned garden community of enlightened middle-class intellectuals, were smaller, with more windows letting in more light, with bright Morris wallpaper and the new bright paintwork much favoured by aesthetic guides like Whistler. A rather cosy 'Jacobethan' or Queen Anne domestic became the general rule for such estates: Ruskinian Gothic was meat too strong for the more delicate stomachs of the 1880s and 90s. Furniture became lighter, almost spindly, with revived Sheraton and exotic Japanese inspiration. Hirsute mid-Victorian males attenuated their whiskers; their consorts likewise attenuated their monstrous crinolines to the more convenient bustle and then to the 'natural' and 'grecian' forms recommended by Oscar Wilde and modelled by Mrs Oscar Wilde. Undoubtedly the decline in fertility was a part of this general social 'refinement'; though exactly how, and whether as cause or effect, it is impossible to say.

Probably the tremendous expansion of the playing of sports was some kind of instinctive compensation. The contemporary expansion of working-class forms of sport was mainly a spectator and professional development; but the middle classes actually played. The Amateur Athletics Association was formed in 1880; the Hockey Association in 1886; the Rugby Football Union had been earlier (1871); golf, croquet, polo, rackets all matured in the 1880s and 90s. Women made their début in Wimbledon tennis in 1884, and the Lawn Tennis Association was established in 1887.

Certainly, at the time, declining fecundity was widely interpreted as evidence of a loss of nerve among the ruling class, a symptom of decadence. Francis Galton, a cousin of Darwin who applied theories of the inheritance of innate superiorities to social policy, chided the middle classes for their sexual renunciation, and argued the expediency of encouraging fertility among the 'civically worthy' and discouraging it among the 'civically unworthy'. With his Eugenics Society propagating alarm about national degeneration, Galton was a particularly effective contributor to the climate of *Kulturpessimismus* among the upper classes which Tennyson's doom-laden prophecies, Ruskin's apocalyptic denunciations and Herbert Spencer's plaintive grumbles had already done so much to bring into being.

V

Old conditions of life were being changed at a palpably accelerated pace after the early 1880s. 'Modern' times were coming into being. The surface phenomena of this change were obvious then as later. The novelist Henry James installed electric light in his apartment in 1895. In 1896 he began riding a bicycle in the country. In 1897 he purchased a typewriter and hired a typist. In 1898 he went to a 'cinematograph, or whatever they call it' to see the Corbett–Fitzsimmons boxing match. The national life-style was becoming urban and secular. Culture and politics were adapting themselves to mass audiences. What was not at all so clear, then or later, was the significance of underlying phenomena. Was the economy declining, growing less efficient, competitive and dynamic, or was it simply changing into a means of responding to different demands which placed less emphasis on spectacular technology?[2] Certainly, American and German technology were making great strides when their British counterpart seemed to be comparatively sluggish. Numbers of undergraduates and technical students per million of total population more than doubled in the United States between 1872 and 1900. By 1914 Britain had only 9,000 full-time scientists compared with 58,000 in Germany. In 1901, there were 4,500 trained chemists in Germany and only 1,500 in Britain. Probably the British performance in this field in comparison with the Americans and the Germans has been underrated: eleven new provincial universities with a strong technical bias emerged between 1871 and 1902 out of the British response, as well as polytechnics. Yet undeniably there was something about British technology that made it unapt for developing large-scale techniques of production which were the key factor in keeping prices competitive. It was entirely appropriate that whereas the characteristic American utopian fantasy of the time was Bellamy's technocratic and futuristic *Looking Backwards* (*If Socialism Comes*) (1888), the correspondingly influential British utopia was William Morris's *News from Nowhere* (1891), arcadian, anti-industrial, medieval.

For all the *Kulturpessimismus* of traditionalists like Arnold and Tennyson and all the symptoms of anxiety of the upper classes, there is no doubt that the established ruling order kept a firm grip on the politics and administration of the State and maintained intact its social hegemony through such vital conditioning agencies as the public schools and ancient universities. The firmness of this grip was certainly in large part a consequence of earlier economic success. Possibly it was the cause in turn of economic failure in the later nineteenth century and beyond. Because it could be argued so persuasively that Britain had been remarkably successful politically in the nineteenth century, this gave the profession of politics and government a tremendous prestige unknown in Europe or America. Enterprise and talent, in this interpretation, were discouraged from going into industry because of an educational bias in favour of the higher morality of the services of politics and the liberal professions as against the lower materialism of markets and profits. Certainly the proportion of the gainfully employed population of professional status – or claiming professional status – expanded considerably in the later nineteenth century. At the same time the number of owners of businesses declined. The school teachers were much the biggest group claiming professional status and as the best way of achieving this they took their tone and line from the public school classical mandarinate.

This morality of liberal professionalism was, in its turn, the prime function of the symbiosis between the aristocracy and the middle classes in the early and middle nineteenth century. Instead of dispossessing the aristocracy of its power as Mill urged and becoming a new kind of radical élite, the middle classes collaborated in preserving traditional social and political forms of the ruling class. They developed the morality of professional service into their equivalent of *noblesse oblige* and equipped themselves with the necessary training institutions in the form of reformed and expanded and new public schools which deliberately clung to classical 'mandarin' curricula. Such was the prestige of these schools that the grammar schools, which provided a cheaper secondary education to a much wider social catchment, followed suit; and so became an extremely important agency of recruitment from below to upper-class social values. (Of the fifty-two great public schools established by 1895, eighteen were founded after 1840; of 216 Headmasters' Conference and Independent Schools, eighty-three are post-1840 foundations.)

Further, the younger generation of industrial families tended, in this atmosphere, to prefer careers in politics, the Civil Service, the universities or to assimilate themselves with the landed gentry, rather than to devote their energies to the family firm. The universities, with their intimate connections with the public schools and dominated by the prestige of Oxford and Cambridge, followed the arguments of Jowett and saw themselves primarily as the trainers of undergraduates for such careers, rather than, as Mark Pattison advocated, as centres of graduate studies and research.

Moreover, lacking dynamic industrial creativeness, Britain came to depend increasingly on income from investments abroad and upon her 'invisible exports' of services in shipping, insurance and general trading and financial facilities. Overseas investments stood at about £1,200 million in 1870, with an income of £44 million; by 1914 they were £4,000 million, bringing in nearly £200 million in income. Of this enormous and quite unprecedented outflow, 40 per cent went into the empire and 60 per cent to foreign countries. This situation had the effect of keeping things going but of masking the real economic problems of the country. Thus no new generation of efficient entrepreneurs and technocrats emerged with sufficient weight to shift the established and inert forces in command of society and politics, with the inevitable consequence of sluggish industrial growth.

This general kind of explanation of the inadequacy of British industrial performance in the later nineteenth century does not lack critics; and within its boundaries there are wide differences of attitude and approach.[3] The arguments against it assert that Britain suffered from inescapable economic disadvantages which had nothing to do with social attitudes. They challenge its premise that British performance must necessarily be matched against the performance of economies like the American or the German with quite different needs and in quite different circumstances. It is arguable, further, that, even if the German and American analogies were valid, fundamental redeployment of British investments and resources would have required a degree of state activity and state supervision totally beyond the bounds of possibility at any time prior to 1914. There was simply no strong body of opinion – and certainly not the trade unions – in favour of it. The nearest thing to it was the Tariff Reform movement in the Unionist Party. And further, it can be argued, in any case British society got quite a good bargain if everything is taken into account: it is just as important to have a good ruling class as it is to have a good economy. The Germans may have had an economy which performed brilliantly, but their political performance, consisting of a series of cynical deals between military, bureaucratic, agrarian and industrial élites, was far from brilliant, and landed them eventually in catastrophe.

However, the 'pessimistic' interpretation became, in one form or another, the standard or received version. It suited the new generation of Liberals and the general social-democratic movement because of its implications of criticism of the nineteenth-century ruling class. It suited the Marxists because it offered a plausible explanation of why Britain did not perform according to expectations: the middle classes failed to do their historical duty. It suited even many Conservatives and Unionists, who could regard the nineteenth-century economy as the creation of inefficient Liberal individualism, and direct their party's economic policy towards alternatives: an imperial *Zollverein* and Tariff Reform in the first stage; later, after the Second World War, integration with the European Economic Community. The arguments are much the same.

More to the immediate point, however, this line of interpretation was becoming during the 1890s the general basis for a new Liberal critique of British society. The younger generation of Liberals were becoming aware of the need for revised intellectual explanations as to why things had gone wrong since 1880. Mill of course no longer sufficed; nor indeed did Morley or Green. They hardly provided anything fundamentally beyond Gladstone himself at Midlothian: that what had happened in 1874 was an untoward event, an unfortunate lapse which did not signify in the long term. Clearly, for the new generation of Liberals represented by young writers like L. T. Hobhouse, C. F. G. Masterman, J. L. Hammond, and J. A. Hobson, it did signify in the long term. 'Imperialism' had already been identified as a particularly virulent political evil, and there was no doubt that it was becoming, from the Liberal point of view, a dangerous social anodyne, a focus of patriotic sentiment, of comfort and reassurance to the reactionary classes, and in its more vulgar and jingoistic aspects, an occasion of unseemly popular misbehaviour, egged on by deplorable populist journalists like W. T. Stead and Robert Blatchford.

Liberalism's next task was to tie imperialism in with a domestic critique so as to produce a general 'scientific' theory or explanation of reaction. This would be done by accounting for imperialism as the product of domestic economic distortions and injustices. The owners of industry, out of reactionary opposition to social reform, refused to make possible a social regeneration through economic re-investment and reconstruction. The first mature formulation of this Liberal theory would come from Hobson in

1902; but already by 1889 he had developed a theory of domestic underconsumption which became the key to the economic interpretation of imperialism (*The Physiology of Industry*, with A. F. Mummery). The argument of this theory runs as follows: capitalism, by its nature, maximizes profits. Because the workers therefore get the lowest wages possible, they lack purchasing power to buy the goods they produce. Therefore the capitalists cannot invest their profits to increase industrial production and they cannot sell their goods to their own workers unless they increase the workers' wages. They reject this solution because they have the alternative of continuing to maximize profits by investing abroad where labour is cheaper and by finding new markets abroad. Hence, imperialism. And hence, Hobson argued, the need to restrain capitalism by taxation devices and various other means to redistribute national wealth more equitably. The only flaw in this argument is that it has never been proved that things actually happened like that;[4] but the underconsumption thesis became nevertheless the core both of social democratic and Marxist criticism of the social and international consequences of capitalism.

VI

The subject of all this middle-class argument was the 'people', the 'lower orders', the 'masses', the 'workers', the 'Democracy'. The majority of them, so far as politics and society at large were concerned, were virtually voiceless. On occasion, as with the great riots of February 1886 in the West End, when Clubland was terrorized and the lord mayor launched a 'ransom' fund for the unemployed, they made their discontent unmistakable. But such occasions were like raids by primitive tribes rather than sustained offensives by disciplined armies: the mob marched back to the East End singing 'Rule Britannia'. Because of their restless domiciliary habits, and a good deal of apathy, a large proportion of adult male workers did not exercise their franchise. Only about 10 per cent of them were enrolled in a trade union by the later 1880s. They were far from being a homogeneous class. Higher paid skilled workers were often much closer to the lower middle class in habits than they were to unskilled labourers. This working-class élite comprised the trade unions and tended to be politically militant compared with the inert mass of unorganized labour. Usually Liberal supporters, they were beginning to move tentatively in the direction of independent Labour representation. They read their Carlyle and Ruskin, and Henry George and William Morris, and sampled the mass of radical and socialist journalism and pamphleteering which began to flourish in the 80s under the auspices of organizations like the Social Democratic Federation, founded in 1884.

In origin this arose out of an effort in 1881 to unite all the multifarious radical groups in a Democratic Federation on the model of the National Liberal Federation. Its founder, H. M. Hyndman, canvassed support from the Positivists, from Karl Marx and from maverick members of parliament like H. A. Munro–Butler–Johnstone and Joseph Cowen. It was heavily middle class in provenance, and in fact the original link between the founding members was Russophobia and support for Lord Beaconsfield and opposition to Gladstone over the Eastern Question crisis of the late 1870s. The Social Democratic Federation which grew out of this earlier body became distinctly Marxist in doctrine; and its object was to convert the mass of the working class to socialism. Ironically, but quite in accordance with the temper of the popular mind, as more middle-class socialists like William Morris came in, most of the working-class Radicals that had originally been there went out. The Social Democratic Federation found it much easier to convert the bourgeoisie than the proletariat.

This became the pattern of the future. Socialism remained essentially the doctrine of a small bourgeois and artisan intelligentsia. The important developments in the working class were essentially indigenous, inherited from the traditional chapel culture of the labour élite and secularized derivations thereof which equated practical Christianity and social justice. These developments centred on immediate means of improving the material conditions of the common people. This demarcation was never absolute. Indeed, there was a paradoxical relationship of creative tension between the two sides which eventually coalesced in the Labour party. The explosion of working-class conscious-ness which expressed itself in the revival and transformation of the trade union movement in the later 1880s and early 1890s would not have been possible without the penetration in depth of a new sense of the possibilities of the situation: crucially, the emergence of the idea that poverty could be eradicated. The pene-tration of this idea owed more to new socialist propaganda than to old working-class culture. Yet socialists never managed to get control of the levers of its implementation.

The new working-class consciousness of possibilities was in many ways comparable to the middle-class Liberal confidence of the 1860s. With the erosion and crumbling of that Liberal confidence in the 1880s and the turmoil and confusion of Liberal efforts at revision and resuscitation, a considerable degree of working-class autonomy and self-determination was in any case to be expected. But the significance of this move towards working class political self-determination in the 1890s should be treated carefully. Orthodox social-democratic historiography places a heavy burden of significance on the 1889 Dock Strike and the foundation of the Independent Labour Party in 1893 as the great deeds of the primitive, heroic prolegomena of the Labour epic of the twentieth century.

In considering the accuracy of this interpretation the first point that must be made is that while the Dock Strike and the forming of the I.L.P. are indeed in a certain political perspective the most important specific events of that time as far as the popular 'movement' is concerned, they were events embedded in a much larger, amorphous social context. In this sense 1889 especially had a symbolic significance, representing the emergence of the idea of but not the reality of an articulate 'mass' consciousness. Like the riots of 1886, it evaporated quickly. But at the same time even such evanescent events were sufficient to impress upon the age that sheer quantity had indeed altered the quality of popular metropolitan and industrial life. Emerson's lament that 'the calamity is the masses' became a *leitmotiv of* the intel-lectuals. What worried intelligent ruling-class observers was that this mass, by the sheer pressure it exerted, would inevitably transform the entire climate of politics. This pressure would transmute social 'mass' into political 'class'. This was happening quite independently of socialist or indeed any deliberate forms of political agitation.

A case in point is popular education. Contrary to general belief, then and later, the Act of 1870 in itself had very little to do with increasing popular literacy[5] and creating a market for cheap bad 'best-seller' literature or for the journalistic enterprises of Newnes's *Tit Bits* (1881) or Harmsworth's *Answers to Correspondents* (1888) or the *Daily Mail* (1896). The cheap 'mass' press was in fact made economically possible by technological advances in printing (linotype and monotype in 1885, straight-line press in 1889) and not by such 'mass' factors as advertising. The *Daily Mail* had actually less advertising than the 'quality' papers, and made a virtue of this fact. In any case the growth of literacy was a phenomenon far beyond the capacity of an Act of Parliament to make or hinder. The 1870 Act had the effect of maintaining rather than accelerating the existing rate of increase of literacy, since it sought out those children who otherwise would probably not have been caught up in the literacy process.

But on the other hand the 1870 Act did create in unforeseen ways very important nucleic institutions of popular class consciousness. In the first place, the creation and expansion to an unexpected degree of a system of education designed to cater for the lower orders encouraged a 'Board school' awareness, which included a very specific sense of relative deprivation. The fact, for example, that practically everyone got, or could get, state elementary education heightened the fact that by 1895 only about five per cent of grammar school pupils were of the working class. As material betterment, job promotion, came to be seen to depend increasingly on educational qualifications, it was clear that such opportunities were going to be extremely limited for Board school children. The effect of this situation was to produce on the one hand a frustrated minority among the working classes conscious of deprivation who, even as they scrambled to embourgeoisify themselves, would very often do so as part of an education in socialism (H. G. Wells and Sidney Webb are classic cases); and on the other a sullen acquiescence among a working-class majority who would tend all the more to fall back on a Board school class consciousness. Board schools could often become the nucleus of characteristic working-class activities and life-styles quite apart from the elementary education they supplied. A good many professional football clubs, for example, in the great age of popular sports expansion with the widespread introduction in industry of a weekly half-holiday on Saturday, had their origins in Board schools.

Trade unionism in the 1880s and 1890s was very much a part of this kind of expanding social awareness. The trade union executive committees became to the working classes what the playing fields of Eton were widely (though quite erroneously) credited with being to the upper classes. The raw materials of agitation were people and facts that had to be deployed. The facts were supplied by the sociologists and by innumerable royal commissions. The Royal Commission on the Housing of the Working Classes in 1885 revealed the alarming incidence of gross overcrowding among the lower paid. The 1891 census showed that one-tenth of the population were living more than two per room; and that this included one-fifth of the population of London. The Royal Commission on Labour of 1891-4 showed that the average annual earnings of adult male manual workers in 1885 were about £60. Less than 2 per cent earned more than £2 a week; and 82 per cent earned 30s. or less. The Royal Commission on the Aged Poor of 1895 showed how more and more elderly people were being obliged to go into workhouses. True, the year 1890 marked an epoch in the administration of the poor law. The old doctrines of lesser eligibility had no relevance to the elderly; and more hospital facilities were provided and generally the regulations were relaxed in a humane direction. Still, no amount of relaxation of poor law regulations would ever reconcile the working classes to the workhouse as an acceptable social institution.

More difficult was the task of deploying the people. The fundamental fact about the mass of the lower classes was still, even as in Disraeli's time, apathy as much as poverty. Visions of State activity on their behalf were not necessarily alluring to people for whom hitherto the State had figured most immediately via the New Poor Law (which Gladstone had thought worth citing in 1887 as one of the great improvements of the age). The State also meant compulsory elementary education to families who would much have preferred to see their children at work earning desperately needed money. Socialist propaganda could not penetrate very deeply at this level, but trade union arguments, helped by hard times, were beginning to bite. The obvious aim was to extend unionism to the mass of the unskilled. The agreed practical target was the eight-hour day as the spearhead of a comprehensive emancipatory programme.

The important new factor was not the idea of 'new' unskilled unionism as such but rather the emergence of a group of militant union executives who sought to capture the T.U.C. and convert it to acceptance of a class strategy and the principle that State intervention on a massive scale would be the means of stamping out poverty. The major figures were Tom Mann, John Burns, Keir Hardie and Ben Tillett. The old guard of the T.U.C., represented by the Chairman of its Parliamentary Committee, Henry Broadhurst, stubbornly stood by Gladstonian principles of 'self-help'. The militant attack in the unions and the T.U.C. itself was well under way by 1886. The first 'new' union, the National Labour Federation, was formed on Tyneside in 1886. The Miners' Federation was formed in 1888. Tillett founded the Dockers' Union in 1887. The victory of the London dockers in their strike in 1889, with a good deal of support from public opinion, was decisive in making the reputation of 'new' unionism. Broadhurst fended off his critics in the T.U.C. Congresses of 1887 and 1889, but in the 1890 Congress at Liverpool the new mood asserted itself, and Broadhurst resigned. Broadhurst's strength as the pre-eminent symbol of collaboration with the Liberals weakened as Liberalism's credit and authority itself faltered. The Liverpool Congress was a turning point. It swung the T.U.C. behind the idea of inclusive unionism and State intervention. This was essential to an effective mass unskilled unionism. The unskilled workers had come to look upon unionization as a means of bettering their position to something like the level of the 'craft' unionists; but they entirely lacked the confidence to depend on themselves and 'self-help'. They needed the State; and with the T.U.C. committed to this policy a revised attitude to Labour's role in politics followed logically.

The foundation of the Independent Labour Party in 1893 reflected a mood of over-confidence. The union side of things promised well. The 1892 elections also seemed to promise better things for the future. Keir Hardie, the president of the I.L.P. and leading advocate of the idea of independent Labour politics, was elected for South West Ham. He had left the Liberals in 1888 and never ceased to push the doctrine that the Liberal party could no longer adequately represent in itself the interests of the mass of the working class. The example of what the Irish Nationalist party had achieved through discipline, organization, and determination was an obvious lead for the Labour interest to follow. Liberalism had, in the words of another I.L.P. member, 'carried the people through one state of development: but as it exists today it is too narrow to be a reflex of the expanding democratic and labour sentiment'. Labour had emerged from the status of a social issue to that of a political issue.

Chapter Ten

THE
POLITICS OF UNIONISM
AND HOME RULE
1886–95

I

The kernel of the Conservative problem was that the party was back to its pre-1874 minority situation. Land and its dependencies clearly, especially after the third Reform Act, could not be the electoral basis of successful politics. Three possible courses of action proposed themselves to Conservatives. First, they could adopt the role of permanent opposition. This idea appealed to many Tories who could not envisage an honest Conservatism in office in an era of democracy; they saw no advantage in making concessions of essential Conservative principle to buy the support of renegade Whigs or Radicals. The second recourse was that proposed chiefly by Randolph Churchill. By exploiting the Liberal Unionists as a 'crutch', Conservatism could limp through a transitional period of difficulty while taking measures to attract a mass support in the democracy which would restore Toryism to its legitimate 'national' predominance. A third recourse was to attempt to exploit all possible sources of strength without compromising the essential traditional nature of Conservatism and thereby keep the landed aristocratic element at its head. Salisbury himself and his nephew Balfour were the chief proponents of this line, and in the short run were remarkably successful.

Chamberlain was vital both to Churchill's and to Salisbury's and Balfour's strategy. There was, of course, the obvious negative motivation of common hostility to Home Rule and desire to preserve the Union. But beyond that, Chamberlain had a valuable stock-in-trade: the 'unauthorized programme'. This had become the focus of 'progressive' ideas in politics. Randolph Churchill aimed eventually to dispossess Chamberlain of his stock and convert it to Tory Democrat purposes. His relationship with Chamberlain was one of intensely jealous and predatory collaboration. Salisbury and Balfour also recognized the value of Chamberlain's stock. They wanted to be able to use their unionist credentials to draw political credit on the strength of it in order to keep Conservatism publicly solvent until alternative sources of credit were ready to be drawn on. Chamberlain, moreover, was dangerously exposed. There was little enough in common with his Whig unionist colleagues. And his Radical running-mate, Dilke, seen by many, including himself, as a destined prime minister, had allowed his irregular private life to get out of hand and ended up in 1885-6 in the divorce court. The rigid moral code of Victorian public life, which tolerated notorious irregularities such as Hartington's liaison with the Duchess of Manchester, would not tolerate the scandal of divorce; and Dilke passed into the political shadows, never to emerge again.

From Chamberlain's point of view, two factors would be decisive. His long-term hopes still centred on Liberalism. His assumption still was that Gladstone could not last long and that once he was gone the distortions he had imposed on the party would be corrected and Chamberlain would return with an enhanced advantage. His immediate hopes were focused on Churchill and the possibility of an alliance in the form of a 'National' party, free of the reactionary stupidity of traditional Toryism and free of the Irish distortion of Gladstonian Liberalism. But after Churchill's smash and clear evidences of Gladstone's determination to pursue Home Rule, all Chamberlain could do was wait until a working relationship between Conservatism and Liberal Unionism developed naturally. This relationship depended upon the willingness of Conservatism as a whole to do a deal for Liberal Unionist support, to make some reasonable recognition of Chamberlain's situation and his need to show his Radical followers concrete evidence of Conservative concessions in the way of 'progressive' policies. On the other hand, Chamberlain needed to educate his following in an understanding that, in a situation where the defection of either group would let Home Rule through in the Commons, polite blackmail was necessarily a two-way process. Many Tories saw no advantage in giving Chamberlain what he wanted as a Liberal Unionist which they would not have given if they had a majority without him. They had the House of Lords to protect the Union. Therefore, why appease Chamberlain and thus lose either way? Being in a weaker position, Chamberlain in the last resort would have to sacrifice Radicalism to the cause of the Union if the choice were forced on him.

Salisbury and Balfour, however, calculated that, quite apart from the Union, certain ingredients of Liberal Unionism would be indispensable to the creation of a majority Conservatism of the future. In an era when politics and administration was becoming a complicated affair and when the House of Commons was no longer primarily a leisurely, gentlemanly club, Conservatism had to take positive steps to be attractive to intelligent young men. The *National Review* had been founded in 1883 with Alfred Austin as editor for just this purpose. W. H. Mallock, who in 1890 became editor of the *British Review*, later amalgamated with W. E. Henley's *National Observer*, was a prominent specimen of the new brand of younger Tory intellectuals. The average elector, moreover, was a rather more sophisticated animal than his counterpart of Bagehot's day. If the Conservative party was ever to redeem itself from the political insolvency of the 80s and early 90s it would have to address itself unflinchingly to the social problems of the modern world. The 'villa Toryism' that had developed strongly in the 70s was a potent electoral factor but it bore with it more of fear and anxiety than confidence. Chamberlain was nothing if not intelligent and confident; and his increasingly close association with the Conservative leadership and the careful balance of give and take which this association involved helped Conservatives like Salisbury and especially Balfour to develop within the party corresponding Conservative applications of intelligence and confidence.

If preservation of the Union was essentially a negative cause, the great positive means of bridging gaps not only between Tories and Liberal Unionists but between Old Tories and New Tories was imperialism. Here was a doctrine which subsumed within itself in coherent relationship foreign policy, military and naval policy, social reconstruction, economic and commercial policy, Ireland. Conservatism's becoming the 'imperial' party under Salisbury and Balfour was inseparably part and parcel of its becoming politically relevant again: 'killing Home Rule with kindness' was essentially as much the application to Ireland of modern policies of social reconstruction, as a programme of special and extraordinary concessions without any wider relevance. This was an argument and an appeal which gave Conservatism, for all its timidities and debilities, an enormous advantage over Liberalism. Salisbury himself warned the Liberal imperialist Alfred Milner about the Conservative party: 'It is a party shackled by tradition; all the cautious people, all the timid, all the unimaginative, belong to it. . . . Yet the Conservative Party is the Imperial Party. I must work with it – who indeed am just such a one myself – but *you* must work with it if you are to achieve even a part of your object.'

However, Salisbury's immediate problems in taking office in August 1886 were to cope with the Irish reaction to Gladstone's failure to pass Home Rule and to cope with the efforts of Lord Randolph Churchill, now chancellor of the exchequer and leader of the House of Commons, to establish himself as the dominant and guiding force in the cabinet.

The Irish reaction was bound to be sharp. In Salisbury the Nationalists knew they had an antagonist worthy of their best invective. One of Salisbury's most notorious 'blazing indiscretions' in public had been his remark during the debates on the Home Rule Bill in 1886 about the relative fitness of the Irish for self-government: 'You would not confide free representative government to the Hottentots, for instance.' Salisbury's important proposition had been that the Irish would not be fit for 'equal treatment' until they were subjected to government 'honestly, consistently, and resolutely applied for twenty years'. As the strong man to initiate this policy of 'giving them a licking' Salisbury chose Hicks Beach, Disraeli's chief secretary for Ireland from 1874 to 1878. Beach's first task was to restore morale in the administration, police and magistracy, badly shaken by Gladstone's Home Rule bid. Many officers, faced by the imminent prospect of a Parnell régime in Dublin, were fence-sitters; Dublin Castle itself was dominated by the Home Rule group about Sir Robert Hamilton, the permanent under-secretary. On the other side, Belfast was still simmering from the Orange riots during Morley's period of office. Salisbury found a powerful cabinet committee on Ireland composed of Beach, Churchill, Matthews (home secretary) and W. H. Smith (Irish chief secretary 1885–6). Chamberlain was a strong influence in the background, advocating a comprehensive Local Government bill for Ireland that would 'break Gladstone's heart and render him completely impotent'. Beach had to strike the right balance between firmness of repression and effectiveness of remedial action. The overriding objective of Salisbury's government was to impose the conviction that Home Rule was not going to be the answer.

This was a challenge the Nationalists had to defeat. Once having received Gladstone's offer of 1886 they would settle for nothing less. The Liberal–Nationalist alliance had led to a decrease in agrarian crime. With parliamentary defeat for Home Rule, the War for the Land began to grow hot once more. Agricultural distress was worse than ever. As world prices fell and the value of Irish production fell with them, evictions for non-payment of rents increased, and a counter-terror of rick-burning, animal maiming and the ride of 'Captain Moonlight' became rampant in the south and west, where, at night at least, the National League was more powerful than the Law.

Coercion was not immediately reintroduced, but it was threatened in decisive terms. A commission under Lord Cowper was formed to advise the government. Redvers Buller, chief acolyte of the Wolseley Ring, was sent to stamp out terrorism in Kerry and Clare. The cabinet committee disputed about how best to deal with the rents problem. The Ashbourne Act of 1885 seemed to offer the best lead for a Conservative Irish policy of giving credits to allow tenants to buy their landlords out. The problem was how, if at all, landlords should be compensated for an intermediate policy of rent abatements. Parnell himself in September 1886 proposed a Tenants' Relief bill providing for a regular system of abatements where good will had been shown and for a suspension of evictions where genuine hardship could be proved. It was a sensible bill and most of its provisions were recommended in 1887 by the Cowper Commission. But the government was not able to respond quickly enough to the initiative and it lapsed.

While Parnell shrugged his shoulders, the running was taken up by more radical Nationalists, led by William O'Brien and John Dillon. In October 1886 the 'Plan of Campaign' was inaugurated under the auspices of the Irish National League. This was a scheme whereby tenants would withhold rents less the abatements claimed and give the money instead to trustees appointed by the Plan, thus forming a fund from which evicted tenants could be subsidized. It was a very shrewdly planned and effective form of 'moral insurrection'. It kept within the bounds necessary to retain Liberal support and was the best possible kind of anti-landlord propaganda. Buller, who succeeded Hamilton as under-secretary, was strongly anti-landlord in his views and pressed Beach in the direction of concession. But the government decided on repression: O'Brien and Dillon were arrested in December 1886 and the Plan was proclaimed as an unlawful criminal conspiracy.

II

As the Irish League's Plan of Campaign menaced Salisbury on one side, Randolph Churchill menaced him on the other. Churchill was convinced, by his previous success in using the Conservative National Union to force Salisbury to abandon the Central Committee and admit him to the cabinet, that the tide of fortune was running his way and that he must not let the initiative slip. With Chamberlain as an ally in the progressive cause and with the ministry dependent on Liberal Unionist support to stay in office, Salisbury, it was reasonable to calculate, was in no strong position to resist Churchill's demand for the next logical and decisive step in the direction which the 'Fourth Party' had mapped out since the early 1880s. But by now Balfour was firmly in Uncle Salisbury's camp; and Churchill's overweening arrogance had lost him much support in the upper levels of the Conservative party where it would matter most.

At Dartford on 2 November 1886 Churchill launched his offensive with a Tory Democratic 'unauthorized programme'. His demands included a smallholdings policy for agricultural labourers, democratic local government reform for Ireland equally as well as Britain, renunciation of coercion in Ireland, a progressive alliance with Liberal Unionism, and a pacific foreign policy and resistance to increased armaments expenditure. This was followed by a great ovation at the Conservative National Conference. Salisbury attempted to blunt Churchill's offensive with some good advice. 'Drastic, symmetrical measures, hitting the "classes" hard' and thereby losing their support, and of 'trusting to public meetings and the democratic forces generally' to carry through legislation for the 'masses', would fail. The 'classes' would not fight on ground determined by Churchill; that was 'not the way they fight'; they would select some issue upon which they could appeal to prejudice and on which they believed the masses to be indifferent; and on that, Salisbury told Churchill, 'they will upset you'.

Churchill disregarded these golden words; or rather, treating them almost with provocative perversity as the scenario for his own political tragedy, he chose to base his decisive bid for dominance on a reduction of the Army and Navy estimates at a time when the naval 'scare' of 1884 was still alive, when Boulanger was riding high in Paris on the crest of a fever for *revanche*, and when Austria and Russia seemed about to come to blows over Bulgaria. The war secretary, W. H. Smith (Churchill's old victim 'Snelgrove'), bore the brunt of Churchill's arrogance. Salisbury and Balfour felt they were on good ground to resist. Recklessly convinced of his indispensability and without consulting Chamberlain, Churchill offered his resignation in December 1886. Salisbury called his bluff and accepted it. No dog stirred in the party or out of doors; and Churchill plummeted to his doom.

It was a testimony to Churchill that there was considerable talk of a coalition unionist government headed by Hartington; instead, with Hartington's approval, Goschen, who had parted from Gladstone as early as 1880, agreed to take over the vacant exchequer. This steadied the Unionist alliance. Chamberlain had hoped for much from cooperation with Churchill, and now would tend naturally to recoil in the direction of negotiating for a deal with the Gladstonians. Goschen, however, would link the right wing of Liberal Unionism closer to the Conservatives; and unless Chamberlain could get dramatic concessions from the Gladstonians, he depended on a Liberal Unionism in being; and so would be neutralized.

Many Gladstonians were eager to seize the occasion offered by Churchill's fall and Chamberlain's isolation to reunite the broken Liberal party. Almost all Liberals still thought in terms of eventual reunion. Only a minority, represented by Morley, thought that Home Rule was worth the supreme sacrifice of indefinite disunion. Only Gladstone's immense authority had carried the party thus far with him. Harcourt and Rosebery were lukewarm at best to Home Rule; many others thought Liberalism was paying far too high a price for it. Harcourt determined to try to get a compromise solution on Ireland acceptable to both Gladstone and Chamberlain. He assumed that good will would overcome misunderstanding. Thus in January and February 1887 Harcourt arranged a series of 'Round Table Conferences' between Chamberlain and the Gladstonians, represented principally by Morley. They failed dismally. Gladstone and Chamberlain in effect each demanded the capitulation of the other. Chamberlain offered Irish provincial autonomy on the Canadian model, but to no avail. The Gladstonians saw no reason why they should concede anything. They saw themselves in a position of strength, with Chamberlain stranded in the political wilderness with his dwindling band. They had already seized Chamberlain's creation, the National Liberation Federation, from him, and transferred its headquarters from Birmingham to London. They were proceeding to 'nationalize' it, making it less of a Radical pressure group, and would increase the 255 branches of 1885 to 716 by 1888. In that year they affronted Chamberlain by ostentatiously holding the annual Liberal Conference at Birmingham itself, the capital of Chamberlain's 'Grand Duchy' of the West Midlands. By-elections were also encouraging for the Gladstonians.

Thus Chamberlain was obliged to fall back upon the Liberal Unionist–Conservative relationship. Salisbury certainly needed all the support he could get early in 1887. The Plan of Campaign in Ireland was spreading apace despite the government's efforts to repress it. A stringent Crimes bill for Ireland was decided on in January. Then Beach's health collapsed under the strain. Salisbury, already harassed by the necessity to depose the failing Stafford Northcote from the Foreign Office and take it over himself, turned to his nephew Balfour, the secretary for Scotland. At first sight it seemed an unlikely appointment. Known to his contemporaries at Cambridge as 'Pretty Fanny', Balfour was notorious for his languid 'aesthetic' attitudes. The Irish were amused. Having wrecked the constitutions of strong men like Forster, Trevelyan and Beach, they supposed they would make short work of 'Bunthorne'[1] Balfour. But in fact Balfour was well suited to the job at hand. Beach still represented essentially a conciliation before coercion attitude. He was passionately concerned. Balfour, a confirmed bachelor, had no apparent passions. His intellectual detachment was a good basis for ruthlessness.

Balfour set about with a Cromwellian strong hand to clear the ground and enable Home Rule to be 'killed by kindness'. The power of the National League had to be nullified by breaking its hold over the tenants. Together with the severe Crimes bill Balfour brought in a Land bill which was a thinly disguised version of Parnell's Tenants' Relief bill of the previous year. Salisbury said of the Irish Land Act of 1887: 'It is the price we have to pay for the Union and it is a heavy one.' Frenzied parliamentary obstruction by the Nationalists led to even more stringent rules of procedure and the introduction of the 'guillotine' to cut obstruction short. The extreme tension of the political atmosphere was further intensified in March 1887 when *The Times* commenced a series entitled 'Parnellism and Crime', brought to a sensational climax on 18 April with a facsimile of a letter allegedly written by Parnell in 1882 explaining why the Nationalists had had to condemn the Phoenix Park murders officially, and while regretting the 'accident' of Lord Frederick Cavendish's death asserted that Burke had got no more than his deserts. Parnell indignantly denied that he had written the letter and a special commission of inquiry was set up.

Chamberlain and Bright both supported the Crimes bill, which the guillotine got through in July. Birmingham Unionist Liberalism, as represented especially by Dr Dale, was unhappy at the return to coercion which Gladstonian propaganda would make the most of. But Chamberlain, by persuading the government to give better terms to tenants in the Land bill despite much Tory grumbling, was able to hold the balance steady. Chamberlain pleased his Radical support in August when he protested against the proclamation of the Irish National League. He was as essentially anti-coercionist as he had been in Gladstone's earlier cabinet. He was ready for appeasement on everything except the main issue of Home Rule. Chamberlain's thinking was running along lines of Irish provincial councils allowing for Ulster federation in Ireland, Irish federation in the United Kingdom, leading eventually to imperial federation. He was glad enough to escape from the embarrassment of being between Balfour and Dr Dale by accepting the government's proposal that he go to the U.S.A. as one of the British commissioners on the Newfoundland fisheries dispute.

For the Conservatives as a whole the Irish problem had rather different implications. For Chamberlain it was a distraction from the real problems of British politics. For Salisbury and Balfour it was the real problem of British politics – the challenge of the masses against the classes – in a particularly exposed and dangerous form. A victory for the Irish insurgency would, in their view, be a signal example of a legally established propertied order being dispossessed by mob violence. It would shake severely the confidence of the British propertied establishment and correspondingly stimulate assault upon it by the forces of radicalism ending eventually in a socialist-directed proletariat. Socialist propaganda in Britain agreed with this perhaps over-flattering diagnosis. 'Bloody Sunday' in Trafalgar Square in November 1887 arose out of an S.D.F. demonstration against the imprisonment of O'Brien. John Burns and R. B. Cunninghame-Graham, M.P., ardent follower of William Morris and ardent Scottish nationalist, were arrested and imprisoned as martyrs to the proposition of an identity of interest between the Irish democracy and the British democracy. This, however, was a doctrine more favoured in Britain than in Ireland, where neither patrician Protestantism of the Parnell (or young W. B. Yeats) stamp nor the provincial petty-bourgeois Catholicism of the Hierarchy or the League or the parliamentary Irish party cherished much in common with Anglo-Saxon atheistic proletarianism.

In any event, Balfour had by the end of 1887 distinctly got the better of the fight. He appointed a vigorous new permanent under-secretary, Joseph Ridgeway, an Irishman who had served with distinction in Afghanistan and the North-West Frontier, and tackled Irish problems in much the same spirit of frontier toughness. Balfour also picked out a young Dublin barrister, Edward Carson, who soon became the most effective and most feared Crown counsel. The very fierceness of the Irish invective against Balfour became a testimony to a certain kind of success. After an affray at Mitchelstown in September 1887 at which two persons were killed, 'Bunthorne' Balfour became 'Bloody Balfour'.

III

On the domestic front, local government reform in England and Wales imposed itself as the first priority. The necessity of doing something comprehensive in this sphere had long seemed obvious. As modern administration increased both in complexity and expense a complete overhaul of the old system of administration by justices of the peace and Quarter Sessions appointed by lords lieutenant could no longer be avoided. Any government in power at this time would have had to rationalize the confusion of centuries of accumulated and piecemeal legislation which had created innumerable and inextricably overlapping jurisdictions and authorities. It was computed in 1883 that there were over 27,000 independent local authorities in England and Wales and that ratepayers were taxed by eighteen different kinds of rates. Extension of the borough suffrage to the counties in 1884 gave a decisive final impulse to reform.

This provided an opportunity for post-1880 Conservatism to re-establish its credentials as a great national party by appealing to both 'intelligence' and the 'masses' by coping sensibly and confidently with an important issue of modern society. On the other hand the Conservative and Whig 'classes' resented sweeping changes in county government which would inevitably tend to compromise their local influence. Salisbury and Ritchie, the president of the Local Government Board, had a delicate problem in deciding at what point old loyalties were being dangerously overstrained and new expectations were being dangerously disappointed. Salisbury himself had no objections in principle to a thoroughgoing bill. As a territorial grandee who owned land in eight counties, with an annual rent-roll (in 1879) of over £30,000, he was immune from the prejudices and anxieties of the lesser gentry. He was confident of the good sense of the average county voter as long as access to intoxicants like the very big sums of money financing the poor-rate (£16·5 million in England and Wales in 1893) was denied them. He was thus quite receptive to appeals from Chamberlain for some major reform with which to comfort and reassure the Liberal Unionists.

The Local Government Act of 1888 abolished a huge number of existing petty jurisdictions in England and Wales and created sixty-two administrative counties (only six of which corresponded with existing historic counties) and sixty county boroughs of cities with more than 50,000 inhabitants. Each county and county borough was to have a council elected by ratepayers and to these councils were transferred the administrative functions of all the multifarious lesser authorities (except the poor law guardians and the school boards) and of the justices of the peace (except control of the police, which was to be shared between the councils and the justices). The government of the 120 square miles of greater London (with reservations in favour of the City proper) was placed by a separate Act of 1889 under a London County Council. The fifty-two historic counties with lords lieutenant, sheriffs and justices of the peace appointed by the Crown survived only as areas for parliamentary elections and, occasionally, for organization of the militia and the administration of justice. There was in fact little political convulsion associated with elections to the new county councils, and on the whole the Act of 1888 belied both the hopes of the Radicals and the fears of the grumbling Tories. Nor is there any reason to suppose that the quality of administration was much improved. After the first flush of novelty only London County Council elections caused much stir (Rosebery was its first chairman). The London County Council became a kind of testing ground for collectivist ideas under the lead of the majority Progressive party, 'municipal socialists' who carefully avoided identification with official Liberalism. They built, for example, the first municipal housing schemes in the world in the 1890s. But in any case the scales had clearly tipped decisively in favour of financial and administrative centralization. The legislation of 1888, and even more the Liberal extension of it in 1894, asserted the desirability of popular local government when its feasibility was already severely eroded. The essential significance of the legislation of 1888 was its appropriateness to the climate of the times.

This appropriateness was precisely the profit and benefit to Conservatism of taking responsibility for seeing the local government issue through. It gave Chamberlain confidence that he could work profitably with the Conservatives. Chamberlain urged the benefit and profit to be coined out of free schools and smallholdings. He could not afford to let the Gladstonians outbid him on social reform. If they delivered more than he could persuade or blackmail the Conservatives into delivering his independent political power base in the West Midlands might well crumble. The Liberal party was in a ferment of trying to decide to what extent its commitment to Home Rule in 1886 disqualified it from this kind of competition. Gladstone and Morley were trying desperately to keep Liberalism 'straight' on 'Irish policy and measures' as the great, necessary central preoccupation of the party. Rosebery, no zealot for Home Rule in itself, agreed on the danger of the party's being allowed to wander amid 'vague Socialistic schemes' and 'vaporous views which at present have no ripeness or consistency', and reluctantly concluded that the Irish commitment alone gave the party 'faith and discipline'. While Morley raged against the 'anarchistic follies' of the London Radicals who were frightening off the 'small shopkeeper', Gladstone at Limehouse in December 1888 warned the Liberals that they were going to be made to keep to the straight and narrow path and there would be no turning aside to indulge in the pleasures of programmes until they had done their duty by the Irish.

Nevertheless, immense though Gladstone's authority was, he was asking too much of the Liberals. Some, like Harcourt, were eager to get on and do useful things like licensing reform to cut down the availability of alcohol. Harcourt urged a 'concurrence' argument that there was no need to postpone desirable reforms until Home Rule was achieved. Younger Liberals insisted on the importance of attracting to the party 'the confidence of that nascent body of opinion in the constituencies which cares little for any Irish policy and concentrates itself on social questions'. The Fabians accused the Liberal leadership of deliberately using Home Rule to fend off reforms that would injure Liberal landlords and capitalists.

By the end of 1890 the Gladstonian Home Rule thesis no longer had the strength to impose the Limehouse doctrine on the Liberal party. Events such as the dramatic London dock strike of 1889 stimulated the 'labour' cause. Parnell in February 1889 had his greatest moment of triumph when he was vindicated by the court of inquiry over *The Times* 'Parnellism and Crime' letters – forged in fact by a seedy Irish journalist named Pigott who fled to Madrid and blew his brains out. Yet Parnell knew that this might well be his last triumph, for Captain O'Shea, the husband of his mistress, having failed to get the benefits he had hoped for from his wife's liaison, was now determined to ruin him. In December 1889 O'Shea filed a petition for divorce citing Parnell as co-respondent. This fuse exploded in November 1890. Parnell was exposed to the horrified gaze of the Victorian public as a sordid adulterer. The Nonconformist conscience, hailed by Gladstone as the 'backbone of the Liberal party', pronounced its anathema in the person of Hugh Price Hughes. Gladstone advised Parnell that for the good of Home Rule and the good of Ireland he should withdraw from the scene. Parnell tried to evade the ultimatum and desperately engineered a vote of confidence by the Irish parliamentary party ignorant of Gladstone's advice. But the Irish Hierarchy, which had often also suffered the sting of Parnell's Protestant and patrician *hauteur*, and which had no desire to see the Irish national movement stray far outside clerical bounds, also pronounced its anathema. The Irish parliamentary party split into bitterly warring factions. Parnell died miserably in October 1891.

This was Phoenix Park all over again for Gladstone, and he wearily prepared to regain the ground lost. But he would need to sweeten the sulking Liberal party with programmatic incentives. In any case the tide was running strongly in the by-elections for Liberalism and there was no doubt that the credit for this was due to the programmatic 'social' Liberal thesis. The Conservative government could not hold the initiative. Chamberlain's constant stick and carrot pressure and propaganda was well-meant, but it had the effect of stimulating domestic ferment, which did Liberalism more good in the constituencies than it did the government. In March 1891, for instance, Chamberlain plucked the issue of old age pensions out of the air of intellectual debate among such as Charles Booth and set it as a cat among the pigeons of politics. The German legislation of 1889, a feature of Bismarck's efforts to head off the Social Democrats, with the costs divided between employers, workers and the state, offered much food for thought in a society where one in seven of people over sixty were obliged to accept some form of parish relief. Chamberlain here was pushing far beyond what the Conservative party of 1891 could possibly respond to, quite apart from the complicated problem of the vested interests of the Friendly Societies. As it was, the government was responding willingly enough on issues like smallholdings and especially free elementary education. The Education Act of 1891 established this in both state and denominational schools at a cost to the national budget starting at £2 million a year. This was a typical government–Chamberlain bargain: the Tories accepted the idea of gratuity; Chamberlain accepted state subsidies to denominational schools.

Despite this, however, and despite the damage to the Home Rule cause of Parnell's disgrace, Liberalism still enjoyed the prerogatived role of 1880. Only in the event of yet another Liberal failure and a much more intimate and effective Unionist alliance would Unionism be granted the equivalent political credit. That more intimate alliance was indeed cemented at the Conservative National Conference in Chamberlain's Birmingham in November 1891. Chamberlain toasted publicly the cause of Unionism and announced that he neither looked for nor desired Liberal reunion. The fusion of radicalism with imperialism had now matured with Chamberlain's visits to Egypt and Canada. The future, he diagnosed, would lie with a great political movement that could comprehend policies of domestic reconstruction in a larger context of a positive approach to integrated British problems as an economic, commercial and military presence in the world. Liberalism, with or without Home Rule, obviously was not, as a whole, capable in Chamberlain's view of rising to that level of national occasion. It would always, in one way or another, be a party of liberty and liberties; it could never, despite the best efforts of some of its most intelligent members, be a party of state.

The Liberal party arrived at an uneasy working arrangement about the relationship between the Home Rule 'single question' thesis and the programmatic social thesis at its annual conference in Newcastle in October 1891. With scarcely concealed distaste Gladstone listened as resolution after resolution was adopted: Scottish and Welsh disestablishment, local option on licensing: land reforms and rural district government; abolition of primogeniture and entails in land; one man one vote; payment of members of parliament and subsidization of election expenses; public control of denominational schools; extension of employers' liability. In return Home Rule was placed piously at the head of the list. Gladstone contributed a unifying note by threatening the House of Lords with dire retribution if it should attempt to thwart the will of the people. Gladstone grudgingly accepted the 'Newcastle Programme' as an expression of the desires of the Liberal party but he did not accept it as a whole or in any part as binding on any future Liberal government.

A future Liberal government became an increasingly near prospect in 1891. Conservative authority in the Commons suffered a serious blow with the death of W. H. Smith in 1891.

Some of Salisbury's appointments, such as Henry Matthews at the Home Office, were unsuited and unsuccessful in commanding parliamentary or public confidence. Such personal factors were straws in the wind of reviving democratic and radical public sentiment. As the Liberal sails began to fill, Chamberlain grew restless. The Newcastle Programme was indeed outbidding him; from now on the 'unauthorized programme' was in eclipse and his old political stock-in-trade correspondingly devalued. Moreover, Hartington succeeded his father as Duke of Devonshire in 1891 and Chamberlain became Liberal Unionist leader in the Commons, and consequently found himself in a much more exposed position. Chamberlain had a brush with the government in April 1892 over his beloved smallholdings policy, when a cunning Liberal amendment in favour of powers of compulsory land purchase, which Chamberlain wanted and which the Tories did not, led to acute embarrassment. By June 1892 Salisbury was warning Chamberlain not to push too hard, rather as he had warned Randolph Churchill in 1886. Balfour in Ireland had achieved much: Irish Land Purchase Acts in 1887 and 1891 and the setting up of Congested Districts Boards in 1891 laid a firm basis for a settlement of Irish agrarian problems. But 'killing Home Rule with kindness' was likely to be a barren policy so long as the Nationalists could look forward to another 1886.

That Salisbury's government got little electoral credit in Britain for Balfour's Irish achievement mattered less than the much more damaging circumstance for the Liberals that Gladstone's Home Rule commitment got little electoral credit in Britain. If the Liberals won, they would win largely on the strength of the Newcastle Programme.

The Gladstonians ended up after the election of July 1892 with 273 seats, the Conservatives with 269. Chamberlain came back at the head of forty-six Liberal Unionists: thanks to judicious electoral arrangements with the Conservatives the Grand Duchy of the West Midlands and sufficient of its appanages was intact. There were seventy-two regular Irish Nationalists and nine Parnellites, and one independent Labour member, Keir Hardie, who won West Ham South. Counting Gladstonians, Nationalists and Labour together, Gladstone had a majority for Home Rule of forty. He had hoped for a hundred. Though reduced to two-thirds of his following, Chamberlain was the victor of 1892. That Chamberlain was not destroyed in the West Midlands was bad enough; but that he was not destroyed in the other main area of Liberal Unionist strength, Scotland, exposed Liberal weakness graphically. Even had the Liberals managed to take another twenty or so seats from Chamberlain's 1886 total it would have made a tremendous difference: Gladstone would have had a majority for Home Rule independent of the Irish Nationalists. His failure to achieve this was crucial. Gladstone needed such a majority in order to establish a moral ascendancy over the House of Lords. As it was, the Liberals depended heavily on the 'Celtic fringe' of Wales, Scotland and Ireland: the Unionists had a majority of seventy-one in the English constituencies.

IV

It was a daunting prospect, but Gladstone, in his eighty-third year, rather grimly formed his fourth and last cabinet. The faithful Morley naturally went back to the Irish Office. Gladstone had much ado coaxing the temperamental Rosebery to take the Foreign Office. Rosebery disliked the Newcastle programme as much as Gladstone; but he also liked Home Rule as little as the chief 'programmatic' advocate in the cabinet, Harcourt, once again chancellor of the exchequer. On top of this, Rosebery was as convinced as Chamberlain of the paramount political claims of the imperial idea; yet, unlike Chamberlain, he was destined to sustain the role of imperial advocate in a party dominated by various manifestations of 'Little Englandism'. He had already caused much offence by publicly announcing that in the event of a Liberal government 'we intend to try the experiment of having a continuous foreign policy . . . I cannot doubt that Mr Gladstone's Government . . . will continue Lord Salisbury's Foreign Policy.' Yet such was Rosebery's general prestige in the country, the darling of fortune and the golden hope of a younger, post-Gladstonian generation, that it would have been impossible to float a Liberal government possessing even a semblance of conviction with so compromised a popular mandate without his adherence. Rosebery consented to come in on the understanding of a virtual autonomy in the Foreign Office. Gladstone, fuming, had to concede. He brought in a brilliant young Q.C. who had distinguished himself in the Parnell affair, H. H. Asquith, as home secretary.

Harcourt made a last effort to cut Home Rule down to size. He pleaded with Gladstone that the 'only chance of holding together our majority such as it is will consist in giving satisfaction at once to the various sections of which it consists'. He proposed therefore that bills should be brought in immediately in the next parliament on 'temperance' reform, village councils with control of schools, one man one vote, payment of members and Welsh disestablishment. Gladstone would not budge. He had already made it plain that he could no longer trouble himself about the 'ordinary exigencies of party'. Home Rule was all he was interested in. Morley put it with candid brutality: 'The Irish are our masters and we had better realize it at once.'

Accordingly the session of 1893 was devoted to a second Home Rule Bill. It differed from the first mainly in that it allowed for reduced Irish representation at Westminster, leaving the Home Rule policy open to the charge of surrendering to the Irish Nationalists not only autonomy for themselves and domination over the Ulster loyalists, but of surrendering to them also the possibility of a decisive voice in British affairs. The course of events took on a predictable, even ritual, character. After furious debates the bill was passed by the Commons on 1 September by a majority of forty-three. A week later, despite Gladstone's menaces, the Lords threw it out by 419 to 41.

The very predictability of the result left the Liberal government helpless. Had there been any doubt their indignation would have had force and popular response; but there had been no doubt whatever since the election results of the previous year. Moreover, the Lords were wise enough to mangle later Liberal bills like Employers' Liability and Parish Councils[2] with tact and finesse, helped by Chamberlain's sagacious advice. Chamberlain in fact virtually took them over and steered them through while the government scowled. All Gladstone could do was to demand a fight with the Lords on a 'Peers *versus* People' or

'Mend them or end them' platform. His cabinet knew better. They knew well there was no scope for another 1876 or another 1880 to be manufactured out of Home Rule. Denouncing his colleagues bitterly as faint-hearts, Gladstone always cited this moment of abnegation as one of the last golden moments of political opportunity. It was the last of the four occasions of his career when he felt sure that he could claim 'insight' that the materials existed for forming a public opinion and for directing it to a particular end. It was certainly the bitter end of the Liberal claims to political prerogative derived from the 1860s.

Undoubtedly his faint-hearted colleagues were right. But on the other hand they had nothing better to suggest than to continue 'filling up the cup' of Lords' iniquitous vetoes on their bills in the forlorn hope that the peers would eventually overplay their hand and provoke public resentment. In the midst of this atmosphere of rather pathetic anti-climax Gladstone in April 1894 found himself isolated on the issue of a big increase in naval expenditure called for, in his view, by the profligate imperialism at the bottom of Salisbury's and Rosebery's deplorable conduct of foreign policy. It was the last straw. Also it was the plausible occasion of a reasonably dignified final exit. Deserted even by the chief anti-jingoes, Harcourt and Morley, in March Gladstone resigned in disgust. He wanted to advise the Queen to appoint Spencer, whose principal qualification was that he was the only man to serve in all four of Gladstone's cabinets; but the Queen, delighted at long last to be rid of him, carefully avoided asking his advice and appointed her least unfavourite Liberal, Rosebery, who, at all events, was sound on foreign policy.

It was an unenviable task for the new prime minister. He headed a government whose existence had depended on one man, Gladstone, in pursuit of one thing, Home Rule. Now Gladstone was gone and Home Rule was out of reach. Moreover, Harcourt, the Liberal leader in the Commons, felt he had superior claims to the leadership of the party than Rosebery, twenty years his junior. Harcourt consented to stay on as chancellor of the exchequer and leader of the commons on terms humiliating to Rosebery: virtually a co-leadership.

Its moral authority and political prestige hopelessly compromised, the Liberal government stumbled on, in the end almost yearning for defeat to put an end to its misery. Asquith at the Home Office was one of its few distinct successes. Rosebery commenced his tenure with offensive tactlessness by announcing that Home Rule would remain in suspension until a majority of the 'predominant member' of the Union, England, consented to it. The last important stroke was Harcourt's 1894 budget. The new naval programme which had forced Gladstone's resignation had to be financed. On the advice of Alfred Milner at the Inland Revenue Board, and contrary to Rosebery's will, Harcourt took the opportunity to inaugurate the principle of re-distribution of social wealth in fiscal policy. Death duties on both real and personal property were combined and subjected to a graduated tax on the lump sum instead of the various sums inheritable by heirs at law. In addition, large sections of the less well-off were exempted from income tax. Gladstone was disturbed by the redistributive implications, and Rosebery deplored the duties as 'class' legislation, and thus contrary to the fundamental principles of true Liberalism. To these accusations Harcourt replied that household suffrage in 1867 and 1884 made inevitable a horizontal class division of parties. He saw his budget laying down guidelines for the Liberalism of the future, a fiscal policy appropriate to an emerging democracy, which would see the end of fiscal privilege.

The first session of 1895 saw the government disintegrating. Harcourt's 'temperance' bill to encourage the suppression of drinking was a disaster. Rosebery offended the Nonconformist conscience by winning the Derby for the second time in his premiership. Gladstone was with difficulty restrained from voting against the Welsh Disestablishment bill. Eventually, to its undisguised relief, the government was defeated in June in a snap vote on alleged deficiencies in cordite, for which the secretary for war, Campbell-Bannerman, was responsible. Salisbury accepted office for the third time on 25 June.

As Liberalism's strength waned, Unionism's waxed. The Harcourt budget of 1894 galvanized many property owners into working and paying for Conservatism to an extent they had not done in 1892. Chamberlain also now seemed a less dubious ally. For his part, Chamberlain amiably but firmly pressed for a treaty about give and take in a coming Unionist government. In September 1894 he announced his negotiating terms: a better Employers' Liability Act; restriction on alien immigration to relieve unemployment (Jews especially, fleeing from pogroms in Russia, were moving westward through Austria and Germany, sparking off the virulent new strain of anti-semitism in which the young Adolf Hitler would shortly be educating himself in Vienna); a better housing policy; an end to private profit on sales of drink (this was known as the Gothenburg system after the Swedish city which had adopted a municipal alcohol monopoly); arbitration in industrial disputes (New Zealand, famous at this time as a laboratory of social experiment, had enacted an industrial conciliation and arbitration system in 1894); an eight-hour day for miners; reduced hours for shop assistants. Old age pensions he had already raised as a problem that would need tackling in the very near future. Over all, he urged the cause of empire as the key to a wider prosperity and the solution to unemployment. In the following month Chamberlain sent Salisbury a 'Memorandum of a Programme for Social Reform' as a formal basis for negotiation: Chamberlain's conditions for joining a Salisbury Unionist cabinet. At Hatfield, Salisbury's seat in Hertfordshire, Salisbury, Chamberlain and Balfour conferred in January 1895 to concert their *coup de grâce* to the moribund Liberal government. There were still considerable difficulties. For example, Chamberlain could not afford not to vote for Welsh disestablishment in March 1895. But the Liberals were even more divided by now. In January 1895 Rosebery piled on the Liberal agony by adding his interpretative gloss as to the relationship between the Newcastle programme and the Liberal government; which was, in effect, purely metaphysical.

In such disarray Liberalism faced the elections. There was no question of possible victory; it was a question of how great would be the defeat. The Liberals lost in all just under a hundred seats. In 1892 they held twenty-three London seats; in 1895, only nine. Keir Hardie, chairman of the Independent Labour party, lost West Ham South, which he had won in 1892. The I.L.P. put up twenty-eight candidates without success; and never recovered from this failure to realize the high hopes of 1892 and 1893. Instead of benefiting from Liberal debility, Labour, despite getting some respectable voting figures, was borne down in the Liberal rout. In England the Liberals held only 112 seats, as against 293 Conservative and fifty Liberal Unionist. English Liberalism increasingly resembled a cluster of beleaguered strongholds: West Riding and the Pennines, the north-east, the south-west and scattered pockets along the east coast. Chamberlain returned at the head of seventy Liberal Unionists in all. Salisbury could face the next parliament with a Unionist majority of 152 in the Commons and an overall Conservative majority of twelve.

Chapter Eleven

NEW DIRECTIONS IN
EXTERNAL PROBLEMS
1886—95

I

What seemed possible and desirable to the directors of British foreign policy after 1885[1] was some kind of useful relationship with a great power or powers which would avoid both the possible dangers of isolation on the one hand and those of a binding commitment on the other. These needs in time became translated into received attitudes governing the conduct of British policy: that the parliamentary constitution made impracticable any alliance involving the distinct obligation of a *casus belli* in a European war; and that therefore the choice would lie between isolation or a relationship short of an alliance. The central theme of external policy after the end of Gladstone's last concert bid in 1885 right up to the beginning of war in 1914 is finding this useful relationship. From 1887 to 1894 the most useful relationship was calculated to be with the alliance of the central powers of Germany and Austria, the link being Italy and the *status quo* in the Near East. From 1894 to shortly after 1900 was a period of difficulty in replacing this earlier relationship, a period thus of isolation deliberately chosen as the least unprofitable of the available options; this lesser unprofitability being moralized later into 'splendid isolation'. After 1900 came a new era of useful relationships. It was launched without any far-sighted design in the Far East by an alliance with the Japanese designed as a means of relieving British burdens in that region; a means of making isolation more tolerable rather than an escape from it. Circumstances logically but unexpectedly led to the linking of the Japanese alliance with a useful relationship with the French which in turn led to one with the ally of the French, the Russians.

Fundamentally the basic British requirement was to remain a Great Power with both independence of action and security of existence. Independence was the means: essentially a matter of being able to look after one's own interests without dependence upon external aid. Security was the end: being able to prevent invasion, keep open communications around the world, deliver seaborne food and raw materials without interruption, all of which meant in practice naval supremacy. Isolation as such was not necessarily a vital danger. Given the security of unchallengeable sea power, Britain's situation was fairly safe.

Naturally a standard British assumption was always that either one power dominant on the continent or a voluntary combination of the continental powers was *prima facie* very likely to be a potential challenge to Britain, because in either case the naval resources of the whole continent might be mobilized against Britain. British policy therefore always attempted to avert, neutralize or in the last resort destroy, such forms of challenge. This policy had been successful against the French. The concert system in Europe after 1815 was the most convenient possible arrangement from the British point of view. The British problem after the final end in 1885 of British efforts to restore that concert arrangement was that the possibility of a serious threat to Britain either from a dominant power or a voluntary combination of powers now had to be taken into account. This sense of a new kind of threat produced the series of naval 'scares' in the 1880s and 1890s which ushered in the era of accelerating competitive armament technologies. An isolation not involving a serious naval threat as in the later 1890s – for the French had given up their challenge and the Germans had not yet begun theirs – was very much to be preferred to a European relationship dictated by the need to cope with a serious challenge to naval supremacy.

Salisbury in 1885 faced the task of picking up the pieces scattered by the wreck of Gladstone's concert. He came to it as adequately prepared as any British foreign secretary in the nineteenth century. He had learned well the lessons of Palmerston's failure in the 1860s and Disraeli's failure in the 1870s. 'The commonest error in politics is sticking to the carcasses of dead policies' (1877). He was equally aware of the implications of Gladstone's failure in the 1880s. He had, specifically, an acute appreciation of the fundamental deterioration of Britain's world position in a situation where neither the Palmerstonian nor the Gladstonian assumptions about directive control could any longer answer: 'Whatever happens will be for the worse and therefore it is in our interest that as little should happen as possible' (1887). Salisbury believed that if Britain could not control events, she would have to go along with them, and no amount of aloofness or isolationism could evade that necessity if it so happened – as it did in fact happen – that those events included a naval challenge.

The measures adopted by Salisbury to modify this situation in the later 1880s and early 1890s were essentially of the same kind and degree as those measures which led to the decision to go to war in 1914. That decision derived from calculations about the dynamic of European power relationships which took on their mature form precisely at this period. Unlike Gladstone and most Liberals, Salisbury was perfectly aware that there was nothing Britain could do to cancel the logic of that European dynamic, which was inherent unto itself and from which none of the principal parties concerned could themselves escape.

The positive alternative to Gladstonism, given the irremediable discrediting of Disraeli's neo-Palmerstonism, was 'imperialism'. Essentially the idea at the bottom of the various applications of imperialism was that Britain could not hope to survive long as a Great Power in the world unless British policy deliberately set out to construct the means of doing this. It repudiated the assumption, common to both Gladstone and Disraeli, that there was some 'natural' relationship between Britain and the external world that would allow this problem largely to look after itself. Imperialism was, in this sense, synthetic and artificial; it was an effort to create form in a formless world. The existing empire, a historical hodge-podge of accident, trade, strategy and conquest, was the obvious source of materials for this construction. There were doubts about the usefulness of some of its major components: was India worth keeping? Did the expense of defending it outweigh its economic value? But in any case could an imperialist policy possibly gain public support in the aftermath of Disraeli's magniloquent 'imperial' gestures by abandoning India? In fact the mythology of India would be indispensable for the demagogic promotion of empire. But one way or another, imperialists would have to make the best of it. By intelligent exploitation of all available resources – economic, human, strategic – Britain could maintain an independent position that would put her out of the reach of any European power or combination of powers. Instead of accepting that whatever happened would be for the worst and that the best that could be done was to try to prevent things from happening, the central argument of the imperialists was that the best hope of security was boldly to take time and circumstance by the throat and bend them to serve the purposes of the national interest.

Obviously imperialism had great attractions to people who wanted positive affirmations instead of rather flyblown Gladstonian pieties. It offered also the possibility of a basis for a constructive domestic policy. Inevitably a school of imperialist statesmanship would emerge. Among the established political eminences Rosebery and Chamberlain already were beginning to see themselves as candidates for the role of historical leadership sketched by doctrinaires such as Seeley, who looked for an English equivalent of the great reconstructor of the Prussian state, Stein, to fulfil the prophecies of *The Expansion of England*.[2] There was by now also a younger Tory generation with pronounced intellectual tastes coming to the fore: Arthur Balfour and George Curzon were decisive in importing imperialist doctrine into the Conservative party which had hitherto been largely innocent of it. This contributed to the new sense of confidence which became noticeable in the later 1880s. Successful resistance to the Liberal Home Rule bid in 1886 had a general stiffening effect on ruling class morale. South Africa was relatively quiet; and in any case Rhodes was working mightily to lure Kruger and the Transvaal into a great British South African entity. Above all, Egypt under Baring's firm rule was becoming a focus of imperial idealism, a showpiece of benevolent authoritarianism. A general forwardness was encouraged elsewhere. A more strenuous and enterprising spirit was evident among the servants of the Indian *Raj*. Roberts took over as commander-in-chief in 1885; Burma was annexed with a fine flourish by Randolph Churchill; Curzon himself, an incessant propagandist of the forward policy, was actually negotiating in 1894 as a private Member of Parliament with the Emir of Afghanistan in Kabul; and Kipling's literary success from 1890 undoubtedly stimulated an immense new public awareness of the sheer dramatic grandeur of the scale of British activities in the world.

Salisbury was not a doctrinal imperialist because he had no faith in positive, constructive blueprints for the future. As a pessimist he tended to agree with the imperialists that imperial consolidation was indeed the only real hope in the long run of staving off Britain's decline. But he was equally sceptical – with good cause, as events were to show – as to whether the project was feasible. He had confidence for the foreseeable future in British capacity to defend the empire, to cope with dangers and problems as they arose by means of resolute tenacity; of not offering any provocation, but of being quite clear where vital interests lay and in being quite determined to defend them. Increasingly Salisbury collided with imperialists who advocated adventures and experiments. He insisted always on solid practicability. His primary aim was to escape from the impasse left by Gladstone. His predispositions were for a good understanding with the French and firm resistance at the Straits to the Russians. He also saw the advantage of working with Bismarck to neutralize as much as possible the anti-British implications of the *Dreikaiserbund*. Bismarck made a point in 1885 of welcoming Salisbury's return to office on the basis of a common anti-Gladstonism; Salisbury responded with appropriate cynicism but also with a willingness to humour the Germans with concessions in East Africa in return for their support in Egypt. Getting out of Egypt on reasonable terms was Salisbury's major concern. In this way good relations with the French could be restored, and thus conditions could be created for a combined Anglo-French or 'Crimean' watch on the Straits.

Events hindered Salisbury in some respects and helped him in others. Bismarck's attempted continental *bloc* never materialized. The French colonial lobby was rebuffed in the elections of 1885 and French policy veered towards a *revanchiste* hostility to Germany. Hence much of Bismarck's cultivation of Salisbury on his returns to office in 1885 and again in 1886. In September 1885 a revolution in Eastern Roumelia – that part of the 'Great Bulgaria' of San Stefano in 1878 which had been returned to the Turks as an autonomous province – proclaimed union with the principality of Bulgaria. Bulgarian nationalists had never accepted the tripartition of the Berlin Congress. Every power except the Bulgarians wanted a reassertion of the *status quo* and hoped that the Turks could do it. But this was beyond them in Bulgaria in 1885 as it had been in Bosnia in 1875. Salisbury took the view which Disraeli would have done well to have taken in 1875: that if the Turks were incapable of asserting their rights the sensible course was to back the insurgents. This had the advantage of being popular with Liberal opinion on the grounds of self-determination. It had also the greater advantage of being contrary to Russian desires. The Bulgarians resented Russian occupation much as Egyptian nationalists resented British occupation. Russian overlordship was repudiated. There was a bitter personal feud between the Emperor Alexander III and Prince Alexander of Battenberg,[3] elected ruler of the new Bulgarian state in 1879. The Russians joined with the Turks in insisting on a return to legality. Bismarck and the Austrians gave support on general *Dreikaiserbund* principles.

Salisbury's line wrecked this 'concert' policy. It was Disraeli's sabotage of the Berlin Memorandum upside down. Liberals were enchanted at the efficaciousness of the 'breasts of free men' as the best barrier to Russian ambitions. When Gladstone came back briefly in 1886 for his Home Rule bid, Rosebery was thus able to smother instinctive Liberal suspicions of his heretical doctrine of the desirability of 'continuity' in foreign policy. The French, moreover, gave Britain support on the understanding of an Egyptian settlement. The 'Crimean' possibilities ripened when the Austrians began to shift ground in an anti-Russian direction. An attempt by the Serbs to stop the Bulgarian union was defeated; and this was a defeat for the Russians also. In April 1886 the Russians were obliged to accept a compromise, proposed by Salisbury, of a 'personal union' between the two Bulgarias. The only consolation for the Russians was their veto of Prince Alexander, who abdicated. Russian threats to invade Bulgaria led to a serious deterioration of Austro-Russian relations. Salisbury, though hampered by Randolph Churchill who argued for abandonment of resistance in the Balkans and the Straits and a consolidation of the British position in Egypt, did his best to bolster the Austrians, who could get no support from the embarrassed Bismarck. This was, as it turned out, the end of the *Dreikaiserbund*.

From the British point of view all this was to the good. Salisbury improved the shining hour by sending Drummond Wolff as emissary to Constantinople to negotiate with the Turks on terms for a British withdrawal from Egypt. While Wolff negotiated with a Turkish government still smarting at Salisbury's patronage of the Bulgarians and with Russian resentment at the British at a fever pitch, Salisbury was being courted by Bismarck and the Italians. The Italians demanded support against the French in the Mediterranean as the price for their renewal of the Triple Alliance of 1882. Bismarck calculated that Salisbury would be prepared to give this in return for Italian support against the Russians and the French in Egypt.

In February 1887 the Anglo–Italian Agreement was concluded. From Salisbury's point of view everything was to be gained by extending it to a wider Mediterranean agreement including Austria in order to guarantee the *status quo* at the Straits. A secret agreement was concluded in March 1887 with the Austrians for diplomatic cooperation with a purely defensive motive. Bismarck was active in promoting it as a promising beginning of a British relationship with the Triple Alliance, especially useful at a time when the French were in the grip of the bellicose war fever focused on General Boulanger. Bismarck squared the Russians with the 'Reinsurance Treaty' to relieve them of anxiety about the Austrians. But Salisbury was as determined as ever to strike a good bargain with the French; and in May 1887 Drummond Wolff finally concluded a convention with the Sultan whereby Britain undertook to evacuate Egypt within three years with a right of reoccupation if necessary. This was the magic formula giving the benefits of control without its burdens. The French, prodded by the Russians, succumbed to the temptation to insist on better terms; and both powers compelled the Sultan to refuse the deal. This was a great mistake on the part of the French and landed them in a renewed passion to force the British out of Egypt, which eventually ended only with the Fashoda fiasco of 1898.

Failure to solve the Egyptian problem threw Salisbury back on the Mediterranean relationship with the Triple Alliance. The British position at Constantinople was now very weak, with the Russians cultivating the Turks over both Bulgaria and Egypt. Salisbury's response was to convert the diplomatic and defensive Mediterranean Agreement of March 1887 into a second Agreement of December 1887. Austro-Russian relations deteriorated further, and Vienna had every motive for cooperation with the British. The second Mediterranean Agreement was an alliance between Britain, Austria and Italy for the defence of the Balkans and the Straits against Russia. Again, it was secret: apart from the exigencies of diplomacy, the Liberals would have repudiated an alliance with the heirs of Metternich. In fact it was a more binding diplomatic commitment than the ententes before 1914.

Salisbury assumed a British capacity for naval penetration of the Straits in the terms of his redefinition of the 1841 Straits Convention in 1878: that is, with or without the Sultan's approval. In any case, the heat went out of the Bulgarian crisis. The British admirals, however, had been thinking of new directions in naval policy which contradicted Salisbury's diplomatic arrangements and the assumptions as to British capacity upon which they were based; and this contradiction underlined a major British problem of relating defence policy to diplomacy.

II

Several circumstances in the middle and later 1880s, modest in themselves, together mark the end of the reign of old assumptions as to what was appropriate and feasible in Britain's external relations. The Salisbury government set up in 1885 the Colonial Defence Committee, first established in 1878 but allowed to lapse. This committee collected information and gave advice about defence problems and drew up memoranda on the general principles of defence policy and the political and strategic assumptions on which its advice was based. The committee made a beginning on what was to become the War Book of 1911-14, a detailed set of instructions to cover all contingencies of national emergency. The C.D.C. had no staff for research or planning; but it was the embryo of later defence planning bodies which did. The Colonial Conference of 1887 at the time of the Queen's Golden Jubilee approved its recommendations for closer imperial defence cooperation, though these did not go as far as Salisbury would have liked. Above all the C.D.C. did not succeed in coordinating military and naval plans – a difficulty which was indeed to remain chronic right up to 1914. Its secretary was G. S. Clarke, the first official person to concern himself professionally with the larger questions of defence policy. In 1904 he became the first secretary of the Committee of Imperial Defence set up by Balfour, the mature form of committee defence planning.

Equally indicative of a new professionalism in relation to defence problems were two of the members of the C.D.C.: the Director of Military Intelligence, an office established in 1885, and the Director of Naval Intelligence, established in 1886. In the services there was a growing awareness of the claims of professional expertise and a growing demand for a greater degree of professional participation in decisions about service policy, disposition and financing. The generals and admirals pressed for a more equal balance between the service chiefs and the civilians, rather along continental lines, where it was recognized that politics was far too important a matter to be left to politicians. This theme became of central importance not only in the armed services: the Foreign Office especially increasingly became a battleground between the forces insisting on the expediency of the claims of the professional expert and the forces insisting on the morality of maintaining the 'constitutional' doctrine of the paramountcy of the politicians responsible through parliament to the people. Clearly, in any case, the growing complexity of government and administration in a modern industrial society would inevitably weight the scales in favour of the bureaucrat and against the politician; but it was in those areas of concern –

armed forces and foreign policy – where the social welfare aspect of things was least and where the consequences of decisions were likely to be most risky and painful that the issues of expediency and morality proposed themselves most starkly.

Contingency planning in these sensitive areas of defence policy was opposed on the grounds that it encouraged militarism, unnecessary expenditure, unwarranted distrust of foreign powers and in general tended to provoke the wars it was supposed to deter. The Liberal party with its strong Cobdenite and pacifist contingents was always prone to this view, though it was not confined to Liberals by any means: Salisbury himself was often sceptical of the professional experts, whether in the Foreign Office or the armed services, on the ground that they had a constitutional disposition to overreact to problems and exaggerate dangers and difficulties. Though Salisbury despised democratic 'public opinion' and had nothing but contempt for Liberal politicians who claimed to speak for it, he also – as in 1866 and 1867 when he resisted franchise reform – had a healthy and indeed perhaps excessive respect for its brute power. He insisted on confronting the Russians at the Straits rather than falling back on Alexandria because he needed to be able to evacuate Egypt as the price of a *rapprochement* with the French; but equally he was genuine in his conviction that public opinion would never understand or forgive abandonment of Constantinople, and that the Conservative party would damage itself irreparably if it countenanced such seeming abdication of greatness.

Nevertheless, Salisbury's scepticism did not prevent his being, as he indicated in the 1860s along with Arnold and Morier, a ready patron of the kind of systematic thinking which was the keynote of the new professionalism. The next major impulse in new directions was the Hartington Commission appointed in 1888, on the organization of the Army and Navy, which presented its report in 1890 (Clarke was the secretary). This was the most important inquiry into defence problems before the Elgin Commission after the South African war; and indeed that latter commission might not have been necessary if the Hartington recommendations had been adopted. These were that a centralized defence council should be set up to make possible combined planning for naval and military forces and that the Army be equipped with a proper general staff. This was the first effort to develop a systematic response to problems of national security. It failed because of entrenched conservatism within the service establishments, represented most vividly by the hoary old Duke of Cambridge who deprecated any changes whatsoever, and because of the dissenting opinions of the future Liberal secretary of state for war. Campbell-Bannerman, Cardwell's former financial secretary at the War Office, faithfully reflected the ingrained suspicion of 'militarism' endemic in Liberalism. He objected that if the Army were given a brain it might want to use it in ways not foreseen by the advocates of a general staff. There was general agreement, at all events, in the new formulation of military policy: the British Army should concentrate its energies entirely on imperial defence and regard the contingency of operations on the continent of Europe as being outside the range of practical possibilities.

But it was the naval issue particularly which exposed the new vulnerabilities of the British position. The naval 'scare' of 1884 inaugurated an era of almost permanent public agitation about the state of the navy. There were occasional fever peaks, as in 1888 and 1893, but the condition did not subside until the surrender of the German High Seas fleet in 1918. The scare arose out of allegations of serious shortcomings in the capacity of the Navy to maintain command of the sea in the face of the French and Russian fleets. Britain, especially since the beginning of large-scale grain imports from America and Australia, now depended more than ever on the security of sea-borne trade. By 1886 it was estimated that two-thirds of bread consumed was made from imported grain. In the two decades between 1871 and 1891 importation of foreign food increased by 88 per cent, while domestic production of food remained stationary and population increased over 20 per cent. Figures like these added a new dimension to an old problem. The last era of naval anxiety had been in the 1860s when French construction caused concern. With the eclipse of France after 1870, the issue had lain dormant; now, with the prospect of a Franco-Russian combination, or possibly even a continental *bloc*, it flared up again.

The naval issue, moreover, drew together the main threads of the British problem in its larger sense. First, there was the technological factor. The tempo of technical change was accelerating to the point where ships became quickly obsolescent. An old wooden line-of-battle ship was in its prime for the better part of a century. By 1896 it was calculated that one small gun boat of the latest model could have destroyed with impunity all the warships afloat in 1850. The conditions of British naval supremacy by the 1880s and 90s placed an entirely unprecedented premium on technological expertise, resources and capacities. New designs of engines and boilers, the steam turbine, screw propellers and torpedoes, new calibres of armament, new capabilities of speed and radius of action and consequent problems of fuel capacity, were now decisive factors. Above all was the accelerating rivalry between the technologies of steel plate armour and armour-piercing projectiles.

Secondly, there was the general debate about the wider implications of imperial defence. At one pole were the navalists of the 'blue-water' school, who insisted that the Navy was the only defence, and once the fleet was lost all was lost. In this view no power hostile to Britain need consider an invasion to reduce her: while the fleet existed, invasion was impossible; with the fleet gone, it was unnecessary, since starvation would do the job just as well and much more cheaply. At the other pole were the militarists of the 'bolt from the blue' school, who insisted that the Navy might well be diverted or weakened temporarily to allow an invasion, and that therefore adequate military defence was necessary.

Until about 1884 this latter school had dominated the debate. Then, contemporaneously with the scare of that year, the blue-water challenge grew more formidable. Steam propulsion and the electric telegraph now made it most unlikely that the Navy could be lured away for long enough to permit an invasion. Moreover, a very powerful school of intellectual support for the blue-water thesis emerged. *Imperial Defence* (1891) by Dilke and Spenser Wilkinson was a major example of the *genre*. But the most famous intellectual prop of the blue-water thesis were the two volumes by the American Alfred Thayer Mahan, *The*

Influence of Sea Power on History (1890) and *The Influence of Sea Power on the French Revolution and the Empire* (1892). This linked blue-water navalism with the imperialist historical doctrine of Seeley. Mahan was in this sense the author of the New Testament of the providential destiny of the 'World Venice'. Other, less anglocentric, readings were of course possible. An enthusiastic and convinced disciple of Mahan was the young German Emperor, William II, who dismissed Bismarck in 1890, and saw visions of a modern, twentieth-century Germany as a world power by means of sea power.

The message had more immediate relevance in Britain. Since about the middle 1880s a school of naval thinking had emerged in France – the '*Jeune École*' – which had put various factors together which resolved themselves in a most formidable equation. They learned from the example of the *Alabama* what could be achieved by commerce raiding – *guerre de course*; to this they added the swift cruiser and the vital new development, the torpedo boat (they would soon be experimenting with the idea of a submersible torpedo boat); they calculated that the new problems of refuelling would make the traditional British recourse of close blockade ineffective; and finally they calculated that the French government would countenance, in the event of a war against the British, the ruthless flouting of international law that the *guerre de course* would involve. The aim of the *Jeune École* was not primarily to sweep the British merchant marine completely from the seas and starve the population dependent upon it into submission; the object was to produce an economic panic by stampeding insurance rates and hence cause price increases and social unrest. This added up to a most serious problem for the Admiralty, for which they had no ready answer. The newly established annual naval manoeuvres concentrated on developing counter measures; but to little purpose, and before long consideration was rather despairingly given to schemes for transferring ownership of merchant ships to neutrals.

Meanwhile, battle raged between the War Office and the Admiralty. In 1886 the director of Military Intelligence advised that an enemy could land between 100,000 and 150,000 men without undue risk. In 1888 Wolseley endorsed this publicly. Naval Intelligence repudiated the Army allegations. The Army's best argument was that the Navy could not win a war. But with military intervention on the continent ruled out and the South African war a long time away, the Army argument lacked immediacy. The blue-water argument was dangerously immediate; and the *Jeune École* was the most convincing possible kind of verification of it. After the failure of Salisbury's effort to get out of Egypt a Franco-Russian combination became a distinct reality. The British admirals, asked by Salisbury to undertake to force the Dardanelles, had to consider the chance of committing British resources in the Mediterranean when the French, in 1888, began transferring their most powerful battleships to Toulon and when the *guerre de course* threat was greatest on the oceanic sea routes. Salisbury, who in any case was an old-fashioned brick and mortar advocate, accused the admirals of funk. Their reply was to demand a sufficient increase in naval construction to ensure command of the sea. This was defined as such strength as would ensure a British superiority over the two next greatest naval forces in the world – which, in practice, meant the French and the Russians. This was embodied in policy by the Naval Defence Act of 1889, which laid down a construction programme for five years.

III

The Naval Defence Act of 1889 signalled British determination to defend her interests as a Great Power by entering a naval armaments race. The two-power standard it laid down was reciprocated in 1891, when a Franco-Russian alliance was virtually a fact. Bismarck's fall in 1890 had led to the German repudiation of the Reinsurance Treaty of 1887 with the Russians; and German policy was committed to the popular 'German' alliance with Austria and to cultivating better relations with the British. Cultivating the British took the form of concessions in East Africa, culminating in the 1890 Zanzibar–Heligoland treaty which established Britain as the dominant power in East Africa at German expense – a complete reversal of the 1885 situation. The Germans saw this as the price they would pay for British adherence to a Quadruple Alliance. In May 1891, however, much to the dismay of the Germans, Salisbury refused to join. He much preferred waiting for the French to come round.

Russian tsardom and French republicanism had little enough in common. The Russians would be very unlikely to do what the French most wanted, fight a war with Germany to allow France to get back Alsace-Lorraine; and, for their part, the French had no intention of fighting a war to get the Russians in Constantinople; but for the time being they had a good mutual interest in baiting the British. The Russians tightened the Central Asia screw again in 1891. Accelerated French and Russian naval construction in the 1890s put increasing pressure on the British position in the Mediterranean. In March 1892 Salisbury was advised in a joint Admiralty–War Office memorandum that the Dardanelles could not be forced unless the French Mediterranean fleet was destroyed first. Forced back on to increasing diplomatic dependence on the Triple Alliance and the Mediterranean Agreement, Salisbury was again, as in 1887, being told that Britain lacked the power to make the Agreement a reality. The defence chiefs were arguing as Randolph Churchill had argued: Cairo rather than Constantinople. Salisbury was still unwilling to accept this, even though he had given up hope of getting out of Egypt. He had given the admirals more ships in 1889 precisely to avoid practising a diplomacy of bluff. Again he denounced the admirals and stuck firmly to the resistance at the Straits involved in the Mediterranean Agreement. He hoped that Rosebery would keep the secret policy intact and resist Liberal pressures towards isolation.

When the Liberals came back in 1892 with Gladstone's fourth and last ministry there was no attempt at another assertion of a distinctly Liberal alternative mode of conducting foreign policy, as in 1880. Liberalism indeed never again, whether in 1886, 1892 or 1905, made a serious effort to do what Gladstone had attempted in 1880. Most Liberals continued to assume that one of the vitally important things Liberalism was about was precisely providing Britain with a new and better and moral kind of foreign policy; and the annoyance and complaint that began with Egypt in 1882 mounted in intensity with every Liberal ministry. There was a widespread feeling that the people and their representatives were being cynically and systematically cheated of what was due to them. Gladstone himself had abated none of his convictions of 1880. His conscience was as tender as ever over Egypt. Europe indeed assumed that Salisbury's defeat would mean significant changes, and the French especially waited hopefully for the concessions on Egypt which Salisbury had refused them.

Yet nothing of the kind happened. Gladstone was in any case obsessed with Irish Home Rule. Moreover, Liberal views and hopes about the Russians had gone sour. But more important was the fact that the very existence of the ministry of 1892, kept in power by Irish votes, depended on the adherence of the temperamental Rosebery, who had been foreign secretary in the 1886 interlude. Rosebery could impose his own terms; and those were for 'continuity'. He made Edward Grey, one of his younger disciples, his under-secretary and spokesman in the Commons. Liberal foreign policy for the future was to be a conspiracy against Liberalism. Gladstone was helpless. Home Rule depended on a Liberal government; and the Liberal government depended upon Rosebery, who was notoriously lukewarm towards Home Rule. The price would have to be paid: the Egyptians had been sacrificed in the 1880s on the altar of Europe; they were now to be sacrificed on the altar of Ireland.

Rosebery conducted policy as far as possible – and in the circumstances wisely enough– without consultation with the cabinet or, if it could be managed, with Gladstone. Rosebery was the first imperialist politician in a position to make important initiatives. He announced during the elections of 1892 plainly enough that 'Mr Gladstone's Government and Mr Gladstone's Foreign Secretary . . . will continue Lord Salisbury's foreign policy as far as we at present know it.' The last phrase was important. Rosebery refused to read the text of the Mediterranean Agreement of December 1887 so that he could deny knowledge of it, which he did to Gladstone, who in turn accordingly reassured the French, whose hopes of great things on Gladstone's return were correspondingly whetted. Rosebery was receptive to Salisbury's view that unless Britain helped to stiffen the Triple Alliance the result would be the 'catastrophe' of a return to the

Dreikaiserbund and Russia on the Bosphorus. The Germans were now beginning to regret their precipitate action against Russia in 1890 as the compensating prospect they had in view of a British alliance revealed itself as a mirage. Rosebery differed from Salisbury in his intense hostility to the French, who speedily discovered that their prospect of Gladstonian dividends was equally a mirage. Rosebery in particular was absolutely determined to stay in Egypt come what may.

This infuriated the Radicals as well as the French. The Radicals never forgave Rosebery; and this more than anything else blighted his later career. The French started scheming about ways of winkling the British out of Egypt by getting in at the Sudan back door on the Upper Nile. The British made a treaty with the Congo Free State in May 1894 in a desperate effort to seal off the Nile from the French. The French, however, with German backing, frightened King Leopold off; and by March 1895, the scheme of an expedition to the upper Sudan was under consideration in Paris despite a warning issued by Grey that Britain regarded any French penetration to the Upper Nile as an 'unfriendly act'. Marchand's expedition from the French Congo to Fashoda was a very long fuse, and would take years to burn to flash point. It was rather like the fuses and counter-fuses being laid against one another by Rhodes and Kruger in the obscure cold war being waged between the ideas of an Afrikaner-oriented and a British-oriented southern Africa. It was as clear on the Vaal as it was on the Nile by 1895 that unless there supervened a radical policy of defusing, dangerous explosions would inevitably occur. Fortunately for their sanity, Liberal ministers were spared the task of having to agree on what the British government should do about it all.

Relationships in the Liberal cabinet were in any case already extremely strained. Harcourt and Morley, the chief 'anti-jingoes', protested strongly against Rosebery. Rosebery's determination on Egypt led him logically to insist in 1893-4 on a British protectorate of Uganda in order to seal off the Sudan and the Nile from the Indian Ocean. Threatening resignation, Rosebery ruthlessly forced this bitter pill down the throats of the choking Gladstonians. The greatest crisis was over the naval estimates. The programme as laid down in 1889 came up for reconsideration in 1893; Spencer, the first lord, and the admirals pressed strongly for a further boost in construction to cope with the great expansion of the Russian and French fleets. Public agitation was at a height again, embodied now in the very effective lobby which institutionalized itself in 1895 as the Navy League. Given the decision made in 1889, and its implications, Britain was committed to a two-power standard (by whatever definition) and this meant inescapably that the estimates would have to reflect the logic of the situation. The Gladstonians could not effectively resist the force of this logic in the cabinet struggles of 1894. Gladstone himself was in fact the only member of the cabinet who did. He saw the swollen naval estimates as a contradiction of everything he stood for in politics: they were the estimates of an armaments race, of imperialism, of a Europe in the grip of militarism and power-politics. All this was true; but Gladstone could not convince his colleagues that anything would be achieved by repudiating these evils by a magnificent gesture of moral renunciation. Gladstone took the opportunity, with extreme appropriateness, to resign. The Queen eagerly appointed Rosebery, and Kimberley took his place at the Foreign Office.

The policy of relating Britain advantageously to the Triple Alliance by means of the Mediterranean Agreement was, however, on its last legs. It collapsed eventually under the insupportable strain of two burdens. Firstly, the Germans were becoming desperate as to what to do. Having launched out on a brave new post-Bismarckian course they were now scrambling back to safety. They did their best to head off and then neutralize the Franco-Russian alliance formally concluded in 1894. 'Neutralization' meant encouraging and assisting an interpretation of it in anti-British rather than anti-German terms. This was not difficult, with the British in conflict with the French in Africa and Siam, and with the Russians increasing the pressure in central Asia. On the other hand this was a poor return for all their recent efforts and they made one last bid to cajole and prod and hustle the British into an alliance with Austria as a prelude to a Quadruple Alliance. They pushed too hard, because they misinterpreted a minor and insubstantial British dispute with the

French over Siam in 1893 as revealing a desperate British dependence on the Triple Alliance. Rosebery would have been prepared to fight at the Straits to keep the Russians out, which was the practical point and implication of such an alliance. But the admirals were still insisting that they could not advise a conflict with the Russians without first being assured of French neutrality. For this German support was needed; but the Germans were busily mending their relations with the Russians, which contradicted the point of an alliance with the British from the British point of view. Obviously the Germans would not fight a great war in Poland against the Russians for the benefit of British imperial security. Thus, for the British, alliance with Germany (in this case through Austria) had no point unless directed at Russia. The Germans wanted it directed at France, where the British had no great need of it; they were afraid of the French fleet rather than the French Army; and in any case had no interest in helping to destroy France as a Great Power for the benefit of increased German preponderance. And in the last resort they could always fall back on Alexandria.

The second insupportable burden which finished the relationship with the Triple Alliance was the material circumstance that it was very unlikely that the British could defend the Straits against the Russians, given that the Turks were increasingly anti-British and given that the Franco-Russian alliance was an established fact. Turkish massacres of Christian Armenians in Constantinople and then in Armenia itself in 1894 and 1895 roused another Liberal agitation of moral outrage along the lines of 1876. British efforts to mount a concert against the Turks failed: the 'concert', in curious contrast to the 1875-6 situation, was entirely devoted to the integrity of the Ottoman Empire. For the Russians the Turks were valuable collaborators; and the French followed willy-nilly. The Germans had no motive for crossing the Russians; and in any case were cultivating Turkey as a promising area of German influence and investment. The Austrians followed suit. For the British the Armenian affair underlined the inescapable truth that there was no point in persisting with a policy which postulated the feasibility of defeating a Russian bid for the Straits. Naturally, the Austrians still wanted the British alliance; but they needed German guarantees of support against Russia which the Germans were unwilling as yet to give.

Amid this welter of contradictions Britain in July 1894 became 'isolated'. This was not the same kind of isolation of failure as that of 1885. The Navy was once again powerful and efficient. Egypt was securely held. Movement of events in the Far East raised more problems for Britain: the Japanese victory over the Chinese in 1895 led to the intervention of the 'Armenian Concert' of Russia, Germany and France, who forced the Japanese to disgorge vital gains. Britain had no particular quarrel with Japanese expansion; on the contrary, there was a strong British disposition to look to Japan as an example of highly desirable Asian stability and efficiency as contrasted with the corrupt and moribund Manchu empire. British 'isolation' from the continental intervention against the Japanese was in any case not genuine; for only the Russians had a serious purpose and a serious prospect of advantage. The French were dragged along, rather as with Armenia, as part of the price that had to be paid for the Russian alliance; and the Germans, again as with Armenia, were primarily cultivating the Russians. In any case, since it was essentially a Russian affair, part of their shift of interest to the prospects offered in Manchuria and Korea, it had the effect of relieving Russian pressure in the Straits and Central Asia, and this was of indirect benefit to the British. True, there was now a naval problem for Britain in the Far East, as the Russians, as patrons of the helpless Chinese, snapped up the strategic areas on the Yellow Sea (Port Arthur being the major base) which the Japanese had been forced to disgorge. But, on the other hand, in the Japanese the British had the possibility of a naval counterweight of far greater consequence than the Italian contribution in the Mediterranean. On balance, given that in any case the old advantages of the concert were irretrievably lost, the new situation of isolation from 1894 onwards by no means represented in itself a seriously slipping international position for the British. Rather, it represented the calculation that for the time being the British imperial system was in no serious danger from it.

Chapter Twelve

VICTORIANISM AND MODERNISM: CULTURAL THEMES AND VARIATIONS IN THE 1880s AND 1890s

I

The general crisis of 'Victorianism' was nowhere more clearly marked than in the broader aspect of culture, of literature and the visual arts, of science, religion, of intellectual debate. In the early 1880s a characteristic cultural consciousness definable as Victorian – the word in fact was appropriately coming into common currency – still remained substantially intact and socially in command. By the later 1890s it was neither intact nor in command. In the intervening years a new kind of consciousness had appropriated the cultural initiative, a consciousness characterized by urges to explore new sensibilities and possibilities. These urges, disparate and often contradictory, shared a common claim to confront the truths of contemporary experience, to be more 'serious', more 'real', more 'honest'. The new consciousness came to be called the 'modern movement'.

The expectation central to Victorian consciousness as it matured in the 1850s and 1860s had been that an equilibrium or accommodation of contending forces, of romanticism and evangelicalism, of religion and science, of aristocracy and democracy, of capital and labour, of city and country, of art and nature, would eventually resolve itself into a coherence of true reconciliation and harmony. Victorians of 'system' such as Mill or George Eliot or Herbert Spencer disagreed about means with Victorians of 'sentiment' like Kingsley, Dickens or Ruskin. But they all agreed as to the ends of the essential cultural programme of their time. The Victorian faith was fundamentally in the homogeneity of society and intellect, a synthesis of progressive politics and moral art. The imaginative writer would collaborate with 'the march of mind'. George Eliot's novels were far from being fictional representations of her loyalties to Comtean Positivism. Yet the structure of her novels, their assured reliance on the rational promise of the future, did relate them significantly to a sense of melioristic and positivistic historical development.

Crucial to the sense of crisis in the later nineteenth century was an awareness of the sheer unprecedentedness of the predicament of a civilization confronted with the cultural consequences of fully developed industrialism and urbanization. The city overwhelmed the romantic creed of the centrality of nature to man's moral being and swamped the Victorian hope to reconcile city and country. More than anything else, the word 'modern' came to carry the charge of the novelty and intensity of this predicament. The phenomenon of a civilization of great cities could no longer be evaded as the determinant factor in shaping social consciousness and the cultural expressions of that consciousness in the future.

Herein lay what came increasingly to be interpreted as the most conspicuous failure of Victorianism: its reluctance to admit the end of the romantic vision of nature and its desperate and futile clinging to a pastoral frame of moral reference. Even Dickens, the first major imaginative writer to accept the unavoidable reality of the city, never reconciled himself to it as the primary source of moral energy. By the 1880s nature had lost its social authority. Its role henceforth would be as the main source of moral criticism of the dominant city, especially of the loss of organic human relationships, of the barren impersonality which became identified as the essential evil of mass urban life.

II

For most educated Victorians, entry into this atmosphere of cultural crisis came earliest through the problem of religious belief, especially as related to the development of natural science. This had always been the most vulnerable of the Victorian defences and it was inevitably the point of resistance that collapsed first. The German philosopher Nietzsche announced in 1889 the death of God, on behalf of Western Christian civilization. His point was not the theological falsity of religious belief but its intellectual insolvency in an age in which the sovereign pressures in advanced societies were secular and materialist. Religious profession remained indeed a formal social fact among the respectable classes in Britain until the war of 1914. But the intellectual élite substantially abandoned belief. What had been an agonizing break in the lives of Matthew Arnold, Arthur Clough and Henry Sidgwick became, by the 1880s and 1890s, an unremarkable commonplace. Secularity among the mass of the urban lower orders was not a consequence so much of loss of belief (there had never been a great deal of it to lose) as of a new environment which had never been encompassed by customary institutions of church or chapel. Traditional habits and webs of community relationships of a relatively static pre-industrial way of life dissolved amid the massive scale of population growth and migration from the land to the cities. Religion dwindled as a social presence.

Intellectual renunciation of belief took the heart out of the efforts to reconcile religion and the 'modern world' characteristic of the Victorian generation. By the 1890s Gladstone's stubborn insistence on the compatibility of Genesis with geology and evolution had become a rather grotesque relic of a debate no longer at the centre of intellectual attention. At the same time the grand Victorian systems of establishing new and sure foundations for ethics, such as the Positivist Religion of Humanity or Herbert Spencer's Lamarckian Religion of Evolution, lost much of their relevance. These systems depended upon the authority of natural science to guarantee the solidity of their sociological theories of a necessarily progressive historical development of human affairs. In this way the ethically good could be conveniently equated with the historically inevitable. But the scientists, particularly the neo-Darwinist followers of Charles Darwin's evolutionary theory of natural selection by random accident, steadily cut away at the foundations of faith in a beneficent historical process.

Science here entered the situation decisively. For the late Victorian generation anxiety arose less out of loss of faith in itself (atheist propagandists like Bradlaugh and Holyoake were thoroughly 'Victorian' in consciousness) than out of an entirely new dearth of consolatory secular alternatives. Most important of all, the scientific triumph of neo-Darwinian evolution dealt a decisive blow at all systems of general explanation of man's place in the cosmos which postulated a meaning, a purposeful intelligence guiding the process. Lamarckian evolution, by allowing the inheritance of acquired characteristics and thus the possibility of accumulated evolutionary progress, was the outstanding example of such a consolatory system. To Spencer, the 'survival of the fittest' meant the survival of the ethically best. Many Lamarckians were loath to give up this comforting assurance and concede victory to the Darwinists with their ethically neutral doctrine that the 'survival of the fittest' meant merely the survival of the fittest to survive in a given environment. One of them was the satiric writer Samuel Butler, who, having passed through a particularly painful religious crisis which he related in classic fictional form, *The Way of All Flesh* (published posthumously in 1903), looked desperately for solace elsewhere. Butler attacked the 'dismal creed' of 'mechanistic' mindless neo-Darwinism and insisted on a 'creative impulse', an instinct of cunning within evolution. Butler's battle against the Darwinists was later taken up by the dramatist Bernard Shaw, whose preface to *Man and Superman* (1903) was a manifesto of Lamarckism and eugenic socialism.

The neo-Darwinist scientific tide, however, could not be stemmed. In this way Darwinism was the greatest factor in compromising the faith in the beneficence of science as an agent and guarantor of progress which had been so prevalent in the earlier Victorian era. This dismayed many sensitive people who, unable to retain faith in a supernatural providential order, sought in vain for an equivalent moral centre which would give meaning and hold together a world otherwise dissolving into nonsensical incoherence. The individual, bereft of both social and moral community, was left exposed and isolated in such a world. This sense of psychological bereavement, of morally isolated individualism, became the fundamental characteristic of modern consciousness. The novelist George Gissing exclaimed, in *The Private Papers of Henry Ryecroft* (1903):

Oh, the generous hopes and aspirations of forty years ago! Science, then, was seen as the deliverer; only a few could prophesy its tyranny, could see that it would revive old evils and trample on the promises of its beginning. This is the course of things; we must accept it.

Gissing's fatalistic pessimism was expressed vividly in such novels as *New Grub Street* (1891), which presented a relentlessly Darwinist view of the survival of the fittest in the literary world, where only adaptation to the debased standards of the new semi-educated mass market for 'best-seller' fiction could save a writer from being crushed in the struggle for life. To the novelist and poet Thomas Hardy the horrifying prospect opened up of a universe without mind, malevolent rather than indifferent. In novels such as *Tess of the D'Urbervilles* (1892) his pessimism grated on the nerves of those – the majority of the literary public – who preferred to hope for the best. Hardy was attacked for the gratuitous 'forbiddingness' of his themes, for insisting that the constitution of the world was 'malignantly topsy-turvy', and that the virtuous, the good and the pure were the predestined victims of a 'conspiracy of circumstances'. In the 1890s this 'conspiracy' metaphor was extended to embrace the whole decade, and *fin-de-siècle* was invoked by many writers as a literal and emotional fact. 'Our thoughts turn ever doomwards,' wrote John Davidson, 'Our century totters tombwards.' Literary affectation certainly played a part in the establishment of this sense, and continental writers such as Max Nordau and Nietzsche fed the mood. But the evidence of decline was actually there in the reverses suffered in the South African war, in the death of those public figures who represented the distinctly 'Victorian' achievement, in the very rapidity of material change.

An extreme sensibility of total despair manifested itself in certain cases of artists and writers. The '*poète maudit*' had always been a feature of the more pathological aspect of romanticism. But by the later nineteenth century a morbid condition called by the French *nostalgie de la boue*, a craving for the gutter, for debasement, a deliberate adoption of the role of outcast, a kind of living damnation of narcotics and alcohol, often ending in suicide, became recognized as a characteristic expression of the times. The poet James Thomson, in his *City of Dreadful Night*

(1874), pictured a world of 'all alike crushed under the iron yoke of fate.' He died of alcoholism and narcotics in 1882. Simeon Solomon the painter and the poets Francis Thompson and Ernest Dowson were others who renounced the world of cities and secularity in lives of conspicuous degradation. The poet John Davidson, one of the first to express an authentically urban, impersonal sensibility in his ironically entitled *Fleet Street Eclogues* (1894 and 1896), could find 'nothing at the root of life', which made it an 'inexorable irony'. He ended his life by suicide.

The Darwinists had but little consolation to offer. The social Darwinists in particular, such as Karl Pearson and Benjamin Kidd, offered instead a horrific prospect of the remorseless struggle for existence between nations and races, in which survival would be accorded to superior societies efficiently organized to use, in Pearson's words, 'hecatombs of inferior races' as stepping stones to a 'higher intellectual and emotional life'.

The spokesman of the official Darwinist school, T. H. Huxley, offered what he could in the way of consolation in the famous Romanes lecture at Oxford in 1893, 'Evolution and Ethics'. He argued that all attempts along the line of Herbert Spencer to relate by analogy the cosmic process of evolution to ethical progress were scientifically incorrect and socially illusory and hence dangerous. The beginning of wisdom was to recognize and accept the essential antagonism of the two, and to realize that ethical advance could only be achieved by resistance to the cosmic process of the survival of the fittest to survive. Huxley offered a modest, rational optimism dependent upon striving to wrest good out of evil: 'the ethical progress of society depends, not on imitating the cosmic process, still less in running away from it, but in combating it'.

> But if we may permit ourselves a larger hope of abatement of the essential evil of the world . . . I deem it an essential condition of the realization of that hope that we should cast aside the notion that the escape from pain and horror is the proper object of life.

Huxley's stoic philosophy, reminiscent of a stark Calvinism, thus provided no easy 'uplift'. Like the parallel 'death of God' consciousness, it threw mankind entirely back upon its own resources. Secularization combined with urbanization. Man had no hope of redemption from either nature or God. The modern intellectual movement was essentially an exploration of the implications of this challenging circumstance.

One further basic social development contributed crucially to shaping the conditions of cultural consciousness in the later nineteenth century. This was the disintegration of the relatively coherent literary and intellectual community of the mid-Victorian era. Compulsory elementary education, the growth of a mass reading public and of a publishing industry geared to cater for its tastes, led to an ever-widening gap between a small, sophisticated 'high-brow' intellectual public and a mass 'low-brow' market for cheap literature dominated by a lower-middle-class or suburban scale of values. A mass, unsophisticated taste inevitably demanded easily assimilable sentiment, romance, naïve realism, melodrama and painless moral uplift: 'fiction false to life and false to art'.

The question of falsification of values was at the very heart of the crisis of late Victorian culture. To some social critics, such as William Morris, there was no possibility of there being any other than false values in a society where the mass of men were deprived of a creative relationship between self and environment by being condemned to live in crowded cities and tend machinery in factories. To most, however, falsification of values was inevitable in any kind of mass society, since true values could be the product only of individual consciousness and moral discrimination. Given, in any case, that an industrial society more or less as it existed was historically inescapable in the foreseeable future, what oppressed contemporary observers who regarded the health of literature as the best diagnostic of the general health of society was the collapse of the cultural homogeneity inherited from the Victorian era which in effect had reached down to cultivate the steadily growing literary public. Dickens, Macaulay, Thackeray, George Eliot, Trollope, Mill, Arnold, Tennyson, Bagehot, Meredith, had, more or less, written for the whole of the educated public. Critical complaint, levelled especially at Dickens, had been that there was rather too much condescension to popular demand in the way of sentiment. Still, the actively attractive literary forces were by and large the 'best' as opposed to the 'mediocre' literary forces; and Mill could die fairly well assured that popular education would reinforce this promising situation.

By the 1880s and 1890s, however, it was clear that the capillary attraction of the higher literature was being overcome by the pressures created by the vast new publishing industry catering for a mass reading public. The pull was now the other way: as the 'educated classes' (in some sense beyond mere literacy) grew quickly to be a much larger segment of the community, so the commanding influence of the 'best' as against the 'mediocre' dissolved. It was now possible, entrepreneurially, to offer the public a wide variety of choices; and, as in the case of journalism, there was a great new public willing, if offered, to choose the literary equivalents of the *Daily Mail*.

Thus the ascendancy of the old literary order crumbled in much the same way and for much the same reasons as the ascendancy of the old political order. This had its paradoxical aspect: many of the great high-Victorians – Dickens, Mill, George Eliot – were radical critics of the contemporary political scene. They had assumed that good literature, like everything else good, would benefit by the passing of the aristocratic dispensation of Church and State. Their inheritors of the 'modern' era shared this general radical assumption as to the badness of the old political order yet could find no comfort in the conditions of the new. Hence a sense of frustration, of political disassociation common among the leaders of the modern movement from the 1880s on, who tended increasingly to combine technical radicalism and innovation with social and political conservatism. The earlier conservatism of Matthew Arnold was in fact an attempt, by recognizing and accepting the interdependent relationship of culture, society and politics, to stave off the fragmentation of the Victorian world and to preserve the hegemonic role of literary intelligence as the cultural expression of the hopes for a hegemonic political role for the enlightened barbarians and the sweetened philistines.

The elements of the Victorian consciousness were thus debased, and critical denunciations of Victorianism grew accordingly sharper. The modern consciousness, concerned to insist on the lofty 'seriousness' of art's purposes and the need for formalistic structure and technical innovation, was fully attuned to an élitist social stance. The idea of resistance to the pressures of a mass or 'bourgeois' reading public became in itself one of the primary tenets of the new consciousness.

Much of the advocacy of the 'modern' was inspired by the anti-bourgeois ideology of French and continental cultural radicalism. The Irish writer George Moore, a disciple of Manet, Degas and the 'impressionist school' of artists in Paris, returned to London as a proselytizer of distinctly French doctrine about the artist as the teller of truth about experience. The novelist Henry James likewise pressed his claims for a new, enhanced status for the novel on the grounds of the achievement in France, led by Flaubert, of the novel as a tightly organized work of art. Both Gissing and Bernard Shaw spoke of literature in England in the later nineteenth century as having got beyond the 'Dickens–Macaulay' and the 'Meredith' stages and being confronted with the salutary 'philosophic fiction' of the Norwegian dramatist Henrik Ibsen and the Russian novelist Leo Tolstoy.

III

Victorians thus at the same time saw the foundations of their cultural accomplishment crumble and a movement of dissidence and subversion arise against it. Those who saw themselves as defenders of the Victorian synthesis of society, morality, art and nature displayed appropriate symptoms of anxiety or defiance. Tennyson's attacks on the 'realists' and 'Zolaism' carried immense weight and helped to create the climate of moral disapproval in which the 'aesthete' and writer of scintillating comedies of society, Oscar Wilde, was convicted of homosexual practices in 1895. Hardy, weary of abuse at the 'immorality' of his novels, withdrew to devote himself from 1895 entirely to poetry. Robert Louis Stevenson was diverted by the pressures of conservative friends from disturbing 'psychology' into wholesome adventure. There was no lack of evidence of a sturdy core who maintained the Victorian faith. The poet Robert Browning remained resolutely cheerful, 'brutally scornful of all exquisite morbidness'. The novelist and poet George Meredith retained intact his faith in nature the redeemer, 'faith that grows in the open air', and his confidence in the beneficent meaningfulness of 'Earth's design'.

Undoubtedly the best example of culturally confident Victorianism was the Royal Academy, the citadel of socially approved and financially well-rewarded painters, sculptors and architects. In the 1880s and 1890s it was at the height of its prestige, adorned by the senatorial figures of Lord Leighton, Sir John Millais, Sir Edward Poynter, Sir Lawrence Alma-Tadema. It had successfully contained the pre-Raphaelite revolt of the 1850s and the hostility of the representatives of the pre-Raphaelite tradition in the later era, D. G. Rossetti, Holman Hunt, Edward Burne-Jones, Ford Madox Brown and William Morris, who settled into the role of an official but not dangerous opposition. The efforts of Ruskin's antagonist James McNeill Whistler to strike a blow at established 'official' art, whether academic or pre-Raphaelite, in the manner of the much more succesful artistic radicals in France had only a limited success. In 1886 Whistler set up the Society of British Artists to challenge the artistic establishment; but this foundered in 1888 when, as he put it, 'the artists went out and the British remained'. The more radical influence of French impressionism led its few English exponents, Walter Sickert, Wilson Steer and Frederick Brown, to found in 1886 the New English Art Club. The London Impressionists held their first show in 1889, which led to Sickert's having to defend their artistic principles against attacks from both the Academy and the counter-academicism of William Morris. A distinctly modern sensibility in the visual arts in Britain developed slowly and confusedly. Even in 1910 the first show of Post-Impressionist artists, organized by Roger Fry, and including paintings by Van Gogh, Gauguin, Manet and Matisse, caused an outcry, and was publicly rejected by many of those very men, such as George Moore, who had campaigned for the 'new' in the 1890s.

A significant reflection of this slowness was the very late emergence in London of a dissident cultural life-style, a 'Bohemia'. Not until the 1890s did a self-consciously *avant-garde* movement develop, with a stock-in-trade virtually imported entire from Paris by the American Whistler, the Irishman George Moore,

Sickert and other aesthetic adventurers. A new generation of dandies inspired by Whistler, Oscar Wilde and the Irish poet William Butler Yeats made the Café Royal and Chelsea and the Rhymers' Club at the Cheshire Cheese into a faintly imitative Montmartre and Montparnasse. There was, on the whole, little sense of conviction as to the seriously subversive capacities, at least in the short term, of the cultural dissidence of the 1890s. Victorianism, it would be generally true to say, was not pushed; it fell. One of the few major figures of the high-Victorian generation who might have developed into something flamboyant along the lines of Baudelaire or Verlaine or Rimbaud, the poet and republican Algernon Charles Swinburne, instead was rescued from this fate in 1879 by his solicitor friend Watts Dunton and immured out of harm's way in No. 2 The Pines, Putney.

The weakness of élitist Bohemia was reflected in the strength of bourgeois suburbia. The confidence of the best-seller market was never shaken. This more than anything else preserved into the twentieth century an appearance of cultural stability which seemed to the post-1914 generations the mark of a lost, golden age. This vast audience demanded above all else to be reassured rather than disturbed. The Victorian ideal of a collaborative relationship between society and art was pressed into this service. It was, in any case, demanding a tremendous amount of Victorians to accept that art should be legitimately a subversive force. To most Victorians, the problems and anxieties of the times seemed to call for more, not less, collaboration. This remained consistently the cultural programme of Liberalism. It was widely assumed among Liberals that a restoration of Liberalism's legitimate political ascendancy would result in a new wholesome integration of art and the march of mind. Thus the politician Charles Masterman called the artists to their duty in *The Condition of England* (1909). Socialism likewise shared this assumption; in an era of imperialism and Toryism, culture would tend towards decadence and pessimism. The strength of melioristic politics would always resist the modernist impulse; and modernism, in turn, tended to feel ill at ease with any melioristic theory of politics and history.

The novelist Hall Caine, a typical exponent of the best-seller genre, took as his model George Eliot's meliorative historicism;

this he larded heavily with melodrama and uplifting religiosity. Another major romantic best-seller, Marie Corelli (*née* Mary Mackay) modelled herself in turn, more faithfully, on Caine, and specialized in reconciling religion and science. At a rather more socially poised level, Mrs Humphry Ward's influential novel *Robert Elsmere* (1888) was a testimony to a wide public demand to be told that a new, purer religion founded on a true understanding of the teachings of Jesus of Nazareth would arise, free from the trammels of orthodox doctrine and ecclesiasticism. Her inspiration was the social evangelism of T. H. Green, to whose memory the book was dedicated. She insisted that science had the power 'of making the visible world fairer and more desirable in mortal eyes'; that one could be assured of the 'unvarying and rational order of the world . . . There is no wanton waste in the moral world, any more than in the material. There is only fruitful change and beneficent transformation.'

Yet for all such evidences of Victorian tenacity, its grip on the levers of directive cultural authority manifestly slackened through the 1890s. The great luminaries of the Victorian constellation were fading out. Dickens, George Eliot, Carlyle, Darwin, Disraeli, Trollope, Newman, Arnold, Maine, Browning, John Bright, were dead by 1890. Tennyson, Huxley, Leighton, Fitzjames Stephen, Millais, Manning, Gladstone, Ruskin, were dead by 1900.

The historians provide an illuminating instance of withdrawal from exposed Victorian positions. More than any other academic group of the high Victorian age, as classics declined in prestige and before English literature had become an established rival, the historians felt entire confidence in their capacity and indeed duty to offer the guidance to the public at large which their historical expertise assumably entitled them to give. Macaulay and Carlyle set the tone and prepared the way. But with the deaths of J. R. Green (1882), Freeman (1892), Froude (1894), Seeley (1895), and Stubbs's promotion to a bishopric the heart went out of this confidence. The new men, such as S. R. Gardiner, renounced the grand expansiveness as well as the 'Whig' crudities of the older generation. Acton and Lecky maintained something of the old grandeur; but the renunciation of the Regius Chair at Cambridge on Acton's death in 1902 by the most brilliant of the younger generation, F. W. Maitland, was a symbolic act. Maitland, an exponent pre-eminently of technical scholarship, resented the 'expectation' that he would speak to the 'world at large'.

The case of John Ruskin, one of the very pillars of the Victorian temple, exposed the fundamental weaknesses of Victorianism at odds with itself in an especially revealing way. Ruskin had preached persuasively to his generation the gospel of a 'true' or 'natural' architecture which would emerge out of the chaos of contending 'styles' and establish itself as the authentic expression of a new, organic society. Ruskin deplored the artificial 'revivalisms' in architecture of his time. Because of his particular dislike of the neo-classical style he has usually and mistakenly been thought of as a champion of the Gothic revival. In fact Ruskin did not advocate a revival of Gothic. He advocated the rediscovery of the basic principles of truth and beauty upon which, in his interpretation, Gothic architecture had been founded. He interpreted Gothic as approaching nearest to the desired harmonious relationship between the art of building and the principles of truth and nature. He wanted his own age to emulate the medieval era by means of a wholly fresh approach to architecture.

In the 1870s Ruskin grew increasingly disillusioned with the state of architecture. The scholarly neo-Gothic of immensely successful practitioners like Gilbert Scott (Albert Memorial, St Pancras Hotel) or G. E. Street (Law Courts, Strand) was too restrictedly revivalist. The more powerful and idiosyncratic designs of William Butterfield (All Saints, Margaret Street and Keble College, Oxford) he found indigestible. The equally powerful but much more aggressively coarse designs of Alfred Waterhouse (Manchester Town Hall, Natural History Museum, Kensington) fitly represented the High Victorian 'rogue Goth' architect completely out of the control of any restraining principles of taste. By the later 1870s Ruskin withdrew into a dismayed melancholy.

The generation which had looked to Ruskin for guidance felt betrayed. Architecture came under a heavy cloud of public and official dissatisfaction in the 1870s. A distinct sense of 'failure' was already well established, and would be fully confirmed during the next two decades.[1] The true, underlying laws, the 'ungraspable abstraction behind style', had indeed not been grasped.

In an atmosphere heavy with disappointment the next generation of architects developed, less ambitious, more exploratory, more sensitive, with a greater emphasis on domestic scale and feeling. The major figure of this 'new eclecticism' was Norman Shaw (Bedford Park Estate, Bryanston, Dorset). Architecture in Britain thus relieved itself of its heavy Ruskinian moral burden, but it had yet to equip itself with a post-Ruskinian equivalent guiding principle. For the 'modern movement' in design this became eventually 'functionalism', the replacement of a concern for style by the demands of relevance. The beginnings of this new or 'modern' trend can be traced in Britain from the generation following on from Shaw: C. F. A. Voysey, William Lethaby and Edwin Lutyens, who followed mainly an aesthetic of craftsmanship inspired by the 'arts and crafts' movement of William Morris. They looked back to the Red House designed for Morris by Philip Webb in 1859 as the key building of the nineteenth century, whose significance had been overlooked in the welter of High Victorian monumental gothicry.

Architectural 'modernism' proper, with a growing confidence in doctrinal functionalism beyond the domestic sphere, assured of its capability to discover original forms adequate to an unprecedented social and cultural situation, manifested itself in Britain most unequivocally in the work of C. Rennie Mackintosh (Glasgow School of Art, 1898–9).

The process was halting and painful, with many dead ends (as the hostile critics, especially of Lutyens, assert). In thus passing through a phase of doubt and crisis into a resolution of the 'modern', architecture was in many ways a pattern of a trend common to all forms of intellectual sensibility in the later nineteenth century.

IV

Seven major modes of modern consciousness can usefully be distinguished as they emerge from the disintegration of the Victorian synthesis. The first to flourish and the first to fade was aestheticism, the 'art for art's sake' movement, which sought to fill the moral void through the only certain reality remaining in the world, the beauty of created art. A 'back to nature' urge attempted to preserve, usually in isolation from the mass of unregenerate industrial society, some sense of human community as the only possible foundation of moral health. An impulse to irrationalism and myth attempted to get back beyond the burden of rationalism and materialism with which mankind had been loading itself and rediscover the true springs of the human psyche, the mythic spirituality of the primitive subconscious. Another impulse was to fill the moral void with action and work, to hold disintegration at bay with an heroic assertion of will. Practitioners of 'realism' or 'naturalistic fiction' inspired by French models such as Emile Zola attempted, by confronting the full tragedy of human experience without flinching, to retrieve thereby a moral sustenance for human existence.

These modes manifested themselves largely before the turn of the century. They represented modernism in a perspective of being opposed to Victorianism. Two later modes emerged in the early years of the new century, though owing much to the earlier phase. One, more or less loosely associated with 'Bloomsbury', expressed centrally an aesthetic of personal relationships, a marriage of the moral truth of art with the 'holiness of the heart's affections'. The other was an extremely ambitious effort to establish an entirely new foundation for human sensibility by radically recasting the nature of language and visual images, to make possible a fresh world of perception and moral renewal by freeing consciousness from outworn and exhausted linguistic and visual traditions of apprehending reality. A more radical experimentalism in one form or another was the decisive mark of this latter phase. This fact shifted the basis of interpretation to a perspective in which Victorianism had ceased to be a plausible enemy. By 1918, in fact, Lytton Strachey's *Eminent Victorians* showed that the heroes of the Victorian era could be mocked as grotesque frauds.

Aestheticism emerged in the early 1880s. It took its 'art for art's sake' motto from Gautier and the Parisian Bohemia. Its philosopher and prophet was Walter Pater, whose gospel was the redemption of the individual, lost in a world of disintegrating creeds and exploded fallacies of progress and certitude, through sensory perception of art and beauty. Art should no longer serve morality in the Ruskinian manner; it should be itself the foundation of morality, since the only graspable truth resided in beauty. The only basis for true knowledge was the sensations evoked by contemplation of the beautiful. This doctrine had a great vogue through the 1880s and 1890s. Whistler and Wilde were prominent exponents of the cult. The idea of the artist's total freedom from the moral restraints of bourgeois philistinism had an obvious appeal. A major text of the aesthetic sensibility was the French 'decadent' Huysmans' *À Rebours*, a monument of pathological romanticism. The scandal-provoking decadent aspect of aestheticism led eventually to the abrupt ending of its vogue in 1895 with Oscar Wilde's conviction and imprisonment. Aestheticism however left legacies of permanent value in the sinuous lines of 'art nouveau' and the art of Whistler and Aubrey Beardsley and the writing of Pater and Wilde. It was important also because it offered an aesthetic of the city, a celebration of the formed and the artificial. Its greatest legacy was its assertion of the artist's moral autonomy, which has since remained a permanent ingredient of modern consciousness.

The urge 'back to nature' testified to an abiding human yearning, extending back, in the Western tradition, to the arcadian myth of the Greeks and Virgil, and recurring at this point with a particularly new intensity. Most of its manifestations were of small communities seeking refuge from an unacceptable world, withdrawing into an agrarian identity with the earth and the rhythm of the seasons. A noted exponent of this mood was the Derbyshire prophet Edward Carpenter (author in 1889 of *Civilization, Its Cause and Cure*) who influenced the young D. H. Lawrence and E. M. Forster. The movement had some affinities with the contemporary garden suburb ideas of Ebenezer Howard and with the land colony schemes run by such organizations as the Salvation Army. It had links with the revival of 'folk' idealism generally, owing much to similar symptoms in Germany with their doctrines of desirable *Gemeinschaft* co-operative communities and undesirable competitive and impersonal *Gesellschaft* ways of life. 'Folkism' was particularly important in England for the revival of a nationalist school of music, led by Parry, Stanford and Elgar and the younger generation of Holst and Vaughan Williams.

Samuel Butler was a keen advocate of village communities, as was W. B. Yeats, who hoped that an Irish cultural renaissance could be founded on preserving Ireland from the contamination of Anglo-Saxon urbanism and materialism.

Most radical of the prophets of a return to nature was William Morris, Ruskin's principal successor as the extoller of the moral virtues of medievalism. Morris advocated a wholesale destruction of cities, retaining only those aspects of technology which saved monotonous and burdensome human effort, and resettling society throughout a huge garden. This was the message of his utopian fantasy *News from Nowhere* (1891). Morris's response to Ruskin's melancholy retreat into insanity was to be converted to Marxist communism and to work for a violent revolution to overthrow bourgeois society and thus allow mankind to get back to nature. Morris's most important practical legacy was the Arts and Crafts movement, of which he was the main inspiration, founded in 1887.

Manifestations of anti-rationalism, mysticism, explorations of myth and its regenerative powers for mankind abounded in the 1880s and 1890s, with many interweavings with both aestheticism and 'back to nature'. One relatively simple aspect of it was a return to dogmatic Christian belief, abjuring anything in the way of rational aids or supports. Roman Catholicism especially enjoyed a vogue with many intellectuals who yearned for a rock of certainty. Huysmans himself ended his days in an abbey; and Wilde, Beardsley and the poet Lionel Johnson were converts. More complex were the various searches for the source of instinctual knowledge and its healing powers. Yeats was attracted by Madame Blavatsky's 'theosophical' mediations of Tibetan Buddhism, and sought for the origins of human creativity in myth, the 'Great Memory' of mankind. Sir James Frazer's *The Golden Bough* (1890), a monument of Victorian evolutionary anthropology, was ironically a major source of materials for such quests.

The literary movement of symbolism with its emphasis on a pre-logical order of language, with gaining the effects of the primitive energy of words used outside the positivist or rationalist discourse of science, had important affinities with this general trend. The imagism of the later era of Ezra Pound and T. S.

Eliot would attempt to give symbolism a harder cutting edge, a more energetic intensity, but it tapped essentially the same sources of linguistic primitivism.

There were remote philosophical currents which contributed something to the irrationalist impulse. The American pragmatist William James asserted the primacy of will and temperament over the intellect. The French philosopher Henri Bergson's criticism of positivistic and scientific conceptions of time had certain similarities to symbolist theories of language. Both William James and Bergson were influential in introducing the concept which in fiction came to be called the 'stream of consciousness' technique, presenting the inner workings of a mind as they truly are, not in a false schematic order.

The creed of action and work had in turn obvious affinities with the irrationalist mode of modern consciousness. But it was fundamentally less hopeful in the sense that it could draw no redeeming moral salvation from instinctual human resources lying in a general subconscious memory. For this reason it was the one mode of modernist response most likely to seek aid by attempting some kind of relationship with contemporary politics, though not with any rationalist or meliorist versions of it. The intellectual, in this view, is at one with the engineer, the soldier, the administrator, the creative statesman, the seafarer, imposing an order created out of moral consciousness upon a primordial and eternal chaos. The atmosphere often tended to be a rather desperate awareness of the ultimate futility as well as the inexorable duty of action. The theme of man dutifully pitting his will against an inimical world was developed with rather windy gusto by W. E. Henley and with more enduring effect by the Polish ex-sea captain Joseph Conrad.

The exponent most characteristic of this mode of modern sensibility was Rudyard Kipling. Kipling's identification with the political cause of imperialism was appropriate enough: it too was a desperate effort to impose will against an inimical world. Kipling's political commitment distinguished him as the one considerable literary figure within the broad category of modern consciousness who used a deliberate attempt to bridge the gap that had opened between high culture and the mass of society as a central motive of his art. He emulated Dickens in his range between the salon and the music-hall. He tried to be popular in the old Victorian way without compromising the integrity of the new post-Victorian purposes. Kipling followed the irrationalists in his denial of the established Victorian conventions about the 'rights' of the individual *versus* society. Society did not function through the laws of melioristic Liberal or Socialist social science; it functioned through custom, convention, religion, law, duties, in-groups codes of behaviour of pack and clan and the sanctions of discipline and leadership derived from them. Kipling's social theory thus approximated somewhat to the contemporary development in Europe of the 'functionalist' sociologists Durkheim, Weber and Pareto, who repudiated the evolutionary positivism of both Herbert Spencer and Karl Marx.

George Moore, the first English disciple of Emile Zola's naturalistic theory of fiction, wrote of 'the idea of a new art based upon science, in opposition to the art of the old world that was based upon imagination, the art that should explain all things and embrace the modern world in its entirety'. 'Realism' in this sense meant largely a minute, objective accuracy of social documentation of areas of life hitherto debarred from polite literature. Moore's early novels, especially *A Mummer's Wife* (1885) and *Esther Waters* (1894), established the genre. The other major practitioner was Gissing (*Demos*, 1886, and *The Nether World*, 1889, as well as *New Grub Street*). Hardy had a certain relationship with this school, at least in the eyes of the public, because of his reputation for 'realism'; though to the purist there was in Hardy too little 'science' and too much 'metaphysical grievance'. Like aestheticism, naturalism had a short life as a movement but a long life as an influence, particularly in breaking down Victorian barriers of respectability as represented especially by the circulating libraries and setting new standards of honest reporting of the human condition.

V

When Victorianism faded away at the turn of the century and the sense of a new era diffused itself in the cultural climate, those modes of modernism which defined themselves against it shifted their bearings. As the mood of modern sensibility turned in a more innovative and experimental direction, the essential cultural demarcation tended to become one of 'innovation' *versus* 'realism'. 'Realism' in a general way had always been the most effective thrust of modern sensibility against Victorianism. But in the post-Victorian era it became the defining characteristic of those writers like Shaw, H. G. Wells, John Galsworthy and Arnold Bennett, who, in sharing loyalties with a melioristic and rationalist – often socialist – view of politics and history, shared also one of the basic defining characteristics of the Victorian sensibility. The moderns of the new generation, whether of the E. M. Forster, D. H. Lawrence, Virginia Woolf and Roger Fry grouping, or of the James Joyce, T. S. Eliot, Ezra Pound and Wyndham Lewis grouping, ceded the grounds of 'realism' to the new school of meliorists and devoted their energies essentially to formal or linguistic or (in the case of Lawrence) apocalyptic concerns. Of these moderns E. M. Forster always remained on the wing closest to the meliorists; and indeed it could be argued that *Howard's End* (1910) was as good a response as could reasonably be expected to Masterman's call in *The Condition of England* for a rally of literature to the cause of political progress. But Forster, true to his culture and calling, could never raise more than two cheers for democracy.

Some veterans of the old conflict against Victorianism suffered great hurt from the new dispensation. Kipling, left at a loss by the failure of imperialism, was struck a heavy blow by the Liberal triumph in 1906. He had nothing left to say until 1914. Others benefited greatly: W. B. Yeats and especially Henry James, whose realism was always of a very distanced kind. James had struggled to take the novel from where George Eliot had left it, disestablish the 'march of mind', abolish traditional conceptions of 'plot' and 'character', accord it the higher status of a morally self-generating, autonomous work of formal art, responsible only for the authentic realization of its inner aesthetic purposes. At last, after a long period of failure, James came into his inheritance.

PART IV

The Search for Adequate Responses: The Unionist Version
1895—1902

Chapter Thirteen

THE
UNIONIST
DOMESTIC BID
1895–1902

I

Salisbury took over the Foreign Office once more as well as the premiership. Balfour became first lord of the Treasury and leader of the House of Commons. The Liberal Unionists were offered four cabinet places. Devonshire, their nominal chief, took the honorific post of lord president. Chamberlain might have had the War Office or the Exchequer if he desired. Both posts had attractions to one so distinctly committed to the idea of recruitment of British power and resources. Instead, to everyone's surprise, he chose to take the Colonial Office, hitherto a post of secondary consideration. Although development of the empire and imperial unity had become central features of Chamberlain's politics, the Colonial Office, paradoxically, was not necessarily the best political point of vantage and leverage for securing imperial ends. It was a good platform for publicity and propaganda, but ultimately the fate of any real prospect of imperial constructiveness would depend upon influence at the centre of the Whitehall machine rather than the peripheries. Chamberlain in effect made himself a hostage to Unionist fortunes. He who was supposedly a great source of strength to Unionism came in fact to depend on Unionism's increasingly dubious strength to underwrite his ambitions. Loyalty – of a kind and to a degree – he could depend upon from Salisbury or Balfour; but among the rank and file of Conservatism there was considerable distrust of Chamberlain's motives and a great deal of resentment at what was felt to be undue deference to the claims for offices and jobs for the followers of the 'First Gentleman of Birmingham.'

The central theme of the Unionist bid to provide new modes of political operation adequate to the challenges of the time is the element of fundamental contradiction integral to it which led eventually to hopeless impasse by 1905. Salisbury had already made the point sufficiently clear in his warning remarks to Milner: the Conservative party was at once the great national party, the only party the imperialist school could hope to work with to serious constructive effect; yet at the same time it was the party of the reactionary, the timid, the cautious, the unimaginative. Important new political departures clearly would be necessary if the Unionist bid were to succeed. Yet many voters voted Unionist in 1895 precisely in the hope and expectation of a quiet political life, of an end to Gladstonian adventures and 'socialism'.

Because he was the greatest imperialist and the greatest constructivist, Chamberlain was bound to suffer most grievously from these inherent limitations. For a long while the sheer spectacle of his energy and exuberance, and the enormous quantity of his achievements at the secondary level of policy – administration, communications, developmental works – obscured the emptiness of his results at the primary level. Chamberlain commenced his tenure at the Colonial Office with a grand scheme to reverse the trend of the pattern of British world trade and to channel it from a foreign to an imperial emphasis. Between 1883 and 1892 British exports to foreign countries increased from £215 million to £291 million; British exports to the Empire decreased from £90 million to £81 million. Britain in 1883 imported goods to the value of £328 million from foreign countries; this rose by 1892 to £423 million. Imports from the Empire decreased in the same period from £98 million to £97 million. By 1902 Britain imported £421 million of goods from foreign countries as against £107 million from the Empire; and by 1901 foreign imports into the self-governing colonies were worth nearly £50 million. These figures were profoundly disturbing to one as convinced as Chamberlain was by 1902 that Britain needed to draw together with the Empire to defend her vulnerable position in an unfriendly world of efficient competitors. 'The days are for great Empires,' he warned, 'and not for little States.'

Unionism's basic strength while it lasted lay in the extent of its capacity to act or propose action in ways impossible or very difficult for Liberalism. It could wage war, conclude alliances, revolutionize defence and education policy, propose that fiscal policy should be founded on expediency rather than principle.

Moreover, Ireland, which had been such a burden to Salisbury's last ministry in the days of the Plan of Campaign and expectations of a Liberal return to power, was now relatively quiescent. Even though the Parnellite and anti-Parnellite factions of the National party were reconciled in 1900, with John Redmond as the new leader, bitter memories remained and Nationalism never again quite recaptured the élan of earlier times. The Liberal collapse removed Home Rule from the category of politically plausible issues. The land question also was largely exhausted as a first-class political cause. Rather, the lead in these years was given by Horace Plunkett's agricultural co-operative movement, fostered by the Irish Agricultural Organization Society founded in 1894. A Conservative M.P. for Dublin County South, Plunkett was a successful mediator between Irish needs and the Unionist government, from whom he got a Department of Agriculture and Industries for Ireland and a Local Government Act in 1898. With the passing of the Parnell era, the vital energies of Irish nationalism tended in the direction of cultural renaissance and search for new approaches.

One of these was Sinn Fein ('Ourselves Alone'), founded by Arthur Griffith in 1905. Griffith advocated a policy of deliberate subversion and physical force and rejection of the parliamentary methods of the Nationalist party. But it would take time and special circumstances for Sinn Fein to make a significant impact on the Irish scene. Douglas Hyde's leadership of the Gaelic League, devoted to the revival of the Irish culture and language without any overt political aim, was a more immediately important aspect of this period of renewal. In the plotting of new national bearings the most important political event in Ireland in the later 90s was the fêting of W. B. Yeats in Dublin in 1898 at the production of his play *The Countess Kathleen*, inaugurating the Irish drama revival. With *Cathleen ni Houlihan* in 1902 Yeats's theatre became a shrine of Irish nationalism. While English politicians, and especially Unionist politicians, could convince themselves that Home Rule had indeed been killed by

293

kindness, Wyndham's Irish Land Purchase Act of 1903 completed the edifice of State aid to tenants buying out landlords inaugurated by the Ashbourne Act of 1885.

Yet events were to expose the crippling limitations of the possibilities for Unionism. Electoral success in 1895 with a Conservative majority independent of the Liberal Unionists led to complacency. It was far too easily assumed that the bankruptcy of the 1880s had been fully and permanently redeemed. This was encouraged further by the disintegration of the Liberal leadership. Rosebery renounced his crown of thorns in 1896 and held himself aloof from the vulgar party fray as the great imperialist statesman awaiting the call to assume national leadership. Harcourt in turn resigned the leadership in the Commons in 1898, disgusted by the prevalent jingoism of the times. John Morley also retired from the fray and devoted himself to the great biography of Gladstone which was to be a reassertion of fundamental Liberal values in an era of faithlessness and renegadism. The most likely contender for the Liberal leadership in the Commons, Asquith, was as yet too junior, and besides, needed freedom to build up a fortune at the bar. Liberal factions, imperialist and anti-imperialist, old-fashioned Gladstonians and New Liberals, luxuriated in bitter conflict. The Nonconformists and the Irish were at daggers drawn over education. *Faute de mieux*, the rather obscure second-ranker of the old school, Campbell-Bannerman, was chosen with more or less reluctance by the Liberals: to most observers at the time, this seemed to confirm the dramatic collapse of Liberalism as a serious political force.

More importantly, there were weaknesses within the Unionist structure which stresses and strains increasingly brought to the surface. Unionism had committed itself to the correctness of the imperialist analysis of Britain's fundamental problems and to the feasibility of imperialism as a policy. Adventurous South African policy alienated the cautious older generation. The war against the Afrikaner republics broke out in 1899, and exposed unexpected and alarming British deficiencies in men and materials. At this crisis in national affairs the political leadership of both Salisbury and Balfour was for a while astonishing in its ineptitude. Salisbury's pessimism became a constant embarrassment; and under pressure Balfour slipped into a rather petulant querulousness. Nor was the general level of ability in the upper ranks of Unionism very impressive. The older generation like Hicks Beach and Goschen and Cross were, as Salisbury, well past their prime. The coming men such as Ritchie and Walter Long were competent mediocrities. The Unionist cabinets were never in themselves impressive: another reality obscured by the public resonance of 'Great Joe'. Education policy offended the important Nonconformist element in Liberal Unionism. Chamberlain's fiscal reform proposals unavoidably involved the political poison of dearer bread.

It was, moreover, a weakness of the Unionist administration – usually much exaggerated in a later, distorted perspective, but a weakness just the same – that Labour was increasingly and unnecessarily alienated by clumsy and insensitive government behaviour. Just as Liberal electoral success in 1892 was in great measure involved in the social movement which produced the 'new unionism' and the successful dockers' strike of 1889, so the much greater Unionist success of 1895 was associated with a marked development of anti-trade-union sentiment and an employers' counter-attack. In 1897 came the lock-out of the engineers. There was a sophisticated development of 'free labour' or strike-breaking labour organization. In 1898 the employers formed a Parliamentary Council to lobby the Commons. In response to this the socialists of the Independent Labour Party persuaded the trade union chiefs to consider the advantages of a more direct participation in politics. In 1900 the unions formed a Labour Representation Committee with Ramsay MacDonald as secretary to build up a greater and more aggressive working-class representation in parliament.

In this atmosphere of developing conflict the Unionist government would have been well advised to exert its influence in the direction of restraint. But on the one hand it did not judge the trade-union interest as sufficiently important to warrant risk of offending the manifestly very important employers' interest; and on the other the government and the Unionist party as a whole tended to share the opinion, widely voiced at the time, that British industrial shortcomings compared with Germany and the

United States were due very largely to the rigidity and restrictionism of the trade unions. The employers' equivalent symbolic success to the unions' success of 1889 was the Taff Vale case of 1901. The Taff Vale Railway Company, having broken a strike in 1900, sued the Amalgamated Society of Railway Servants for damages incurred during the dispute. The court found for the company; and though this judgment was reversed by the Court of Appeal it was eventually upheld by the Judicial Committee of the House of Lords. This judgment was in fact the culmination of a series of legal tests as to the clarity of the legislation of the 1870s in protecting the funds of trade unions from such claims for damages. Balfour refused to offer the unions legislation to give them the protection they had always assumed they enjoyed. Doubtless, from the point of view of the immediate balance of political advantages involved in the issue, Balfour's refusal was justified; but in the longer term, the Taff Vale case assumed a symbolic significance which would have repaid a little investment by Balfour in 1901 with handsome dividends.

These flaws and the kind of short-sightedness exposed by such issues as the Taff Vale affair, together with Liberal debility, account for the persistent political sub-plot of the era: the idea of escaping from orthodox party limitations altogether by creating a new axis about which politics could revolve and serve the country more efficaciously. Churchill and Chamberlain in the 1880s had dreamed of a 'national' government emancipated from both Old Tory stupidity and Gladstonian distortion. Rosebery shared much of this attitude. At the turn of the century, incited by the revelations in the South African war of widespread incompetence and mismanagement, came the 'National Efficiency' movement. The 'Co-efficients', a group brought together by the Webbs in 1902 as a select dining club to discuss the aims and methods of imperial policy, spanned a wide spectrum of political opinions. The membership included the Liberal front-benchers Haldane and Edward Grey, the Conservative Milnerite Leo Amery, Leo Maxse the Conservative journalist, Sidney Webb, H. G. Wells, Hewins the economist, Bertrand Russell, the geopolitician Halford Mackinder, who succeeded Hewins as Director of the London School of Economics, and the former New Zealand minister of labour Pember Reeves, who in turn succeeded Mackinder. Eight years later, when the Liberal government in its turn had reached something of an impasse, Lloyd George was to propose in 1910 a 'National Settlement' to put politics on a new, non-partisan and more effective footing. But as long as peace lasted, orthodox party lines remained strong enough to resist these challenges. Both the Unionists and the Liberals were fated to make their respective bids on the basis of such autonomous sources of strength as they could bring to bear.

In many ways Balfour best exhibits the advantages and limitations inherent in the Unionist position. His uncle Salisbury was too much of the older generation, his great partner Chamberlain was too much an outsider. Balfour, from beginning to end of the Unionist bid, was uneasily poised between a clear intellectual awareness of the inescapable necessity of doing certain things, particularly in the spheres of defence, encouragement of scientific and technological development and secondary and higher education, and an equally clear and often paralysing awareness of the difficulties and dangers involved. He was as deeply committed as his uncle to the desirability of preserving as much as possible the traditional dispensations of politics and society; at the same time he realized that new classes of economic and social intelligence would have to be mobilized if Britain were to respond adequately to the problems of being a successful society and a successful power, and that this intelligence would inevitably be translated into political claims. Moreover, this awareness of the need for new forms of managerial intelligence had the effect of helping to blind Balfour to the need to take due account of social movements running in what seemed to him a contrary direction: generally, a developing working-class consciousness; specifically, the new power and influence of the trade unions.

On top of this, there was for Balfour the constant problem of working with the wilful Chamberlain, easily the most celebrated and popular and execrated member of the government. Chamberlain had already played a major part in destroying the unity of one great party; he would soon destroy the unity of the other. Balfour had to try to guide Chamberlain's immense demagogic energies into channels good for Unionism and harmless to Conservatism. Although in many ways intellectually adventurous, Balfour always remained at bottom a good party Conservative. Chamberlain felt no deep sense of obligation to the Conservative party. He was always a Nonconformist and a provincial; he could know or share nothing of emotional loyalty to the party of the Church and of the traditional ruling order. It was the best means at hand towards the end of national reconstruction. Increasingly for Chamberlain its drawbacks as a means would come near to outweighing its advantages.

II

Meanwhile there was a great deal about which Balfour and Chamberlain could cooperate. They were in general agreement about the need for breaking with the Victorian past and about the crucial role of government policy in achieving this. Balfour responded positively to Chamberlain's programme of 1894 of 'Social reform in a Conservative spirit'. He accepted Chamberlain's arguments for a comprehensive Workmen's Compensation Act, passed in 1897. This embodied the important new principle of automatic compensation for industrial accidents by employers, for whom the costs involved would become a normal charge of trade. Chamberlain's success with this issue in fact underlined a very important aspect of Unionist political advantage at this time over Liberalism. Asquith had brought in an Employers' Liability bill in 1893 in an attempt to solve the question. This bill failed not so much because of amendments by the Lords as because the Liberals could not bring themselves to accept that a special privileged legal position could be granted to any particular social group. Hence they insisted that an injured workman could not be presumed to be entitled to compensation. He would have to prove his employer's liability. At the heart of this legislative policy were Liberal principles of self-reliance and the idea that the moral stature of the individual must be an inner, personal thing and that paternalism must never be the guide of social policy. This 'fraternalism' was as much a feature of the thinking and influence of Green and Toynbee as it had been of

Mill. Chamberlain's advantage was to be able to cut through this Gordian knot of inhibition by a bold stroke of expediency. He ignored every consideration but that of the convenience and utility of asserting that compensation should be based on injuries sustained in the ordinary course of employment and not through acts or defaults. For many Tories this represented 'Socialism pure and simple'. Some complained that Chamberlain had 'annexed' the Conservative party, and deplored the 'dominating will' of the colonial secretary. But Salisbury and Balfour replied firmly that on social questions Chamberlain was the 'spokesman of our party'. This was true also on the issue of old age pensions.

Chamberlain and Balfour alike were receptive to new expressions of social and political intelligence. H. G. Wells, the embodiment of the 'new man' of the suburbs, of the South Kensington science schools, abandoned himself to an almost idolatrous worship of Balfour's mind and capacity for visionary ideas. The Fabian socialist group centred about the Webbs and Shaw was one example of the influences working in broadly the same direction. Haldane, the Liberal imperialist, busied himself in arranging for the Webbs to gain an entrée to the highest political circles, where they cultivated Balfour especially. A new school of political economists, represented by W. J. Ashley and W. A. S. Hewins, was another contributory influence. They followed Toynbee and Cunningham in insisting on the primacy of the historical method, with its implications of empiricism and expediency. Though they failed in the short-run to overturn the established orthodoxy of political economy, they became important in helping to formulate ideas in high places about economic and social change. Chamberlain, who shared Balfour's enthusiasm for the cause of higher education, was instrumental in founding Birmingham University in 1901 as one of the new 'vital ramparts' of Britain's 'industrial defences'. He brought Ashley in to help man the ramparts as head of the first school of commerce in a British university and to supply him with expert economic advice. Hewins, the first director of the London School of Economics from 1895, left to become the secretary of the Tariff Commission set up by the Tariff Reform League in 1903.

Chamberlain had decided in 1897 that Birmingham should have a university which would be a model of new forms of higher education, designed expressly to adapt themselves to new social needs, especially in the fields of industry, technology, trade, transport, medicine and agriculture. His main inspiration for this was, appropriately, his imperialist teacher Seeley, whose recommendations on higher education policy pointed primarily to the example of Germany. The ultimate success of a policy of imperial consolidation and reconstruction would depend on the training of a new élite not merely for government but for an era in which the relationship between the state and science would be the secret of national survival. Oxford and Cambridge would remain essentially seminaries of statesmanship. All the more vital was it, therefore, that the provincial and London universities should develop themselves into seminaries for the application of scientific and technological intelligence to State policy. For Seeley as for Arnold, State and science were functions of the same fundamental values: order and reason. Thus Arnold, as an inspector of schools, advocated the necessity of government intervention through a Ministry of Education and a system of truly public secondary schools to inculcate these values among the mass of the population. The public debate about British technological backwardness in the 1870s and 1880s now began to have impressive effect. A good deal of technical education had been developed, both at the secondary school and polytechnic levels, helped by the Technical Instruction Act of 1889. The teaching of scientific subjects was introduced in elementary schools in 1890. But Britain still had a long way to go to match Germany in the quality of scientific instruction.[1]

At the higher level Britain as yet had nothing to compare with great institutions like the Massachusetts Institute of Technology or the Technical Institute at Zürich, or especially the new Physikalisch-Teknische Reichanstalt established in 1895 at Charlottenburg. This famous foundation stimulated even further British awareness of German scientific and technological superiority, and especially the close links between government and science policy. Already, in 1894, the Cowper Commission had recommended the establishment of a scientific research institute in London. In 1895 the demand grew for increased government grants for scientific research and instruction at the universities. In 1897 the British government expended £26,000 in grants to universities: the Prussian government at the same time expended £476,000.[2] In 1897 a committee under Lord Rayleigh proposed the establishment of a National Physical Laboratory. It was in this climate of emulation that Chamberlain decided to launch his Birmingham scheme. He was adept at extracting endowments for it from industry, helped no doubt by the stimulation of such propaganda as E. E. Williams's *Made in Germany* (1896), a widely-selling 'scare' story of successful German trade rivalry. Chamberlain was also the great provincial counterpart of the metropolitan movement launched in 1903 to establish a 'Charlottenburg' in London, a cause in which Rosebery took a great interest. This eventually emerged as the Imperial College of Science and Technology.

In 1895 the Bryce Commission on Secondary Education reported on the existing provision of education between the elementary and higher levels. There was a general recognition that the requirements of the times were much more serious and exacting than in the days of the Clarendon and Taunton Commissions of the 1860s. Then the notorious fact that in Britain a much smaller proportion of the population of secondary school age went to secondary school than in France or Prussia did not have the added urgency of the circumstances of the 1890s. Inevitably the whole question of State provision of secondary education was opened up. Without considerable expansion in the secondary level the new schemes for the development of higher education could not hope to prosper. By now it was received wisdom that the prosperity and success of a modern society depended on the quantity and quality of its provision of secondary education. The Bryce Commission's recommendations of a comprehensive central authority to formulate policy and the constitution of local authorities to administer secondary education on a county or county borough basis set in train a debate which came to a climax in the 1902 session.

III

The Education Act of 1902 was Balfour's great contribution to domestic Unionist policy and was unquestionably the most important domestic achievement of the Unionist government. To a great extent the enormous political fuss associated with its passage obscured its true significance, which had to do with the beginnings of direct State responsibility for providing cheap secondary education. The fuss was essentially about the fact that the logical and sensible consequence of putting secondary education under a central authority for policy and under country authorities for administration was to bring the existing elementary system into the same framework. This meant abolishing the 2,500 school boards provided for in the Act of 1870. These boards had largely become the darlings of provincial Nonconformity, and were thus a vested Liberal and Radical political interest. They carried a considerable sentimental charge, compounded of the ideas of democracy, anti-centralism and community control. Many school boards in fact were running secondary departments in their schools although this was legally dubious under the provisions of the 1870 Act. An obvious alternative to central control was to give the school boards the task of running the new secondary system. This recourse would not be palatable, however, to the Conservative party. More importantly, the effect of including elementary education in the general framework envisaged for provision for State secondary education was to revert to the original proposal of Forster's bill in 1870 of providing voluntary – mainly Church of England – schools with local finance from the rates. That had been anathema to Nonconformity in 1870, and Nonconformists had been able to block it. It was still anathema in 1902, but they were unable to block it.

The reason for this was in one sense very simple: the bill of 1902 was a Conservative Bill passed by a Conservative majority in the House of Commons with the blessing of the Church of England and (to the fury of Liberal Nonconformists who had supported Irish Home Rule against some of their deepest instincts) the Roman Catholics, whose schools would benefit incidentally.

However, there were many other factors involved apart from the Conservative majority. The Church of England and the other voluntary bodies, certainly, were in desperate financial straits: over half their elementary schools were virtually bankrupt, kept in being by bazaars and jumble sales. There were more than 10,000 of these schools, and it would have cost the state about £30 million to replace them. The churchmen would not consider handing them over to the State and making religious guidance a matter of subsidiary provision: whether Anglican or Roman Catholic (or, for that matter, Wesleyan), they were more than ever convinced that religion must encompass the whole of the child's school life. They were convinced that the kind of minimal 'non-denominational' religious instruction provided for in the Cowper–Temple clause of the 1870 Act was worse than nothing at all. These schools would have to get money from some public source; the simplest recourse was frankly to integrate them completely with the envisaged State system and 'put them on the rates'. For Toryism this represented an irresistible combination of principle and expediency: what was good for education was good for the Church and good for the Conservative party. The government, moreover, was in a good position to cope with controversial legislation. The House of Commons was dissolved in the autumn of 1900 and in the 'Khaki Election', capitalizing on patriotic emotion engendered by the South African war, the Conservatives and Unionists maintained intact their ascendant position of 1895.

To Balfour the existing educational system in England was 'chaotic', 'ineffectual', 'utterly behind the age', making England the 'laughing stock of every advanced nation in Europe and America', putting the English 'not merely behind our American cousins but the German and the Frenchman and the Italian'; and he was quite clear that it was 'not consistent with the duty of an English Government to allow that state of things to continue without adequate remedy'.

This was very much the language of the movement for 'National Efficiency'. Educational improvement was seen increasingly as an integral part of a comprehensive improvement of social conditions, along with improvements of public health and national physique through an emphasis on social or preventive medicine, improvement generally in the machinery of government and administration. This aspect of the educational question was most aptly represented by Sidney Webb, who as chairman of the L.C.C.'s Technical Education Board was strategically placed to influence the London Education Board, and Robert Morant, a very able and intensely ambitious officer of the civil service who since 1895 had been preparing a *coup d'état* inside the Education Department to gain effective direction of its policies.

Webb and Morant agreed on the necessity of putting all forms of education under the direction of a vigorous central authority not merely for purposes of efficiency in administration but as a means towards the propagation of a national ideology. They deplored the elective school board system, with its assumption that education should be subject to democratic popular judgement instead of being controlled by informed expert opinion. To the Webbs and the Fabians generally, compulsory education was one of the elements in their project of a 'National Minimum', a set of standards in every sphere of life below which no member of society should be allowed to fall (whether he liked it or not) in the interests of the general social good. Bad education was like bad health, bad housing, unemployment, bad hygiene; part of an intolerable slovenliness defacing public life that would have to be abolished by the enforcement of adequate standards of social discipline. This was a view widely shared in circles at the time who stressed the need for more coercive and authoritarian modes of governmental guidance of well-meaning but ill-informed democracy. Morant was one of the many heirs of Toynbee's social idealism, to which he added his own kind of authoritarian twist. He wanted State education to weld the nation together in common regenerative purpose by allowing for a minority of exceptionally gifted working-class children to join the mass of fee-paying middle-class children in publically administered secondary schools. He felt a vocation for a 'High Priesthood for the masses'. Morant's eventual control of the Education Department in 1903 inaugurated the era of educational policy as a commitment to an ideal of popular enlightenment, no longer as a matter of administration and finance, bricks and mortar.

Morant gave to State education a missionary function of propagating a form of secular religion.

Morant and the churchmen, led by Bishop Talbot of Rochester, set out to persuade Balfour to grasp the educational nettle. It was a daunting prospect in many ways. The bees would be set buzzing in the ecclesiastical hive. Chamberlain and the Liberal Unionists would be gravely affronted. The Liberal party would be offered a politically very remunerative issue which would help offset many of its liabilities. In any case the issue became unavoidable in 1900 when a legal judgment (known as the Cockerton judgment) established that existing school boards were not competent to offer education beyond the elementary level. This was a great fillip to the advocates of a county council system for elementary as well as secondary education. Talbot discreetly arranged a dinner at his episcopal residence to allow Morant to get at Balfour. Morant cared little for the religious issues or for the Church schools as such, but he realized that rate aid for them could be the bait to hook Balfour, who needed something to offer the Conservative party, badly in need in turn of stiffening at the time of setbacks in the war in South Africa.

Morant used the war against Chamberlain. He went off intrepidly to confront the colonial secretary in his Highbury lair in December 1901. Chamberlain deplored any departure from the compromise of 1870. His view was that since neither educational party could overcome the other, recognition of this should be the basis of educational policy. He had accepted this in 1891 when Church schools got extra State money. But now Chamberlain was caught in his own Education League trap of 1870. Then the great strength of his case had been the desirability of a uniform national educational system; now he was resisting that idea and clinging to the kind of rival dualist system which simply could not stand up to intelligent critical appraisal in 'modern' social and international circumstances. When, after threatening Morant with a great crusade of Nonconformist 'rate-martyrs', Chamberlain asked why voluntary schools should not get additional grants out of State funds as in 1870, thus avoiding recourse to rates, Morant replied crushingly: 'Because your War has made further recourse to State grants impossible.'

Chamberlain had no answer to this. He extracted the concession that the granting of rate aid to voluntary schools should be a matter of local option; but he could get no other concessions to help allay Nonconformist agitation and the inevitable weakening of Liberal Unionism as a political force.

Morant's Education bill, steered by Balfour with great resource and persistence, was finally guillotined through in December 1902 against frantic opposition led in the Commons by the Welsh Liberal David Lloyd George and out of doors by Dr Clifford of the Westbourne Park Baptist Chapel. Some zealous Nonconformists, mainly in Wales, went to prison rather than pay rates for the use of Church schools.[3] The school boards were abolished and voluntary schools were incorporated into an integrated system of elementary, secondary and technical education administered by county or county borough councils under the general direction of the central Education Department. Chamberlain was not able to maintain the local option concession, much to Morant's satisfaction. The really important new departure was the provision of State secondary education. By 1914 there were 1,123 secondary schools in England and Wales inspected by the Board of Education; these were attended by nearly 200,000 pupils, one-third of whom came from elementary schools and held free places. Five hundred of these secondary schools were controlled directly by county or county borough authorities. This represented in fact a disappointing shortfall on the planning estimates. Transfers to secondary schools from elementary schools were in 1913 only 25 per cent of what had been expected. However, in such matters it is the first step which counts.

IV

The old Queen, an inconsolable widow for forty years, died in January 1901 and was succeeded by her rather unsatisfactory and raffish son, Albert Edward, who chose to take the title (to the annoyance of Scots nationalists) of Edward VII. Victoria's death at the beginning of the new century and after the longest reign in British royal annals (sixty-three years) snapped the strongest link with the past in the general public mind. She had become the 'Grandmother of Europe'. She was indeed the grandmother of the German Emperor William II and the grandmother-in-law of the Czar Nicholas II, and the complex web of her dynastic relationships encompassed almost all the non-Catholic thrones. Victoria had recovered the popularity she had lost through her obstinate seclusion and withdrawal from the public functions of the monarchy. But though she left the monarchy much more secure in public esteem than in the days of her wicked uncles, she left it also bereft of real power and influence. This was the result not of any lack of assiduity in business or shrewdness in affairs, but rather of the insensible accumulation of constitutional limitations on the sovereign's practical as opposed to theoretical freedom to act. Since, with the development especially of democratic sentiment and a fairly smoothly functioning two-party political system, the monarchy increasingly was no longer in a position to exploit opportunities and to command success as George III had usually managed to do, the logical alternative was to withdraw constitutionally to a position where failure was no longer risked. This effectively was the central constitutional development of Victoria's reign, though the process was formally elevated into constitutional principle in the reign of her grandson George V. The major aspect of her own political views was her increasingly virulent dislike of Liberalism and a feeling not far short of hatred for Gladstone; but these sentiments bore with them little more than political nuisance value. She welcomed Salisbury back in 1895 with undisguised and almost embarrassing pleasure; but her support was no more assistance to Salisbury than her hostility had been an obstacle to Gladstone.

The new king lacked his mother's obsessive capacity for political vigilance. He lived for the pleasures of the table, the bed, the wardrobe, the turf and the casino; and his flamboyant hedonism cost him no general unpopularity in an era distinguished for its determination to launch the new century in a fittingly brash style of luxurious materialism. Edward VII travelled restlessly and loved amusing society and full dress occasions, tastes which could be put to diplomatic use; and his public manner of hearty *bonhomie* made him an excellent advertisement for Britain in the more fashionable watering-places of the continent such as Marienbad (where he struck up a useful friendship with Campbell-Bannerman) and the Riviera. He could make his opinions count in the armed services and in diplomacy: Fisher at the Admiralty and Hardinge at the Foreign Office were two of his protégés. Such serious influence as he possessed was generally exercised through able favourites, especially the smooth political 'fixer' Reginald Brett, Viscount Esher, who was able to use the royal favour to lever himself into a position to do a great deal of useful backstairs work in the spheres of defence and military reform.

Following the election success in 1900, Salisbury, under pressure, relinquished the Foreign Office. The reconstructed ministry reflected the patrician unwillingness of Salisbury and Balfour to recognize the need to make gestures of concession to the restless Conservative rank and file, who immediately joined with the jeering Liberals in dubbing the ministry 'the Hotel Cecil' because of the prominence of several of Salisbury's relatives.[4] The important changes were that Lansdowne succeeded Salisbury at the Foreign Office and Selborne succeeded Goschen at the Admiralty. Salisbury in any case was hardly capable of sustaining the burdens of administration much longer. He stayed on feebly until the coronation of Edward VII (postponed from 1901 to 1902 because of the serious illness of the King) and then resigned in July 1902. He died a year later. Balfour was called on to form a ministry. This was a foregone conclusion. Chamberlain happened to be incapacitated at the time, badly injured in a cab accident; but there was no real question of his making a claim to the succession. He had accepted that his political destiny meant that the highest prize of politics should be out of his reach. To underline the point, the King neglected even to make a gesture towards his old comrade in pleasure 'Harty Tarty' Devonshire, whose political prestige rested largely on his having declined thrice to undertake to form ministries.[5] Devonshire stayed on to lend his massive ducal dignity to the political scene. Chamberlain remained at the Colonial Office, where he was in the midst of presiding at the Colonial Conference of 1902. One of Balfour's protégés, George Wyndham, the Chief Secretary for Ireland, was promoted to cabinet membership: as it turned out, the beginning of the tragic end of a once promising career. Another appointment which turned out to be momentous was C. T. Ritchie's transfer from the Home Office to replace the retiring Hicks Beach at the Exchequer, where he was to prove a painful thorn in Chamberlain's side.

Indeed Chamberlain's position and prospects at this political juncture were much less brilliant in reality than they seemed to the superficial view. Though clearly the dominant personality in the Commons after Gladstone's departure, and very much the strong man of the Unionist electoral campaign in 1900, where he aroused both for and against himself extraordinarily violent public emotions, Chamberlain had little to show for his immense efforts. The Colonial Office in personnel and resources simply was not capable of achieving the sort of spectacular imperial results that Chamberlain demanded of it. Nor did he get much support in the cabinet, and the Treasury, affronted by his assertiveness, was consistently hostile to him. Quite apart from the circumstance that South African policy left much to be desired in the way of being successful and being seen to be successful, his plans for imperial construction had run into awkward snags.

Chamberlain commenced his tenure at the Colonial Office with the idea of developing an imperial free trade entity, an imperial *Zollverein*, with the implication involved in the German word – that political and defensive union would follow somehow naturally on economic union as in the case of the German example. The great tactical advantage of this approach from the British point of view was that an imperial economic policy based on 'free trade all round' would not conflict with existing British economic orthodoxy; on the other hand, strategically, from the point of view of British protectionists and crypto-protectionists like Chamberlain, once an imperial free trade *bloc* were institutionalized, the protectionist votes of the colonial governments could change the imperial entity into protectionism against the foreigner. Chamberlain assumed that he could persuade the colonial governments to renounce protection for their own developing industries for the time being against all comers but eventually only against Britain. This assumption did not survive the Colonial Conference of 1897. The colonial governments had no intention of making a serious sacrifice for the cause of imperial unity by exposing their industries to unrestricted British competition. Britain had no means of enforcing free trade upon the self-governing colonies as she could on non-self-governing possessions like India. The Canadians took the lead in proposing an alternative: instead of an imperial free trade area an imperial preference area, that is, the empire governments reciprocally offering each other especially favourable commercial terms not available to outsiders. The Canadians had in mind getting preferential advantages for their wheat as against the United States in return for offering the British lower industrial tariffs. The other self-governing colonies were quite prepared to give sympathetic consideration to this proposal.

This was the most that Chamberlain could achieve. Moreover, existing British commercial treaties with Germany and Belgium bound Britain not to do precisely what the Canadians proposed. In other words, the colonies would consider an imperial commercial policy only at the price of Britain's abandoning free trade as the basis of fiscal policy. Chamberlain managed in 1897 to persuade the cabinet at least to reciprocate the Canadian tariff offer by denouncing the German and Belgian commercial treaties standing in the way of imperial preference; but persuading them to abandon the principle of free trade was quite another matter. The economic experts of the Board of Trade were sceptical: Britain's trade with the empire was a declining proportion of her world trade. Kipling wrote some stirring verses in praise of the Canadian tariff, and Chamberlain for the time being had to be content with that.

On the social reform front also, Chamberlain was running into serious snags. He had supposed in 1895 that he could crack the old age pensions problem and pull off a brilliant political coup which would establish Unionism's reputation with the working classes unassailably. But again the facts were stubborn enemies. The Rothschild Committee Report of 1898 found many insuperable difficulties. The position of the powerful and influential Friendly Societies was a mass of bristling complications. Chamberlain insisted that a way must be found and succeeded by 1899 in getting the government to pledge its determination to pursue the issue. A significant twist was given to the issue in 1899 by Henry Chaplin, the head of the old protectionist agricultural interest. As chairman of a parliamentary committee on old age pensions, Chaplin stressed the point that the only feasible source of finance would be some form of revised tariff policy. This point was not lost on Chamberlain. The Chaplin Committee recommended a minimum pension of 5s. per week for all necessitous and deserving persons over sixty-five years. Lloyd George got Chamberlain to pledge his support for this. But the expensive war in South Africa damaged his old age pension chances as mortally as his education chances. In any case in 1901 Hicks Beach, in one of his last strokes of Gladstonian financial rigour before quitting the Exchequer, pointed out to the cabinet that annual government expenditure, excluding extra expenses incurred by the war, had risen alarmingly from £105 million in 1895 to £147·5 million in 1902: an increase of 40 per cent. In the period 1883-90 the increase had been 5 per cent, and between 1890-95, 15 per cent. This galloping acceleration could not go unchecked, Hicks Beach argued, without increasing the taxation yield either by raising the income tax to a level involving very serious social implications and serious political hurt to Unionism, or by recourse to higher revenue duties with equally hurtful and unacceptable implications for the sanctity of the reigning free trade orthodoxy. By 1902, unable to turn one way or the other, Chamberlain was at an impasse on old age pensions: he denounced the 'extravagant expectations' of a scheme for a noncontributory pension of 5s. a week for everyone over sixty; and thereupon, in what his biographer Amery described as a 'fateful hour', relapsed into inactivity, 'let slip a great opportunity', and renounced the leadership of the social reform movement.

By 1902 Chamberlain's political position was decidedly slipping; he was a frustrated and hence a dangerous politician. His war had caused considerable strain and tension in the cabinet, where he now had few strong friends. Irish Home Rule seemed moribund, and this weakened the old sense of urgency in Conservative and Unionist links. The Education Act had dealt a mortal blow at Chamberlain's Liberal Unionist political power base, and he was bound to cast about for a new one. His imperial and social reform projects were running into very heavy weather. Chamberlain's last throw in the context of existing political and fiscal attitudes was at the Colonial Conference of 1902 when the colonial ministers were gathered for Edward VII's coronation. Chamberlain's hopes for a Council of Empire to consolidate political relationships and his hopes for integrated imperial defence were dashed. He rebuked the colonial premiers for their failure to rise to the great occasion. It was as depressingly clear as ever that the self-governing colonies were not going to make any serious sacrifices, financial or otherwise, for the cause of imperial federation.

It was difficult to get Chamberlain and British imperialists generally to understand that such enthusiasm as there was in the colonies for imperial federation usually meant something rather different from what it was interpreted to mean in Britain. Disraeli had been wise enough in the 1870s not to take it seriously; now Chamberlain was staking his reputation on the thesis that Britain could no longer afford not to take it seriously. In the meantime colonial nationalism was thirty years more mature. Colonial ideas about imperial defence and imperial foreign policy meant in fact the opposite of what British imperialists hoped to get out of a coordinated imperial defence and foreign policy. The brash imperialism of R. J. 'King Dick' Seddon of New Zealand, often cited as the apogee of colonial willingness to serve the greater interests of Empire, had within it a very significant charge of colonial nationalism: it was a view of Empire in which New Zealand's voice and interests would count for more, not less; and accordingly would restrict rather than enlarge Britain's freedom of action as a Great Power. Britain wanted to mobilize imperial resources of men and material for British directed policies and purposes on the assumption that its fortunes could be equated with those of the whole Empire. The colonials wanted to get maximum security at minimum cost to themselves and effectively a veto on British foreign policy: in other words, no war to preserve the European balance of power without colonial consent, which would in almost any circumstances be most unlikely. The self-governing dominions prosecuted war in 1900, 1914 and 1939, only because, in effect, they were free, if they wished, not to. A coordinated and centralized Chamberlainite imperial defence and foreign policy structure would, paradoxically, have contradicted the very point of Chamberlainite purposes, which were essentially British (and increasingly Europe-oriented) and not colonial imperial purposes.

On the other hand, the colonial delegations were much more positive and forthcoming on commercial matters. They took up the Canadian reciprocity scheme of 1897 with enthusiasm and pressed it on the British. Laurier, the Canadian premier, tempted the British by raising the 1897 preference to Britain from 25 per cent to 33½ per cent. Britain was free to respond but it was a most delicate domestic political issue. Already shrewd Liberals were sniffing the breeze for a whiff of the old devil Protection. The Board of Trade was as clear as ever that imperial preference would not be a very good economic deal from Britain's point of view. Chamberlain was poised agonizingly between this advice on good commercial business and the cause of Empire. The Canadian delegation routed the ill-prepared Board of Trade officials in economic argument; anti-free-trade economists like Ashley and Hewins were pressing their doctrines on Chamberlain (who, though a businessman, was no economist). It was as clear as anything could be that there could be no closer union of the empire without a major departure in British fiscal policy.

In his agony Chamberlain seized on a fortunate circumstance. In the budget estimates for 1902 the rigidly free-trade Hicks Beach had proposed a temporary financial expedient as one of the extraordinary necessities to cover the enormously increased expenditure caused by the South African war. This was a registration duty (last imposed in 1869) on imported corn of 2s. per quarter. It gave the Canadians a golden opportunity to ask for a reduction in the duty on imports of their corn. Chamberlain vigorously supported the Canadian request for preference and managed to get the cabinet to agree to it. This at least was a positive British response and a clear breach in principle in the strict doctrine of free trade. It could be the acorn from which a splendid imperial oak might grow. But while Chamberlain was away in South Africa early in 1903 Ritchie, the new chancellor, who was an old 'fair trader' of the 1880s and 1890s, but now a converted zealot to Treasury orthodoxy, abolished the Corn duty; and Chamberlain's last throw in the context of existing political arrangements came to nothing. Balfour was aware of the significance of what was happening; but did not think he could risk Ritchie's resignation from the Exchequer so soon after Hicks Beach's retirement. Chamberlain returned from South Africa a very frustrated and dangerous politician indeed.

Chapter Fourteen

UNIONIST EFFORTS TO SAVE THE EXTERNAL SITUATION 1895–1905

I

On his return to the Foreign Office in June 1895 Salisbury faced a testing group of problems. So did Chamberlain at the Colonial Office. The difference between their positions was broadly that whereas Salisbury's problems were of other people's making Chamberlain's were largely and necessarily of his own making. For Salisbury, as the last great representative of the traditional aristocratic ruling order – indeed, the last prime minister in the House of Lords – the highest ambition was to avoid trouble. Chamberlain, a very self-conscious representative of a new bourgeois briskness, efficiency and hard-headed, business-like treatment of governmental problems, assumed that Britain's future in the world would not be secured merely by negative policies of putting off distasteful decisions but would depend upon willingness to go out looking for trouble and defeating it.

Salisbury's problems were immediately in the Near East and Venezuela and secondarily on the Nile, the defence of India and in the Far East. Chamberlain's problems were immediately in South Africa and secondarily in the general prospects of imperial federation.

In the Near East the Ottoman Empire was convulsed with the Armenian national revolutionary movement. Kurdish irregulars suppressed ferociously an insurrection in Sassun in 1894. Rosebery failed to achieve a united European intervention. In Macedonia, Greek, Bulgar and Serb *comitadjis* challenged Turkish authority. Crete was about to burst into revolt under the influence of Greek irredentism. In October 1896 an Armenian demonstration led to massacres in Constantinople. The Ottoman Empire seemed to totter on the brink of dissolution. The Russians, anxious for the security of the Straits, were preparing an expedition to occupy the Bosphorus.

Venezuela was in dispute with Britain about the boundary of British Guiana. In July 1895 the Cleveland administration in the United States intervened, asserting that Britain was violating the Monroe Doctrine and insisting that the dispute be settled by arbitration. Salisbury came to the conclusion that it would be best to humour the Americans, who were obviously seeking occasions to enter the international arena. Rather exaggerated hopes for a future Anglo-American world policy were common form among imperialists: Chamberlain and Kipling, both married to Americans, cultivated relations with the United States. It was clear that no serious British interest would be served by resisting American claims to hegemony in the Caribbean. The British won the material victory on the issues under arbitration; the Americans won a moral victory at the expense of the Venezuelans. The same attitude governed British policy during the Spanish-American War of 1898: Spanish resentment was harmless; American resentment counted. The British were happy to let the Americans believe, erroneously, that Britain had blocked an attempted European mediation. British appeasement reached its natural conclusion in the Hay-Pauncefote Treaty of 1901 which conceded formally to the Americans a Caribbean hegemony which Britain had neither power nor desire to challenge.

The Near East offered no such easy solutions. Salisbury in fact was at the end of his tether with the Turks. He had given up all hope of effective resistance to the Russians at the Straits. The military and naval advice was as insistent on this as ever. The director of Naval Intelligence advised the cabinet in October 1896: the 'one way in which England could not only maintain herself in the Mediterranean at all, but continue to hold India . . . is by holding Egypt against all comers and making Alexandria a naval base'. Salisbury ruefully admitted that Britain had 'backed the wrong horse' from the Crimea onwards and braced himself for a Turkish collapse and a scramble for partition. But none of the powers were anxious to participate. With the Russians Salisbury's natural recourse was to hark back to the good Conservative days of the 1844 accord between Aberdeen and Nicholas I. He announced that as an 'old Tory' he had no objections to a good bargain with the tsardom. The Russians were not impressed by this: 1844 had not prevented 1854. Besides, the Russians much preferred security of the Straits provided by the compliant Turks and the alliance with the French; their plan for a descent on the Bosphorus was a last resort to head off the British, whose military and naval abdication they did not suspect. The French had no desire to see the Russians in Constantinople. The Austrians were delighted to agree with the Russians to put the Near East 'on ice' while the Russians turned their attention to the Far East. The bottom had fallen completely out of the Anglo-Austrian policy established in 1887. It was the end of the 'Eastern Question' for the British. The Germans were cultivating the Turks as a promising sphere of influence, and encouraged projects such as the Anatolia–Baghdad railway to this end. The one positive achievement was that the powers agreed to give Crete autonomy under a Greek prince. In any case the Turks displayed amazing powers of recuperation, and in 1897 with their German trained and equipped forces routed the Greeks who had injudiciously declared war.

Now Britain was committed beyond recall to 'holding Egypt against all comers'. This gave the question about what to do with the Dervish régime on the Upper Nile an added urgency. It was not a threat to Egypt but it was equally not a stable, reliable entity. The French had abated none of their obsessive determination to force the British to give Egypt up or at least to gain some compensation. They decided to force the issue by sending Marchand on his march from Brazzaville in the French Congo to establish a French presence on the Upper Nile in defiance of Grey's warning of March 1895. This decision was made in November 1895. Marchand eventually set out from Brazzaville in March 1897. French policy was in fact hopelessly self-defeating: the more the Franco–Russian alliance made effective British security at the Straits impossible, the more the British would cling to Egypt. With the Marchand expedition the French were putting a noose around their own necks. The British decision to destroy the Dervish régime was taken in March 1896, when they were unaware of the French plans. The decisive push was given by the collapse of the Italian bid to take over Abyssinia at the battle of Adowa at the beginning of March. Behind the victorious Emperor Menelek were the French. Kitchener, since 1892 Sirdar of the Egyptian Army, was dispatched with an Anglo-Egyptian force to forestall a Franco-Abyssinian presence on the Nile. Proceeding deliberately, he took Dongola in September 1896 and then set off for Khartoum.

As it happened, Marchand, toiling with his little expedition across the watershed of the Congo and Nile basins, reached the Nile at Fashoda three days after Kitchener had crushed the Khalifa's army further down river at Omdurman outside Khartoum on 2 September 1898. Kitchener confronted Marchand on 9 September at Fashoda and a diplomatic war of nerves began which the French had no chance of winning. The Russians had their hands full in the Far East, pressuring the Chinese to give them virtual control of Manchuria. The British and the Germans had just signed an agreement about ultimate disposal of the colonies of bankrupt Portugal. French morale in any case was debilitated by the scandals of the Dreyfus Affair. On 2 November they decided to withdraw Marchand. It was a purely self-inflicted humiliation. Like the Russians with their fears of aggressive British penetration into the Black Sea, the French completely underestimated how successful their battleships at Toulon had been in dissolving British confidence in the Mediterranean. The French, in fact, were the gainers; they got rid of a futile policy while the British were burdened with extra responsibilities which desperately stretched Egyptian finances.

However, the fillip of prestige was welcome enough to the British, increasingly under pressure in Asia and South Africa. The government of India was nervous of the state of its outer defences in Persia, the North West Frontier and Tibet. Chinese defeat at the hands of the Japanese in 1895 had weakened Peking's suzerain influence, never very strong, in Tibet; and British practitioners of the 'Great Game' were sure that the Russians were moving in. When Curzon assumed the viceroyalty in 1898 he set about a vigorous policy of countermeasures, including the Younghusband mission to Lhasa in 1904.

Opinion by now had come generally to agreement that, despite the burdens of defence, the security of India was a vital British interest. The English originally went to India for trade and the profits thereof. This motivation had not basically changed since. As much as in the Younger Pitt's day, British policy was British trade. Chamberlain indeed was reaffirming this principle in every speech he made. The exigencies of trade dictated political stability and social prosperity. Since the eighteenth century British power in the form of the East India Company and since 1858 the British government directly had alone been able to secure stability and encourage prosperity and the growing markets that went with prosperity. Not until the first meeting of the Indian National Congress in 1886 was there a sign of a revived indigenous desire to share power with or even replace the British Raj. With the construction of the great strategic and commercial railway network from the 1850s and the opening of the Suez Canal India became a unified and increasingly prosperous and important economic entity despite the chronic poverty of the mass of the fast-growing peasant population. By 1913 India was the world's greatest exporter of cotton yarns next to Britain; and had in fact replaced Britain in the valuable Chinese market. India, from being dependent on the British market, diversified successfully in continental Europe, the Far East and the United States. In turn, India absorbed around 75 per cent of her imports, mainly quality cotton goods, from Britain, though in the 1890s cheap Belgian steel surpassed imports of British steel. The importance of British cotton exports to India and the dependence of Lancashire on the Indian market led the British government to forbid tariff protection to the Indian cotton industry and to impose on top of this an excise duty on Indian cottons to offset the small revenue duty on imports from England. This was widely resented by nascent Indian public political opinion, and did much to encourage anti-British nationalism; but, in the short-term, it was a vivid illustration of the practical benefits to Britain of being in political control of a vast economic market in a period when her great industrial competitors (for Indian custom among others) and even her self-governing colonies were erecting protective tariffs against British goods.

The basic economic fact about India was that in terms of international trading balances, it provided by far the largest surplus item in the British account. By 1914 one-tenth of total British overseas investments were in India. This was only half, proportionately, of what it had been in 1870; but absolutely it was a significant amount. It was a capital British interest to maintain the stability of such a vital factor in world trade. Had an indigenous Indian government been able to do this, no doubt the benefits to Britain would have been even greater, for she maintained expensive military and naval establishments in India and because of India above and beyond the Indian Army itself. The only losers would have been those British families who made their careers out of the Indian civil and military services; but these were an infinitesimal factor in the grand balance of interests. The fact was in the 1890s that without British rule India would dissolve in anarchy. In a world of crumbling indigenous régimes in Turkey, Persia, China, Morocco and elsewhere, imperialists had a good argument when they pointed to Egypt and India as examples o areas contributing to both their own and world prosperity by means of externally-imposed régimes guaranteeing stability and a measure of sensible administration. Japan was as yet the one example of an indigenous non-European régime managing to construct a modern industry.

By 1895, on the basis of this industry, Japan had emerged as a serious factor in the balance of international power. Almost immediately the Japanese faced the problem of how to cope with the Russian thrust in the Far East. The Russians started constructing the trans-Siberian railway in 1891. They were leaning heavily on the Chinese. Witte, the Russian finance minister, had great plans for commercial development of northern China along the lines of British development in the Yiang-Tse basin. Salisbury could only pretend to applaud this and attempted to get the Russians to agree to European economic cooperation in China on the basis of its territorial integrity. Apart from French loans the Russians had no need of European cooperation; they needed virtual control of Manchuria in any case as the shortest means of linking the Siberian railway with Vladivostok in the Pacific Maritime Province. On top of this, a Far Eastern party in St

Petersburg dreamt of a great new Eastern Empire including North China and Korea which offered greater rewards and fewer risks than the traditional prize of Constantinople. They had the ear of the new Tsar, Nicholas II, as reactionary as his father Alexander III but lacking all his father's strength of character and caution. Russia, dominant in Turkey, Persia, Central Asia and China, allied with the French in Indo-China and secure at the Straits and given every encouragement by Germany and Austria, glad to have the heat taken off their eastern borders and the Balkans, would, in this view, bestride all Asia and establish a decisive ascendancy over the British in India.

By February 1898 it was clear that the Russians were determined to transfer their temporary occupation of Talienwan and Port Arthur on the Yellow Sea (which the Japanese had been obliged to disgorge in 1895) into a permanent occupation. The Germans had already in 1897 obliged the Chinese to agree to a compensatory lease of Kiao Chow bay. When in March 1898 the Chinese finally succumbed to Russian pressure and conceded the lease on Port Arthur the British were forced to the rather humiliating recourse of demanding compensation like the Germans. They leased Wei-hai-wei, mainly for the benefit of British public opinion. The British did not at this stage think of striking a bargain with the Japanese as the two major powers on the Asian perimeter; the Japanese were thinking in terms of benefiting from a partition of China rather than of preventing it, and hoped to strike a good bargain with the Russians over Korea. The British, particularly Chamberlain, who was growing increasingly impatient of Salisbury's caution and passivity, thought rather of a bargain with the Germans.

Again and again, from 1898 to the end of 1901, Chamberlain pressed both the cabinet and the Germans for an alliance. The major difficulty was that what essentially the British had to offer the Germans was the proposition that the *status quo* ought to be defended. They wanted an alliance of world conservatism. As far as Europe was concerned there were advantages for the Germans in this. They wanted to preserve the Habsburg Monarchy as a Great Power, and they wanted to keep Alsace-Lorraine. In these terms, pan-Slavonic Russia and *revanchiste* France were the radical subversive powers. The Germans were prepared to fight the Russians and the French for the purposes of German policy; but they were not prepared to fight them for the purposes of a *status quo* desired by the British, who in any case would be sitting tight and safe on their island. But in larger, global terms, and indeed ultimately in European terms as well, the Germans were far from desiring a conservative *status quo*. They saw themselves as a young power whose immense industrial and technological achievements on top of her military and cultural reputation gave valid historical credentials for advancing from the position of foremost continental power in Europe to that of a world power on terms of equality with the greatest of other world powers.

These arguments were already firmly established in the German public mind, and few Germans even among the Social Democratic party membership resisted the claim for a 'place in the sun' for Germany. Behind their claim was a considerable amount of resentment and sense of disinheritance: Germany had been the victim of historical misfortune, and while she remained dismembered and impotent, the other powers had shared the world out. Germany was a latecomer at the carve-up; and the German case was that in fairness the possessing powers ought to make appropriate concessions to German claims.

German resentment tended to focus on Britain for several reasons. First, because the British were the most conspicuously successful world power, the Germans usually found them across their path in every quarter of the globe. From this German viewpoint, the British were a great world dog in the manger, sitting on their vast possessions and grudging the few scraps the Germans had managed to snap up. This resentment flared up strongly whenever the British protested about German naval construction. The Germans found British legalism and morality about the rights of small nations hypocritical. Moreover, many Germans inclined to question British world prerogatives in any case on the grounds of British unfitness. The very fact that Britain was a conservative power clinging to the *status quo* indicated that her great days were over. She was now decadent. German industry was challenging the British for their markets. Though a 'Germanic' people (this was one of the arguments Chamberlain constantly put forward as the basis of a 'natural' Anglo-German alliance) the English were hopelessly infected by the shallow materialism of the French enlightenment. Like the French (irredeemably inferior in any case as 'Latins') the utilitarian and rationalistic English merely possessed a civilization; only the Germans possessed a higher, spiritual *Kultur*. Hence another argument for German prerogatives in the world. Thus for the *weltpolitisch* Germans Britain was both a model to emulate and a power whose acceptance and recognition of German claims to world equality would be the greatest desirable historical accolade for Germany, and at the same time a suspicious, grudging power determined to maintain a world supremacy against the just claims of Germany. The half-English Emperor William II was a very representative German in this emulation/resentment psychology. Certainly, British policy never wavered from a clear recognition that British independence and security in the world were logically contradicted by German claims to equality in the world; to that extent German resentment had a basis of justification.

This German resentment first impinged seriously on British public consciousness in January 1896 when the Kaiser with deliberate provocativeness sent a telegram to President Kruger of the South African Republic of the Transvaal congratulating him on the successful defeat of a hostile invading force without having to ask the help of any friendly power. The invading force was the mounted filibuster led on 29 December 1895 by Dr Jameson, an old friend and confidant and agent of Cecil Rhodes, the premier of the Cape Colony, launched from Mafeking with the object of joining forces with an expected insurrection of Uitlanders in Johannesburg against the Transvaal government; and the reference to friendly powers was a direct challenge to British claims of paramount authority over the external relations of the South African Republic.

II

In South Africa Unionist efforts to save the British external situation were the most crucial in terms of the consequences of success or failure and they faced the greatest difficulties in execution. Elsewhere dangers might be more apparent than real: the Ottoman Empire did not collapse, the Russians did not seize the Bosphorus; the French backed down at Fashoda; and Russian schemes in Asia might well (as indeed they did) come to grief.

But the difficulties for Britain in South Africa were of a more fundamental kind. There it was not merely a case of avoiding trouble, or of preserving the *status quo*. It is not too much to say that if British policy failed in South Africa the wider hopes of the new school of national reconstruction would eventually fail also. Chamberlain, Rhodes and Milner in different ways and different degrees were united in the conviction that South Africa was the key to success or failure of imperial policy, and hence of the chances of Britain's bid to retrieve the situation of bankruptcy left by the failures of the Disraeli–Gladstone era. In global terms it was the 'heartland' of the 'world Venice's' empire. The Cape was the hinge of the oceanic sea routes. The Cape was inseparable from the interior; and the supreme object of British imperial policy was to win the interior and create a great British South African entity. This would be only secondarily a matter of economics: the key would be population, the peopling of the relatively empty[1] interior *veldt* with settlements of immigrant British, purposefully and systematically planted. South Africa then offered Britain opportunities to turn occasion to advantage which neither Canada nor Australia or New Zealand offered. The other colonies of settlement were the products of chance; South Africa might be made the product of design.

The vital heart of this envisaged interior was the Transvaal. All the surrounding areas were in one way or another pre-empted: only the Transvaal offered the decisive opportunity which would make all the difference. Rhodes had already secured the northernmost area by defeating the Matabele who had been driven out of the Transvaal and across the Limpopo by the Boer trekkers in the days of Kruger's father. The territory of the British South Africa Company south of the Zambesi was proclaimed Rhodesia in May 1895, but it was still largely undeveloped and not a factor of decisive weight. The great gold-bearing reefs which Rhodes insisted were up there never came to light. In the south the colony of Natal was also safe for the imperial idea. Its white population was solidly British. Unfortunately it was small, less than 50,000 in 1891. But it sufficiently counterweighed the preponderantly Afrikaner white population of the Orange Free State, with nearly 80,000 whites. Cape Colony itself, with a white population approaching 400,000, had passed the point where population policy could make decisive shifts of balance. The Afrikaner majority would remain a permanent and probably increasing factor. 'The Cape, then, must be outweighed by a British Transvaal. The Transvaal was the agate point on which the balance of power in South Africa would turn.'[2] In 1898 it had a total white population of something like 290,000; and of 51,000 whites living in the Johannesburg region, only 6,200 were Afrikaners. The Uitlanders, outsiders attracted to the Rand by the gold reefs, were mainly British.

In South Africa the *status quo* was not merely inadequate for imperial purposes; it would in the long run be inimical. Left to themselves, the South African colonies and Afrikaner republics would merge gradually into a loose entity essentially independent of British purposes and requirements. With Afrikanerdom in the ascendant in the Cape and without a countervailing Englishdom in the Transvaal Afrikaner attitudes and ideas would become the permeating representative and received attitudes and ideas of South Africa.

Thus an attempt, heroic in scale and nature, to reverse the tendencies and implications of the *status quo* was required in South Africa. This is what distinguished Chamberlain's chief concern decisively from Salisbury's concerns. And this is what made Chamberlain's almost embarrassingly insistent demands both on Salisbury and the cabinet and on the Germans directly for an Anglo-German alliance so exceptionally inappropriate. Chamberlain was asking the Germans to commit themselves to a world conservatism in order to make it easier for Britain to adopt a revolutionary policy in South Africa. Hence in South Africa British policy as guided by Chamberlain, Rhodes and Milner was aggressive, and its aggression was aimed centrally at the destruction of Kruger's Afrikaner Transvaal Republic.

Kruger's republic was ruled by a narrow-minded Calvinist

oligarchy whose mentality had more in common with the seventeenth than the nineteenth century. Its treatment of the blacks was brutal even by South African standards. Its attitude to the gold-grubbing Uitlanders of the Rand was an unsavoury mixture of greed and hypocrisy. Transvaaler hatred of the British was notorious and they cultivated apocalyptic visions of a South Africa purged of the pestilential British presence.

An imperial policy with the object of destroying that republic would get little support in the Cape and would foment much resentment; and if the destruction of it were a long-drawn-out and messy operation, imperial policy might well be self-defeating. The Rand capitalists would prefer British rule to Boer extortion, but above all they did not want their profitable investments put at risk. If Rhodes could pull off a sharp coup, well and good; if not, it would be best to keep paying Kruger's blackmail. Thus the mode of execution would be of crucial importance.

Rhodes was convinced that Kruger's régime was a hollow pretence which would crumble with minimum pressure applied decisively at the right point at the right time. Rhodes was given to sweeping a map of Africa from the Cape to the Zambezi, saying: 'That's my dream – all English.' A Liberal in politics (he gave £10,000 in 1891 to the Liberal election coffers in aid of Home Rule for Ireland, which he saw as the germ of a gigantic system of English-speaking federation), Rhodes made and lost several huge fortunes in diamonds, gold and general investments as the sinews of the war for a united British South Africa. A mystical imperialist and Anglo-Saxon racialist, he wanted Seeley to become the head of a college based on Jesuit techniques for training a future secret society of the elect imperial ruling élite. The Rhodes scholarships at Oxford were the eventual outcome of these ideas. In 1890, in alliance with the unsuspecting Cape Dutch leader, Hofmeyr, he became premier at the Cape. He planned to bring Kruger down by employing the Trojan horse of the disaffected Uitlanders on the Rand, who, without civil or political rights, felt themselves exploited by the greed and corruption of the Transvaal régime. A rising of these 'helots' with judicious external assistance would be enough. Schemes to this effect were discussed in 1895. The Colonial Office of the Liberal government was not without discreet awareness of them, though heavily deprecated. Nor was Chamberlain unaware of their general tenor after taking office in June 1895.

Chamberlain in general shared Rhodes's optimistic assumption as to how easily Kruger could be disposed of. But unlike Rhodes he trusted more to time and steady pressure. As long as the Uitlanders were given sufficient encouragement of imperial sympathy and support they would eventually and inevitably, by sheer weight of numbers, do the trick. And if Kruger tried to stop immigration to the Rand Chamberlain would have a good case for intervention on the grounds of the London Convention of 1884. On the other hand, Chamberlain would not wring his hands in moral outrage if Rhodes managed to topple Kruger with a minimum of expeditious chicanery. He did not know, or want to know, precisely what Rhodes was up to, but he trusted Rhodes to know what he was doing.

The great and constant difficulty of Chamberlain's position was that he could not openly avow his central aim. The moralism of British public opinion could not swallow a policy of British aggression. Chamberlain had to carry with him an often doubtful cabinet, and he had to cajole an often doubtful House of Commons. Hence Chamberlain constantly had to whip up a conspiracy theory of Boer aggression. Milner later actually believed this. But the point was, it did not really matter whether there was or was not a serious pan-South African Afrikaner anti-British conspiracy: since the *status quo* in any case was just as inimical to British imperial purposes in the long-run, conspiracy was irrelevant. And since any policy hostile to the Transvaal would alienate the loyalties of the Cape Dutch, those loyalties were bound to be alienated to some extent. The delicate problem of imperial policy was how to smash Kruger without creating deep or permanent alienation among the Cape Dutch. Again, absolutely minimum force with absolutely maximum effect was of the essence. Moreover, the greatest moral strength the imperial case had – that imperial rule would be much more enlightened and humane for the vast black majority of the population – was precisely the kind of argument best calculated to unite all national sections of the white population in hostility to imperial policy.

The worst thing that could happen was for Rhodes's coup against Kruger to misfire; and that is what did happen. At the last moment there was a hitch at the Johannesburg end of the conspiracy. Dr Jameson ignored Rhodes's orders not to proceed and launched his filibuster into the Transvaal with much more courage than judgement. The 600 or more riders were ignominiously rounded up and Kruger won a splendid propaganda victory. Rhodes had to resign office and the political alliance with Hofmeyr and the Cape Dutch was badly compromised. Chamberlain also was badly compromised. The Kaiser's provocative telegram congratulating Kruger and the furious British public reaction was a godsend to him. In the subsequent parliamentary inquiry Rhodes was able to assert that a feature of Kruger's anti-British conspiracy was to place the Transvaal under German protection. In any case the Liberal government had been under no illusions about Kruger's good will and good faith. There was much more 'continuity' between the Colonial Office under Lord Ripon and under Chamberlain than most Liberals imagined. And the Radical Labouchere, who might have done Chamberlain great hurt if he had had his wits about him, instead set off on a wild goose chase to prove that the whole thing was a conspiracy of Rand capitalists. This, heavily spiced with anti-semitism, became the central Radical interpretation of the origins of the South African War: the Radical equivalent of the imperialist bogey of a pan-South-African Afrikaner anti-British conspiracy. The South African question was made to fit into the theory of the economic origins of imperialism which J. A. Hobson and others were formulating as the mature and scientific Liberal explanation of the nature of political reaction, and which was to achieve classic and continually reprinted form in his *Imperialism* of 1902.

Chamberlain's policy was in disarray, and he now realized that Kruger would be a much tougher nut to crack. Too many possible enemies had been alerted. Chamberlain still had faith in the ultimate efficacy of steady pressure together with the passage of time, though increasingly he tended to the conclusion that the pressure would have to be increased sharply to convince Kruger that Britain was prepared if necessary to go to war to preserve imperial paramountcy in South Africa. Kruger concluded an offensive and defensive treaty with the Orange Free State in March 1896 (which he was perfectly entitled to do under the London Convention of 1884) and started arming via his Delagoa Bay railway to Lourenço Marques in Portuguese Mozambique. In September 1896 the Transvaal Volksraad passed an Aliens Immigration Restriction Act to cut off the flow of Uitlanders. In 1897 Chamberlain demanded the repeal of the Immigration Restriction Act as contrary to the London Convention and increased the British garrisons at the Cape and Natal to 8,000 men and twenty-four guns. The Volksraad gave way and repealed the Immigration Act.

In August 1897 Chamberlain sent Sir Alfred Milner as High Commissioner in South Africa and Governor of Cape Colony. He thus injected, without fully realizing it, an entirely new element into the very delicately balanced situation in South Africa.

Milner saw further than most men but he saw narrowly. He despised the evasions and compromises inherent in political life which Chamberlain had to stoop to. Milner's only contact with the democracy had been as an unsuccessful Liberal parliamentary candidate in 1885. He was the purest specimen of the intellectual ruthlessness and the claims for the prerogative of informed intelligence fostered in Jowett's Balliol. What Milner saw clearly in South Africa was the hopelessness, especially after the Jameson fiasco, of expecting that time was on the side of imperial policy or that the existing intensity of pressure would bring Kruger down. His radical determination to reverse the trends inherent in the *status quo* not only meant eventually a clear-headed acceptance of the inevitability and hence desirability of war, but a willingness also to tumble everything in South Africa into an imperial crucible, by advocating a revolutionary new approach to the question of the black majority and by advocating ultimately the suspension of the Cape constitution along with the annexation of the Transvaal.

Thus Milner was very soon advocating pressure to the point of war with the Transvaal if necessary as the unavoidable means to the greater end. He never quite understood that this was an impossible policy for Chamberlain to press in cabinet and the

Commons. Chamberlain had many other things on his mind. He was oppressed by Salisbury's debility in the handling of foreign policy. He had negotiations on hand arising from his proposals for an imperial commercial union made at the Colonial Conference of 1897. All protective tariffs between empire states would be abolished. This was to be the first step towards imperial consolidation and federation. The encouraging response given by the Canadians and the atmosphere of colonial cooperation strengthened Chamberlain in his view that a war in South Africa between English and Afrikaners should if at all possible be avoided. But in the end Chamberlain could not resist the force of Milner's logic and only hoped that Milner would be more efficient at coming to conclusions with Kruger than Rhodes and Jameson had been. In this he was not disappointed.

Kruger was triumphantly re-elected President of the South African Republic in February 1898. Chamberlain's hopes that moderate Transvaalers might see that Kruger was leading them into trouble were disappointed. Milner on the other hand was glad to accept the challenge. This he did in a speech at Graaf Reinet in March in which he announced that war in South Africa would be prevented only by Kruger's recognizing the necessity of reform and of assimilating the institutions and 'temper and spirit' of his republic to those of the 'free communities' of South Africa. He pressed Chamberlain to get an agreement with the Germans over the Portuguese colonies in order to block Transvaal armament through Mozambique. Chamberlain and Balfour in turn forced the reluctant Salisbury to agree that German blackmail on the Transvaal was worth paying. But by the end of 1898 Milner was convinced that the chances of winning the great game without war had passed. He was dejected by lack of general public awareness of what the real issues and the real stakes in South Africa were. Increasingly he grew impatient to force things to a crisis.

Chamberlain pinned his last hopes of peaceful success on a meeting between Kruger and Milner at Bloemfontein, arranged by the Orange Free State President Steyn in May and June 1899. Chamberlain hoped for a successful compromise on the issue of giving the Uitlanders full voting rights. Kruger hedged, offering concessions on Uitlander rights in exchange for British re-nunciation of suzerainty. He was advised shrewdly by a young Cape Dutch, English-educated lawyer, Jan Smuts. Milner wished to avoid achieving a compromise, which in his view would merely obscure the permanent realities of the situation. He thought war and annexation of the Transvaal both inevitable and desirable, the sooner the better. Chamberlain still did not want war but was losing hope of being able to avoid it. Preparations for the possible dispatch of an army corps were commenced. Sir Redvers Buller was nominated to command. Kruger's offers were refused in September. He was faced with the choice between surrendering to Chamberlain's assault or of surrendering to Milner's battery. Kruger exclaimed in tears at the end of the Bloemfontein con-ference: 'It is my country that you want . . . I am not ready to hand over my country to strangers.' Chamberlain finally agreed with the generals that active war preparations were necessary. The cabinet decided to send 10,000 troops to reinforce South Africa. Salisbury and others like Hicks Beach had no enthusiasm for the adventure but they were overcome by Chamberlain. The Transvaal and Orange Free State governments dispatched an ultimatum and declared war on 12 October 1899.

Having got his war, Milner now required that it be finished quickly and cleanly. He accepted philosophically that the forces of the Republic and the Free State would enjoy the initial advantage. Frontier towns were quickly invested: Ladysmith, Mafeking (defended by Colonel Baden-Powell, author of *Aids to Scouting*, 1899), and Kimberley (where Rhodes, convinced that Kruger would not dare to risk war, was stranded on his way north). The British garrisons were inadequate for an offensive, and Milner's military adviser Sir William Butler, an Irish Roman Catholic Home Ruler who shared fully the Radical thesis that the war was an evil capitalistic conspiracy of Rhodes and the greedy financiers of 'Jewburg', was far from being an enthusiastic organizer of the military potential of the Cape. Indeed, to Milner's indignation, the Cape government, intensely embarrassed at conflict between English and Afrikaners, took the line that the war was an imperial affair, and that the Cape would maintain a virtual neutrality.

The government calculated that Buller's army of 50,000, together with the troops already in South Africa, would be a sufficient force to disperse the Afrikaner commandos, which Army Intelligence estimated at a maximum of 48,000, including a proportion of untrained men.[3] Wolseley, gratified by the smooth efficiency of his mobilization procedures, offered two full army corps; but this was thought excessive. The general British expectation was that the campaign would be finished by Christmas. The Afrikaners under Joubert committed their main thrust into Natal, and Buller decided to concentrate his attention in that quarter. He left Methuen in the far west of the theatre to relieve Kimberley and push up into the Transvaal. In the centre he sent Gatacre to push the Orange Free State forces back and follow up the line to Bloemfontein.

By the middle of December Buller was floundering in defeat and confusion. Methuen and Gatacre had equally little luck. The 'Black Week' of British defeats (10–15 December 1899) stunned the confident public. British training was inadequate, British armament was inadequate (the Afrikaners had excellent Schneider-Creusot and Krupp guns), and British generalship was inadequate. Wolseley suffered the ultimate indignity of seeing his favourite lieutenant discredited and replaced in the supreme command in South Africa (without Wolseley's being consulted) by the despised 'little Hindoo', Roberts, with Kitchener as chief of staff.

This pair arrived in January 1900 and, leaving Buller to try to repair his reputation in Natal, organized a direct and heavily reinforced offensive from the Cape Province into the Free State and the Transvaal beyond. Colonial contingents from Canada, Australia and New Zealand, sniffed at by Wolseley who wanted to keep the war a preserve of the Home Army, were now welcomed. Roberts defeated Cronje and entered Bloemfontein on 13 March and overran the Free State. It was annexed to the British Crown as the Orange River Colony on 24 May. Mafeking was relieved after a much-publicized but not very serious investment. Hysterical rejoicings in Britain revealed the depth of British public anxiety at the spectacle of the hitherto successful defiance by a few farmers of the might of the British Empire.

Roberts defeated Botha, who had succeeded Joubert as Transvaal commandant-general, and captured Johannesburg in the Transvaal on 31 May and the capital, Pretoria, on 5 June. By this time Buller had managed to push the Afrikaners out of Natal and joined forces with Roberts on 4 July. The Transvaal was annexed as the Transvaal Colony on 3 September.

Kruger fled to Lourenço Marques and left for Europe to drum up sympathy and support. He got a great deal of sympathy but no support, for even had the continental powers been disposed to meddle they had no way of getting directly at the British in South Africa as long as Britain maintained supremacy at sea. The Russians had their hands even fuller in the Far East: the anti-western 'Boxer' rising in Peking broke out in June 1900. Public opinion in France, still smarting from the Fashoda humiliation, was furiously anti-British. In Germany also there was much agitation on behalf of the 'Teutonic' Afrikaners. In both countries anti-semitism added spice to sympathy for the cause of small freedom-loving peoples struggling against brutal oppression. The passage of the second German Navy Law in 1900 was helped greatly by the practical demonstration to German public opinion of German impotence to influence world affairs without an adequate navy. Until Germany had such a navy her colonies and her expanding oceanic commerce were at the mercy of the British. Apart from turning British embarrassments and preoccupations to advantage in getting their way in a minor dispute over the Samoan Islands, the German government in fact defied German public opinion and gave Chamberlain more delusory hopes of securing an alliance. The Kaiser refused to receive Kruger; he came to England in January 1901 to be at the death bed and funeral of his venerable grandmother Victoria and exuded friendliness and sympathy. The Germans had no intention of concluding an alliance to suit the British but equally they had no motive for crossing the British by joining any continental league against them which would serve French or Russian interests but not German interests.

Chamberlain and Milner were not at all getting the war they wanted. Their best chances went down the drain with Buller's reputation. Roberts's retrieval of the situation by June 1900 left them with only second-best chances. Afrikaner disaffection in the Cape was serious but containable. The key thing was that the Transvaalers seemed to be thoroughly demoralized: the annexed Transvaal was at last the blank page upon which Milner was free to write what he wished. Anglicization and industrialization – if necessary speeded up by importing temporary coolie labour – were to be the decisive directives of his policy of reconstruction. Roberts assumed that the war was over and went home to succeed Wolseley as the last commander-in-chief of the British Army. He left Kitchener to clear up the military mess. But to the extreme inconvenience of Kitchener and to the reduction of Chamberlain's and Milner's chances to fourth- or fifth-best category, the war had yet another eighteen months to go.

Still hoping for help from Europe, encouraged by the disaffection of their Cape brethren, unwilling to submit to Milner's demands for unconditional surrender, the Transvaal Afrikaners quickly recovered from their defeat in regular warfare and adopted guerrilla methods. Small commandos raided British outposts, harassed lines of communication, penetrated deep into the Cape Colony, blew up railway tracks, ambushed convoys, and captured General Lord Methuen. Kitchener was provoked into harsh measures of repression. He built a system of blockhouses and camps where Afrikaner families cleared out of disturbed areas were concentrated under supervision and divided between 'tame' and 'wild' Afrikaners. Farms and all other means of shelter and succour for the guerrillas were ruthlessly destroyed. In the end Kitchener had about 300,000 troops suppressing the guerrillas. The Afrikaners claimed that 26,000 died in the concentration camps; the British official estimate was 18,000. In a situation when the British were losing four times as many men through disease as through fighting these figures were not surprising. But they exposed British policy on its most vulnerable flank. The camps were a disaster for Milner, who disapproved of them. They widened and deepened the already dangerous division between English and Afrikaners in the Cape. They gave the government's opponents in Britain a heavy stick with which to beat the imperial policy.

The initial phase of patriotic enthusiasm in Britain which

sustained the government in the 'khaki election'[4] of 1900 had worn off. Most Liberals in the Gladstonian tradition deplored the war but were unwilling to denounce it while British troops were in the field against enemy armies. The Liberal imperialist minority approved the war, and the 'Oxford group' among them led by Haldane and Grey, who shared Milner's intellectual pre-dispositions, formed themselves into a 'voluntary bodyguard' to protect Milner from his political enemies. Campbell-Bannerman kept a balance between the two Liberal sides. But with the ending of the regular war in 1900 most Liberals felt that the time had come for negotiations and compromise leading to recon-ciliation. For Milner, compromise and reconciliation after war was no better than compromise and reconciliation before war. He wanted not merely to defeat the Afrikaners but to get the Afri-kaners to admit their defeat in an unconditional surrender and hand their country over to Milner to reconstruct. The longer the irregular war continued by the refusal of the Afrikaners to submit the stronger were the feelings in Britain that a negotiated peace should be sought. Thus the guerrilla war was fatal to Chamber-lain and Milner: they could get Britain into war by pleading the case of Afrikaner conspiracy and determination to destroy Britain's position in South Africa; but they could not keep the war going with general public acquiescence using that argument in a situation where British armies had destroyed Afrikaner military power. They were trapped in the predicament that their real motives for war were now contradicted by their ostensible motives for war.

Anti-war or 'pro-Boer' agitation in Britain got under way as Milner, quarrelling with Kitchener, was increasingly seen to be in difficulties. Even his friends like Asquith and Haldane and Winston Churchill counselled a less rigid insistence on all or nothing. These waverings resulted from the strength of the pro-Boer campaigns mounted by such as the young Welsh Radical M.P., David Lloyd George, who established a national reputation by daring to beard Chamberlain in a meeting in 1901 at Birming-ham, from which Lloyd George escaped with his life by disguising himself as a policeman. Welsh Liberalism and Irish Nationalism both had an idealized picture of the Afrikaners as a small democratic people resisting English domination. Campbell–Bannerman tilted the Liberal scales decisively by denouncing the concentration camps as 'methods of barbarism'.

Chamberlain and Milner no longer had a firm grip on the way things were going. The Afrikaners, led by the personable and gallant Louis Botha and the equally personable and gallant Jan Smuts, had built up a great credit in Britain with the people who would form the next Liberal government. A majority of the British public would be quite content with a South African solution based on negotiation and reconciliation, which meant in effect a reaffirmation of the *status quo*. Increasingly Chamberlain and Milner saw the threat looming before them that the 'great game' was being lost through the combination of Afrikaner guerrilla resistance and British public weariness of war and inability to understand and to share Chamberlain's and Milner's original aggressive motivation.

The Afrikaners, finally worn down, submitted at Vereeniging on 31 May 1902. In form Chamberlain and Milner won; in substance they lost. The Afrikaners submitted, but they protested; and they had good expectations that the Unionist government had lost much public credit and might well not survive the next elections. Afrikanerdom, which Milner had set out to break, was stronger and more effectively led than ever. Milner faced an impossible task. Time was running out as the Unionist government, now headed by Balfour after Salisbury's retirement in July 1902, began to crack up. With his 'kindergarten' of young and enthusiastic disciples he set desperately about the tasks of anglicization and industrialization. After much ado he managed to get agreement from the government (approved also by his Liberal friends Asquith, Grey and Haldane) for the importation of Chinese coolies to get the Rand mines working again. Even this was to rebound against him: Labour in Britain resented the exploitation of cheap labour for the benefit of Rand millionaires; humanitarians were offended by harsh conditions of employment. In fact the coolies were much better off than they would have been in employment anywhere else and were specifically attracted to South Africa by the relatively high wages offered; but such explanations, like the equally reasonable explanations of high mortality rates in concentration camps, cut no ice. Increasingly Milner became a man fewer and fewer politicians in Britain cared to compromise their political credit by defending. The Liberal imperialists (or 'Limps') formed themselves under Rosebery's leadership into the Liberal League in 1902; but even they were chary of identifying themselves too closely with a policy that had turned sour.

Chamberlain himself despaired of ultimate success. A visit to South Africa at the end of 1902 convinced him of the futility of Milner's full-blooded policy of English supremacy. He came around to the hope that, after all, the imperial purpose in South Africa might be served on the basis of reconciliation and English and Afrikaner equality. After all, Botha was a very different proposition from Kruger. Milner could not agree. Anything short of supremacy would ultimately be useless. But in any case by now Chamberlain was dreaming of a great alternative programme which would redeem the imperial policy from its South African bankruptcy. In 1905 Milner reluctantly agreed to the restoration of representative institutions to the Transvaal. The 'great game' in South Africa was now decisively lost. Milner resigned his offices in March 1905 and returned to Britain to see the Unionist government, from which Chamberlain had already resigned in 1903 to launch his Tariff Reform crusade, crash in ruins and to see his bitterest political enemies returned triumphantly to power.

III

While the imperialists' 'great game' was being played and lost in South Africa, the Unionist government played their great game of world politics. Because this game was defensive rather than offensive and because the object was to avoid losing rather than to win, they (and their 'continuity' Liberal imperialist successors) kept successfully in play longer. The end result was in fact not all that different. War to the finish in 1914–18 did much the same mortal damage to the imperialist cause at large as did the failure to get quick and clean victory to the imperialist cause in South Africa. Grey worked as hard to avoid war in 1914 as Milner worked to get war in 1899. These policies were perfectly consistent and complementary.

The Unionist cabinet in 1900 was determined to pursue the goal of putting the imperial chances in the world on a credible footing. Salisbury and Hicks Beach, the two major opponents of the forward policy, were pushed aside. Both were against war in 1899. Hicks Beach, as chancellor of the Exchequer, protested at the financial burdens which threatened the stability of Victorian fiscal assumptions. Higher direct taxes on incomes caused by war expenditure would become permanent peace-time levels if the new demands for naval construction proposed by the Admiralty were accepted and if the Army reforms pressed for following the revelations of military inadequacy in South Africa were put in hand. Higher indirect taxation would mean a return to protective tariffs. This indeed was the logic Chamberlain was soon to follow.

A cabinet revolt in 1900 by Goschen (Admiralty), Hamilton (India) and Lansdowne (War), supported by Balfour and Chamberlain, obliged Salisbury to give up the Foreign Office, where he had been stubbornly blocking all efforts to get him to try to conclude a deal with the Germans. The Russians occupied Manchuria after crushing the Chinese 'Boxers' in Peking. The cabinet rebels' recourse was Chamberlain's old panacea of a German alliance. Salisbury's negative instinct was perfectly sound. The Germans would not allow themselves to be made use of by Britain against the Russians in the Far East, where they had no serious interests at stake, and thus expose their long eastern frontier to danger. Lansdowne succeeded Salisbury at the Foreign Office. Since Britain's major rivals were the Russians and the French, a German alliance seemed natural. The German government, after all, had refused to countenance Russian and French proposals for mediation in South Africa. It took Lansdowne the best part of a year to realize that he had nothing to offer the Germans which they needed. His greatest weakness as a foreign secretary was that he never realized that what they did want – in effect British subordination in a German system of Europe and British acquiescence in German naval equality in the world – would contradict the whole point of trying to come to an agreement in the first place.

Two new factors were beginning to obtrude upon British consideration of policy. The first was that the French were becoming more amenable to agreement. The second was that the Germans were becoming very serious about their naval programme and 'world policy'.

The French were now free of the Egyptian burden of resentment they had been loading themselves with ever since 1882. Given their refusal to accept the *status quo* over Alsace-Lorraine, their first priority inevitably would be readiness for conflict with Germany. It was out of the question for France to risk conflict with the greatest naval power as well as the greatest military power: therefore, since the recent obstacles in the way of better relations with the British were being removed, a move in that direction was sensible. The French were in any case unable to sustain their ambitious naval plans against Britain. They were too expensive and drained resources from the undernourished Army. After 1902 the French Navy ceased to be a major maritime force. The serious point of the Russian alliance was to help preserve French independence in Europe against Germany. Its merits as a way of baiting the British had always been secondary. Now those merits were losing their attraction. Moreover, French dependence on the Russian alliance left them vulnerable to Russian pressure in the Far East. If the French refused to support Russia financially and diplomatically in Manchuria and Korea, the Russians would throw them over on German mercies in Europe. The French had no more desire to fight a war for the benefit of the Russians in the Far East than for the benefit of the Russians in the Near East. But in 1901 British approaches to the Japanese to form a united front against Russian pressure made the French aware that it would be convenient to reach a good understanding with the British to avoid unnecessary entanglements in the Far East.

Getting an alliance with the Japanese was pursued at the same time as the German alliance negotiations. The British would have preferred above all an agreement with the Russians to preserve the Far East *status quo*, with reasonable delimitations of economic spheres of interest. Failing that, and failing an agreement with the Germans, the Japanese were the last resort. The Admiralty pressed for an alliance. The Japanese had a large and efficient navy, with six capital ships in commission and one under construction. In the Far East Britain had four capital ships against six Russian and French, with three more Russian ships under construction. Japan would make all the difference. As with the Hay-Pauncefote Treaty with the United States, the Japanese alliance was a response to the fact that the two-power standard of British naval supremacy laid down in 1899 was beyond British capacity to maintain.

The cabinet, Balfour especially, would much have preferred further efforts to get an arrangement with the Germans. In the end it was Salisbury's anti-German attitude which tipped the scales in favour of the Japanese alliance. Even more significant for the future was that the major motive force for the alliance with Japan bearing on Lansdowne from the Foreign Office professionals was the strongly anti-German attitude of the assistant under-secretary Francis Bertie. Lansdowne paid far more attention to the professional experts than did Salisbury; and it was an important factor for future British policy that a group of younger professionals was now coalescing and preparing to replace the older generation bred up in Salisbury's days and ways at the head of the Service. The predispositions of this group were for good understandings with the French and the Russians as a means of checking the expansionist ambitions which they analysed as the basic purpose of German policy.

The British–Japanese alliance concluded in January 1902 committed either party to come to the aid of the other in the event of one of them being at war with more than one great power. Britain recognized Japan's special interests in Korea. It was the first formal alliance involving a *casus belli* contracted in Britain since 1856. For that reason, then and later, it was accorded an exaggerated significance. It did not mean the end of British isolation from Europe. But certain of the implications involved in it led in that direction. The alliance made it possible for the Japanese to consider the possibility of war with Russia as a last resort knowing that the French would be held back by the British. In 1901 the Dual Alliance was extended to include reciprocal obligations if France or Russia should be attacked by

Britain. The Russians further insisted that they and the French announce a joint agreement on China as an answer to the British and Japanese. French desire to avoid unnecessary entanglement with the British led them to seek accommodation on various matters under current dispute. The British would be responsive for the sake of settling disputes and for the sake reciprocally of not getting unnecessarily entangled with the French because of the Far East; more important than both these considerations by now, however, was the opinion gaining ground in the British Foreign Office that a good understanding with the French was desirable for anti-German reasons. For Chamberlain the mirage of a German alliance had been a most painful disappointment.

The issue of German naval construction programmes began to feature in British public affairs in 1902. The Admiralty began to revise its traditional habit of computing naval requirements in terms of the French and Russian fleets. The violence of anglo-phobia in Germany, and especially in the propaganda of the large and influential German Navy League founded in 1898, also began to be taken into account. It was difficult for the English governing order to understand the demagogic basis of agitation for a great navy in Germany. The German Navy was an imperial service, unlike the Prussian, Bavarian, Saxon and Wurtemburg armies; its officer corps was heavily middle class, whereas the soldiers were striving to maintain the aristocratic character of the Army officer corps. The Navy was the focus of much of the national sentiment of the German professors and the educated middle class generally. It was thus 'popular' and politically attractive. In deciding on naval policy Britain could not ignore the 'malignant hatred of the German people or the manifest design of the German Navy'. In immediate terms the French and Russian fleets were still the major rivals to Britain; but with the running down of the French Navy from 1902 and the destruction of the Russian Pacific and Baltic fleets in 1904–5 by the Japanese, the full significance of German fleet policy would become strikingly manifest.

The *entente* with France and later with Russia did not result alone from the pressure of the German naval threat. British policy, after all, was genuinely pacific except in South Africa and thoroughly defensive and conservative, and consequently aimed to secure an *entente* with every power in the world except the Afrikaner Republics of South Africa. The British alliance with Japan was part of a policy of achieving an understanding with the Russians. Lansdowne never ceased to hope that he might somehow strike the elusive bargain with the Germans. Britain had been trying to re-establish the 'liberal alliance' with the French ever since its disruption in 1882. Broadly speaking, Britain would achieve *ententes* with powers who calculated that the British could deliver to them something they wanted. It so happened that this was the case with the French in 1902 – or rather, with their masterful ambassador in London, Paul Cambon. Negatively, the French wished to avoid possible embarrassing consequences of the British–Japanese alliance; but they also wanted positively to gain British support in Morocco which they were planning to absorb to round off their North African empire, British consent for which they proposed to purchase by selling up their Egyptian claims. The British were in a quandary as to how to cope with Russian penetrations in Persia and Afghanistan facilitated by the new French-financed Tashkent strategic railway. Fear for India spurred them to better relations with the French as a step towards better relations with the Russians.

Neither the French nor the British entered into these questions with any deliberate idea of emerging as an anti-German *bloc*. Britain had no continental army and its fleet was as useless as ever for the defence of Paris. A naval threat from Germany would certainly make the British aware of the supreme usefulness of the French Army. But since the whole point of British naval policy was to preserve British independence and security by maintaining a sufficient maritime supremacy, dependence on the French Army would be equivalent to British naval bankruptcy and defeat. In any event the French would fight the Germans only to preserve their own independence; and a Franco-British combination against the Germans required that the Germans should threaten both British independence on sea and French independence on land. This the Germans were beginning to do by 1905.

The British came round to the idea of doing a deal with the French on Morocco at the beginning of 1903. The indigenous régime was crumbling and the British were aware that they had no means of stopping the French from taking control. Providing they could get arrangements to safeguard Gibraltar's strategic role and providing the French could square the Spanish, the British were willing to countenance a French takeover. In fact Lansdowne was rather glad that the French were willing to take on the burden of 'dealing with so helpless and hopeless a country'. This British shift was decisive for the French Foreign Ministry. Once the initial inertia was overcome the *entente* rolled forward with comparative ease. Chamberlain favoured it. The new King Edward VII, highly francophile, favoured it. The rising generation at the Foreign Office favoured it. The French Foreign Minister, Delcassé, favoured it. There was some doubt in France as to whether an *entente* with Britain was compatible with the alliance as extended in 1901 with Russia. Delcassé insisted there was no incompatibility and set out to fulfil the idea he had cherished since 1888 of a British–French–Russian combination to save Europe from German domination. The idea of extension to include Russia was welcome to the British, especially Balfour, who had got himself into a panic about Indian defence problems. Curzon, the viceroy, was trying to conduct an aggressive foreign policy of his own and his relations with the home government were deteriorating to the point of resignation. But Lansdowne was not thinking in Delcassé's terms about an anti-German combination. For him it no more ruled out a similar agreement with the Germans than the Japanese alliance ruled out agreement with the Russians. For their part, the Germans were convinced that a Franco-British *entente* would weaken the Dual Alliance and thus conduce to their benefit. The Russians indeed were not happy about it but were by now (February 1904) engrossed in war with Japan. After an exchange of visits between Edward VII and President Loubet the *entente cordiale* was concluded in April 1904. In any case, the French and the Japanese were faced with the task of actually securing their prizes.

The Japanese found it impossible to get the Russians to come to a sensible arrangement. The reckless expansionist party in St Petersburg overruled the cautious Witte, who resigned in

August 1903. The Russians confidently decided that they had no need to share with the Japanese but could take all. This was not the situation which Lansdowne had envisaged in 1901–2; but there was nothing to be done about it but hope that the Japanese knew what they were doing. Fortunately for the British this was indeed the case. Japanese armies drove the lumbering Russians out of Manchuria and captured Port Arthur. They destroyed first the Russian Pacific fleet and then they destroyed the Russian Baltic fleet off Tsushima in May 1905. By this time, however, the French as well as the Russians were in serious trouble.

The French were bound to be in trouble either way. Russian victories in the Far East against Japan would have drawn Britain in to rescue the Japanese diplomatically if not militarily. But as it happened Russian defeats and consequent revolutionary outbreaks in Russia which paralysed her as a great power offered the Germans an opportunity they did not have the strength of will to resist. While ostentatiously offering sympathy and comfort to the Russians and proposing a Russo-German alliance that would in effect cancel the Dual Alliance, the Germans decided to break the French will to resist German ascendancy in Europe and remain an independent great power. They decided to make use of Morocco as the wheel upon which the French would be broken. Their case was plausible. Morocco was an independent state and the French were shamelessly taking it over. The Sultan in December 1904 made a last effort to repel the French. The Germans would stand on the principle of the independence and integrity of the Moroccan Empire. If they could force the French to surrender their Moroccan objectives, particularly as approved and consented to by the British and Spanish, that indeed would be the end of France as an independent great power. For the Germans it would be the grand slam: end of the Franco-Russian alliance, end of the Franco-British *entente*, France accepting the permanence of the loss of Alsace-Lorraine and collaborating as a junior partner in a German system of Europe. Accordingly the Germans applied pressure on the French with an unsparing hand. They expected that the British would prudently move away from the target area; but instead the British for the first time seriously started thinking about the consequences for their interests and security of a French collapse in Europe.

But as yet the British were not thinking of military intervention alongside the French in Europe. The conclusions of the new Committee of Imperial Defence set up by Balfour in 1902 as part of his intense concern to pull British military, naval and strategic thinking together in the aftermath of the Boer war were still aligned with the 1891 Stanhope doctrine on the Army and blue-water doctrine on the Navy. These doctrines now began to come under more critical scrutiny. For the time being British diplomatic support sustained the tottering French and helped them to arrange a conference of the powers to be held later at Algeciras in Spain which would have the effect of Europeanizing the crisis and dissipating much of the direct intensity of the German pressure. The conservative pacific Rouvier ministry in France, bewildered by the brutality of the German assault, supposed that Delcassé's impatient recklessness had provoked the crisis. Delcassé resigned on 6 June 1905, a few days after the annihilation of the Russian Baltic fleet at Tsushima. On the same day the Kaiser raised his Bismarck-substitute, Count Bülow, to the rank of prince. It was a victory, but it turned out to be empty and costly. The French were shaken and confused, but by no means broken.

The British could come to two conclusions about this. Lansdowne, representing what was by now an old-fashioned orthodoxy, drew the moral that the French were not to be trusted to stand firm. With Sanderson, the permanent under-secretary at the Foreign Office, he was prone to be critical of the French and uncritical of the Germans. The Russian defeat by the Japanese removed the threat to India, which in any case was covered by a renewed version of the Japanese alliance, and this removed in turn a major British motive for the *entente* of 1904. But on the other hand, the younger school in the Foreign Office drew the moral that the Moroccan crisis revealed the true intentions of the Germans and the necessity to draw closer to France and Russia. Hardinge was appointed ambassador in St Petersburg in 1904 and was to replace Sanderson as permanent under-secretary in 1906. This difference of opinion represented a clash between an old empire-oriented outlook and a new Europe-oriented outlook.

This clash in turn involved revolutionary implications for military, naval and strategic thinking.

Debate over defence between the end of the South African War and the shock of the Moroccan crisis of 1905–6 rehearsed the themes which would be of decisive significance in the years leading to 1914. Unlike Salisbury, Balfour was deeply concerned with contingency planning, and one of his first priorities on succeeding Salisbury in 1902 was to try to put British defence thinking on a proper footing. His major contribution in this direction was the setting up in 1902 of the Committee of Imperial Defence, which replaced the Defence Committee of the cabinet. The new committee would deal not merely with problems submitted to it by cabinet, but would, it was hoped, be a permanent body which would centralize thinking about defence problems. It would have a mind of its own and include the service intelligence chiefs. By 1904 it was equipped with a permanent secretariat headed by Sir George Clarke. As Balfour explained to the Commons, the C.I.D. differed 'fundamentally' from everything that had ever existed in the past.

Concurrently, the needs and functions of the armed services underwent thorough reappraisal. A commission under Lord Elgin was appointed to investigate the shortcomings of military organization. Lord Esher, a member of the commission and an influential political *éminence grise*, became chairman of the War Office reconstruction committee in 1903, whose report in 1904 recommending sweeping changes in Army organization including an Army Council (to replace the commandership-in-chief) and a general staff was accepted by the government. Selborne at the Admiralty revolutionized naval organization. Receptive to new ideas and aware of British technological weakness, he altered systems of entry to the service and training of personnel. He established the Royal Navy War College and introduced modern equipment and a system of fleet reserves. His major ally in the service was Admiral Sir John Fisher, who became First Sea Lord in 1904. Between them, Selborne and Fisher were responsible for the decision to commit naval policy to the basis of the all big-gun capital ship, the first of which, *Dreadnought*, was laid down in 1905. They were responsible also for the decision to streamline the fleet by getting rid of masses of obsolete ships and for deciding to shift the balance of British naval power. Fisher began moving ships from the Mediterranean to home waters, where they inevitably took on the function of counterbalancing the new German fleet, greatly augmented in effectiveness by the recent construction of the canal from Kiel in the Baltic to the North Sea.

Naval questions like these were complicated and gave rise to bitter controversy, but the Navy did not raise problems as crucial as conscription or whether or not Britain should attempt to be a great continental military power as well as the greatest naval power. The Duke of Norfolk's commission on the role of auxiliary forces concluded in 1904, in agreement with similar recommendations by the Elgin commission, that a home defence army capable in the absence of the whole or the greater proportion of the regular forces of protecting Britain against invasion could be raised and maintained only on the principle that it was the duty of 'every citizen of military age and sound physique to be trained for national defence and to take part in it should emergency arise'.

This added rank 'brick and mortar' and 'bolt from the blue' heresy revived from the past to a new heresy: national military service through compulsion and conscription. Balfour's government, in deep trouble from the tariff reform issue among other things, backed away in horror from this political poison. They were highly embarrassed when Roberts, discharged from the commandership-in-chief, decided to become the leader of a movement to advocate the idea of national service and resigned from the Committee of Imperial Defence. The blue-water school, led by Fisher, accused the national service advocates of being secret planners of large-scale military intervention on the continent under the guise of repelling an invasion which they knew could never happen. Fisher argued that Britain could not afford to be both the greatest naval power in the world (which was in any event an unquestionable necessity) and a great military power. The only sensible army reforms would be along the lines of regarding the Army as a projectile to be fired by the Navy. But already, by September 1905, the Military Intelligence chiefs were attacking Fisher's assumptions that support for France against Germany would have to be essentially naval in character, and were coming round to consideration of the need to do something better: if not a large conscript army to match the French, then such an expeditionary force as would effectively 'give support to the French Armies in the field'.

Chapter Fifteen

THE
UNIONIST IMPASSE
1903—5

I

Chamberlain's frustration exploded in May 1903. Ritchie's budget plans involved the dropping of the Corn duty, which was Chamberlain's last hope within the existing frame of politics of keeping alive the prospect of Britain's being able to reciprocate colonial offers of tariff preference.

Balfour had not felt able to resist Ritchie on the point. Ritchie was being quite deliberate. It was well appreciated that protectionist opinion was now lifting its head with a real sense of new possibilities in the air. Solidly behind Ritchie was Treasury opinion. The idea was to stamp out the reviving evil of protectionism before it had a chance to gather strength. Hence the necessity of killing the Corn duty, even though it had originally been imposed purely as a revenue expedient by Hicks Beach.

In his Birmingham bailiwick on 15 May Chamberlain took up Ritchie's challenge in a startling public pronouncement. Empire was the key to British prospects in the new century. This was the old theme, as old as Seeley. What was new was Chamberlain's thesis that trade and commerce were in turn the key to empire. It was the true business of British statesmen to do what they could 'even at some present sacrifice', to keep the trade of the colonies with Britain, and to promote it even if in so doing trade with foreign competitors was somewhat lessened. Chamberlain denied that he was a protectionist in any familiar sense. His point was that all familiar orthodoxies, free trade or protectionist, had ceased to be relevant because Britain's situation was 'absolutely a new situation'. There had been nothing like it in British history. Never before had the British people been in the position to make this kind of choice bearing in mind the stakes involved. Chamberlain wanted a great public debate to consider the two alternatives of acceptance or rejection of the prospects of an imperial destiny. This speech inaugurated what was soon to be known as the Tariff Reform movement.

It was extremely important for Chamberlain to urge that old labels from the past struggles over fiscal policy be abandoned, because they would have the effect of compromising the proposition that was central to his imperial policy. The essence of preference policy was giving the colonies tariff reciprocity on what Britain imported from them: that is, very largely, raw materials and especially foodstuffs; and such reciprocity logically demanded the imposition of tariff barriers on importations of foreign produced foodstuffs. Thus imperial preference inescapably involved taxes on food. This is what Chamberlain was hinting at in his remarks on 'sacrifices'. Chamberlain as yet had to hint about this because it was a matter of the utmost political delicacy, and had to be imparted to the public mind as gently as possible.

'Protection', on the other hand, such as had been envisaged with the emergence of the Fair Trade movement in the 1880s and the Conservative party conference resolution of 1887, was essentially about protecting British industries from the competition of the manufacturing industries particularly of Germany and the United States. Such protectionism for the most part fell over backwards in its fervour for a fiscal policy of cheap food importation, and took care to dissociate itself from the embarrassing support of reactionary squires like Chaplin, who would support protectionism in any shape or form in the eventual hope that protection for British agriculture would thereby become a respectable cause again. There was in fact a very great deal of latent or actual enthusiasm for this kind of industrial protectionism to be tapped politically at the beginning of the new century.

Thus the great problem for Chamberlain was that most of the protectionist public enthusiasm he needed to tap politically was directed at cross purposes to his imperial preference proposals. He was not quite as yet a convinced industrial protectionist. He still regarded himself as a free trader who saw the necessity of modifying free trade on a basis of logical expediency for the greater and higher purposes of a policy of imperial construction. Chamberlain became an industrial protectionist because that was where popular protectionist sentiment largely was. Imperial preference could never be the rallying cry of a great mass political movement. For Chamberlain taxes on food were a necessary evil for his economic imperialism in much the same way that smashing Kruger's republic was a necessary evil in his South African imperial policy. They were both policies of *raison d'état*. The British public, imbued with self-righteous moralism, could not be won over on such grounds. Therefore Chamberlain had to be devious and cunning. This was the bargain ultimately struck by the two anti-free-trade factions; but it was not to be concluded without considerable time and trouble.

Much the best way, tactically, for Chamberlain to reveal the food tax implications of his imperial preference proposals would be to link them with a social reform programme: protective duties would provide finance otherwise not available, or available only through prohibitively increased direct taxation, for expensive measures of social amelioration. Old age pensions were at the head of this agenda, and it was under cover of this issue that Chamberlain chose to come out into the open. Liberal free traders were well aware of the shape of things to come. One of their back bench parliamentary spokesmen was Lloyd George, who as a 'pro-Boer' had specialized in baiting Chamberlain in the hectic and violent days of the 1900 election.

This time, however, Chamberlain was quite willing to be hooked. Lloyd George assumed that, if he could tempt Chamberlain to bite at the old age pensions bait on the food tax hook, Chamberlain would be hauled out of the political waters to gasp and die, revealed to the horrified gaze of the free trade public as an advocate of taxing the food of the struggling masses. Chamberlain envisaged quite a different scenario. The protectionist fish was much bigger and more powerful than the complacent free traders imagined. This leviathan would in fact drag free trade into the political waters and drown it. Thus, when later in May 1903 Lloyd George flicked the hook baited with old age pensions, Chamberlain rose and snapped at it with careful deliberation.

The only way of getting the funds necessary for an old age pensions scheme, Chamberlain made clear, would 'involve a review of that fiscal system' which he had 'indicated as necessary and desirable at an early day'. Later, more explicitly, Chamberlain added: 'Therefore we come to this – if you are to give a preference to the colonies . . . you must put a tax on food. I make hon. gentlemen opposite a present of that.'

Now Chamberlain was out in the open. Liberals of all factions rejoiced to have a political target more promising of triumphs and rewards than anything since the days of faltering Lord Beaconsfield at the time of Midlothian. Chamberlain's own enthusiastic cohorts rejoiced that battle with musty Victorian doctrinaire fiscal and political orthodoxy was now frankly joined. People like Leo Amery, Leo Maxse (owner and editor of the *National Review*) and the journalist J. L. Garvin, who became one of the most formidable Tariff Reform propagandists, entered into the fray in a spirit of youthful zest and crusade.

Far different was the spirit of Balfour. As prime minister and leader of the Conservative party he had to consider the consequences of Chamberlain's pronouncements for the government and the main body of its support in parliament and in the constituencies. Personally, Balfour was quite sympathetic to Chamberlain's demands for a national reconsideration of fiscal policy. He was inclined to query the expediency for Britain of free trade in a world where Britain alone of the greater economic entities remained wedded to it. Even though debate might establish that free trade was indeed the more expedient alternative for Britain, Balfour despised the quasi-religious fervour of the mass of free trade sentiment which objected on grounds of muddled morality and historical mythology to the question's even being explored. But at the same time Balfour had to recognize that a great deal of Conservative opinion in and out of the government firmly adhered to free trade on the grounds both of principle and of political expediency: it was good political economy, and any departure from it would be disastrous for Unionism because the country at large simply would not swallow the arguments of Tariff Reform. Already indignant free trade Tories like Lord Hugh Cecil and Randolph Churchill's son Winston were bombarding Balfour with protests and warnings. Their arguments stressed that cheap food for the people was a true 'Disraelian' Tory policy; and that protectionism was the characteristic policy of selfish 'Brummagem' middle-class manufacturers, who, as in America, would flood the lobbies of the House of Commons with touts if protection were ever conceded. Old Hicks Beach and Goschen were scandalized, and so were the more vociferously free trade members of the cabinet, Ritchie, Balfour of Burleigh and Lord George Hamilton.

Balfour had to weigh the various factors in the equation very carefully. In the first place, though Chamberlain had not presumed to challenge Balfour's succession to his uncle Salisbury in 1902, Chamberlain clearly had seized the political initiative. Whether loved or hated, the colonial secretary had unmistakably captured the public imagination and the headlines. Balfour increasingly faced the prospect of being in much the same situation as Granville and Hartington in relation to Gladstone from 1876. In the second place, Chamberlain's claims that there was a great mass of public sentiment waiting for just some such chance for giving support to a major new political initiative might very well be true. The mass of evidence of social and governmental inadequacies emerging from the various committees and investigations provoked by poor British performance in South Africa added up to a formidable agenda of national reconstruction. Balfour would have to be careful not to put himself in the position of resisting Chamberlain and giving to Chamberlain by default the real leadership of Unionism. The central intellectual essence of Unionism, after all, was the testing of assumptions inherited from the High Victorian era to assess their continuing adequacy for new circumstances. Chamberlain had a very strong intellectual case to which Balfour, an intellectual in politics, was peculiarly susceptible.

Nevertheless, as against this, there was the question of keeping the Unionist government in being in order to make the necessary adjustments of national policy possible; and the key to this was maintaining the unity of the Conservative party. Balfour above all was obsessed by the overriding necessity of not being a second Robert Peel. Conservatism was the foundation not merely of the

Union and the integrity of the United Kingdom; it was the foundation of all possibilities of national reordering and reconstruction. For if Liberalism were to be allowed to get back into power because of the collapse of Unionist unity the consequences, in Balfour's view, would be profoundly disturbing. The mass of Liberals were Gladstonian in general outlook. Presumably, they would infect any future Liberal government with their political debility, their feckless insistence on the 'rights' of people even at the expense of the higher interests of society at large and the State: the irresponsibility of the Nonconformists in putting their own petty and selfish sectional interests above the cause of an effective and efficient system of State education was as good an example of Liberalism's provincialism and incapacity to be a truly 'national' party as could be asked for. Their 'softness' and inability to resist what to Balfour were the spurious claims of Irish nationalism could well lead to a situation where a Liberal government, dependent on Irish votes to stay in power, would attempt to force Home Rule down the throats of the majority of people in Britain and the Irish Unionist minority. This situation could well destroy the political morale of the British people and provoke civil war in Britain as well as Ireland. As for defence questions, Campbell-Bannerman, who would be the next Liberal prime minister unless Rosebery could somehow contrive to block his path, was the notorious author of the dissenting minority report of the Hartington Commission, arguing against a general staff. It was well known that many Liberal imperialists, who continued to look to Rosebery for leadership and who belonged to the Liberal League, especially Grey, Haldane, Fowler and even the more circumspect Asquith, regarded the prospect of Campbell-Bannerman as prime minister with undisguised alarm as a standing menace to basic national interests. For Balfour only a united Conservatism as the heart of a united Unionism keeping a firm grip on the levers of the power of the British State could keep out the Liberals; and this negative consideration would have to take priority over Chamberlain's plea that the stakes of empire justified the immense risk of throwing the whole political *status quo* into the crucible.

The Tariff Reform movement, none the less, was inevitably

going to be the greatest single dynamic force within parliamentary Unionism, and, therefore, presumably within constituency Unionism. Many Unionist members saw in some bold fiscal initiative a way for Unionism to redeem the inadequacies of its performance during the South African war. These were the kind of people who listened to Kipling's excoriations of British national flabbiness in poems like *The Islanders* (1902), and who hungered for masterful leadership. A meeting of the parliamentary party in June 1903 revealed no less than 130 convinced Unionist Tariff Reformers. A later meeting of Unionist Free Traders mustered only sixty members as the nucleus of a Unionist Free Food League. To some extent Balfour was paying the price of his back benchers' exasperation with the nepotic and feeble government reconstructions of 1900 and 1902. Chamberlain was preparing a massive propaganda machine to convert the constituencies. Although the idea of food taxes was as yet distinctly unpopular, the idea of protectionism in a more general way was not. Chamberlain's tactic was to exploit the latter in aid of the former.

Balfour initially had hoped to preserve party unity by adopting a central stance and requesting ministers not to engage in public debate. But with the party beginning to split beneath them, the ministry could not long maintain this posture astride the two sides of the case. Balfour determined, first, that his overriding duty and responsibility was to maintain Unionism for as long as possible as the directive force of national life and politics. Second, he determined that he could not stand pat on free trade, but would have to keep a working relationship between Unionism as a whole and Chamberlain's Tariff Reform crusade. His Unionist ministry would be, in some way and to some degree, a ministry of fiscal reform. That would mean letting the extreme free traders go. This made sense in terms of the weighting of opinion in the party generally, in terms of the national interest which orthodox free trade very conceivably was not serving, and in terms of Balfour's own personal predilections. Balfour calculated that he could keep his ministry in being without Chamberlain on the one side and without the free trade zealots on the other so long as he could keep the old Duke of Devonshire in.

Though he had long ceased to have any of the practical importance in affairs he had possessed as Marquess of Hartington, the Duke had established an extraordinary public reputation for integrity, political honesty and plain dealing. Balfour quite reasonably calculated that he could preserve public confidence in his government if the public saw that the Duke himself had confidence in it. The Duke would be an indispensable steadying influence. The Duke was a free trader but no zealot and amenable to arguments of the higher interest of keeping Unionism and all that it involved since 1886 intact. Without the Duke the Unionist free traders would have no leader of national stature, and would therefore be neutralized. Chamberlain himself would be no problem. He had no motive for crossing Balfour because his whole campaign depended ultimately in carrying Unionism with him; he had nowhere else to go since Liberalism was solidly free trade. It seems certain that Balfour and Chamberlain agreed that Chamberlain should resign from the ministry and lead his crusade in a private capacity and that his son Austen should come into the cabinet as his representative; and that Balfour would regard the Tariff Reform movement as an advance guard or 'pioneer' of fiscal reform conquering public territory which Balfour would then occupy and consolidate with the forces of loyal Unionism.

Meanwhile, in August Balfour offered his colleagues a compromise fiscal solution for public consumption, that of retaliation against countries which erected unreasonably high tariff barriers against British trade. This did not break decisively with free trade principles nor did it involve dangerous food taxes. Balfour trusted that this would be enough for the time being to keep both wings of the party substantially together. At the same time Balfour determined that the criterion for continued membership of the cabinet would be 'hearty acceptance' in principle of some moderate degree of fiscal reform in the future. But he did not make this clear until after he had virtually dismissed the three free traders in the cabinet on 14 September – Ritchie, Balfour of Burleigh and Hamilton. In collusion with Balfour, Chamberlain announced his intention to resign. Balfour calculated that if Chamberlain went out on the one hand and Balfour could interpose a statesmanlike moderation between the out-and-out free traders and the Duke, he could keep the Duke in and preserve the credibility of the ministry. For a short time Balfour seemed to have succeeded; but the dismissed free traders convinced the Duke that Balfour's 'moderation' was merely a cover for collusion with Chamberlain; and the Duke took the first opportunity to resign and in October became president of the Unionist Free Trade League. Balfour's attempt to make of himself and the Duke a bridge that would hold the two wings of the party together had failed. The split was now beyond repair.

With both Chamberlain and Devonshire gone, Balfour's ministry was merely a shell. Milner declined to leave South Africa to replace Chamberlain at the Colonial Office. Chamberlain's son Austen took Ritchie's place at the Exchequer but could lend none of his father's grandeur to the government. Balfour was short of good replacements; the new men he brought in, Arnold-Forster at the War Office and Lyttelton at the Colonial Office, were comparative lightweights. From now on Balfour was reduced merely to holding on to office as long as he decently could and to hoping that possibly a Devonshire–Rosebery alliance might at least head off the horrid prospect of a Campbell-Bannerman Liberal government committed to and in the hands of the Irish.

II

The Chamberlain faction was the majority faction of Unionism: that was put beyond all doubt at the annual meeting of the National Union of Conservative Associations at the beginning of October 1903 in Sheffield. There Balfour announced his compromise tariff retaliation policy as the official Conservative fiscal policy. But once the Duke resigned the initiative was wholly in Chamberlain's hands. Chamberlain had no difficulty asserting his control of his own Liberal Unionist party organization. At Glasgow on 6 October Chamberlain launched his propaganda campaign to convert the British public to a realization that the key to their future as citizens of a great and independent country lay in the development of Britain's links with a larger world entity such as the empire provided, and that the key to establishing these links lay in a tariff policy of imperial preferences and the food taxes they involved. From Glasgow he went on to Greenock, and then to Newcastle, Liverpool and Leeds in the first stage of a tremendous demagogic campaign without political precedent. Chamberlain took care to link a general programme of protection with his food taxes proposals. He painted a lurid picture: agriculture 'practically destroyed', 'sugar has gone, silk has gone, iron is threatened; the turn of cotton will come'; these industries 'and the working men who depend upon them' were 'like sheep in the field'; and the home trade was being hit as well. In this way he secured the support of the powerful Harmsworth press, led by the *Daily Mail*. Harmsworth was convinced that the pill of imperial preferences would never be swallowed by the public unless sugared with increased duties against foreign manufacturers. Chamberlain had other influential champions in the press: Amery in *The Times* and Garvin in the *Daily Telegraph* were in situations of vital strategic advantage. Pearson, founder of the *Daily Express* in 1900 and controller of a great provincial press empire, was also a convert to the cause. He purchased the *Standard* and made it into a Tariff Reform organ. Only the *Spectator* among leading Unionist papers supported the Unionist Free Trade League; and the attempts of this minority group to purchase *The Observer* were frustrated by Harmsworth, who bought it in 1905 and later appointed Garvin as its editor, who made it into the most influential of all the Tariff Reform journals.

But Chamberlain was still fighting an uphill battle. He was basing a great propaganda campaign on economic issues. It was difficult for him to project an ideal of empire on this basis of statistics, percentages, indices of production, exports and imports. Cobden and Bright, in their great anti-corn-laws agitation, did not have to do this. They appealed not to interest and ad-advantage and to fear but to hope and justice. The future they pointed to was one of golden prosperity relieved of all occasions of domestic and international class or power conflict; a version of an earthly paradise. In complete contrast, Chamberlain was appealing precisely to interest and advantage. But he appealed also for a willingness to accept that progress was not guaranteed and automatic as in Liberal free trade theory. Chamberlain was arguing that opportunities of interest and advantage must be seized in order to make it possible for Britain to survive in a world of future rivalry and conflict in which the race would be to the swift and the prize to the strong. Chamberlain, in short, was offering himself as the English statesman who would fulfil Seeley's imperial prophecies. This was, fundamentally, the reason for his failure. The sacrifices he was asking were far too great. He demanded, in effect, that they renounce the reassuring comforts of the central Liberal intellectual tradition of the nineteenth century, which, whether in terms of Mill or Cobden or Green or Morley or Spencer or Hobson or indeed socialist versions of it as with Morris, offered in one way or another an ultimate reconciliation of forces, involving less and less anxiety, ultimate harmony and repose, an end to strenuous conflict.

Strenuousness was of the essence of Chamberlain's offer. He offered the historical analysis of Seeley, the kind of authoritarian state envisaged by Arnold, the kind of informed expert intelligence fostered by Jowett and represented with almost frightening intensity by Milner, the kind of revived and reformed aristocracy of leadership demanded long ago by Carlyle. Chamberlain was demanding nothing less than that Edwardian boards of directors should become captains of industry and emulate Abbot Samson of *Past and Present*. All this indeed was of the logic of National Efficiency and of Unionism, and all of it was at the heart, for example, of Balfour's and Morant's policy on education. But education had the saving grace of being a moral issue in a way that the economics of empire never could be.

A second fundamental weakness in Chamberlain's argument was that the conditions and prospects of British industry by no means sustained indubitably the analysis of crisis essential for the protectionist aspect of his programme. The wave of industrial self-criticism that went parallel with the general sense of national inadequacy provoked by the failures of the South African war, expressed especially in books like Williams's *Made in Germany* (1896), Mackenzie's *American Invaders* (1902) and A. Shadwell's *Industrial Efficiency* (1906), and the famous article in *The Times* of 1902 on the 'Crisis in British Industry', set off a debate which failed to come to any clear conclusion either way. There was simply not enough precise quantitative data in an aggregative form available at the time to sustain large-scale assertions about the state of the economy. It was one thing to assert that Britain was in something that could plausibly be described as an industrial crisis; it was quite another thing to prove conclusively that this was caused by unfair foreign competition. Much of the crisis propaganda in any case contradicted the tariff reform arguments by laying the blame on inefficient British management. Entrepreneurial weaknesses were very probably the major factor in the difficulties of the British iron and steel industries. The same was true of coal. But on the other hand cotton, Britain's major export industry, was affected neither by inadequate management nor by foreign competition but by the decline of the proportion of cotton goods entering world trade as more countries supplied a greater percentage of their own needs.[1] Cotton on the whole remained a buoyant industry. Tory Lancashire, one of the great bastions of Conservative electoral strength, in turn depended for its buoyance on cotton; and Chamberlain's protectionism would tend to compromise this desirable *status quo*. The woollen textile industry in fact reversed the downward trend of its export trade in fabrics after the turn of the century, and British success in exploiting world markets more successfully than foreign competitors was very noticeable. The boot and shoe industry responded very successfully to foreign competition in the pre-1914 years; and by 1913 the *Economist* exulted in the 'Victory of British Boots' on the evidence of the trade figures of 1903–12 compared with those of 1890–1903. Engineering displayed a much more mixed pattern of success and weakness. Trade between Britain and Germany (mutually one another's best customer) showed clear British superiority in textile machinery, agricultural machinery, boilers and machine tools; as against German superiority in (by 1913) motor cars, cycles, implements and tools, arms and unenumerated machinery. There was certainly no convincing evidence either of a general entrepreneurial weakness or of a general inferiority in the face of foreign competition: British engineering in many respects remained outstandingly superior. In the field of electrical products the British industry recovered from a bad patch after 1903, resumed its earlier advantage, and Britain ceased to be a net importer of electrical machinery. In cables Britain was not at a competitive disadvantage; and the British export position for telegraphic equipment was always good. And though the electrical industry as a whole was more an offshoot of American and German industries than an indigenous growth, this situation would not have been materially improved by tariffs. Chemicals was more clearly an industry suffering from the impact of foreign competition from about 1900, as was glass, but here again the evidence was mixed. And in mercantile shipping, despite strong German competition, there was little evidence that British supremacy in ship building was in danger of being compromised, and the British maritime industries retained their overwhelming predominance up to 1914.

It was indeed unfortunate for Chamberlain's campaign that its inauguration in 1903 coincided with the beginnings of a marked upward trend in the economy after a period of depression which had done much to foster the fears and anxieties which found expression in the call for industrial protection. This upward trend was particularly important in cutting the ground beneath Chamberlain's hopes of rallying working-class support for his campaign. He got almost no support from official working-class leadership in politics or unionism. Much of the ideology of the movement of national and imperial reconstruction associated with Tariff Reform was critical of the trade unions as hindrances to rational efficiency. The T.U.C. was resolutely Cobdenite, as were the cotton workers, who nourished an orthodoxy which had rejoiced at the destruction of Indian efforts to protect its cotton industry against Lancashire. Although many Socialist intellectuals like Bernard Shaw were attracted to Tariff Reform because of contempt for the outmoded Victorian nonsense of free trade, others such as the Webbs avoided becoming embroiled in the issue, to the regret of their enthusiastically pro–Chamberlain associate W. A. S. Hewins. The Webbs were more interested in getting Balfour to agree on a Royal Commission on the Poor Law.

Herein lay another weakness in Chamberlain's position. Although Tariff Reform had as its central object the consolidation and integration of the empire, it had the effect of splitting pro-imperial opinion in Britain. Indeed, Chamberlain and his protégé Amery expected that the Liberal imperialists of the Liberal League would 'want to follow Joe'; and there were some defections to Tariff Reform. Milner was a convinced Tariff Reformer. But Amery was hurt and surprised at the failure of Grey, Asquith and Haldane to come across. Grey possibly was tempted; but in any case their chief, Rosebery, failed to give a decisive lead on the issue. Rosebery's initial reaction had been friendly enough, and a Rosebery–Chamberlain conjunction was a frequent topic of speculation in the middle of 1903. But, impressed by the cautious scepticism of Asquith and Haldane, Rosebery withdrew from the brink.

The Liberal imperialists insisted on efficiency in industrial management as the central British problem. With efficiency, tariffs would be unnecessary; and a protective policy which in effect protected inefficient British industry from efficient foreign competition would be the greatest possible economic disaster for Britain. Instead, Rosebery and his Liberal imperialist followers concentrated on the 'Charlottenburg' scheme of a university of science and technology as a symbol of a new era of technological and industrial efficiency and as an alternative to Chamberlain's tariff schemes. This in turn drove Chamberlain, hitherto closely in sympathy with the kind of development represented by Charlottenburg, to deprecate its significance. Thus Tariff Reform weakened the links between 'efficiency' enthusiasts as well as imperialists. Indeed the 'Co-efficients', including most of the leading advocates of imperialism and national efficiency, disintegrated under the strain of the tariff question. Chamberlain was leading a crusade, and its fuel was fanaticism. Out of fanaticism came dogma and anathema. In 1904 a group of Tariff Reformers formed a secret club called the Confederates – 'a kind of political Mafia', as the *Nation* called it – with the avowed purpose of driving Unionist free traders out of public life. This provoked intense and long-lasting bitterness. Many Unionist free traders renounced their party allegiance. Winston

Churchill and J. E. B. Seely, two of the party's most promising younger men, crossed the floor of the Commons in 1904.

In an atmosphere of increasing acrimony, with Unionism floundering but clinging to office, Chamberlain in 1904 found it difficult to sustain the initial momentum of his movement. He expected that once it became clear that the government's credibility was destroyed, as it now unquestionably was, Balfour would have to dissolve the House of Commons and after the inevitable Unionist defeat Chamberlain would become *de facto* leader of a new Tariff Reform Unionist party. He would then soon recapture office from the incoherent Liberals, who would be capable of no more than putting in a caretaker government in the manner of the Tories between 1846 and 1874.

Two things foiled Chamberlain's plans. First, Balfour, with agile obstinacy, clung to office despite every humiliation until December 1905. Doubtless he had no desire for an early election while Chamberlain's crusade was in the first flush of its impetus. In any case, he needed time to complete various projects he had on hand, principally concerned with defence, which he did not trust the Liberals to do justice to. Secondly, this time thus provided by Balfour allowed the Liberals a chance to develop a new unity and a new confidence.

III

Campbell-Bannerman's election to the Liberal leadership in the House of Commons in 1899 did little to heal the wounds which had excruciated the Liberal party since Rosebery's painful tenure of the premiership. Though he had grown somewhat in stature since the latter period of the South African war and the struggles over the education question, Campbell-Bannerman still was not a convincing alternative prime minister. Nor would he be likely to have a chance of impressing himself on the public mind as such so long as Rosebery waited ostentatiously in the political wings for the call to national leadership. Undoubtedly Rosebery had ambitions, like Chamberlain, to be the great imperial statesman. Unlike Chamberlain, however, he lacked the nerve and the character to launch out on the great gamble. His loyal imperialist following led by Grey and Haldane urged him without avail to act boldly and decisively. Campbell-Bannerman, bearing the toils and burdens, resented Rosebery's olympian aloofness as well as his imperialism and determined not to make way for him. Chamberlain resented him as a rival for the leadership of the imperialist cause. Balfour resented him as the advocate of a new axis of national politics above and beyond the existing obsolete and harmful party system.

Rosebery's only serious chance of exercising decisive political influence in fact was frankly to set out to build up an imperialist Liberal party that would either oust Campbell-Bannerman and overwhelm the Gladstonian Little Englanders or could conceivably coalesce with dissident Unionist and Liberal Unionist forces dissatisfied with Balfour to form a central national and imperial political *bloc*, possibly in conjunction with Milner and Chamberlain. Winston Churchill for a while was keen on this project. But Rosebery disdained to work for political effectiveness in this way. His major concern was always to preserve the purity of his independence from party ties. When Asquith clashed with Campbell-Bannerman over the latter's notorious 'methods of barbarism' remark, Rosebery failed to come to Asquith's support. Consequently all his initiatives came to nothing. Great hopes were excited by his speech at Chesterfield in December 1901 in which he called for the Liberal party to throw over its Gladstonian heritage and transform itself into the vehicle of a policy of national efficiency. Most loyal Liberals regarded this as an insult to their party's historic past; and suspected, correctly, that the Chesterfield programme owed more to Sidney Webb's current influence on Rosebery than Rosebery was willing to admit. A little later Rosebery called for a formal repudiation of Gladstone's policy of Home Rule for Ireland. This was asking far too much of the Liberal party as a whole and was giving his own followers no practical and plausible lead.

Consequently, when in 1902 and 1903 politics were transformed by the impact of the fiscal issue and Chamberlain's initiative, Rosebery was left stranded, waiting for the crown that no one would or could hand to him. He was never thereafter a considerable political force. He went off to plough his 'lonely furrow' and left those who had invested their political credit in his future, such as the Webbs, very much at a loss.

This left Campbell-Bannerman in a much stronger position, especially *vis-à-vis* his Liberal imperialist critics, led by Asquith. Liberals irreconcilably opposed to the idea of Campbell-Bannerman as prime minister were reduced to such shifts as thinking of recalling one or other of the great proconsuls, Curzon, Cromer or Milner, as the head of an imperialist coalition; or perhaps of a Devonshire Free Food ministry. But there was no substance to such wishful fantasies. When Chamberlain set out on his great stump campaign, Campbell-Bannerman had the wit to depute Asquith to dog him from place to place and challenge relentlessly Chamberlain's claims and assertions. No one was better at this debating technique than Asquith, whose brilliant defence of the Free Trade case elevated the campaign into a political gladiatorial contest which fascinated the public. This helped not only the cause of Free Trade and Asquith's own reputation and the morale of Liberalism, but it helped Campbell-Bannerman also to consolidate his leadership by forging links between the two alienated sectors of the party.

This process continued throughout 1903, 1904 and 1905. Campbell-Bannerman further enhanced his prospects by taking care not to rest content with a merely negative Free Trade orthodoxy. He injected a considerable programmatic element into Liberalism in addition to standard sectarian policies on such things as education and licensing: a smallholdings policy, payment of M.P.s, curtailment of the House of Lords' veto on legislation. In general he conveyed, to the increasing satisfaction of the Labour interest, that his resistance to Tariff Reform did not by any means signify his satisfaction with the degree of social progress and social justice achieved hitherto in the fiscal framework of Free Trade. This went down well with the Labour and union chiefs in the post Taff Vale judgment era. Campbell-Bannerman gave conspicuous support to efforts in the Commons to get legislation to protect unions from the consequences of the Taff Vale decision. He was also responsive to Labour demands for more working-class representatives in the Commons. Labour pressure in by-elections led to the Liberal chief whip, Herbert

Gladstone, concluding a secret pact with Ramsay MacDonald in 1903 for Liberal and Labour electoral cooperation. The L.R.C. was given a free hand in thirty constituencies. The Liberal leader pleased Labour even more by his forthright condemnation of Milner's 'Chinese Slavery' policy in South Africa, which was felt as an affront especially by the trade unions, who shared with their brethren in Australia and New Zealand a peculiar horror of the importation of cheap, and especially non-European, labour. Finally, Campbell-Bannerman soft-pedalled the Home Rule issue by insisting that it could only be put through in cautious stages. This was a very good mix for the electoral purposes of Liberalism as Balfour's ministry slid helplessly down the slope to disaster. By-elections foretold unmistakably the impending Unionist defeat.

By the middle of 1904 Chamberlain sensed that his Tariff Reform campaign was in danger of being becalmed in 'doldrums'. He and his son Austen tried unavailingly to persuade Balfour to resign and to lead the Unionist party in the forthcoming elections with a fiscal policy which the Tariff Reformers could support. But Balfour had no intention of delivering himself and his party into the hands of the Chamberlains. The party as a whole was not ready to swallow food taxes, which were clearly the main cause of Unionist by-election defeats.

Thus Chamberlain had to set off at the end of the 1904 session on another great stump tour no nearer to a working alliance with Balfour and the Unionist party. He launched his second tour with a great rally in the Albert Hall in July at the first annual general meeting of the Tariff Reform League. He compared his agitation with that of Cobden and predicted an even greater success. But the old sanguine bounce had gone. Chamberlain was now seventy and the strain was telling. He wrote to Selborne:

> It will not be easy to make an Empire and it is well that all who desire it should know the difficulties.
> But they are no greater than those confronted by the makers of the United States.
> They *can* and *must* be overcome if we have as much faith, determination, and courage as Washington and Hamilton.
> Sometimes I think we are of inferior fibre – and then only do I despair.

Kipling helped Chamberlain to launch out on the second phase with his famous lines 'Things and the Man', exalting Chamberlain as a latter-day Joseph – 'Once on a time there was a Man' – who was the prophet of a latter-day Israel in the Egyptian bondage of Free Trade. Chamberlain cast about him for a formula which would capture Balfour for the cause.

The tug-of-war continued through to the Conservative Party Conference at Southampton in October 1904. Chamberlain could not repudiate Balfour because he needed the power of official Conservatism behind his campaign; Balfour could not repudiate Chamberlain because Tariff Reform was the majority opinion of Conservatives. Since Chamberlain had the numbers on his side, he dragged Balfour a little way towards him. Though Balfour stuck to his 'Sheffield' programme of retaliation and no food taxes, he put forward a scheme for colonial consultation linked to new elections. Though the Chamberlains regarded this as impracticable, it was at least a gesture towards the idea of accepting colonial pro-preferences opinion as a factor in resolving British fiscal policy. The Conservative Conference duly passed a pro-Tariff Reform resolution; but Balfour deftly side-stepped the fiscal issue by devoting his speech to problems of foreign policy relating to the Russo–Japanese war. Indeed Balfour nimbly side-stepped all efforts to pin him down, whether from Chamberlain insisting on an early election to save his campaign from frustration or whether from Morley challenging anyone to put Balfour's quibbling and evasive fiscal policy on 'a sheet of notepaper'. Balfour responded in January 1905 by putting it on 'a half sheet of notepaper', where it still remained not enough for Chamberlain and too much for Morley.

IV

The Unionist government staggered on. Balfour had bad luck with his appointments. Wyndham, the Irish secretary, was anxious to perfect his important Irish Land Purchase policy which completed the dismantling of Gladstone's efforts in the 1881 Land Act to establish an 'English' relationship between landlord and tenant and accepted the concept of a 'peasant' landownership. He wanted as his permanent under-secretary an able and energetic officer of the Indian Civil Service, Sir Anthony MacDonnell. Balfour and Lansdowne both advised Wyndham against this appointment because MacDonnell was a Catholic Home Ruler. But Wyndham insisted and offered to take the brunt of any trouble. MacDonnell indeed fulfilled Wyndham's requirements with respect to Land Purchase, which worked excellently, but with an Indian disregard for the niceties of constitutional doctrine regarding the Civil Service and a laudable desire to rise above the bitterness of Irish politics, he meddled indiscreetly in schemes for 'devolution', a species of covert administrative Home Rule promoted by Lord Dunraven, one of the main inspirations behind the Land Purchase scheme, and a body called the Irish Reform Association. When the Irish Unionists became aware of what was afoot a scandal erupted. Wyndham, rather a graceful dilettante in politics as in literature, was careless in not keeping a sharp eye on his subordinate; MacDonnell in any case was rather inconsiderate in his behaviour to his chief. Wyndham became the target of virulent Orange agitation. After holding out for eighteen months his nerve eventually cracked and he resigned at the beginning of 1905. A good deal of Orange resentment was directed at Balfour, as Wyndham's defender and protector; and this contributed to the gradual undermining of his position as party leader. MacDonnell hung on like a limpet to await a more sympathetic Liberal government.

Even in Balfour's most particular area of concern, defence, matters did not go well. St John Brodrick's army reform schemes were clearly not making progress. They failed to answer the old British military problem of providing adequate contingents and replacements for overseas service. Such was the general erosion of Unionist political credit that he found it immensely difficult to find a suitable war secretary in the cabinet reconstruction of 1903. Arnold-Forster, the eventual appointment, a Tariff Reformer whose promotion pleased Chamberlain and a noted theorist of military policy, found the practical problems of army reform intractable. Results in the military sphere by no means matched the achievements in the Admiralty, where Esher and Clarke worked very effectively with Fisher and Selborne and his successor in 1905, Cawdor, to put the Navy on an entirely new footing of efficiency.

On top of these embarrassments and weaknesses of administration, Balfour had endless trouble with the flamboyant Curzon in India, whose adventurous frontier expeditions kept the cabinet in a constant state of anxiety. The wilful viceroy was quite beyond the control of the new secretary for India, St John Brodrick. On taking up a second tour of office in 1904, Curzon found himself at odds with the commander-in-chief in India, Kitchener, who needed fresh employment after winding up the South African operation. Kitchener demanded changes in the Indian military organization. The Indian system left executive command in the hands of the commander-in-chief but reserved administrative control to the Indian government. This involved, in Kitchener's view, wasteful and inefficient duplication of effort. It annoyed the autocratic Kitchener intensely that the administrative chief of the Indian Army was a member of the Viceroy's Council like the commander-in-chief. Kitchener was as wilful as Curzon and more devious. After furious wrangles, in which Curzon's frustrations over larger policy matters in which he was in conflict with the cabinet clearly unhinged his judgement, the viceroy resigned in August 1905; a resignation which the weary Balfour accepted with relief.

The dying Unionist government's last notable legislative spasms were the Licensing Act of 1904 and the Unemployed Workmen and Aliens Immigration Acts of 1905. The Licensing Act was designed to settle the vexed question which had plagued public life for decades of compensating publicans whose licences were withdrawn through a fund provided by levies on the Trade. Hitherto arguments for compensation had assumed that the finance would come from public funds. But the legal position was doubtful, and naturally such proposals were furiously resisted by the anti-Trade forces, always very powerful in the Liberal party. Balfour accepted arguments for a reduction of licences in areas obviously over-endowed with public houses competing vociferously for trade; but he would not accept that licences were some sort of tainted form of property and that a government in abolishing them was under no obligation to consider compensation. Balfour argued that compensation by the Trade itself, the remaining publicans benefiting from the suppression of the superfluous licences, was a sensible compromise. The Act broke the legal impasse holding up desirable liquor reforms and worked well.

The Unemployed Workmen Act was a rather wavering government response to demands for action to relieve unemployment, which was acute in some industries and localities in 1904 and 1905. Keir Hardie urged the setting up of a Ministry of Labour and a system of local authorities charged with relieving unemployment by undertaking public works and agricultural projects. George Lansbury in Poplar set up farm colonies for London unemployed with private money supplied by a wealthy disciple of the doctrines of Henry George. Under pressure of agitation and a march of Leicester unemployed on London, Balfour rather grudgingly allowed a bill to pass empowering local authorities to establish committees to help unemployed workers to find work, but he vetoed the crucial principle Hardie was fighting for of public money being used to create jobs.

The legislation restricting the immigration of aliens was in fact much more likely to please the average working-class voter than reform of the legal status of a minority working-class interest like the trade unions. A Royal Commission set up in 1902 in conjunction with inquiries on deteriorating national physique and sweated labour and related social evils recommended legislation to stem the flow of immigration of destitute persons, largely Jews fleeing from persecution in Eastern Europe. There were objections that Britain's honourable tradition as a refuge for the politically persecuted should be maintained. But opinion generally was hostile to large-scale, and especially large-scale Jewish, immigration. Anti-semitism was a characteristic feature of radical attitudes, and had become especially virulent at the time of the South African war, that conspiracy of 'Jewburg'.

After the session of 1905 Balfour was at the end of his tether. Chamberlain and the Tariff Reformers were insisting on an election as soon as possible and Balfour could not resist this importunity without risking serious danger of a Tariff Reform secession on a vote of confidence. During the session Balfour suffered the ultimate humiliation of being obliged to lead his supporters out of the chamber to dodge the even more embarrassing consequences for the Unionist party of the Tariff Reformers' insistence on a free vote on a crucial fiscal motion. By November 1905 Chamberlain made it unmistakably clear that Balfour's appeals for unity and forbearance between the Unionist factions no longer carried any weight or authority. But Balfour had held on long enough to give new defence initiatives a reasonable chance to survive Campbell-Bannerman. Although army reform hopes were still very much in the balance, Esher and Clarke at least had succeeded in putting the War Office itself on a secure basis for the future. The new Liberal war secretary would have excellent prospects of success if he chose to take advantage of this preliminary work. Although the Liberal leader had been querulous and indignant about the arrogance of Esher and Clarke and the dangerously unconstitutional implications of the C.I.D., there was reason to believe that he could be neutralized by Asquith, Grey and Haldane. Haldane in fact was much involved in the back-room intrigues of defence reorganization; and he took the initiative in getting Asquith and Grey to agree in September 1905 to a compact (known as the Relugas Compact because it was agreed at Grey's fishing lodge in Sutherland) that none of them would join a Campbell-Bannerman ministry unless Campbell-Bannerman himself consented to exile in the House of Lords. Although he did not know of these manoeuvres, Balfour's obvious tactic, given the inevitability of a Unionist defeat, was to strengthen the hand of the Liberal Leaguers by resigning without dissolving the Commons. Campbell-Bannerman thus would form his ministry not as the triumphant leader of a Liberal majority but as the rather insecure leader of a minority party which still bore the scars and wounds of more than a decade of acrimonious disputes. The King, moreover, was privy to the scheme to force a peerage on Campbell-Bannerman. Balfour resigned on 5 December 1905, and the great Unionist bid to provide adequate responses to Britain's problems ended in an ultimate exhaustion of complete impasse.

PART V

The Search for Adequate Responses: The Liberal Version
1905—15

Chapter Sixteen

THE
LIBERAL
DOMESTIC BID
1905—11

I

To the surprise of both Balfour and the arch-intriguer of the Relugas Compact, Haldane, Campbell-Bannerman had little difficulty in forming a convincing Liberal ministry. Asquith needed a Liberal government as much as a Liberal government needed Asquith. He was clearly the heir apparent. He had already sacrificed Milner for the sake of his brilliant future prospects. He would not now compromise those prospects by insisting that the leader of his party accept the role of *roi fainéant*. Campbell-Bannerman appreciated this, and knew that if he chose not to be bluffed by the Relugas group, Asquith, at least, would have to accept his terms. Campbell-Bannerman disliked Haldane intensely, and in any case regarded him as politically expendable. Grey he also disliked but regarded on balance as an asset to be cultivated. Asquith thus shared with Campbell-Bannerman a desire not to expose unnecessarily Liberal sectarian divisions. For his part, Campbell-Bannerman could not afford to refuse to form a government in the manner of Disraeli in 1873. He needed to be able to prove that Liberalism was capable of assuming the responsibilities of power without obvious strain. Moreover, if he did refuse, there was the possibility that Balfour would seize the opportunity of advising the King to have recourse to Chamberlain or Rosebery or Lansdowne as heads of some sort of imperialist coalition government.

Asquith duly performed excellently as the weak link of the 'Limps'. He overcame the obstinacy of Grey by means of Haldane. He surrendered his claim to the leadership of the House and persuaded Haldane to surrender his claim to the lord chancellor-ship and to accept instead Campbell-Bannerman's rather sardonic offer of the War Office. Campbell-Bannerman was inclined, as an old Gladstonian, to stick only at the prospect of Grey at the Foreign Office. Grey in any case was reluctant to take office at all. Only after a prudent refusal by Cromer, who in any case had long ago, like Milner, given up the Liberal party as a lost cause, did Campbell-Bannerman offer the Foreign Office to Grey; and only the heavy pressure of both Asquith and Haldane could prevail upon Grey to accept with Campbell-Bannerman still in the Commons.

Thus the Liberal Leaguers were in, somewhat to their dis-comfiture. Henry Fowler, another of their group, got the Duchy of Lancaster. On the other side, the Gladstonian Old Guard was represented by the new prime minister himself; John Morley, who went to the India Office to fulfil a new instalment of Liberal progressivism in the spirit of Ripon in 1880; Ripon himself now took the Privy Seal; Sir Robert Reid, an old crony of Campbell-Bannerman's, became lord chancellor (as Lord Loreburn). Elgin got the Colonial Office with the rising young convert to progressive Liberalism, Winston Churchill, as his under-secre-tary. Gladstone's son Herbert went to the Home Office. Harcourt's son Lewis (Lulu) was brought into the cabinet in 1907. Bryce became Irish chief secretary, and the Nonconformist Augustine Birrell was put in charge of education to right the wrongs of 1902. Two of the new cabinet were conspicuously *novi homines*: John Burns, the maverick Battersea ex-socialist 'Labour' chief, be-came president of the Local Government Board (with Charles Masterman as his under-secretary); and the notorious Welsh Radical, Lloyd George, was given the Board of Trade. Campbell-Bannerman's cabinet gave every appearance of being a stronger body than Salisbury's of 1895 or Balfour's of 1902. The known quantities of weight and opinion were fairly clear: the Glad-stonians had a majority but Campbell-Bannerman could not last very long and then, it could be assumed, the Liberal Leaguers would be in a position of greater strength. Of the largely un-known factors Lloyd George was the most intriguing. He was rather in the position of Chamberlain in Gladstone's ministry of

1880; and indeed his subsequent career had about it a great deal of the pattern of response to national problems set by Chamberlain.

The elections for a new Commons were held in January 1906. Campbell-Bannerman put into operation the concurrence theory of Liberalism as advocated hitherto most prominently by Sir W. H. Harcourt. Instead of attempting to impose the concentration doctrine of the Home Rulers as against the efficiency and imperial doctrine of the Leaguers, Campbell-Bannerman succeeded in restoring Liberal electoral credibility on the basis of Harcourt's recommendation to wait on political events and let Liberal political activity be determined primarily by their Conservative and Unionist opponents. By challenging free trade their opponents had provided Liberalism with the broad unifying principle and focus of loyalty which Liberalism had been unable to provide for itself.

In his election manifesto Campbell-Bannerman stressed the 'time-honoured principles of Liberalism – the principles of peace, economy, self government and civil and religious liberty'. Free trade was at the heart of all these principles. In foreign policy, Grey would not tolerate any drum-beating for a 'new' alternative to the Unionists, so Campbell-Bannerman contented himself with renunciation of the 'undesirable characteristics' of militaristic Unionism while undertaking to continue the *entente cordiale*, thus allowing a ritual obeisance in the manner of Gladstone in 1880 to the doctrine of 'substantial continuity' without departing from the 'friendly and unprovocative' methods of earlier Liberal governments. Ireland would be gradually prepared for a wider degree of self-government, though Home Rule proper would be subject to endorsement by a further general election. Thus Home Rule would take its place naturally as one of the major duties to be discharged by a restored Liberalism. 'Chinese slavery' in the Rand would be abolished: this was the issue next to Free Trade most harped upon. There were vague references to certain 'long delayed' social and economic reforms; though in fact John Burns was the only member of the new cabinet to go so far as to advocate old age pensions as a desirable object of Liberal policy. The trade unionists were to get their legal status protected;

and the wrongs of the Unionist Education and Licensing Acts were to be righted.

The Unionists, riven by sectarian disputes and a party more at war with itself than with the Liberal enemy, expected to lose; but they did not expect to lose as badly as the Liberals had done in 1895. Chamberlain, an acute judge, predicted a Liberal majority of not more than eighty. He did not envisage any fundamental change in the basic conditions of politics: a temporary Liberal strength was a function of a temporary Unionist weakness. But the tale of the polling results was devastating to the Unionists. An electoral shift of seismic proportions engulfed Unionism in a landslide. In Great Britain as a whole there was an electoral swing of something like 9 per cent towards the Liberals, who now, with their Labour allies, engrossed over 55 per cent of the total vote. Chamberlain's bastion of the West Midlands alone resisted the general trend. Lancashire collapsed with the arrival of class politics overlaying traditional religious sectarianism as the foundation of public life. The Lancashire swing against the Unionists was almost 13 per cent. London also collapsed at the other end of the Unionist electoral axis. Class politics, already well established, now bit deep, and Liberalism reaped the benefits of an aroused working-class vote. Balfour himself was defeated in Manchester by Winston Churchill. The tale of unseated Unionist chiefs read like a list of the French chivalry at Poitiers.

In the end, the Liberals found themselves 377 strong. In addition they had two flanking *corps d'armée*: the Irish Nationalists came back with their usual contingent of eighty-three members, and there were fifty-three 'Labour' members, twenty-nine of them products of the secret L.R.C.–Gladstone arrangements, the remaining twenty-four mainly miners' representatives in the Burt Liberal–Labour tradition. Thus the new government could count on a grand total of over 500 supporters in the new House. Droves of unheard of and rather surprised Liberals surged in to public life, not invariably (as with the case of Horatio Bottomley) to its benefit. There was an unprecedented turnover in membership: no less than 220 Liberals and thirty-nine Labour members were new to the Commons. One distinctive feature of the new House was the unprecedented number of 157 Nonconformists, nearly a quarter of the total House, including sixty-five Congregationalists and thirty-seven Wesleyan Methodists.

The starkest measure of the Unionist defeat was that their shattered forces now merely amounted to the same number as the Nonconformists. They comprised Tariff Reform 'Whole Hoggers', Balfourites and Free Fooders in variously calculated computations, which the most reliable estimates conclude (taking account of leading Unionists temporarily without seats immediately after the elections such as Balfour himself, Bonar Law, Alfred Lyttelton, who soon equipped themselves with more reliable constituencies) to be seventy-nine in the first category, forty-nine in the second and thirty-one in the third. The former distinction between Conservatives and Liberal Unionists was now otiose. The wreck of the Unionist ascendancy was so complete as to produce shocked stupefaction or exhilaration rather than despair. Balfour defiantly declared in the midst of the rout that it would remain the duty of the 'great Unionist Party' to 'still control, whether in power or whether in Opposition, the destinies of this great Empire'. This was a reference not merely to the Unionist majority in the House of Lords but, more significantly, a statement that Unionism would not respond to 1906 in the manner of Peel's responding to 1832 or of Conservatism's responding to 1880: there would be no apologies, no strivings towards fundamental adjustments and accommodations, no revisions of the received 'national' doctrine of legitimacy. Balfour thus recognized and accepted what had emerged as the decisive characteristic of the electoral implications of 1906: the reality of class and class interests as the major political determinant. Hitherto Unionism had benefited from middle-class manifestations of this; now Liberalism was reaping the benefit of working-class manifestations.

II

The great new power of Liberalism was far from monolithic. It comprehended a very complex and heterogeneous assortment of values, loyalties, assumptions and expectations. On the one hand there were ancient Gladstonians like the apostle of Temperance

Wilfrid Lawson, who remembered the glad days of April 1880 and saw the hand of the Lord chastising the hosts of the Evil One. Gladstonian financial orthodoxy looked forward to an era of retrenchment in government expenditure and a reduction in graduated taxation rates. On the other hand was a greatly augmented group of New Liberals who looked forward to an era of social reconstruction and a stepped-up graduated taxation policy, led by Masterman, Chiozza Money, Charles Trevelyan, Josiah Wedgwood and Herbert Samuel. They saw Liberalism as the means of rescuing the mass of society from 'normal' conditions. Lloyd George became their cabinet spokesman. Behind them was a greatly augmented pool of civil servants eager to apply the administrative resources of the State.

The Irish were led by veterans who had grown grey at Westminster in the service of Home Rule: Redmond, Dillon, T. P. O'Connor, Healy, O'Brien, men increasingly remote from the new movements in Irish nationalism which would find expression in more radically populist or 'folkish' republicanism represented in its extreme form by Sinn Fein. Redmond and his party would stand or fall on their ability to deliver Home Rule to Ireland by means of the new Liberal ascendancy in Britain. From their point of view the colossal Liberal majority was a mixed blessing. On the one hand it would give Liberal ministers confidence, especially in confronting the House of Lords; on the other hand, it made Liberal ministers invulnerable to threats of a withdrawal of Irish parliamentary support. The immediate Irish problem was to keep the Liberals up to the mark and not allow them to relegate Home Rule to some comfortably remote future. The lack of enthusiasm of the British electorate generally for the Home Rule cause gave Liberal ministers every incentive for dragging their heels. The tactical problem that would shortly confront the Irish was how to respond to the government's intention to bring in a bill greatly enlarging Irish control of local affairs but stopping short of Home Rule. The Irish dilemma was that such a devolutionary scheme might be as much an impediment to full Home Rule as a prelude to it. There was the great danger that it might work too well and answer all requirements short of those of heroic myth or nationalist metaphysics.

The 'Labour' group had rather a different problem. There was a huge gap between their claims and their actual circumstances. Ostensibly they represented the 'working-class', whose newly maturing class consciousness was unquestionably the most significant phenomenon of the election. In reality they were a sectional pressure group, a satellite to the Liberal sun. The leaders of the I.L.P. section, Keir Hardie, Ramsay MacDonald, Snowden and Henderson, had little in common with the 'Lib-Labs' and even less with the 'Labour' spokesman in the cabinet, Burns, widely regarded as an opportunist renegade. Unlike the Irish, who had one clear overriding objective, the Labour members' energies and preoccupations ranged between a total Socialist reordering of society to very practical legislative details about improving the status of trade unions and the conditions of labour. Somewhere in the middle of this wide spectrum was the problem of exactly how 'Labour' should relate to 'Liberalism'. It could remain an established and accredited sectional interest group within the Liberal fold, like Nonconformity; or at the other extreme, it could set out, as the accredited representative of 'the people', to establish its independence and eventually aim at displacing Liberalism as the party of the left. Most Labour people in 1906 did not like the first alternative, yet they could not seriously envisage the second. Liberalism in 1906 performed quite adequately the functions of a 'class' party. For the time being the 'movement' would remain uneasily poised on this fundamental issue.

Nevertheless, not very far beneath the surface of the situation in 1906, masked by the sheer massiveness of the Liberal majority, lay the basic dilemma for Campbell-Bannerman's government in implementing a political programme which would preserve and continue Liberalism's restored hegemonic political role. If, as 1906 suggested and later elections in 1910 were to confirm, the working-class vote was the 'last best hope of Liberalism', Liberalism's primary aim must be to make certain that that vote be retained. Yet how could Liberalism, in origin essentially a party of subscription to principles such as those underlying the Radical Programme of 1885, principles repudiating the legitimacy of the idea of class and class interest in politics, reconcile its origins and essence with this new necessity?

The quintessential dilemma for Liberalism was indeed of this kind; and can be observed strikingly at the very heart of those representative manifestations of Edwardian Liberalism usually interpreted as displaying most convincingly Liberalism's adequacy for its new 'progressive' class role in politics.[1] Lloyd George's famous 'table of the law' speech at Newcastle in October 1909, in the midst of the excitement over the famous budget of that year, beneath the surface of the rousing radical rhetoric, exposed a fundamental political evasiveness. Lloyd George's argument, as directed against the House of Lords, was in effect as follows: if the moneyed classes of society do not submit to the whips of Liberalism, they will be made to submit to the scorpions of 'the people'. This was the kind of argument about reform made by Whigs in the 1820s and 1830s; and Liberalism historically was the resolution of that tension, just as Labour was to be the resolution of the Edwardian tension. Lloyd George's rhetoric in effect invited a party of the Left to fulfil the logical implication of his argument. Such a party did not exist prior to 1914. The period between 1908 and 1914 is characterized by the development of Labour's capacity to fulfil this role but not of a will to do it. The major example of this ambiguous process was the decision in 1908 by the Miners' Federation that M.P.s elected under its representatives' scheme should henceforth belong to the Labour party rather than the Liberal party. This had its origin in the conflicts of the South Wales miners, in a phase of declining production and decreasing wages, with their employers, who were nearly all Liberals and Nonconformists. It made little difference to the voting habits of miners as a whole and certainly did not represent a takeover of Liberalism by Labour. But, in a period of rapid expansion of trade unionism – between 1906 and 1914 affiliated trade union membership of the Labour party increased from 904,500 to 1,572,400 (and total trade union membership by 1914 was over four million) – there was a corresponding increase in the financial possibilities of independent political action. There was a considerable increase also in the number of local Labour party branches and the number of Labour members elected to local government authorities. But all this still amounted to a growth in capacity rather than in motivation to fulfil Lloyd George's implied definition of a party of 'the people'.

Liberalism itself, by definition of its component parts, was not capable of doing this. It was not merely that Asquith and the moderate men like him would not allow it. Lloyd George himself, the spokesman of the 'left' of the party, looked to by C. P. Scott of the *Manchester Guardian* to do for twentieth-century Liberalism what Gladstone had done for the nineteenth century, would in 1910 be proposing a coalition with the Unionists. Just conceivably, if Liberalism had been able to push through in 1910 a fourth Reform Act along the lines of the Act of 1918, hegemony might might have been preserved longer. But it did not have the strength and determination to do this. Hence, paradoxically, the more effectively Liberalism performed its 'progressive' function as defined by such as Lloyd George, presenting Liberalism to the possessing classes as the lesser evil, concessions to which would save them from the greater evil of socialism, the more tightly it pulled the noose of eventual supersession on the Left about its neck.

Thus, there is in the political situation between 1906 and 1914 a curious but not mysterious contradistinction to be made between a hegemonic party successful in maintaining intact its hegemonic status – indeed, as is often pointed out, Labour was doing less well in general between 1910 and 1914 than it had been doing between 1906 and 1910 – and a party which was destined eventually to have its hegemonic credentials quite suddenly withdrawn. It is essential that the political performance of Liberalism in its last era of greatness between 1906 and 1914 be correctly interpreted in the light of this duality of profitability and impending bankruptcy.

III

Even more than in 1880 there was, initially, considerable doubt as to what, beyond the fulfilment of immediate and relatively straightforward engagements such as the 'Chinese slavery' issue or the legal status of the trade unions issue, Liberalism most appropriately might do. In 1880 at least the external side of things seemed to offer a clear and straightforward path of action, whatever may have been the quandaries about the domestic sphere. But in 1906 even foreign affairs offered no clear light of guidance. It was one thing for Campbell-Bannerman to assert against the sophistries of efficiency-mongers and strategists and power manipulators that the essence of foreign policy was 'How to make those love us who now hate us'; it was quite another matter to find a mode of applying such a doctrine to the Germans at Algeciras. Grey in any case insisted on the 'continuity' thesis, so as far as the Liberal government was concerned foreign affairs was largely ruled out as a profitable line of political investment in the loyalty and enthusiasm of the party rank and file.

On the domestic side there was much debate about how to interpret the meaning of events and thus the likeliest way ahead. There was, in the first place, great dispute about what the election results themselves really signified. Some observers could see in the Liberalism of 1906 only a heterogeneous collection of outmoded and musty attitudes left over from the Victorian era: Cobdenite Little Englandism, Gladstonian economy, Nonconformist provinciality.

It was the same unawareness of subterranean shifts of opinion which led the Unionists into hopeless miscalculations about their electoral prospects. When in 1897 C. P. Scott of the *Manchester Guardian* invited L. T. Hobhouse to join the staff he gave as his reason the conviction that the relations of Liberalism and Labour would govern the future of politics, and that 'the great problem was to find the lines on which Liberals could be brought to see that the old tradition must be expanded to yield a fuller measure of social justice, a more real equality, an industrial as well as a political liberty'. There was now, in this interpretation, a whole new dimension of politics, adding a social depth to the traditional two-dimensional politics of the old ruling class. This was the era of a flowering of democratic idealism, as witness for example the inauguration in 1903 of the Workers' Educational Association, by Toynbee Hall out of the Co-operative movement. By 1906 it had branches in eight cities.

It was certainly significant that Scott hoped to make foreign affairs the focus of Liberal and Labour symbiosis in a common front against imperialism and jingoism. This was clearly, along with Free Trade after 1903, the easiest way of allying old-fashioned Gladstonians with the new advocates of collectivism and thus preventing dangerous fault lines opening on the surface. Out of such an alliance in the external sphere would develop a joint commitment to a vigorous policy of domestic reform and social justice. Here Hobson was the major influence by way of the Rainbow Circle, a group of 'progressive' social and economic thinkers whose ideas gained wide currency through the *Daily News* and the *Speaker*. Ten of its twenty-five members were elected to the Commons in 1906. This circle was important in formulating influential new concepts of positive state action, particularly with respect to taxation policy, which marked a significant stage of divergence between the two parties.

Another formative group of this kind was the League of Liberals against Aggression and Militarism. Its executive committee included C. P. Scott, G. W. E. Russell, Harold Spender, F. W. Hirst, J. A. Hobson, H. N. Brailsford and J. L. Hammond. This group planned to work together with the I.L.P. Hobhouse's *Democracy and Reaction* (1904), one of the major radical documents of the time, attempted to pull political theory away from the reactionary allurements of German idealism and back into the progressive English tradition of the 'plain, human, rationalistic way of looking at life and its problems'.

With his huge majority behind him, Campbell-Bannerman was a very different figure from the rather dim old gentleman of former years. He overshadowed Rosebery. He established a personal ascendancy in the Commons by brushing Balfour aside in a famous incident at the opening of the 1906 session: 'enough of this foolery'. The government plunged into the business of restoring politics to its proper and natural Liberal condition. But it was not long before unexpected difficulties cropped up. Abolishing 'Chinese slavery' turned out to be a more complicated task than anticipated, and the government had grudgingly to accept that it could only be done by stages in accordance with contractual obligations rather than by a decisive stroke of moral assertion. The trade union issue revealed a different kind of problem. The government's proposals for legal protection were ignored and the bill was virtually commandeered by the Labour section. Campbell-Bannerman legitimized this by supporting the unofficial version of the bill rather than the official one. The trade unions were by the former to be given special sectional privileges: full immunity for liability for damages. The bewildered Liberal rank and file followed the prime minister's lead, to the indignation of Asquith, a lawyer, and Sydney Webb, who strongly advocated retaining a reasonable degree of union liability. Liberalism was being false to itself under the pressure of a vociferous interest group. Burns correctly described it as an 'insincere majority'. Education also proved difficult. Birrell's Education bill, designed to liberate education from the 'injustices' of 1902, provided that every school maintained by public money should be under the exclusive management of the representative local authority. This was expressly framed to hurt the Anglican or Roman Catholic schools which got rate money in 1902. The bill provoked a sharp outcry, with the Irish Roman Catholics in league with the Tories. Some members of the cabinet were notoriously unenthusiastic for their bill. In the face of hostile amendments by the Lords the government sullenly abandoned the measure. But though the Lords had no compunction in offending the Nonconformists they thought it might be dangerous to challenge the new force of Labour in the aftermath of the great electoral upset. The Tory majority in the Lords, like the Liberal majority in the Commons, let through the Trade Disputes bill with heavy misgivings.

Otherwise the government did well enough. It had to give up the idea of repealing the Aliens Act of 1905 which, though offensive to progressive consciences, was popular with the xenophobic and anti-semitic public at large; but Herbert Gladstone got through an improved Workmen's Compensation Act, Lloyd George a good Merchant Shipping Act. The social efficiency movement started to bear legislative fruit by grafting to the emergent growth of radical humanitarianism. Regular medical inspections of elementary schoolchildren were provided for. The government found itself the rather reluctant author of a measure permitting provision of meals to elementary schoolchildren.

This act was accorded the distinction by A. V. Dicey in the second edition of his famous *Lectures on the Relation between Law and Public Opinion in England during the Nineteenth Century* of being the first of the deplorable socialist departures from old principles of individual responsibility and true Liberal political morality which became the rule rather than the exception in the following years. Certainly, the medical inspection and feeding of school-children has been justly interpreted as 'the first elements of the welfare state'.[2]

A settlement of the Transvaal and Orange Free State questions was another item high on the Liberal agenda. The keynote of Liberal imperial policy would be to replace the coercive attitudes of Unionism with conciliatory approaches appropriate to a party of progress and humanity. In India Curzon's high-handed and unpopular partition of Bengal was eventually rescinded. Eldon Gorst, Cromer's successor in 1907 in Egypt, also had much ado to appease nationalist agitation. But inevitably South Africa took the centre of the imperial stage.

The Unionist colonial secretary, Lyttelton, had already introduced a system of representative but not responsible government in the former Afrikaner republics. There was in fact despite much mythology to the contrary no chance that the Liberals would do other than grant immediate responsible government; the only question was whether to do this by adapting the Lyttelton constitution or by scrapping it and starting afresh. Campbell-Bannerman was keen to make a clean break as a political gesture against the 'Limps', all the more so if he could not seriously challenge 'continuity' in foreign affairs. There was also as an incentive to decisive appeasement the dire precedent of the muddle Gladstone had got himself into in 1880-81 over the Transvaal. The Transvaal Afrikaners under Botha and Smuts in alliance with the British colonials were clearly going to take over the Transvaal one way or another in any case; there was a united front of whites who feared above all Liberal efforts to do something serious for the interests of the black majority.[3] Their fears for white supremacy were in fact too flattering to the Liberals, who had no stomach for conflict with their erstwhile heroes of anti-imperialism. Liberal ministers were content to let Smuts believe that he had converted them to a magnanimity to which in reality they had no alternative.

In 1907 Botha's party, Het Volk, won the Transvaal elections, and power passed back to the Afrikaners. The Indian immigrant population began a campaign of passive resistance, led by a lawyer, Mohandas Gandhi. At a constitutional convention in 1908 a scheme for a South African Union (favourable to Afrikaner interests) was agreed on as opposed to a federation on Canadian or Australian models (which would have favoured the British interest): the Liberal government duly swallowed this and put through the South Africa Act in 1909. Afrikaner predominance was finally established in the Union elections of 1910. This marked the final bankruptcy of the old, Chamberlainite, ideal of empire as a form whereby Britain could impose an imperial authority in the world. Henceforth the empire would be militarily and strategically a burden rather than a source of strength. Gandhi, after having got the better of Smuts in South Africa, would soon be moving to India, where he would get the better of the British in due course. The final pious touch was added by sending Gladstone's son Herbert out as first governor-general of the new Union in 1910.

Any lingering scruples the Liberal majority may have had about the likely fate of the blacks were dissolved in the pleasure of humiliating their chief jingo bogeyman, Milner. That rebarbative statesman had the temerity in the Lords to denounce Liberal policy. He immediately found himself at the receiving end of a furious censure motion in the Commons. The Lords took up the challenge on behalf of Milner and repudiated the Commons' censure.

Incidents such as this did nothing to pour oil on the troubled waters of relationships between the two Houses of Parliament. Balfour and the Unionist leadership had in any case decided that they should not treat all Liberal legislation with the tender regard they had chosen to apply to very sensitive items such as the Trade Disputes bill. The Unionists, shattered by electoral disaster, badly needed occasions of morale-building assertiveness; and they had good reason to believe that the more moderate elements in the government relied on Lansdowne in the Lords to deal fairly stringently with such things as the Education bill. The Lords in fact were on firm ground here, for the public as a whole were bored and irritated by the sectarian vindictiveness and fuss of the Nonconformists.

It would take more, however, than the balm of amendments in the Lords to heal the wounds of stricken Unionism. They still had to try to come to some conclusion about fiscal policy. The 'Whole Hog' Tariff Reformers had emerged much the strongest faction in the party, but they did not have an absolute majority over the Balfourites and the small but even more resolute group of Free Fooders. Convinced as ever that they represented the future, the Whole Hoggers pressed ahead ruthlessly with their bid to take over the party and commit it unequivocally to tariff reform and food taxes. Whereas the Balfourite centre group were strong in the elements of traditional Toryism, landowners, country gentlemen, the civil and military services, the Whole Hoggers were both younger and much more heavily representative of industry and new money. The Canadian-born Glasgow ironmaster Andrew Bonar Law was a typical rising star among the Chamberlainite ranks, as also was the swashbuckling young F. E. Smith.

Chamberlain himself, now, like Gladstone twenty years before, an old man in a hurry, pressed home his advantage over Balfour. In an exchange of notes in February 1906 known as the 'Valentine letters' he pinned Balfour down to agreeing to a party meeting to seek an acceptable formula on the tariff issue. Since the primary objective of the Balfourites was to preserve the party in being above all else, Balfour yielded to the Tariff Reform pressure sufficiently to satisfy Chamberlain while preserving enough basic ambiguity to make the Free Fooders feel that all was not lost. Because of the weight and determination of the Chamberlainites it was clear that Balfour would be eventually driven into a corner. At the Imperial Conference of 1907 the colonial premiers came with their usual offers of reciprocity. The Liberal government, somewhat embarrassed, declined their gifts. Balfour, however, responded enthusiastically, to the pleasure of the Chamberlainites and the dismay of the Free Fooders. At last he committed Unionism officially to a moderate version of Tariff Reform. The great question was whether the Tariff Reformers could translate their party advantage into solid and lasting national political advantage for their cause.

In the aftermath of his ascendancy over Balfour, Chamberlain, on 17 July 1906, suffered a severe stroke which left his mind alert but completely disabled him physically. His active political career was finished. He lingered on until 1914 to witness the temporary triumph but ultimate failure of the Tariff Reform bid to capture Unionism. His son and political heir, Austen, was no adequate substitute. He was as incapable as Balfour of the necessary demagogy. But Balfour's position was by no means strengthened by Chamberlain's removal from the scene. Joseph Chamberlain could never aspire to the leadership of Unionism; but Austen Chamberlain, of Rugby and Trinity and without a Radical background and in an era where Liberal Unionism had ceased to be a meaningfully distinct entity from Conservatism, could; and from now on Balfour would be exposed to the harsh test of political utility without the protective if rather suffocating embrace of Great Joe.

IV

The government was trying to cope with its own difficulties. The Lords, emboldened by their success over education in 1906, did great execution among the Liberal bills of the 1907 session. Ministers could get no further with education and found it equally difficult to drum up impressive public indignation at the sorry fate of their Licensing Bill, yet another assault of the Alliance against the Trade, which died in the Commons at the mere threat of Lords' amendments. Campbell-Bannerman, exasperated, tabled a resolution asserting that the Lords' powers to amend or reject bills from the Commons should be so restricted as to ensure that the deliberately expressed will of the popular house should prevail within the limits of a single parliament. He proposed further that the limits of a parliament should be reduced from seven to five years (ostensibly as a corresponding Commons' concession, but in fact as a blow for democratic principle). This was in fact a much more radical approach to the problem than the plan previously approved by the cabinet which provided that in the event of a deadlock between the Houses, there would be a joint vote in which the Commons would sit entire but the Lords would be represented only by a delegation of one hundred.[4] The cry against the Lords was taken up by Churchill and led by Lloyd George, already building up a formidable reputation as the major Liberal pace-setter. The president of the Board of Trade performed with great *éclat* over the railways dispute of 1907, averting a costly strike and cajoling owners into concession. By 1908 Lloyd George had established very persuasive claims to promotion in the impending event of the government reconstruction not far distant as Campbell-Bannerman's health deteriorated under the increasing burdens of office.

Among these burdens the Irish were not least. The Nationalist chiefs were extremely dissatisfied with the interim measures offered by the government. Bryce and the permanent under-secretary, the tenacious MacDonnell, found their Irish Devolution Bill provoking hostile Nationalist agitation on the one hand and Orange riots in Belfast on the other. Bryce was glad to get out to the Washington embassy at the beginning of 1907 and leave Birrell to face the Irish music. The Devolution Bill provided for a mainly elected central Irish Council to take over local government organs without legislative powers and disposing of a fund from the imperial exchequer of £650,000 per annum. The Nationalist response was to hold an Irish National Convention of 2,000 delegates in May 1907 which rejected the government's proposals as too little and in any case too dangerous for the cause of ultimate Home Rule. Birrell added fuel to the fire of Nationalist resentment by accepting the Lords' amendments to the Evicted Tenants' Bill. Redmond and the Nationalist leaders were clearly not delivering results; and consequently were coming under increasing pressure from more radical Irish opinion.

Labour also was burdensome. The parliamentary Labour group were as determined as the Irish to keep up maximum pressure on the government. Rising unemployment levels spurred them to demands for some sort of 'right to work' legislation. Their pressure tended to expose serious divisions within Liberalism between those (like Burns at the Local Government department) who thought the principle both useless and dangerous and those (like Burns's under-secretary, Masterman) who were in favour of 'going forward boldly in some large and far reaching scheme of social reform'. In a debate at the beginning of 1908 the Liberal party split on the issue, 116 rebels joining the Labour members to give them a considerable moral victory and encouraging them to press on with related issues like the eight-hour day. This split, like the two Labour victories at Liberal expense at by-elections in 1907 at Jarrow and Colne Valley, was annoying rather than disturbing to the Liberal ministers; but it helped greatly to contribute to the general sense of frustration and malaise which had come over the Liberal majority by 1908.

This sorry situation it would be Asquith's task to restore. Campbell-Bannerman was dying, his grip on events slipping fast. Asquith was the unchallenged heir apparent. The King insisted on going abroad for his usual round of resorts, and eventually in April 1908 Asquith found himself kissing hands as prime minister at the Hotel du Palais, Biarritz. Asquith entered into his inheritance without any marked enthusiasm among the generality of the Liberal rank and file. He had been too much of a Liberal Leaguer for their taste. Nor did the puritans in the party (of whom there were many) approve his penchant for dining and wining and the influence upon him of his socialite second wife, born Margot Tennant, which made him by 1908 a different figure from the dour north country product of the stern and unbending Balliol of Jowett. Asquith made his way in politics as he had at the Bar, by sheer, economical executive efficiency and smooth application. But more was needed than these talents to fill Liberalism's sails and get the party out of the doldrums. The 1908 session found the government once more at the mercy of the Lords. The Licensing Bill failed again. Education was finally given up as a lost cause. Other things being demanded vociferously within the party – land reform, Welsh disestablishment, Irish Home Rule – were beyond the government's power to command.

The situation was all the more frustrating because the Unionists generally took care to discriminate between legislation it might be unpopular at large to block and Liberal partisan legislation as with the drink and education issues where popular feeling was much less prone to be excited. The miners' eight-hour day and old age pensions came into the former category. The important principle involved in the miners' case was that this was the first legal restriction on the length of the working day for men. The old age pensions issue, so long under debate and the first major breach in the Poor Law, depended for its success by 1908 on being non-contributory to get around the Friendly Societies, and on seriously underestimated miscalculations as to how much it would cost. It provided a pension of 5s. a week for necessitous and worthy persons of seventy years or over. The Unionists in the Commons put up no resistance. Asquith took the prudent and unusual step of designating it as a money bill to save it from spoiling amendments in the Lords. He had calculated the costs, taking into account savings on pauper relief, at £6 or £7 million a year; by 1914 pensions were costing nearly £13 million. Unquestionably, old age pensions was the one item of the Liberal social reform programme widely popular among the working class because it removed the dread of the workhouse. The percentage decrease in pauperism of the aged was nearly 75 per cent between 1906 and 1913. There was a decrease of 95 per cent in outdoor relief.

With old age pensions and school meals and medical inspections, Liberalism may fairly be said to have fulfilled the prophecies of the older generation of social workers like Charles Booth. The very young and the very old had been given the protection of the State. This was in accordance with Liberal principles about the legitimacy of giving help to people presumably unable to help themselves. Now, after 1908, would begin a second phase of the New Liberalism led by two politicians, Lloyd George and Winston Churchill, not hitherto much associated with intellectual social reform circles, who would take Liberalism into the 'untrodden fields' of State provision for the vast mass of the working population. National insurance on the German model was the next great objective. The motives and expectations of a new Liberal mood are revealingly expressed by Churchill in urging Asquith to further effort in December 1908:

I believe that there is an impressive social policy to be unfolded which would pass ponderously through both Houses and leave an abiding mark on national history. I care personally and I think the country cares far more about these issues than about mere political change; and anyhow I am confident that there is a great work to be done and that we are the men to do it.

Lloyd George and Churchill were the two major beneficiaries of Asquith's cabinet reconstruction upon becoming prime minister. Lloyd George took Asquith's place at the Exchequer and Churchill took Lloyd George's place at the Board of Trade and entered the cabinet. Grey stayed at the Foreign Office and Haldane at the War Office, where he was very successfully implementing a revolutionary reform of the Army with immense implications in foreign policy. Morley retired to the Lords but remained at the India Office where, in cooperation with the Viceroy, Minto, he was preparing the important Indian Councils Bill of 1909, increasing the powers of legislative councils in India, making a majority of their members elective, and increasing native Indian representation at the highest levels.

The reconstructed cabinet had to find a way out of the doldrums. What, most appropriately and effectively, would be the means of doing this? Home Rule for the Irish would fill no political sails in Britain, and disestablishment for the Welsh was too sectarian to raise much wind. One obvious recourse was that well-tried political wind-machine, franchise reform. Each phase of Liberal strength and vitality hitherto had been marked by a great measure to extend the franchise. The Act of 1867, though snatched by the adroit Disraeli, owed its existence as much to the forces of Liberalism as did those of 1832 and 1884. Surely now was the great opportunity for Liberalism to fulfil itself and recruit its strength by completing the great edifice of Reform? Thereby Liberalism could reassert more convincingly than in any other way its prerogatived political status. Much could be done. Under the existing dispensation, about 40 per cent of adult males did not exercise the franchise. The registration system was chaotically complicated, and moreover still lay in the hands of the agents of political parties. Being registered for the right to vote was still, as of old, the reward of known loyalty to a political party rather than the disinterested exercise of a citizen's rights.

It was undoubtedly the most telling indication of a fundamental Liberal debility in this era that Liberalism was inhibited from making a determined initiative on franchise reform. It was clear that any reform measure would involve the question of votes for women, now emerging as a major political issue. Some Liberals were hostile to votes for women out of sentiment and because they were convinced that superstition and emotion would make the female vote a bastion of reaction. Others were against female suffrage unless accompanied by a general extension of the franchise, on the ground that female suffrage on the existing registration would favour women of the wealthy classes. Another major inhibition was the Irish. It was well appreciated that the question of redistribution, as in 1885, could not be divorced from the franchise for the very simple reason, again as in 1885, that the Conservatives, with the House of Lords behind them, would insist that the two must go together. The point of this was that, for their own reasons, neither party had insisted in 1885 that the Irish representation be reduced proportionately to the decline of Irish population since 1846. This would mean that the Nationalist contingent at Westminster would be reduced drastically.[5] The Unionists would now insist on this if the Liberals raised the question of reform. The Irish in any case would resist furiously any proposal for reform, and hence redistribution, before Home Rule put them firmly in the saddle in Dublin; once there, they cared little what happened at Westminster. Thus the Liberal government was trapped in the situation where the condition for getting the democratic elixir of franchise reform was swallowing the political poison of Home Rule. Reform thus was an issue which tended to paralyse Liberal motivation and will rather than generate energy and confidence.

What else? Dissolution was considered, but rejected as a dangerous gamble in the absence of any big issue to restore morale. Free trade would not again have the impact of 1906. The Lords had not raised popular wrath against them. Increasingly the Liberal government began to focus its hopes on financial policy. Old age pensions was a pointer in this direction: as a money bill the Lords, by constitutional convention which left control of the public purse exclusively to the Commons, could not amend it. Strictly, they could reject it, but so outlandish a possibility was not seriously thought of. Hence emerged the idea of a budget in

1909 which would rescue Liberalism from its frustrations. Asquith announced in December 1908 that finance was 'an instrument of great potency and also of great flexibility', a 'partial solvent of what, under our existing constitutional conditions, would be otherwise insoluble problems'.

Political exigency chimed in well with financial necessity. More money was badly needed. Old age pensions were proving more expensive than anticipated. A deficit of nearly £16 million loomed if the tax system remained unaltered. McKenna, newly appointed to the Admiralty and expected to be a force for economy, instead agreed with the admirals and pressed demands for a huge expansion of naval construction to keep ahead of the accelerated German building programme. Lloyd George accordingly presented proposals in 1909 for increases of taxation amounting to some £16 million for the current financial year which would yield a total revenue sufficient to meet the estimated government expenditure of £162 million. There would be a new tax on motor cars and petrol, increased taxes on spirits and tobacco, increases in the upper brackets of income tax liability to a maximum of 1s. 8d. in the pound with a new super tax on incomes over £5,000, an increased scale of death duties, new duties on licensed premises, taxes on unearned increments of land values and the capital value of undeveloped land. Lloyd George also proposed that surpluses should no longer be automatically applied to the reduction of the national debt but might be used for financing a Development Commission to encourage improvements in transport, research in agriculture and afforestation.

Certainly this was a budget which would please Liberals, as it was intended to do. It would hurt their traditional enemies, landlords and brewers. But though it can be regarded as the first 'modern' budget, designed deliberately to use financial policy as a means of manipulating the relationships of social interests, the tax proposals were far from revolutionary or ruthless. There were no indications of general democratic enthusiasm. The main criticisms arose out of interpretations of the underlying social implications of stressing direct as opposed to indirect taxation and the stepping up of graduation. There was particular concern in orthodox circles about the proposed abandonment of the principle that surpluses went automatically towards debt reduction. The Irish were annoyed at the increased duties on their whiskey. To its amazement the government became aware that there was a distinct possibility that the Lords would reject the Finance Bill. The explanation of this extraordinary and quite unexpected result lies not in the budget provisions themselves but in the way the budget became inadvertently the focus of several distinct strands of political passion in 1909.

In the first place, the budget tended to get entangled with the issue of restricting or abolishing the Lords' veto, the very impediment it was designed to avoid. This happened because renewed Liberal enthusiasm equated the two issues and Unionist counter-enthusiasm followed suit. The Lords were again, in 1909, provoking Liberal outrage by their amendments and rejections. They mutilated an Irish Land Bill extending the provisions of Wyndham's 1903 Act. The Irish Nationalists were particularly keen on the matter of the Lords' veto because they well knew that crippling the powers of the Lords was an indispensable prerequisite to the ultimate attainment of Home Rule.

A more general influence added both flavour and colour to the already potent political stew. 'Socialism' had become a bogey with which the comfortably circumstanced classes of society frightened themselves. Rosebery, ever in search of great issues which would break up traditional party lines, drummed up the scare, using such things as Victor Grayson's victory at the Colne Valley by-election as grist to his mill. Old Chamberlain also, from the shades of Highbury, sounded the anti-socialist alarm. The budget was the thin end of the socialist wedge. To most Unionists the combined assault on the constitution of socialists and Fenians appeared as yet another manifestation of the anti-'national' conspiracy evoked by Disraeli. Then 'cosmopolitan' Liberalism was at the heart of the conspiracy; now Liberalism was reduced to the role of lackey to more sinister, extreme forces.

Much the most important influence bearing on the Lords, however, was that of the Tariff Reform movement. Austen Chamberlain, Bonar Law, Garvin and their followers were convinced that the decisive chance of forcing the issue to their advantage had arrived. Their argument was that the 1909 budget exposed the fatal limitations of free trade finance, which could only raise sufficient revenue by attacks on capital and the means of capital accumulation. The gap between the two great political parties had now widened markedly on this question. Liberal economists who approved the budget, following Hobson's under-consumptionist doctrines, stressed the need to create popular consuming capacity by redistributing capital; Unionist economists (and dismayed orthodox Liberals) stressed the countervailing doctrine of the vital importance of not eroding the capital foundations of the productiveness of private industry. The Tariff Reform message was clear: only through a protective fiscal system could the required revenue be raised without mortal damage to the free economy; the clear implication of free trade finance was that it must head in the direction of socialism; and therefore the fundamental issue which emerged out of the budget of 1909 was a choice between Tariff Reform or Socialism. For this reason the Lords must throw the budget out and force an appeal to the electorate to give them the chance of making this fundamental choice. Moreover, if an election were forced, Liberal ministers would be put on the spot, for they would have to honour their pledges to the Irish Nationalists to introduce a Home Rule Bill; which, according to Unionist calculations, would tend to divide rather than unite the Liberal party.

The Tariff Reformers were certain that the tide was flowing their way. Probably they might not win the election. But if the government's majority could be reduced to 1892 proportions, dependent on the Irish and Labour, that would be enough for the time being. Tariff Reformers were doing well in by-elections. They controlled the Unionist party. Most Unionist Free Fooders who remained were against rejection by the Lords but were unable to stem the feeling in favour of forcing an election on the budget. Balfour himself decided to go with the Tariff Reform tide in August 1909. He had no option otherwise if he wanted to retain the leadership.

By this time the political atmosphere had become extremely warm. Lloyd George, hitherto cultivating a new reputation for responsible statesmanship, was unleashed by Asquith and set off on rousing demagogic excursions. At the Edinburgh Castle public house at Limehouse in July 1909 Lloyd George delighted 4,000 of the faithful with some fiery rhetoric at the expense of landlords. At Newcastle in October, in the 'table of the law' speech already noted as carrying, beneath the rhetoric, not particularly comforting long-range implications for Liberalism, Lloyd George fastened on some incautious ducal public pronouncements: 'a fully-equipped duke costs as much to keep up as two Dreadnoughts'. Possibly he was being deliberately provocative. In daring the Lords to reject the budget and thus call up the genius of popular revolution he could produce immediate dividends for Liberalism. Other ministers were indeed coming round to the conclusion that a veto by the Lords could, in Churchill's candid words, be a 'great tactical advantage' for the government.

The Finance Bill eventually passed the Commons in November 1909. Lansdowne in the Lords proposed that 'this House is not justified in giving its assent to the Bill until it has been submitted to the judgement of the country'. On 30 November, by 350 votes against seventy-five, the Lords threw out the budget. Rosebery advocated rejection though characteristically he abstained. Asquith and the other former Roseberyite ministers formally parted company with him, and the Liberal League, long moribund, quietly passed away. Asquith announced the dissolution of the Commons and elections in January 1910. He also, following the precedent of 1832, asked the King what his response would be in the event of a request for the creation of sufficient Liberal peers to ensure the passage of the Finance Bill through the Lords. The King replied that he would countenance a procedure so repugnant to his feelings only after the return of a Liberal majority in a further general election after January 1910. This response dismayed the Liberal ministers, who wanted to be able to feel assured that they had this ultimate sanction at their disposal. The party as a whole was under the general misapprehension that Asquith had in fact obtained a royal undertaking that the Lords would if necessary be coerced by a mass creation of peers. Ministers pinned their hopes on an electoral rally to Liberalism.

The elections destroyed the overall Liberal majority. The Liberal and Labour proportion of the British vote dropped from

55·1 per cent to 51·6 per cent. Unionists gained over a hundred seats from Liberals; and Labour dropped from fifty-three to forty seats. The L.R.C. had put up seventy-eight candidates. Labour in 1909 had suffered another legal setback known as the Osborne Judgement, which ruled that trade unions could not compulsorily levy funds for political purposes. This cramped the Labour electoral effort. Labour's consolation, however, was twofold: they lost less heavily than the Liberals, and now the whole Labour parliamentary contingent was united under the auspices of the L.R.C. Hardie, MacDonald and Snowden had resigned in any case from the I.L.P. under the pressure of its socialist zealots, and for the time being had nowhere to go but back into the Liberal government's fold. The Irish Nationalists retained their usual contingent less only one. They did not like the budget, and their support for the government was entirely dependent on its good behaviour as defined by Redmond and his increasingly restless party. The Unionists returned 273 strong, regaining their majority of the English constituencies and forcing the Liberals to depend for their 124 majority on the 'Celtic fringe' and Labour.

The Liberal ministers were desperately disappointed. They had expected to drop many of their marginally held seats. A repetition of 1906 was hardly to be expected. Yet they hoped that the House of Lords, representing privilege and reaction, would have aroused more of a radical spirit among the electorate than appeared to have been the case. Indeed, a record 86·6 per cent of the registered electors voted, compared with 83 per cent in 1906. But this was not converted into Liberal strength.

On the other hand, the Tariff Reform Unionists could not claim an unqualified success for their appeal. They were now in complete control of the Unionist party. The Balfourian *via media* had eroded into nothingness. The Free Fooders were proscribed. But it was seriously disappointing to the Tariff Reformers that they failed to re-establish convincingly the old Conservative dominance in London and Lancashire. In fact, this moment was to prove the zenith, and the beginning of the decline, of the fortunes of the Tariff Reform movement.

Undoubtedly it was the Irish Nationalists who emerged with the greatest advantage. They could, if they wished, by voting against the government, turn them out. Eight Nationalists in fact broke away from Redmond to form an advance guard of such a blackmailing tactic. They had the government committed to Home Rule; and they had, in the budget issue, a providential means for striking decisively at their victorious enemy of 1893. However lukewarm for Home Rule the bulk of Liberals might be, they were committed for their own purposes to destroying the absolute veto power of the Lords; and once that power went, Home Rule could get through. The Irish insisted that the larger question of reforming the constitution of the upper house must be left until later: the veto must go first, come what may. Since the Irish had genuine motives for not liking the budget their votes for the Finance Bill would be in the nature of a concession for which they would exact full reciprocation. If the Irish voted against the Finance Bill the Liberal electoral appeal would be converted from a failure into a disaster. Yet that very failure deprived the Liberal ministers of their entitlement to press the King for guarantees of the means to coerce the Lords; which guarantee in turn was vital for the purposes of the Irish.

V

The Liberal ministers were in a state of confusion and despondency. Some, between the devil of the Lords and the deep blue sea of Home Rule, were for resignation. Asquith's prestige slumped badly when he revealed to his dismayed followers that he had neither requested nor obtained a guarantee from the King that sufficient peers would be created. The idea was canvassed of negotiating Unionist support to get the budget through and calling the Irish bluff. But all such manoeuvres opened up vistas even more distressing than the painful existing situation. The government recovered its nerve and decided to press ahead with the question of the Lords' veto powers, leaving a larger reform scheme until later.

The constitutional issue and its concomitant dependencies of Home Rule and Welsh disestablishment, moreover, was not necessarily foremost in the minds of many Liberals, whose priorities had to do with labour exchanges, unemployment and a complete reform of the Poor Law following the Report of the 1905 Commission at the beginning of 1909. Lloyd George wanted to put through his plans for a comprehensive project of social insurance. Winston Churchill's system of Labour Exchanges to facilitate re-employment was in fact inaugurated at the beginning of 1910 as the first step in the direction of a comprehensive unemployment insurance. Both the Report of the Poor Law Commissioners and the Minority Report of the Webbs offered much food for political thought. The majority commissioners advocated reforms more or less within the existing administrative framework. The Minority Report, highly imbued with the Webbs' national efficiency doctrine, advocated that the principles of relief of the poor should be turned inside out into a standard system of social welfare services based on the starting point of the service socially necessary, rather than from the distressed circumstances of the poorest classes of society. This, an 'environmental' approach to social problems, was far too authoritarian for the Liberal government to swallow; and the social reform programme continued along lines of insurance against evils rather than compulsory prevention of evils. Thus, amid the constitutional turmoils of 1910 and 1911, the National Insurance Act of 1911 brought the social welfare policy of the New Liberalism to culmination.

This was Lloyd George's last great domestic political achievement. The circumstances of 1910 combined with Lloyd George's career in politics and personal predispositions created a situation very revealing for the present and significant for the future. It had long been recognized, especially by shrewd Unionists, that in outlook Lloyd George was much more of the Chamberlain stamp of statesmanship than an orthodox party Radical. Even more of an outsider than Chamberlain, he had no deep-rooted loyalties to particular ideas or institutions. He would be much more likely to break parties than to make them. As long as circumstances dictated that he make his way in politics by such orthodox issues as anti-imperialism in 1900 or education in 1902 he could give every impression superficially of being a mainstream Liberal. Then, so long as Liberalism retained something of the political ascendancy conferred by the 1906 election and while mainstream issues like the budget dominated the political scene and while the Liberal leader retained his personal ascendancy intact, Lloyd George's deeper heterodox tendencies would be obscured. But once, as with the election of January 1910 and the first serious damage to Asquith's prestige, Liberalism and its leader shrunk in stature and authority, circumstances would confer on Lloyd George wholly new opportunities for the exercise of a much more idiosyncratic mode of political behaviour. Already, by the cabinet reconstruction of 1908, he was placed in a position of much greater potentiality.

The essential irony of the situation was that, up until 1908, it had been generally assumed that the end of the Campbell-Bannerman 'Harcourtian' dispensation at the head of Liberalism would be logically followed by the ascendancy of its traditional rival, a 'Roseberyite' Liberal League dispensation. Asquith as leader with Grey and Haldane still going strong was supposed to reflect this decisive shift. Yet in fact the shift that took place was quite different. Liberal imperialism was as much discredited by the failures of the South African policy as was Chamberlainite imperialism. The two imperial conferences of 1907 and 1911 finally ended any lingering hopes of economic integration and defence and political integration. The appearance of 'Liberal League' continuity and authority was sustained in reality by the fact that the forces of genuine strength and potentiality represented by Lloyd George and his henchman Churchill were willing, from 1911, to sustain Grey's foreign policy. Whatever they were, as their later careers amply indicated, both Lloyd George and Churchill were neither Harcourtians, Roseberyites, nor indeed any easily definable species of Liberal. They were statesmen of genius in search of great roles to play in politics. Lloyd George made his first tentative initiative in this direction as the 'normal' machination of party politics seized up between the two elections of 1910.

In April Asquith introduced the Parliament Bill providing for the exclusion of the Lords from financial questions, the restriction of the Lords' veto power on other legislation so that the will of the Commons should prevail within the limits of a parliament, and the shortening of parliaments to a maximum of five years. Asquith announced that if the Lords should reject the Parliament

Bill he would recommend another dissolution; but he would make no such recommendation to the King except under such conditions as would ensure that in the new parliament the judgement of the electorate would be carried into law. In other words, if the Lords rejected, the government would resign unless the King undertook to create peers in the event of the government's securing a majority in the constituencies. Already the Liberal ministers were accused of being accomplices of the Irish; now, in the eyes of outraged Unionists, they were going to force the King to become an accomplice also. By now the budget itself was a minor affair: the Lords passed it on 21 April without a division.

Suddenly, on 6 May, Edward VII died. The new King, George V, lacked his father's cosmopolitan confidence. Conscientious and virtuous, he came into the line of succession to the throne only on the unexpected death of his elder brother the Duke of Clarence in 1892. His training had been exclusively in the Navy and he was not in a position either by taste or ability to impose on the critical political situation anything in the way of a royal mediation. Instead, the politicians took the occasion of the new reign to agree to a 'Truce of God'. This was institutionalized in June 1910 in a formal Constitutional Conference to try to bring the two sides together to reach some compromise agreement. There were twenty-two meetings between June and October. Asquith and Lloyd George were the chief Liberal representatives; Balfour, Lansdowne and Austen Chamberlain represented the Unionists. There was much futile debate on reforming the Lords and on getting around Irish Home Rule. Neither party was willing to sacrifice any serious points of principle, though Asquith remained hopeful that some formula could be found that would avert a serious collision. Deadlock was complete.

This deadlock provoked Lloyd George to attempt to negotiate a 'national settlement' on his own initiative. Oppressed by the difficulties he was facing in his national insurance project from the lobby influences of the insurance companies and the medical profession, the idea of what great things might be achieved by replacing sterile party squabbling with fruitful party cooperation captured his imagination. Lloyd George at this point looked back to the 'efficiency' ideas of the turn of the century and forward to the coalition ministry of 1915. In a memorandum composed in August 1910 and developed further in the following months Lloyd George argued that politics was essentially, like any practical business, a matter of management by the best available talents. With rhetoric very reminiscent of Rosebery's efficiency propaganda of 1900, Lloyd George emphasized the necessity of both great parties in the State bringing their resources of talent 'into joint stock in order to liquidate arrears which, if much longer neglected, may end in national impoverishment, if not insolvency'.

Many were attracted by this idea of a 'grand settlement', Churchill among them. Asquith was given only the vaguest idea of what was afoot. Indeed, Lloyd George had already discussed with Balfour the desirability of promoting Asquith to the Lords very much in the spirit of Asquith's earlier plans for Campbell-Bannerman. But again Balfour was not prepared to run the risk of sacrificing the historic identity of the Conservative party in the way that Lloyd George was prepared to repudiate historic Liberalism. Clearly, the concept of 'national government' was premature.

Thus, after the interruption of these official and unofficial negotiations, partisan politics was once more, towards the end of 1910, free to follow the course determined by its own untrammelled logic. Asquith preferred an immediate dissolution but the King would agree only after the Parliament Bill had been rejected by the Lords. The King also attempted to avoid having to give an undertaking to create if necessary enough Liberal peers (something like five hundred) to swamp the Lords. But Asquith and the cabinet stood firm and threatened immediate resignation. The royal undertaking was given, rather resentfully. The Parliament Bill was sent up to the Lords where it was duly (in effect) rejected. Asquith thereupon dissolved the parliament and a second general election was held in December 1910.

The new elections solved nothing. One less Unionist, three less Liberals, two more Labour and two more Irish Nationalist members were returned than in January. The result was a stalemate. The Liberals had hoped to increase their numbers by at least thirty. In fact their total proportion of the vote in Britain dropped slightly. But in any event the Liberal government clearly could still count on a majority of more than a hundred on the two great issues it had set before the constituencies, the Lords' veto and Home Rule for Ireland.

The Parliament Bill was reintroduced in the new House of Commons in February 1911. The main provision was that if a bill passed twice by the Commons and rejected twice by the Lords were to be passed a third time by the Commons it would thereupon be transmitted for the royal assent regardless of the Lords. The bill went in May to the Lords, who made amendments unacceptable to Asquith, who thereupon revealed officially that he had received guarantees from the King that the necessary number of peers would be created if the Lords proved recalcitrant. Amid the brilliant junketings of the coronation and the imperial conference the Unionists wrestled with their consciences. They split into those led by Balfour, Lansdowne and Curzon, who advocated the expediency of surrender, and those led by Austen Chamberlain, the new Lord Salisbury and the Irish Unionist leader Edward Carson, who resolved to 'die hard'. Party enthusiasm for the diehard (or 'last ditch') cause focused on the octogenarian Lord Halsbury, the former lord chancellor. Majority sentiment both in the shadow cabinet and in Unionism as a whole approved resistance and repudiated Balfour's advice to capitulate and, by clear implication, his leadership. Eventually, on 10 August, sufficient peers ('hedgers') were induced by Curzon to vote for the bill to save it from the Halsbury 'ditchers'; the government got a majority of seventeen, and the wholesale peerage manufacturing was avoided, to the great disappointment of many obscure Liberal hopefuls.

Meanwhile, Lloyd George's National Insurance Bill, delayed in the confusions of 1910, was now embroiled in the atmosphere of bitterness and recrimination engendered by the constitutional crisis. National Insurance was the logical completion of the pattern of the Liberal government's social reform programme and the appropriate conclusion to the first era of the Liberal bid to respond adequately to the domestic aspect of great national problems. Insurance against unemployment and health insurance for workers in the building, shipbuilding and engineering trades, notoriously vulnerable to seasonal fluctuation, were the necessary consequences of the balance of forces within Liberalism. On the one hand the New Liberals argued the need, following the diagnosis formed by C. P. Scott as early as 1897, that the crucial thing was to conciliate the working class and to pre-empt socialism. It was impossible to reconcile the Poor Law with a democratic franchise. On the other hand the Old Liberals would not accept the dismantling of the Poor Law with its built-in assumption of Victorian principles of self-help and individual independence, and the inescapable necessity of punishing improvidence and fecklessness. John Burns, to the fury of his erstwhile Labour comrades, had become a pillar of this attitude. Neither New nor Old Liberals had strong enough stomachs to swallow the ruthless authoritarianism of the Webbs. Therefore alongside the existing Poor Law had to be erected a parallel system of institutions for the relief of social distress, of which National Insurance was the most complicated and controversial. Lloyd George had to incorporate the Friendly Societies and the commercial insurers; he had to mollify the suspicious medical profession. Liberalism got relatively little political credit from the workers, who resented the compulsory contributions involved. The majority of workers in any case were not covered by it. For Lloyd George this was a 'necessary temporary expedient', a substitute for a comprehensive overhaul of welfare services that would eventually come with the abolition of the Poor Law. By 1911, social Liberalism had gone as far as it could go.

Chapter Seventeen

LIBERAL RESPONSES
IN FOREIGN AFFAIRS
1905–11

I

Grey's accession in the place of Lansdowne to the Foreign Office was a guarantee that there would be no attempt by the Liberal government to implement what the great majority of the Liberal party understood to be a 'Liberal' foreign policy. As Josiah Wedgwood, the Radical M.P. for Newcastle-under-Lyme, put it in 1911, looking back over the years since 1905: 'The Foreign policy of the Government is not a Liberal foreign policy. It is not merely a continuation, but it is an accentuation, of the foreign policy of our predecessors.' Haldane at the War Office equally was a guarantee that the military reforms of Esher and Clarke and Balfour's projects for defence planning centred on the C.I.D. would not be sacrificed on the Liberal altars of peace, retrenchment and reform. The new First Lord of the Admiralty, Tweedmouth, was of a more 'moderate' stripe, but by no means inclined to challenge the admirals' demands for ships and money, and in any case not of the political weight to divert general government policy one way or the other.

Thus 'continuity' in a general sense prevailed; but, equally important, there were several factors of decisive novelty. In the first place, the Foreign Office of 1906 was a very different department from that presided over by Salisbury and Lansdowne. Secondly, the implications for Britain of the international situation were new: margins of profitability directed British attention away from imperial defence towards Europe. Hitherto the 'balance of power' had concerned the British primarily as it impinged on Africa and Asia and the Straits; now it concerned the British because of the way it impinged directly on Britain. In the first situation British policy had devoted itself to coping with its imperial rivals, the French and the Russians. In the second situation British policy devoted itself to coming to understandings with the French and the Russians as the means of a counterpoise of European power against the threat of German domination.

The Foreign Office itself changed in two important ways. First, the increasing pressure of business tended to increase the responsibility of the officials handling it. This was generally true of the whole Civil Service, and was part of the tendency in a complex administrative state for the bureaucracy to become more influential and to gain an increasing control over the initiation as well as the implementation of policy. The Civil Service, from being mere servants of the politicians, now were to be guardians of State interests; and in no department were these responsibilities more readily assumed than in the Foreign Office. This was not entirely because, as a Radical politician complained, the Office itself and the traditions of its staff were 'far too aristocratic in tone and illiberal in principle'. But its aristocratic character did have much to do with its peculiar administrative structure which excluded the purely clerical division established as a result of the Northcote–Trevelyan recommendations of 1853. This meant that much more important matter circulated among junior levels of the staff; and when the sheer pressure of materials to be processed forced a delegation of responsibility, greater opportunities of initiative and decision devolved upon junior staff at the Foreign Office than at most other great departments – opportunities of which juniors like Eyre Crowe took full advantage. At the other end of the hierarchy, the permanent under-secretary under the new administrative arrangements became much less a mere executive subordinate of the secretary of state and became much more of an equal personage. Sanderson, the last of the self-effacing under-secretaries bred in the days and ways of Salisbury, who neither requested nor expected his officers to have opinions about high policy, retired in February 1906. His successor, Hardinge, fully intended to have opinions about the conduct of policy and to do his best to get those opinions translated into policy. Indeed, Hardinge's appointment was specifically engineered in the Office because, as Mallet, who was in turn to be engineered into Grey's private secretary by Hardinge, put it to Bertie, Hardinge's crony and now ambassador at Paris, 'the importance of having someone who will keep the Liberals straight is overwhelming'. The other candidate, Eldon Gorst, was not considered so reliable for this purpose; so he was shunted off to replace Cromer in Egypt in 1907.

'Keeping the Liberals straight' meant precisely keeping policy immune from the 'sentimental' influence of Cobdenism and especially of the government's backbench radical supporters, with their philanthropic view that British policy should be, in the words of Arthur Ponsonby, a 'detached, disinterested, humanitarian' effort to uphold 'the freedom of downtrodden peoples' at the expense of 'Empire and armaments'. Grey the Office chiefs recognized as 'sound'; they were worried about Campbell-Bannerman and the 'Gladstonian' majority of the ministry – Loreburn (the most constant and unforgiving critic in the cabinet of Grey's relationship with the Foreign Office), Morley, Bryce (along with Loreburn, very Germanophile and critical of the French *entente*), Lewis Harcourt, very much, in this respect, his father's son. To some extent Morley, who might have made himself a formidable nuisance to Grey, was neutralized by being at the India Office which, combined with his Gladstonian zeal for financial retrenchment, made him a natural ally of efforts to relieve pressure on Indian defence by doing a deal with the Russians, which suited the Foreign Office even though they had quite different motives for dealing with the Russians. But Grey's greatest advantage as against his unsympathetic colleagues was that none of them was particularly interested in foreign affairs. Compared with Lansdowne, Grey was very rarely supervised or interfered with in cabinet; and correspondingly, Grey was able to conduct policy with far less reference to his colleagues. Grey often, in the coming years, passed into the sphere of policy consultation where lack of officious zeal to inform shaded into a preference for not informing which in turn shaded, on certain vital matters, into deliberate withholding of information to a degree which merits the term deception.[1]

But the important factor in the Liberal government was not so much Grey's willingness to withhold information when it suited him as his colleagues' willingness, in effect, to let themselves be duped. The basic fact was that those ministers who resented the attitude and the assumptions of the clique around Grey at the Foreign Office could mount no convincing intellectual contradiction of the anti-German policy advocated most strongly by Bertie, Mallet and Crowe in an era of international affairs distinguished by German behaviour in the accelerating tempo of power conflicts represented most critically by First Morocco (1905-6), First Bosnia (1908-9), Second Morocco (1911) and Second Bosnia (1914). Equipped essentially with nothing more than Cobdenite assumptions that nothing stood in the way of a natural and inevitable ultimate reconciliation of conflict and harmony of interests in a world of rational men capable of good will except bad faith and misunderstanding, Liberal ministers preferred to avert their eyes from the spectacle of an international scene too inexplicably and irrationally violent to be contemplated without despair. The Unionist ministers who had waged war in South Africa and concluded the alliance with the Japanese were not so intellectually constituted; and hence the 'healthy' relationship between Lansdowne and his colleagues. It is highly significant that the colleague who gave Grey most trouble was his closest friend and Liberal imperialist confrère, the secretary for War, Haldane: argument was possible because they shared common ground. Haldane, emotionally Germanophile, disliked Grey's increasingly hard-line pro-French commitment, and devoted himself, unavailingly, to persuading his German friends to drop a policy – their naval programme – which would guarantee British hostility. He never seriously questioned the legitimacy of that hostility.

There was, consequently, little or no political feedback from the cabinet to the Cobdenite radicals,[2] nor in return from the radicals back to cabinet level. The necessary articulation would have had to be a willingness on the part of Grey's cabinet colleagues to force upon him, in the face of the expert testimony of the Foreign Office, the Admiralty, the War Office, the Committee of Imperial Defence and the India Office, acceptance of the propositions, first, that Germany had every right to claim a position of world equality with Britain, and that no considerations of

British security entitled Britain to deny or resist that German claim; and second, that the reason for apparent German hostility lay precisely in the dog-in-the-manger character of British policy, and once that was dropped German hostility would fade away also. Grey's cabinet colleagues were not willing to enforce these doctrines on him. They did not, in short, have the courage of their backbenchers' convictions. That unwillingness, not Grey's 'deceit', was the core of the Liberal government's 'betrayal' of Liberalism's duty to the external world in the era from 1906 to 1914.

II

The 'military conversations' with the French which Grey approved in January 1906 did not cause military cooperation with the French Army; they were the consequence of a decision already taken in 1905 that such cooperation might well be desirable, and that therefore it would be necessary to have some idea of French military dispositions. Grey informed Campbell-Bannerman of the conversations, and the prime minister correctly judged their implication: 'I do not like the stress laid upon joint preparations. It comes very close to an honourable undertaking: and it will be known on both sides of the Rhine.' But he let himself be persuaded by Haldane that what he knew to be the case would not be the case; and he acquiesced in permitting that the cabinet as a whole was not informed of them, and knew nothing of them until the facts came out in 1911. Cambon, the French ambassador, was perfectly aware that several Liberal ministers would have been 'astonished' to know of such consultations and would certainly have objected to them.

The decision to consult with the French about possible military cooperation against the Germans arose out of the Morocco crisis of 1905, which a conference of the powers was trying to resolve at Algeciras in early 1906. The question of Morocco in turn had become a European crisis because of the way it fitted into German requirements. The Germans were devoting themselves to two main objectives. First, they were pursuing a 'world policy' based on naval power which had the effect of offending the

British very seriously. The pugnacious Fisher was already talking of 'Copenhagening' the German fleet before it became a serious menace. The Germans, convinced of their right to have as big a fleet as they were willing to pay for, took such threats far more seriously than did the British public. Secondly, the Germans were trying to preserve their position as the central power in Europe from the dangers of 'encirclement' inherent in such a situation and to restore the advantages of centrality which it had been the essence of Bismarck's policy to exploit. That meant breaking the Franco-Russian alliance, for with defeat in the Far East the Russians had to come back to the Near East and Europe. Russian policy wavered between adventurous pan-Slavists who wanted to challenge Austria in the Balkans and Germany at the Straits and as the general protector of the Ottoman régime, and conservatives who wanted a return to the safety of the Three Emperors' League. If the Germans, making use of the Morocco question, could crush French resolution to remain a resistant Great Power, Russia, weakened in any case by defeat and revolution, would have no option but to conform to a triumphant new German dispensation of Europe. The French, determined to resist and without a powerful Russia to call on, put all the pressure they discreetly could on the British. On 10 January 1906 Cambon, as Grey wrote, 'put *the* question to me directly and formally': could France rely on British aid in the event of war with Germany? After all, the French were going ahead in Morocco as a consequence of the *entente* with Britain. Grey replied that if a war should break out on such a question arising from the *entente*, British public opinion would be 'strongly moved in favour of France'; but he could not, without further consultations with his colleagues, give a more binding answer. Grey was 'much upset' by the occasion, and the Office, led by Mallet, the most violently anti-German of them all, rallied vigorously to keep him 'straight'.

This incident was for Grey like the first numbing shock of a plunge into ice-cold water; but he grew more comfortable and inured as time went by. It was Grey's great achievement that, having accepted the elementary logic of the Morocco crisis, he accepted its implications without any self-deluding reservations.

The crucial implication was that what the Germans were trying to do in Europe was even more vital from the point of view of British interests than what they were trying to do in the way of 'world policy'. The implication of 'world policy' centred on relative naval strength. This became from Grey's point of view increasingly a side issue. It did not cease to be important, because it touched Britain and British public opinion very directly, and it imposed on the government increasing and unwelcome financial burdens. But Britain could, if necessary, keep the required margin of superiority against Germany comfortably enough by jettisoning finally the old Two Power standard of 1889. Britain, in other words, would not go to war with Germany over the issue of naval programmes.

The question that Grey had to face was: would, or should, Britain go to war with Germany for the sake of the 'balance of power' in Europe, which in practice meant the preservation of France as a Great Power and, as a necessary corollary, the preservation of the Franco-Russian alliance? And if the answer to this question was Yes, could Britain make the necessary contribution in the application of power by essentially naval means, as the admirals argued, using military force in a diversionary strategy – say, against Schleswig-Holstein – or by essentially military means, as the generals argued, by sending over to operate with the French Army such a proportion of the British Army as would make a decisive contribution to an ultimately successful result? And what would, in that case, constitute such a proportion of the British Army?

These were the questions at the heart of British foreign and naval and military policy in the years from 1906. The answers arrived at were, first, that Britain would go to war to preserve France and the European balance against a German dominance if circumstances were such that there was no alternative means of redress. Secondly, it was decided that for this purpose a sufficient military force would be dispatched to the left wing of the French Order of Battle, and it was decided that two extended army corps of six infantry divisions and one cavalry division, 150,000 men in all, would constitute such a force, amounting in bayonet strength to seventy-two battalions of infantry.[3]

These conclusions were virtually fore-ordained by the end of the Algeciras conference in March 1906, when the Germans, isolated except for the rather embarrassed Austrians and the pathetic Moroccans themselves, climbed down. This was the first major rebuff the German Empire had received in international affairs since its foundation. Grey was convinced that the lesson to be learned from the Morocco crisis was that above all else the French had to be supported. Hitherto, the *entente*, as negotiated by Lansdowne, had been a means of getting rid of French resentment. Lansdowne never thought of it as committing Britain necessarily to support of the French. Nor did he assume that the *entente* with France conflicted with his constant efforts to get an equivalent *entente* with the Germans. To interpret the *entente* agreement on Morocco as putting the British under an obligation to help the French against the German effort to stop them was a natural French manoeuvre; the important thing is that Grey accepted this French interpretation, and thus converted the *entente* from a convenient means to a finite end – good relations with France – to an end in itself, the corner-stone of a balance of power policy, infinite in scope and possibilities.

The doctrinal codification of this fundamental shift in foreign policy was formulated in the classic 'Memorandum on the present State of British Relations with France and Germany' by Eyre Crowe, circulated on 1 January 1907. In this Crowe, an expert on Germany with a particularly valuable insight into the influence in German affairs of demagogic 'national' movements like the pan-German League and the Navy League, argued that the opposition into which Britain must be driven to resist any country's aspiring to a European dictatorship 'assumes almost the form of a law of nature'. He thereupon argued that the circumstances of Germany pointed either to a clear-cut aim at 'general political hegemony and maritime ascendancy' or to a much more general and diffuse German ambition to exploit legitimately her energies and potentiality to maximize her interests in Europe and the world, 'leaving it to an uncertain future to decide whether the occurrence of great changes in the world may not some day assign to Germany a larger share of direct political action over regions not now a part of her dominions, without that violation of the established rights of other countries which would be involved in any such action under existing political conditions'. Either way, Crowe concluded, British policy must be the same: faithfulness to the general principle of the balance of power, faithfulness to the *entente* with France and recognition of the desirability of a corresponding *entente* with Russia, wariness of any future German proposals for a 'close understanding', without at the same time bearing any immutable ill will for Germany. Above all, Crowe recommended an intelligent firmness, such as was shown, with excellent results, to the French over Fashoda in 1898, to any German efforts in the future to repeat the Morocco adventure.

That the Germans would in fact try to repair their Morocco setback by a second campaign to break the forming counterpoise on either side of them was implicit in Crowe's analysis. For the Germans not to make such a bid would be tantamount to acceptance that the new alliance system of Europe was dominating them by imposing strict limits on their freedom of action rather than, as with the original Bismarckian development of the system, that Germany used the alliance system to secure and maintain a European hegemony.

Grey certainly accepted the validity of this analysis. To what extent he did so under the influence of Mallet and Crowe especially and to what extent their influence merely reinforced a pre-existing disposition can never be known. Indeed, Grey would have liked to make an honest man of himself in cabinet and in parliament by a French alliance. But neither the cabinet nor parliament would have countenanced so disturbingly logical a procedure. By this time Grey was too anti-German even for Hardinge's liking. In the post-Algeciras situation there was much effort by parties of good will on both sides to restore good Anglo-German relations. Liberals who wanted retrenchment or who were pushing for social reform measures resented increased defence expenditure and demanded an effort for a settlement with the Germans. Loreburn and Lloyd George pressed constantly for this in cabinet. Grey displayed conspicuous lack of enthusiasm to foster this; and concentrated his attention on following up the next logical course open to him, an *entente* with the Russians.

By 1907 Grey's commitment to the French was complete. His constantly reiterated claims of full freedom of action were mere exercises in public relations. When Campbell-Bannerman, in conversation with the French prime minister Clemenceau in Paris in 1907, remarked that he did not think British public opinion would countenance British troops fighting on the continent, Clemenceau's dismay provoked Grey to swift reassurance.

The Russian *entente* was indeed the next predestined step. Nicolson, its prime advocate, was sent off in May 1906 to get it at St Petersburg. The negotiations were conducted on two levels. One, for the consumption of the cabinet and parliament, was settlement of outstanding disputes in Tibet, Central Asia, Persia, the Near East. The other, the major motive in the minds of Grey, Hardinge and Nicolson, was to restore Russia as a major factor in Europe and as a part of a counterpoise neutralizing Germany. The 'balance of power' motive would never have secured general public endorsement. Even the resolution of conflicts approach ran into grave difficulties. *Entente* with France was, after all, a good enough Liberal cause, redolent of Gladstone. But *entente* with Russia had ceased decidedly to be a good Liberal cause ever since the murder of Alexander II in 1881. Liberals were incensed by anti-semitic pogroms. Nicholas II's dismissal of the recently established Duma in 1906 incensed them even more. When in 1908 the Anglo-Russian *entente* was to be formally consummated by a meeting of Edward VII and Nicholas II on their yachts at Reval, Keir Hardie proposed a censure motion which gathered fifty-nine dissident Liberal and Labour votes.

Morley, the secretary for India, insisted on putting his oar in, but he was useful in two ways. By being allowed to believe that India was the key to the whole negotiation his vanity was flattered; as a Gladstonian anxious to reduce Indian defence costs he could be relied on to quash any efforts by the government of India to protest against undue concessions to the Russians. Persia became the focus of trouble, where Russian behaviour and British connivance at it indeed gave the Radicals every cause for moral indignation. The dispute exposed an ironical situation. On the one side, the strange alliance of Russophobe Radicals and the Indian Raj advised by none other than Lord Kitchener protested at the preponderant role being conceded to the Russians in a partition of Persia into spheres of influence. On the other side was the Foreign Office, willing to offer up Persia as a sacrifice on the altar of the European balance of power, and Morley, the official keeper of the Gladstonian conscience.

The Russians were not enthusiastic about the *entente* with the British but were willing to pick up any advantages being offered. But in a larger sense the *entente* fitted in to the preponderant directive forces in Russian social and political development. The régime had to restore its prestige after the Far Eastern disaster. This meant encouraging 'national', or pan-Slavonic, opinion. Pan-Slavonic enthusiasm led inevitably to a general anti-Germanism and especially to anti-Austrian policies in the Balkans, where the Jugoslav (South Slav) agitation centred in Serbia under the newly established pro-Russian and anti-Austrian Karageorgevich dynasty offered a tempting focus of aid and encouragement. The Straits question also proposed itself to the Russians as a possible source of badly needed dividends. In the *entente* negotiations the British had made it clear to the new Russian foreign minister, Isvolsky, that they would have no objections to the Russians securing a revised Rule of the Straits if they could get European consent. This sent Isvolsky off on his European pilgrimage and especially to Buchlau[4] in Moravia to deal with the Austrian foreign minister, Lexa; and thereby Isvolsky landed himself in dire trouble, for an official Straits policy which needed Austrian consent was not compatible with a pan-Slavonic policy, even if unofficial, which the Austrians were bound to attempt to suppress. In exchange for Austrian support on the Straits Isvolsky agreed to countenance an Austrian annexation of Bosnia and Herzegovina, occupied by the Austrians since 1878 on behalf of the Sultan but now the focus of intense Serbian Jugoslav agitation. Isvolsky thus made himself a hostage to fortune. For the Austrians, Bosnia was a bird in hand, the ultimate annexation of which had never been in doubt. Now, with the Emperor Francis Joseph's diamond jubilee impending, here was every reason to expect some spectacular demonstration; and the motive for thwarting Serbian hopes was an even stronger incentive. Moreover, the 'Young Turk' revolution which had just deposed Abdul Hamid aimed at restoring to Turkey all its rights, including Bosnia, and the Bulgarians were willing to chime in with Vienna and proclaim the end of the Turkish suzerainty. Thus the Austrians would not wait for Isvolsky to realize his European investment; it was up to him to do the best he could. The Austrians went ahead and proclaimed the annexation of Bosnia and the Herzegovina in October 1908.

This set off a European uproar. The Serbs were frantic with resentment. The Russians were furious at the blow against Slavdom. The French followed this cue. The British took a high moral line about the sanctity of the Treaty of Berlin. The Italians immediately demanded Albania in compensation. The Germans were offended at not being consulted.

The importance of all this was that, once they got over their initial annoyance, the Bosnian crisis offered the Germans a second great opportunity to break the Franco-Russian alliance and the new Anglo-Russian *entente*, this time by turning the heat on the Russians. Their performance now more than validated Crowe's analysis. Already the Germans and French were on bad terms over French recapture of German deserters from the Foreign Legion from the German consulate in Casablanca. The French did not ask the British government what their intentions would be in the event of a war with Germany; but as it happened, Asquith, Grey and Haldane had already decided to assist the French.

III

Anglo-German relations had in any case also taken a turn for the worse, after the brief post-Algeciras relaxation. The Amending Law of 1908 to the German Fleet Law of 1900 involved a considerable acceleration of replacement policy and consequently a very important concealed addition to German naval strength. This was prompted to a considerable extent by the shock of the *Dreadnought* of 1905 and the *Invincible* of 1906, a new type of all heavy-gun battle cruiser, fast and relatively lightly armoured. The German response, engineered by Tirpitz, was very formidable. British public opinion was aroused. The Unionist press started off a campaign to replace the obsolete two-power standard with a two-keels-to-one standard against the Germans. The Liberal press, while admitting the need for a margin of superiority, reminded the government of the existing immense superiority of the British Navy and of its pledges for reductions in armaments and the pressing need for social reform. The government wanted to restrict naval estimates for 1908-9 to the same level as for 1907-8, but Tweedmouth and the admirals demurred. Tweedmouth and Fisher threatened resignation and forced the anti-navalist ministers, Lloyd George, Harcourt, McKenna, Morley, Burns and Crewe, to disgorge nearly £1 million. In the heat of the dispute the rivalry flared up between Fisher and his bitter service critic, Admiral Lord Charles Beresford, who opposed Fisher's policy of wholesale scrapping of old ships and concentration of the battle fleet in home waters at the expense especially of the Mediterranean. Public remarks by Esher in defence of Fisher involving indiscreet references to the Germans and their Kaiser provoked the Emperor William to write indignantly to Tweedmouth defending German fleet policy and denouncing British presumption to decide for Germany how big Germany's Navy should be. Rumours of the Emperor's astonishing outburst and of an inept reply by Tweedmouth led to allegations of German efforts to influence British policy, which in turn fanned the flames of demands for increased British estimates.

On assuming the premiership Asquith replaced Tweedmouth with McKenna to appease the Radicals. Lloyd George at the Treasury and Churchill now in the cabinet were in a much stronger position to lead the social reformist cause against 'bloated armaments'. The admirals, however, convinced McKenna of the need for at least four, and possibly six, dreadnoughts to be laid down in 1909. Hardinge attempted in the course of a meeting of King Edward and his nephew at Cronberg in August 1908 to convince the Emperor William that Anglo-German relations would be embittered seriously unless naval rivalry could be slackened. His effort was very ungraciously received. This hardening of the German position reinforced Grey's support for Fisher against the cabinet economists. In turn the Kaiser was provoked to another characteristic private tirade against British interference in German affairs which, published in the *Daily Telegraph*, caused another sensation both in Germany and Britain and provided more fuel for the fires being stoked by the 'scare' press.

This led by the end of 1908, as the Bosnian crisis developed, to the most formidable navalist agitation any government had faced. Asquith was under great pressure to adopt officially the two-keels-to-one German standard: instead he redefined the two-power standard: a margin of superiority in capital ships of 10 per cent over the combined strengths of the two next strongest powers. This pleased the navalists. The admirals themselves, more realistic, depended on diplomacy to replace the two-power standard. Hence they keenly supported Grey's *entente* policy. Thus the admirals were in a position to please both Grey and the Foreign Office on the one side and the social reformers on the other. Asquith, under equally heavy pressure from the economists and social reformers, delayed a decision on the actual content of the new programme. This was the situation as the miasma of crisis looming out of Bosnia enfolded Europe in 1909.

Meanwhile, Haldane at the War Office was engaged on what was, from the foreign policy point of view, a rather more positive and important exercise in policy. The Navy, after all, could lose a war and could thus lose the Empire and possibly Britain itself. But the Navy could not preserve the French Army from defeat by the German Army, or win a European war; and increasingly British foreign policy and British strategic policy became geared to the necessities of that objective.

Haldane entered the War Office in December 1905 with a fairly clear idea in his mind as to what he wanted. He caused offence among the anti-militaristic Liberal faithful and annoyed Campbell-Bannerman by election speeches which stressed the point that there were political obligations 'higher even than that of economy' and insisted that 'the business of Government was to preserve the Army and Navy in as strong a position as possible.' Though not generally popular in the Liberal party or government, Haldane was in a position of advantage in several respects. Like Grey, he was aided by the fact that the concerns of his department were not matters of interest to the mass of Liberals. The Navy was in a rather different position here, for Liberal sentiment always tended to look upon the Navy as a bulwark of liberty while they distrusted the Army as a potential threat to it.

Thus whereas the First Lord of the Admiralty would have to fight hard to get what his admirals wanted from a Liberal cabinet, he could remain fairly assured that in the end he would not do too badly: no Liberal government would willingly or easily repudiate the principle of the necessity of British maritime supremacy, though they might well insist that the objective could be achieved at less expense than the Admiralty estimated. The Army, on the other hand, tarnished and discredited by its mediocre performance in South Africa, could rely on no such sentiments of sympathy and understanding. In the first place, there was no clear principle or understanding as to what the Army was for. Liberals would not contemplate a repetition of a war like that in South Africa anywhere else in the empire. It is doubtful if the Liberal government would have received support from the Liberal rank and file if it had been faced with the need to suppress serious nationalist insurrections in India or Egypt, or, more to the immediate point, in Ireland. The idea of ever again sending a British army to the continent in the Wellingtonian or Crimean manner was to the vast mass of Liberals in 1906 preposterous. And thus, if by elimination the only conceivable function of the Army was home defence, the only question of principle would revolve around the extent to which invasion was possible in view of the admitted reality and necessity of British naval supremacy. Hence, for many Liberals, invasion was impossible while Britain remained supreme at sea; and hence the more money spent on guaranteeing naval security, the less money needed to be spent on the Army. Within this context of assumptions, the only possible argument for some kind of positive view of military policy depended on the proposition that naval security was unreliable and that invasion was a real possibility, and thus an army for home defence was essential. This argument got entangled with the agitation led by Lord Roberts for compulsory military service along the lines almost universal on the continent.

Debate surged around this theme. The admirals, convinced believers in the purest of 'blue-water' doctrine, were determined to corner as much defence finance as possible, and attacked the

Roberts thesis. Fisher's refusal to agree to schemes of coordination with the Army was a major stumbling-block to British strategic planning and did much to compromise the usefulness of the C.I.D. There was some very effective pro-Roberts propaganda. Erskine Childers, a clerk in the House of Commons who had served in South Africa, had published *The Riddle of the Sands* in 1903, fruit of his sailing expeditions along the German coast. Northcliffe put his weight behind Roberts, and one of his journalists, William Le Queux, published the widely-selling *The Invasion of 1910* in 1906. Conscription was anathema to Liberal and general democratic sentiment.

With a Liberal government in power, all the Unionist efforts at military reform under Brodrick and Arnold-Forster were automatically cancelled. This suited, as it happened, both Esher and Clarke in the back rooms and Haldane himself in the front room. This identity of view was Haldane's second advantage. Although he was working against the grain of Liberalism, he was working with the grain of the social and bureaucratic establishment. As Esher admiringly remarked, Haldane believed in 'force as the foundation of Empire'. A third advantage was that Haldane knew that Roberts had no chance in his bid for conscription, which in the circumstances was a vast irrelevance; but though the conscription campaign was at cross purposes to the sort of Army Haldane and his allies wanted, Roberts performed a useful function in a general way of keeping up propaganda among the public for some kind of positive military policy, and, even more important, providing a lightning conductor which tended to divert anti-militaristic resentment away from Haldane; the noise and fuss of his agitation became a kind of smoke screen behind which Haldane could operate almost unobserved. Most Liberals, like Campbell-Bannerman, feared the National Service League much more than they feared Haldane. Finally, perhaps Haldane's greatest single advantage was that his plans did not involve large increases in the Army estimates. In fact, while by 1914 the total services budget had increased from the 1905 figure of £63 million (44 per cent of the total budget) to over £80 million (39 per cent of the total), the Army share of it had declined markedly: the estimates for 1914 were less actually than those in 1905. The

Army share of the services budget was 48 per cent in 1905 and only 36 per cent in 1914.

Haldane wanted, first of all, to create 'a highly organized and well-equipped force' of regulars which could be 'transported with the least possible delay' to France – though for official purposes he stipulated 'to any part of the world'. He wanted also to form a second-line non-regular force which could constitute a general reserve but whose ostensible function would be home defence. He wanted to create a general staff. He wanted also to reorganize supply, medical services, transport and officers' training systems.

The Territorial and Reserve Forces Act of 1907 created the second-line force by amalgamating the old Yeomanry and Volunteer organizations. As the title of the Act indicated, the precise role of this force was ambiguous. Haldane concentrated on the home defence side of things, but justifiably suspicious Radicals tried unsuccessfully to pin Haldane down as to whether in fact the Territorials could be used as a reserve for operations outside Britain.

A general staff was established by 1909, thus at last implementing one of the two major recommendations of the Hartington Commission in 1890. The other, to integrate naval and military planning, was as yet still unrealized, despite the efforts of Clarke at the C.I.D., mainly because of the stubborn resistance of Fisher, who insisted on keeping the Navy's plans very much to himself. The admirals, obsessed with expectations of an immediate clash of battle fleets, had no intention of subordinating their plans to the requirements of cooperation with the Army. Clarke's quarrels with Fisher on this score led to his resignation from the C.I.D.

The Expeditionary Force was the centrepiece of Haldane's new army. Consultations with Grey at the time of the Moroccan crisis ensured that there would be no real doubt about the essential function of this force: it would be to post itself on the left flank of the French armies in the event of a war between France and Germany. This, however, could never be its avowed purpose. The purpose avowed by Haldane was that its primary task was to defend the empire, especially India. The *entente* with Russia was rather awkward from this point of view. But since the Radicals never trusted the Russians anyway and since Morley was ready to swallow it (he was even made temporary chairman of the C.I.D.) all in the end was well. Both Unionists and Radicals who had any knowledge of military questions were highly dubious about this, but Haldane remained unshaken in his testimony. When under extreme pressure from Lloyd George and Churchill in cabinet Haldane did let slip indiscreet admissions, these were ignored as irrelevant or mere bluff. Haldane's most effective camouflage was in fact the sheer unwillingness of the mass of Liberals even to contemplate the conceivability of Britain's engaging in a continental war.

Thus, by the time the Bosnian affair was transformed by Germany in 1909 into a European crisis, Britain was engaging in an excited and open public debate about what sort of response should be made to the accelerated German fleet programme and was being equipped by subterfuge and deception with a military striking force intended to permit her to intervene in a European conflict.

IV

The Serbian government refused to recognize the Austrian annexation of Bosnia and the Herzegovina. In Sarajevo and other Bosnian cities, Serb secret nationalist societies fomented agitation against Austria. The Serbian Army was mobilized. The Russian government also did not recognize Habsburg sovereignty in the two provinces. Russian public opinion was excited, much as it had been at the time of the Bulgarian affair of the 1870s. The Austrian chief of the Army staff, Conrad, wanted a war to eliminate Serbia once and for all as the inspiration of South Slav disaffection. The Russians were in no military condition to intervene on behalf of the Serbs. But Lexa wanted neither war with Serbia nor humiliation of Russia. The Germans decided on the latter for their own purposes. In March 1909 the Germans stepped in and presented the Russians with a request for a 'precise answer – yes or no' within a certain time as to whether or not they would recognize the annexation and drop support for Serbia; if not, events, as the diplomatic formula went, would be left to take their course. The French, who had hoped desperately that the Germans would mediate in the old Bismarckian tradition rather than throw all their weight behind the Austrians, were unwilling to fight, especially as the Russians were unable to anyway. Isvolsky was driven to the wall as Delcassé had been in 1905. The Russians had to swallow their humiliation. The French had scrambled out of trouble in 1906 by their ability to fight in the last resort. This ability the Russians did not have in 1909; but the moral they drew from the Bosnian crisis was not to join the Germans but rather to be ready for them next time. The Germans gained nothing in the end but a costly diplomatic triumph which resolved nothing.

For Grey, Bosnia fitted into a pattern of expectations deduced from the Moroccan crisis: Germany was aiming at a hegemony in Europe by a policy of breaking the nerve and will to resist of any powers striving to remain independent of her. If Britain were to stand aside and let this happen, her turn would eventually come: 'if we sacrifice the other Powers to Germany we shall eventually be attacked'. The British grew stiffer in their resolve to keep the *ententes* in being and increase their counterpoise effect on Germany. The Germans, increasingly aware of this and now a little nervous at having thrown Bismarckianism finally to the winds so recklessly, made overtures to Britain: Bülow offered not to increase the existing German naval programme if in return the British would commit themselves to a 'benevolent neutrality' to Germany in the event of Germany's being at war with either France or Russia or both. Grey interpreted this as an attempt to split the *ententes*: the German proposal 'would serve to establish German hegemony in Europe and would not last long after it had secured that purpose'.

The importance of the Bosnian crisis for Britain was that for the first time the naval issue and the widespread public concern associated with it came into phase with the European balance of power issue. Radical critics of Grey found themselves in an awkward situation. They could argue that Germany was merely defending herself against *revanchiste* France or pan-Slavonic despotic Russia; but they could not plausibly argue that the German High Seas Fleet was a defensive force. The purpose of the German Navy Law of 1898 and every addition and amendment to it since was to wrest from Britain her exclusive oceanic hegemony. It was natural and inevitable that the British public mind should assume that the power threatening Britain must be a general threat to peace and international morality. Increases in the British fleet to maintain superiority over Germany would do nothing to help to preserve the independence of France and Russia. Yet it was much better camouflage for Haldane's military policy than the mythical requirements of the defence of India. Unless the Germans would make serious naval concessions – in short, renounce the whole policy which under Tirpitz had guided the German naval programme since 1900 – this assumption in the British public mind would remain firmly planted, and no amount of Radical denunciation of Grey would shake it. That denunciation would begin to take effect only after the German fleet had steamed in to surrender at Scapa Flow.

In fact the disposition of political forces in Germany made it impossible for the Germans to decide on one rational course or another. The Emperor and Tirpitz and the powerful Navy League would never concede defeat for their naval plans, and all Bulow's and later Bethmann-Hollweg's efforts in this direction were ultimately futile. On the other hand the Germans would not accept the logical Bismarckian corollary of this: good relations with Russia and refusal to support Austria. The basic demagogic impulses in Germany were instinctively anti-Slav and ideologically anti-British. In the absence of an intelligent directive mind at the centre of German policy-making, these impulses went unchecked and Germany was bound to want to have it both ways. These determinants governed the development of international affairs through the second Moroccan crisis to the final explosion over the second Bosnian crisis in 1914.

The British government in these circumstances was in no position to resist the navalist agitation, drummed up especially in the Unionist press. McKenna and the admirals had asked for six new dreadnoughts in 1909; Lloyd George, Churchill and the economists stuck at four. Asquith attempted a characteristic compromise: four immediately and four later on if developments seemed to warrant them. But this compromise was swept aside by the agitation, with its catch-cry of 'We want eight and we won't wait'. The eight were conceded. The 1909 budget was part of their price to the Unionists.

Throughout 1910 the futile talks with the Germans about naval limitations meandered on to final collapse in May 1911. Lloyd George, pinning his hopes for domestic policy on a *detente*, was bitterly disappointed by the failure of his bid in 1910 for a national coalition, and faced now the unpleasant prospect of conflict over the Lords and Home Rule without any compensating external settlement. Also in May 1911 the French occupied Fez, the capital city of Morocco, which was about to be reduced formally to the status of a French protectorate. The German reaction to this initially was not at all in the spirit of 1905. They no longer sought to prevent a French takeover, but they wanted to make a demonstration which would guarantee them some substantial compensation from France as the price of acquiescence. They had their eyes on the French Congo. The French were quite prepared to do a deal on this basis. But the Germans, nervous of aroused national opinion, overplayed their hand by sending a gunboat, *Panther*, to Agadir as a symbol of their determination. From this point developments got out of hand, and what had started as a routine diplomatic negotiation between Germany and France ended up as a critical confrontation between Germany and Britain. Grey and the Foreign Office interpreted the situation as the familiar one of Germany overbearing the weakening French. The *entente* was in danger. In fact Caillaux, the new French prime minister, was genuinely anxious for reconciliation with the Germans, an end to armed rivalry, and social reforms. To that extent the *entente* was indeed in danger. Caillaux's allies, the socialists led by Jaurès, like their British counterparts, disliked the Russian alliance and wanted friendship with Germany. To Caillaux's dismay he found across his path not merely his own nationalists led by Clemenceau, Poincaré and the military, but the officious British, coming to his rescue.

By now the difficulties over the naval issue with Germany had exasperated Lloyd George and Churchill. Either they could resign in protest at what they considered British unreasonableness or they could stay on and vent their exasperation against the Germans. Since they had no answer to Grey's argument that maritime supremacy was vital for Britain and was incompatible with German maritime equality, they were forced in the latter direction. It was assumed that the Germans wanted Agadir as a naval base. There were fears that the French might weaken and conclude an agreement with the Germans without reference to British interests. Lloyd George let fly in quite the best Palmerstonian manner in the course of a Mansion House speech in July. The references to foreign policy in the speech, vetted by Grey, warned the Germans not to throw their weight about on Morocco. This was to be Crowe's version of a Fashoda rebuff to the Germans. The Foreign Office were enchanted at the new Lloyd George they had discovered. Nicolson, now under-secretary in place of Hardinge,[5] was impressed by Lloyd George's and Churchill's combativeness.

The Germans were rudely shaken out of their assumption that they were settling up Morocco sensibly with the French. There was an explosion of anglophobe sentiment. They interpreted Lloyd George's speech as a deliberate attempt to wreck a Franco-German *rapprochement*: convincing proof of nefarious British designs to encircle Germany and choke her legitimate ambitions to make her way in the world. Grey in turn was shaken by the explosion that had been set off. He seriously thought a German attack on the fleet was possible and alerted McKenna. Already in any case the French military had seized the opportunity to perfect their project for cooperation with their British counterparts. Henry Wilson, the supremely francophile Director of Military Operations in the new general staff, concluded arrangements on the day before Lloyd George's speech. For the first time the British military and naval apparatus was confronted with the concrete likelihood of having to prove its capacity. A small group of ministers – Asquith, Grey, Haldane, Lloyd George, McKenna and Churchill – supervised proceedings of the C.I.D. in a 'historic' meeting on 23 August 1911. Their other colleagues were carefully not informed. Arrangements between the Army and the Navy to transport the Expeditionary Force to France were at last, much to the discomfiture of the Navy, decided on. The British military staff had in effect determined on a strategic commitment to go to the aid of the French in the event of a

Franco-German war. They would do their best to persuade the politicians to honour this commitment. Already, in October 1910, Henry Wilson had predicted that though most British regimental officers neglected to familiarize themselves with the topography of Belgium, they would probably 'be buried there before they are much older'. A War Book had already specified action to be taken by every government department in the contingency of an outbreak of hostilities. Prospect of war was suddenly no longer in a remote distance. Cambon reported to Paris on 6 September 1911: 'Militarily, England is ready.'

Amidst violent recriminations between the British and the Germans, with both Lloyd George and Churchill now distinctly bellicose, the French settled quietly with the Germans in November. In exchange for two strips of territory giving access from the German Cameroons to the Congo river the Germans abandoned their claims in Morocco. Though the French generals were glad to profit from British bellicosity by completing arrangements for possible military cooperation, French policy had no desire to prolong the confrontation. The Russians had no more intention of fighting for Morocco in 1911 than the French had of fighting for Bosnia in 1909. At the same time Agadir provoked a resurgence of French national feeling. The appeasing Caillaux fell from power in 1912 and the resolutely *revanchiste* Poincaré formed a ministry of patriotic solidarity. For Germany the consequences were even more profound. Aroused national opinion was now running ahead of official policy. Bethmann-Hollweg, denounced to the applause of the Crown Prince for allowing Germany to be humiliated, could not resist Tirpitz's demands for three keels a year instead of two. The Army in turn put in bids which could not be resisted. German demagogic impulses on the one hand and the armed services on the other were getting beyond the control of the Reich government.

In Britain the consequences were of a different order. The Radicals had been confronted with the conceivability of war, and they refused to accept it as rational or sane. C. P. Scott, on behalf of the Manchester Liberal Federation, protested to Grey that Liberal opinion was 'dismayed' to learn that in the recent negotiations between the German and French governments about Morocco, 'this country was so intimately involved that had war broken out between France and Germany, we must in all probability have been a party to it'. Scott and his friends denied that 'any British interest of such magnitude was at stake as to justify war or the threat of war'; and they were further unable to discover that there was 'anything in the treaty obligations of this country' which could be construed as obliging Britain 'to support France by force of arms in a quarrel not our own'. Scott urged Grey to make it plain to the French that the *entente* 'is not to be understood as an alliance, and that it leaves us perfectly free to enter into similar negotiations with other European powers and notably with Germany'. This theme was taken up and pressed vigorously on Grey in parliamentary debates. The circumstance that war between France and Germany was never in fact likely did not make these criticisms any less embarrassing to Grey.

In cabinet he had greater problems. Those ministers who had been excluded from participation in or consultation about the contingency preparations for war in 1911 were indignant when they discovered what had happened. Their leader was Loreburn, who regarded himself as the only upholder of true Liberal doctrine apart from Harcourt since the death of Campbell-Bannerman. Morley and Burns, though well-meaning, were useless; and with the loss of Bryce, Elgin, Ripon and Herbert Gladstone, Asquith and his Liberal League clique were freed of the restraints of party principles. Lloyd George and Churchill were unreliable opportunists. In fact Churchill in October 1911, after a spell in the Home Office, eagerly replaced McKenna at the Admiralty. McKenna had lost Asquith's confidence by refusing to arrange to transport the Expeditionary Force at short notice to France. McKenna now joined Loreburn, Harcourt, Morley and Crewe in complaints to Asquith, not merely about recent secretive and unconstitutional procedures, but also on account of the original military conversations with the French in 1906, which had now come out in the open. In some very unpleasant cabinet recriminations Grey was supported only by Asquith, Haldane, Lloyd George and Churchill. They were obliged to agree to a strict formula laying down that no military or naval arrangements entered into with other countries could directly or indirectly commit Britain to military or naval intervention and that such arrangements should henceforth not be entered into without the previous approval of the cabinet.

Majority opinion in the cabinet and in the Liberal party at large coalesced as a result of the crisis of 1911 into a formidable movement. A large group of about eighty members of the parliamentary party, led by Noel Buxton and Arthur Ponsonby, formed themselves into a Foreign Affairs Group to keep a sharper eye on Grey. Grey certainly took care to behave henceforth very circumspectly, a task made easier by the fact that he did not get on well with his Russophile under-secretary, Nicolson. More important was the consequence that these recriminations prevented any chance of the C.I.D. managing to get a real grip on the planning and formulation of war contingency policy. Liberal politicians could not admit frankly the needs and purposes of such planning; and the Committee remained essentially a debating club, with the generals and admirals largely free to go their own way. Thus the C.I.D. turned out to be the worst possible kind of body: settling none of the main issues but making many people, including cabinet ministers, think it had.

Out of doors there was a surge of moral revulsion against Liberal involvement in a war policy, tapping the same sources of energy as the movement of hostility to imperialism and the South African war. Hobson, Hobhouse, H. N. Brailsford, Lowes Dickinson, Bertrand Russell, J. L. Hammond, G. P. Gooch, E. D. Morel, rallied intellectual support. The veteran dissenter from the great days of Gladstone and Bulgaria, Leonard Courtney, became chairman of a Foreign Policy Committee to agitate for greater public control over the main lines of foreign policy. Philip Morrell put up money; R. C. K. Ensor, the Fabian and *Manchester Guardian* journalist, became its secretary. Ironically, as these movements of Liberal feeling gathered form and momentum in the party, the leadership at the highest and most decisive level needed to make them effective had moved in the opposite direction. Buxton, Ponsonby, the intellectuals, the journalists led by Scott of the *Manchester Guardian*, A. G. Gardiner of the *Daily News*, F. W. Hirst of the *Economist*, H. W. Massingham of the *Nation*, needed the leadership of Lloyd George, or better still,

Lloyd George and Churchill. There was no one of anywhere near equal calibre in the opposition to Grey's conduct of affairs. Loreburn had no great weight in the country. Morley's reputation was fast fading. The others, Harcourt, Crewe, Samuel, Burns, Birrell, McKenna, lacked the necessary stature. But the very crisis which provoked the party revolt against the inner cabinet establishment also had the effect of converting its natural leaders to that establishment. Having failed in his 1910 project of a national government, Lloyd George consoled himself with a national foreign policy which Unionism was bound to support. Clearly in any case he was finished with orthodox, sectarian Liberalism of the kind needed to fuel a crusade against war. In the short run this saved Asquith, Grey and Haldane; in the long run it was their ruin.

Thus by 1911 Lloyd George and Churchill had once more, as in 1908, given a decisive tilt to the character of the Liberal cabinet. It was this tilt which led Loreburn to warn C. P. Scott in 1911: 'Always remember that this is a Liberal League Government.' And it was a Leaguer who told the French historian Elie Halévy, who had remarked on the mysterious disappearance of the League which had been founded with so much publicity in 1902: 'But the Liberal League did not vanish. What happened is simply that in 1905 it absorbed the Liberal Government. That is why we went to war in 1914.'[6]

Chapter Eighteen

THE LIBERAL IMPASSE
1912–15

I

Liberalism now had to honour its post-dated political cheques: one, a very large and onerous consideration, was for Irish Home Rule; the other, a lesser consideration, was for disestablishment of the Church of England in Wales. Both these questions would consume Liberal energy without replacing it. Irish Nationalism and Welsh Nonconformity were profitless investments in English politics. It was a question by now as to whether English Liberalism was a profitable investment for Irish Nationalism. The younger generation of Irish nationalists was getting restless and impatient; the Nationalist political leadership now had a last chance to extract Home Rule from the Liberals and get it through the House of Lords before the end of the 1910 parliament. If they failed, for one reason or another, they would give the 'irreconcilable' extremists an opportunity to seize the initiative despite the circumstance that the bulk of Irish opinion was far from wanting a republic in the image of Sinn Fein. Welsh Nonconformity was by now a dry sectional interest in Wales itself, let alone in British politics as a whole.

The Liberal government embarked on this programme, moreover, embarrassed and compromised by its inability either to satisfy itself or give satisfaction on three fundamental issues which were dangerously vital and indeed ultimately lethal to Liberalism. The first was the question of the franchise. Given that Home Rule would have priority, the obstacle of Irish resistance to redistribution would be removed; but the obstacle of Liberal inability to confront resolutely the issue of female suffrage remained; and the Franchise and Registration Bill introduced in

June 1912 to enfranchise all adult males on the basis of one man one vote foundered on this rock. Liberalism badly needed to maximize its potential electoral strength. Already its parliamentary ranks of 1910 were being eroded by Unionist by-election successes, and its dependence on Labour and the Irish Nationalists cruelly underlined. Enfranchising the residual third of the adult male population and abolishing the estimated half-million plural votes would unquestionably be a stout blow for Liberalism. The essence of the 'Progressivism' of J. A. Hobson and L. T. Hobhouse was the demand that Liberalism identify itself with the cause of the masses against the classes; whereas the whole disposition of the Liberal government as encapsulated by Lloyd George in 1909 was rather to mediate between the classes and the masses, much as Liberalism had done under Gladstone from the 1860s to the 1880s. Whether or not franchise reform would have saved 'progressivism' for the future, the government's inability to satisfy itself by getting legislative results was a telling symptom of a larger political debility: Liberalism, whether suicidally or misadventurously, was entering into a general condition of impasse.

The second compromising issue contributing to this general condition was Labour in the particular context of intensified industrial unrest characteristic of the years between 1911 and 1914. Again, the question is not so much whether the Liberal government could or should have done something decisive about this as rather that within Liberalism there was a disturbing consciousness of fundamental indecision as to what could or should be done. Low rates of unemployment, a huge rate of expansion of trade union membership (the total membership of all unions increased by over 60 per cent between 1910 and 1914, and that of the 'new unions', dockers, seamen and general labourers, by over 300 per cent), and the influence of syndicalist ideas from the U.S.A. and France opposed to political and parliamentary methods, all interacted positively to conduce to a rash of disruptive and highly publicized strikes. In 1912 nearly 41 million working days were lost through strikes, compared with an annual average of 7 million in the preceding five years; in 1913 there were 1,459 individual strikes, compared with an average number of

600 in the preceding six years. The railway and transport workers' strikes of 1911 and great national coal strike of 1912 set the pattern; the Triple Alliance of miners, railwaymen and transport workers of 1913 with threats of concerted industrial action represented the maturity of a vital sectional force to which the government had formulated no idea of usefully relating. Sidney Buxton at the Board of Trade was deputed by the cabinet in 1913 to propose such a means of relating by some system of government encouragement for facilitating industrial agreements or for intervening uninvited in industrial disputes, but came up with nothing convincing; nor did his successor in 1914, Herbert Samuel. The government did something to encourage Labour's parliamentary interest and discourage syndicalist influence by the Trade Union Act of 1913. This helped political Labour to overcome some of the disadvantages imposed by the Osborne judgment of 1909 forbidding unions to make compulsory levies for political purposes, such as the payment of M.P.s. The miners' strike in 1912 provoked the government to push through (without Unionist opposition) a Minimum Wage Bill for coal mines; but the Port of London dock strike led by Ben Tillett and defeated by the resolute Lord Devonport, chairman of the newly established Port of London Authority, produced no such remedy. Lloyd George was increasingly impatient with this inhibitiveness. He complained to Masterman: 'I don't know exactly what I am, but I am sure I am not a Liberal. They have no sympathy with the people.'

Lloyd George was restlessly beginning to thrash about for a great cause that would put new life into the dry bones of radicalism. The old programme stemming from 1906 was now wound up. He had set the National Insurance system going in July 1912 with the first benefits for sickness and unemployment due to commence in July 1913. This was more of an anti-climax than otherwise to the great Liberal effort to transform the foundations of society. Most workers did not receive any benefits, and those who did had cause to complain. Indeed, some unions gained militant membership by offering to protect workers against employers who tried to shift the whole burden of contributions on to unorganized workers.

The thought of a parliamentary prospect in which nothing big or wholesome could be seen beyond the dreary wastes of Irish Home Rule or – for all that he was a Welshman – Welsh Disestablishment was to Lloyd George profoundly disturbing. He thought in 1912 he had found it in the land question. In this he looked back yet again to the example of Joseph Chamberlain and he intuitively responded to a contemporary mood of 'back to nature'. This was a reaction against the artificiality of the dominant aesthetic modes of the previous era. Garden suburbs, the folk music revival of the new generation of musicians led by Ralph Vaughan Williams and Frederick Delius, the ale-quaffing and wine-bibbing heartiness of Chesterton and Belloc, boy scouts, Georgian poets in the hedgerows and at sea, the early novels of D. H. Lawrence, the fame of Count Leo Tolstoy, were all contributory influences to a cultural atmosphere which produced also characteristic social and political manifestations. Land reform, the return of the land to the people, had always been an ingredient of the radical wing of Liberalism. Now the dispute with the House of Lords had revived it. Moreover, the question of urban land values, and their implication for industrial reforms, employment, and cheap housing, was also involved. Lloyd George told his crony Riddell, the owner of the *News of the World*, that he was convinced that the 'land question is the real issue'.

The third compromising issue was war. The crisis of 1911 made it clear that the Asquith–Grey–Haldane clique with their new recruits Lloyd George and Churchill were perfectly capable of trying to get the country into war with Germany. Since going to the Admiralty in fact Churchill was as rampantly bellicose as he had been vociferously Cobdenite in his earlier Radical phase. Could the rest of the cabinet withstand so formidable an aggregation of political talent and reputation if it came to the point? And if they could not, could the Liberal cabinet retain the confidence of the parliamentary party, not to mention Labour and Irish Nationalists, especially with the pacifistic elements of the Foreign Affairs Committee and similar forces out of doors so thoroughly aroused and alerted by the Agadir affair? For that matter, was a Liberal government capable of retaining the confidence of the country in the conduct of war? Unquestionably, in any event, Liberalism would not go to war with anything like enthusiasm or even, possibly, solid resolution. The reality of British participation in a great European war would have a shattering impact on Liberals' confidence in the fundamental validity of its social-scientific intellectual inheritance stressing progress and ultimate reconcilability of competing interests. From any point of view, war for Liberalism would not merely contribute to a situation of impasse, it would be very likely in itself to constitute total and hopeless impasse.

II

In such circumstances, disabled on franchise, adrift and dissociated from industrial Labour, exhausted in any case as far as social reform was concerned, and menaced by the impending possibility of war, the Liberal government addressed itself to Home Rule and Welsh Disestablishment. The great obstacle of the House of Lords was now removed. To that extent the Liberal government of 1912 enjoyed an enormous advantage over the Liberal government of 1893. But it also had great disadvantages. In the first place, it did not have the commanding leadership of Gladstone. Asquith was a Home Ruler in much the same spirit that Sir William Harcourt had been. It was preferable, marginally, to coercion; and it fairly reflected the balance of what could be reasonably demanded on the one side and reasonably conceded on the other. Asquith could not on this issue nor on any other offer inspiring leadership. Morley by now was in the background. None of the powerful ministers betrayed much enthusiasm for the cause. They had been happy to leave Birrell in the Irish Office ever since the beginning of 1907. Churchill's interest tended to focus on the idea being promoted by some imperial federationists for Irish Home Rule as a model for an extension of 'Home Rule All Round' in the United Kingdom and the empire. It had, thereby, lost its old Gladstonian centrality for many Liberals. Moreover, there were now new factors in the Irish equation which compounded the initial disadvantage of the Asquithian character of the Liberal initiative.

The first of these was the change in the leadership of the

Unionist party in the House of Commons. Balfour had offended too many of his followers by his opposition to the tactics of the diehards of the party over the House of Lords veto. Leo Maxse was running a 'Balfour Must Go' campaign in the *National Review*. This was not important, but it wounded and irritated. Balfour had earlier offended Austen Chamberlain by endorsing the idea of a referendum on the Tariff Reform proposals in exchange for a referendum on Home Rule. Although some rather naïve Tariff Reformers like Bonar Law thought this would be an advantageous bargain, to Chamberlain it looked rather like a last wriggle by Balfour to shift the burden of food taxes from his back by handing them over to the uncertain sympathies of the electorate. Balfour in any case was tired and wanted to go. The Unionist leadership ever since 1903 had been a bed of thorns. Balfour sensed, correctly, that the attitudes and assumptions of the era of Salisbury in which he was bred were no longer appropriate to a new political dispensation. The Unionist party, with its strong industrial and business element, was quite a different body from the old Tory party, even in alliance with Liberal Unionism.[1]

In November 1911 Balfour abdicated. Two candidates vied for the succession. Austen Chamberlain laid claim to the place his great father had never presumed to aspire to. He represented the pure milk of the Tariff Reform word. His rival, Walter Long, a less orthodox Tariff Reformer, represented the squirearchy and the Old Families. These two cancelled one another out. Neither could command a convincing majority, and both agreed to stand aside for a compromise candidate whose merit was his relative obscurity. Thus, to his great surprise, Andrew Bonar Law, former parliamentary secretary to the Board of Trade, became the Unionist leader in the Commons. Law's campaign was managed with great dexterity by his young fellow-Canadian, Max Aitken, who had become an M.P. in 1910 and was shortly to become owner of the *Daily Express*. A dour Presbyterian, Law entered politics late after making a career in Glasgow banking and iron. Like Chamberlain he represented new forces of business in Conservatism; unlike Chamberlain he had loyally supported Balfour in giving way over the Lords' veto. He cared strongly for only two things: Tariff Reform and Ulster. His Ulster Presbyterianism and his lack of the normal ruling-class attributes of Conservatism both stood him in good stead. Circumstances made it impossible for him to maintain food taxes as an integral part of the Unionist programme. There was too much else at stake; food taxes were unpopular and were a hobble on the effectiveness of the party; and the lesser orthodoxy of Tariff Reform would have to be sacrificed, temporarily, to the greater cause of the Union and the fight against socialism. With the House of Lords' veto power in effect abolished, Unionism would have to fight all the harder to protect the great 'national' interests of the established order. For this purpose, the Unionists selected well in Law: he was above all a fighter and, in his dour way, a fanatic.

The second new factor in the Irish equation was that it was more than a quarter of a century since Gladstone had introduced the first Home Rule Bill. In that time, the forces of Unionism in Ireland had rallied. In the three southern provinces of Leinster, Munster and Connaught, Irish Unionism was largely an English or Anglicized upper layer of landowners, businessmen and professional men; closely-knit, wealthy and careful to maintain influential links with the Unionist party in Britain. Their most prominent representative was the Dublin barrister Edward Carson. This group included many Catholics, and thus deprecated resistance to Home Rule on a sectarian basis. In the northern province of Ulster half of the entire population was Protestant, many of them Presbyterian settlers originally from Scotland, amounting to about a quarter of the total population of Ireland. These were not the old English Ascendancy: they were a population as firmly rooted in Ireland as the contemporary plantations of New England were rooted in North America. They constituted a great interest. They were determined to remain, like the Scots and the Welsh, in relationship with the English within a British framework. Compared with Unionists in the South, they were in a position, if they chose, to look after themselves. They possessed a geographical basis for an alternative Irish state. And their Unionism, unlike that of the southern Unionists, was strongly sectarian in character. Wholly opposed to majority Catholic rule from Dublin, the Ulster Protestants looked for support and encouragement from the Unionist party. Now that the Lords no longer shielded them, they shared with the Unionist party a realization that the Liberal government would have to be impressed by public manifestations of a massive strength of anti-Home-Rule feeling.

Hence in 1912, as the time came for the introduction of the third Home Rule Bill, an impressive series of rallies and demonstrations was organized. Winston Churchill visited Belfast in February 1912 and managed only with difficulty to address a Home Rule audience. In the same month reports appeared of Ulster Protestants drilling. The point of this was to convince the Liberal government that the Ulster Protestants would, if forced to, fight to preserve themselves from Dublin Catholic rule. Because of the mass Unionist strength in the north, Ulster became the focus of resistance; and Carson transformed himself into an Ulsterman to lead it. Home Rule forces countered with equally massive demonstrations as Asquith introduced the Home Rule Bill in the Commons on 11 April 1912.

The bill was as cautious and modest as the Liberal ministers dared propose. It provided for an Irish legislature and a reduced Irish representation of forty-two members at Westminster. The imperial parliament at Westminster would retain control of defence, foreign affairs and certain other financial and police matters, and would have the power to amend or repeal any legislation of the Irish parliament. Redmond and his followers decided to accept what they could get without complaint: once operative, the system could no doubt be modified.

That things would turn unpleasant was indeed very likely. The Unionist leadership in Britain echoed Randolph Churchill's old slogan: 'Ulster will fight and Ulster will be right.' F. E. Smith in particular distinguished himself in reckless advocacy. Then, in the 1880s, that slogan had been a manoeuvre of politics; now, the question was whether there might be an Irish civil war. The Irish Nationalists, insisting on a united self-governing Ireland and quite unwilling to consider partitioning off the Unionist areas in Ulster, bent every effort to convince the Liberal government that these threats were bluff which could be safely called. Increasingly, Liberal ministers became less certain of this. The Nationalists were genuinely convinced that Ulster resistance was elaborate bluff: in this respect, as in many others, they betrayed an old-fashioned respectability fast being overtaken by events. The Orange extremists in Ulster matched the Sinn Fein republicans in their ultimate willingness to resort to violence. Moreover, the Unionist leadership as a whole did nothing to counsel restraint, since in reality the capacity of Ulster to frighten the Liberal government was the only strong card the Unionists held.

The logic of the Unionist position was first to try to convince the Liberal government that Home Rule would be more trouble than it was worth. Ulster would in effect constitute a veto against the partition of the United Kingdom. If the government's nerve held on the main principle, the Unionists' second line of resistance was to argue the case for Irish partition, leaving the predominantly Protestant areas in Ulster in the Union and conceding Home Rule to the rest. This was indeed anathema to orthodox Nationalism and, officially, to orthodox Liberalism, and even more so to Sinn Fein republicanism; but it had the merit of being a rough approximation to the balance of forces involved in the question. The Liberals justified their Home Rule policy on the basis of the rights of majorities: a pro-government majority in the Commons, a pro-Home-Rule majority in Ireland. Yet the Unionists had a good argument in their proposition that in the last resort majority rule can only function on the basis of a decent respect for minority opinion. Would British Liberalism countenance a civil war in Ireland fought in order to coerce a million loyal British subjects into subjection to a rule they detested?

It was at this point that the Liberal ministers' nerve began to crack. Churchill was visibly weakening on the issue of partition by July 1912. The Nationalist leaders felt they had good cause to distrust Lloyd George's resolution. For Asquith, partition would follow naturally from the Harcourtian starting point: the Ulster loyalists, just as much as Irish nationalism, had a case which could be reasonably demanded and which could be reasonably conceded. Asquith's official position, as announced in Dublin in July 1912, was that Ireland was 'not two nations, but one nation'. The question was how long Asquith would sustain this opinion in the face of manifest contradiction from a quarter of the

Irish population. Nor was the utilitarian strain in Liberalism impressed by the mystical Nationalist premise that Ireland was somehow uniquely sacred and could not be subject to the same principle of expediency which prevailed about the political unity or partition of any other geographical area of the earth's surface. Belfast was linked economically with Glasgow and Liverpool rather than Dublin. Against the Nationalist argument that the Protestant plantations of Ulster were colonizing invaders and hence had no right against the claims of the indigenous population was the argument that all history was a process of invasions and colonizations, and that the Irish themselves had not hesitated to contribute to the invasion and colonization of the New World, where the first British plantations were a little later than the Ulster plantations of the early seventeenth century.

In the end, because of its intrinsic strength as approximating to the balance of force of the contending parties, the argument for partition carried the day: six of the nine counties of Ulster remained in the United Kingdom while the remaining twenty-six Irish counties formed the Free State and then the Republic. But this compromise was arrived at more than nine years after Asquith brought in the third Home Rule Bill and the first proposals were made by Unionists for exclusion of some parts of Ulster from its provisions. Carson made this the official Ulster policy at the beginning of 1913, and though his motive was still to make Home Rule impossible by raising the issue of Ulster exclusion – he was convinced that Ireland could not be economically feasible without Belfast – in fact Carson made the first step on the road to the compromise of 1921 and partition in 1922. It was one thing for Liberals to insist, as Gladstone had done since 1886, that the Irish minority had no right to block self-determination for the Irish majority; it was quite another thing for Liberals to be faced with a demand by the Ulster Protestants for the same right of self-determination against a united Ireland as the Irish Nationalists had demanded against a united British Isles. Many Liberals would welcome the opportunity to arrive at a compromise through partition as a temporary expedient. In between lay Asquith's decision not to countenance partition. In September 1912 a great rally of Protestant Ulstermen presided over by Carson pledged themselves in a solemn Covenant[2] to defend the Union and never to accept Home Rule. Then began the procedure governed by the Parliament Act of 1911.

The Commons passed the Home Rule Bill on 16 January 1913. The Lords rejected it on 30 January. The Commons passed it a second time on 7 July 1913, and the Lords rejected it a second time on 15 July. By this time the Ulster resistance movement was mounting to a climax: on 12 July 1913 (the day of Orange celebration for the Battle of the Boyne) 15,000 Ulstermen at Craigavon resolved to resist coercion by force of arms. By the end of 1913 about 100,000 Ulster Volunteers were enrolled and drilling. A retired general, Sir George Richardson, nominated by Lord Roberts, took command. Churchill was publicly advocating concession to Ulster sentiment. Lloyd George in private advocated it. Loreburn, now resigned from the lord chancellorship, a noted former opponent of the exclusion of Ulster, now appealed for a conference of the parties to find a compromise solution. Asquith conferred secretly with Bonar Law, and started putting pressure on Redmond in November 1913. Lloyd George hinted that Nationalist intransigence might lead to the break up of the Liberal government, and with it the Nationalists' last hope of any substantial measure of Home Rule. Asquith's proposals to Bonar Law and Carson for a temporary exclusion of most of Ulster from the provisions of the Bill to be followed by automatic inclusion after a certain period were rejected. The bill had only to be passed once more by the Commons to become law automatically under the Parliament Act. Churchill by now was talking of resignation if Ulster were not at least temporarily excluded. The King, worried about the loyalty of the Army in the event of active coercion of Ulster, pressed Asquith either to make concessions to Ulster or hold another general election. The contingency of the King's dismissing the ministry was not beyond conjecture.

By February 1914 Asquith, as he made clear to Redmond, had come to the conclusion that the painful reality of two nations in Ireland would have to be admitted to the extent of an autonomous Ulster within Home Rule Ireland. After a cabinet on 9 February Birrell, the Irish Secretary, reported to Redmond that there was 'great difference of opinion disclosed'. The Nationalist leaders watched with increasing consternation as the Liberal government's resolution to put Ulster resistance to the test weakened.

On 9 March Asquith proposed that individual Ulster counties might opt out of Home Rule for six years. Carson rejected a 'stay of execution' and dramatically left to take up command of the Ulster resistance. Both sides in Ireland were arming and drilling. A movement to raise Irish Volunteers in response to the Ulster Volunteers was gaining ground in the South, much to the disquiet of Redmond and Dillon, who feared that it would pass into the control of dangerous extremists. At the end of 1913 the Irish Volunteers numbered less than 2,000; by July 1914, they were about 160,000 strong, a third being in Ulster itself. Meanwhile the Ulster Volunteers were daringly running arms to Larne and distributing them throughout their movement. Civil war seemed imminent.

III

Welsh disestablishment, introduced in the Commons by McKenna (now Home Secretary) the day following Asquith's Home Rule Bill, proceeded on an almost parodically parallel course with that of the fateful Irish Bill. It too went through the Lords twice. It was finally passed by the Commons on 19 May 1914 and went on to await the royal assent. It was some consolation to Welsh nationalism in an era when compulsory elementary education had anglicized the new industrial working class, especially in South Wales. But the heyday of Welsh Nonconformity as the vital expression of Welsh national sentiment was in any case over, really since the end of the 1880s. The old, indigenous Welsh culture, already severely eroded by industrialism, was dragged further down by its identification with a declining religious confession. Already less than half Welshmen were Welsh speakers. It was also, no doubt, some consolation for Nonconformity at large, especially after the failure to right the wrongs of the 1902 Education Act; but in a more revealing way, the success of Welsh Nonconformity in ridding Wales of an Anglican Establishment in the manner of the Irish in 1869 only exposed all the more starkly the extent of the failure and disappointment of English Non-conformity in fulfilling the fond hopes and expectations of the movement to disestablish the Church of England which had seemed so irresistible in the 1860s and 1870s, and which Joseph Chamberlain and John Morley had not disdained to put at the spearhead of the radical assault in the early 1880s. No one would fight to prevent the four Welsh dioceses from being withdrawn from the province of Canterbury or resist the abolition of all ecclesiastical jurisdictions in Wales or die to preserve the seats of Welsh bishops in the House of Lords.

Meanwhile Asquith's government was embarrassed by the muck-raking agitation of G. K. Chesterton's brother Cecil, who had recently succeeded Hilaire Belloc as the editor of a weekly paper, *Eye-Witness*. He set his sights at four eminent members of the ministry: Attorney-General, Sir Rufus Isaacs; Liberal chief whip, Master of Elibank; Postmaster-General, Herbert Samuel; and Lloyd George himself. The 'Marconi Scandal' of 1912 and 1913, on its merits a minor affair of reprimandable (except in the case of Samuel) errors of judgement in the grey area between inside political knowledge and possible financial advantage,[3] became a heated issue because it fed on, and in turn helped to feed back to, the febrile political atmosphere of the House of Lords crisis and the Home Rule crisis. With the Chestertons and Belloc there was a quite virulent strain of anti-semitism at the expense of Isaacs and Samuel; and Lloyd George was a well-hated man in many quarters. The Marconi affair appeared to many a portent of the decadence of a new plutocratic generation, where old standards of integrity had decayed and 'monopoly capitalism' was squeezing out the 'small investor'. Lackeys of this exploitive system were politicians like Lloyd George and Isaacs, without 'bottom'. Unionist opinion naturally interpreted the affair as a manifestation of Liberal political corruption in the widest sense. The best evidence of this intensity of feeling is Kipling's vitriolic poem *Gehazi*, provoked by Asquith's appointment of Isaacs to the lord chief justiceship in 1913. Asquith in fact might have left Lloyd George and Isaacs (Elibank had already resigned quite independently of the affair) to be torn to pieces by the dogs who were hounding them; but instead he chose deliberately to save them by putting the weight of the Liberal party machine behind them. There was much to be said for saving Lloyd George and smothering a scandal at the critical time of the third Home Rule Bill; though later Asquith must often have regretted this particular combination of expediency and magnanimity.

Moreover, the Marconi scandal was not the only awkward problem vexing Asquith in 1912. The failure of the Franchise and Registration Bill and another version of it in 1913 brought in its train a frenzied and destructive 'suffragette' agitation led by Mrs Emmeline Pankhurst and her daughter Christabel. There was much damage to property by arson and explosives. A zealot mutilated the Rokeby Venus by Velazquez in the National Gallery. Asquith himself and other ministers were assaulted or threatened with assault. Many of the militants were arrested and imprisoned. Inside prison they caused almost as much scandal as outside by going on hunger strikes and arousing popular sympathy by being forcibly fed. The government's answer to this tactic was McKenna's 'Cat and Mouse' Act of 1913, which allowed for release and rearrest as convenient; that way no martyrs would be created. But one fanatic achieved martyrdom on Derby day 1913 by flinging herself in front of the King's horse. Some observers at the time and later interpreted suffragette violence along with the Ulster Volunteers and the industrial syndicalists as forming part of a pattern of extremism amounting to a pathological social morbidity. But in fact the situation in 1912-14 was distinctly less charged with violence than the situation of the 1880s. There was nothing like the ride of Captain Moonlight, the murder of Mountmorres or Leitrim or Frederick Cavendish and Burke; there was nothing like the great West End riots of 1886. Paradoxically, the Irish crisis in 1913-14 was notable for its order rather than its disorder: men marched and drilled but did not kill each other. Carson espoused the Ulster Covenant as a safety valve for emotion, not as an incitement to action. It was the breakdown of this pattern of confrontation, not a continuation of it, which led to the Easter Rising of 1916. The great strikes of 1912-13 equally were notable for order and discipline rather than the contrary. Most of the participants were in any case shortly to be in uniform, fighting for King and Country.

IV

The really dangerous manifestations of violence were international rather than domestic or Irish. For the moment they remained under the surface. The Germans increasingly felt themselves under intolerable pressures. The aftermath of the second Moroccan crisis left them as incapable as ever of resolving their basic dilemma. The emperor and the navalists would not give up the 'world policy' and the conflict with the British inescapably involved in it. On the other hand the German situation in Europe seemed to be deteriorating dangerously. French national morale revived after the scandals and disputes of the Dreyfus Affair; the Third Republic under the stern Lorrainer, Poincaré, conspicuously gained in confidence. French military thinking now stressed the offensive spirit; and revised plans envisaged a decisive thrust into Germany through Lorraine. It was now much less likely that the French would flinch from commitment to Russia in the manner of 1909. Would the Russians flinch once more from their commitment to France in the manner of 1911? The Russians were reviving from their prostration after defeat and revolution in 1905 even more conspicuously. Economically Russia was booming. Her great military reform programme would give Russia a completely retrained and re-equipped Army by 1917. The Germans wavered as to whether they should ingratiate themselves with this potentially immense force or whether they should take the first opportunity of pre-emptive strike before Russian resources and development put Russia beyond the reach of German power.

The indispensable requirement of a return to good relations with Russia and Bismarckian principles would be renunciation of the cause of Germandom in the Danube basin, and necessarily, along with this, renunciation of the cause of Magyardom, ever since the days of 1866 the most reliable of all the allies of Prussia. This was demagogically impossible in Germany: and since the Serbs would not renounce their objective of a Jugoslavia and the disruption of the Habsburg monarchy which this would necessarily involve, Germany was bound to support Austria against Serbia. It was problematical how long the Austro-Hungarian monarchy could survive unless it took decisive steps to neutralize the South Slav problem: either by war to reduce Serbia to insignificance or by some form of fundamental reconstruction of the monarchy to appease Slav claims against the Germans and the Magyars, along the line of 'Trialism' as advocated by the Habsburg heir apparent, the Archduke Francis Ferdinand. The latter alternative was unlikely so long as the Magyar politicians maintained their supremacy in Hungary and their effective ascendancy in the councils of the Common Monarchy. Thus an Austrian war to reduce Serbia was much the more likely contingency. If the Russians insisted on supporting Serbia and the Slav cause, the Germans might well find themselves in a situation where their nervousness about the Russian colossus in general, their inducements to make a pre-emptive strike against it, the cause of Germandom and Magyardom in the form of the Austro-Hungarian monarchy, and the lethal threat to that monarchy involved in the South Slav movement, would make of an Austro-Serb quarrel an irresistible temptation for Germany to try conclusions with the Russians.

Compared with this perilous equation of conflict, the western manifestations of power rivalry were relatively insignificant. The French would not go to war directly on the issue of Alsace-Lorraine, let alone Morocco; but once involved in a war with Germany, Alsace-Lorraine would naturally become the central focus of French ambitions. The key to French policy would lie in French willingness to support the Russians against Germany. Similarly, the British would not go to war with Germany directly about naval rivalry. The British, once over their initial naval panics, were quite confident of their ability to outbuild the Germans. Though Fisher's tour of duty as First Sea Lord ended in 1910, his work in galvanizing the Navy to cope with a new technological era was substantially complete. If the British were involved in a war with Germany, naturally the fleet issue would be in the forefront of British war aims; but the key to British policy would lie not in the naval issue but in willingness to support the French against Germany.

These were the fundamentals of the post-Agadir international scene. In Britain the Radical outcry against Grey led to some tactical manoeuvres. There was much talk of better relations with Germany. The Russians infuriated Liberal opinion even more by invading northern Persia at the end of 1911 to suppress the Persian reformist régime: the *entente* of 1907 seemed hopelessly compromised. Grey's critics dreamed of getting rid of him while Grey cemented his position by cultivating an axis of identity of views with Lloyd George. Harcourt consoled himself at the Colonial Office by pushing strongly for colonial concessions to Germany at the expense of the Portuguese. The government offered gestures of general good will. Negotiations about the Portuguese colonies were resumed; negotiations also about the Baghdad Railway, which the British, increasingly disillusioned by Russian policy in Asia, were no longer concerned to resist so long as British interests in the Persian Gulf were protected, particularly supplies of oil fuel, now vital to the Navy.

It was decided to send Haldane to Germany at the beginning of 1912 'to feel the way in the direction of a more definite understanding'. All he got was the standard German offer: a slowing down of the tempo of the fleet programme in return for British neutrality in the event of a Franco-German war. Then the Germans ended hopes of a naval accord by publishing their new Navy Law in March 1912. The Germans continued to insist on having a Navy so formidable as to make any British attack on it too risky to be contemplated with any ease of mind. The British responded by removing more battleships from the Mediterranean and concentrating them in home waters. This involved naval conversations with the French to match the earlier military arrangements. The French transferred their battleships at Brest to Toulon: the Austrians had commenced a dreadnought programme which would give them four first-class capital ships by 1914. By this transfer the French left protection of their Atlantic and North Sea coastlines to the British.

The penultimate phase of international developments centred about a further dismemberment of the crumbling Ottoman Empire, which the Young Turk party were trying desperately to modernize and reform. Austria and Bulgaria in 1908 had given the cue. In 1911 the Italians, emulating the French in Morocco, seized Tripoli. In 1912, exasperated by stubborn

Turkish resistance, they bombarded the Dardanelles and occupied Rhodes. The Turks closed the Straits. This pinched the
Russian economy very painfully; and intensified Russian determination to secure her vital interests there. The Balkan states of
Serbia, Bulgaria and Greece joined together for a final partition
of Turkey-in-Europe. Russian sentiment approved this crusade;
Russian policy attempted to restrain it. The Austrians watched
with dismay as preparations for a Turkish partition proceeded.
They knew all too well that, from the point of view of Serbia, a
successful partition of the Ottoman Empire would be the prelude
to an attempt to partition the Habsburg Empire. The Turks were
forced more and more to dependence on German support. The
First Balkan War broke out in October 1912. The Serbs, Bulgars
and Greeks were everywhere victorious over the Turks. Turkey-
in-Europe virtually disappeared.

This crisis gave Grey the opportunity to please radical sentiment by giving the defunct concert of Europe a last airing. All
the great powers agreed at a conference in London to take the
peace-making out of the hands of the victorious Balkan powers.
Eventually in May 1913 the Balkan states were induced to accept
the London proposals for a settlement. But in any case they
quarrelled among themselves: the Bulgarians attacked the
Greeks and the Serbs, were defeated in the Second Balkan War
in which Romania intervened against them as well and this
allowed the Turks to get back Adrianople and save a last corner of
Turkey-in-Europe. German influence was now more than ever
firmly entrenched at Constantinople and the Russians came
finally to the conclusion that Russian interests at the Straits could
only be secured by war. The only consolation for the Austrians
was to insist on the creation of an independent Albania; and even
to get the Serbs out of Albania took a partial Austrian mobilization. As it was, Serbia was doubled in size and population.
Moreover, anti-Hungarian irredentist enthusiasm was kindled
in Romania, which added yet another threat to Austro-Hungarian
integrity. For the Serbs, the Turkish round was over; now the
Austrian round was to begin. The Austrians had either to scotch
the South Slav idea or to abdicate not merely as a great power but
to renounce their very existence as a state. There were no

historical precedents for this kind of abdication or renunciation. Austria-Hungary would fight to preserve itself. Could the Russians afford, in the name of the defence of Slavdom and Orthodoxy and the popular stability of the czarist régime, not to intervene on behalf of the Serbs to revenge their humiliation of 1909? Could the Germans, in turn, afford to let the Austro-Hungarian monarchy come apart at the seams? And could the French, in turn, afford not to support the Russians if the Russians were threatened again by the Germans? And could, finally, the British afford not to stand by the French in such a case?

V

The attention of the British public was directed not at these matters but at the latest stage of the Irish crisis. In December 1913 the government took steps to ban the importation of arms and ammunition into Ireland and their coastwise transport. Asquith, having failed in his negotiations with Bonar Law to find any common ground, now approached Carson; but had to report to the cabinet that Carson refused 'anything short of the exclusion of Ulster'. Now the Army was growing restive at the prospect of being ordered to coerce Ulster and disarm the Volunteers. The British Army officer corps was rich in Ulster Protestants. The director of military operations, Henry Wilson, protégé of Lord Roberts and architect of military liaison with the French, was one such: a loyalty that was eventually to cost him his life at the hands of Sinn Fein gunmen. Wilson, a very political soldier, acted as liaison between the Unionist politicians, the Ulster Volunteers and the Army chiefs. Strains and tensions in the Army led Seely, who had replaced Haldane at the War Office in June 1912, to summon the holders of the major commands in Britain and Ireland to confer with him in December 1913. Himself a soldier, Seely was, like his former colleague on the Unionist benches, Churchill, temperamentally sympathetic to the Ulster cause. His intention was to keep the Army steady, but in fact his ambiguities about what limits of coercion would be ordered left the generals more unsteady than ever.

Carson's rejection of Asquith's compromise proposal of March

1914 to allow Ulster counties to exclude themselves for up to six years from the provisions of the Home Rule Bill led ministers to waver back to the line that Carson would have to be tamed by a show of strength. The cabinet decided to take precautionary measures to forestall any possible attempts on the part of Ulster Volunteers to occupy military depôts of arms and ammunition. Dispositions to move troops to secure exposed depôts led the commander of the troops in Ireland, Paget, to offer the alternatives of obedience or dismissal to his officers; which in turn led to many officers at the Curragh barracks outside Dublin resigning their commissions. Brigadier Gough and fifty-seven officers of the 3rd Cavalry Brigade preferred to accept dismissal if ordered north. The cabinet reacted by relieving Gough and two other senior officers of their commands and refusing to accept the resignations of other officers. In fact the troop movements went off without incident, but Churchill ruined the effect of quiet firmness by provocative fleet movements. There was much public scandal, embarrassing to the government, of a 'mutiny at the Curragh'. In the stress of events Seely made undertakings to Gough to the effect that the Army would not be called on to enforce the Home Rule Bill in Ulster, which the astonished Asquith felt himself bound to repudiate. Seely and Sir John French, the chief of the imperial general staff, resigned. Asquith personally took over the War Office in a bid to steady the badly rocking ministerial boat.

The government's show of strength thus misfired. The Unionists made the most of a 'plot' to coerce Ulster which had been foiled by patriotic officers. Seely clearly had no stomach for decisive action against the Ulster loyalists. Ministers wavered back to a conciliatory, compromise line: Grey offered the possibility of some federal solution. The notorious Larne gun-running of April 1914 was played down discreetly. The Home Rule Bill passed its third reading in the Commons on 26 May; it would now become law regardless of the Lords. Asquith decided to push through the compromise he had offered in March and put the Ulster militants in the tactical disadvantage of having to initiate violence rather than swallow the 'stay of execution'. This was designed, as introduced in the Lords on

23 June, to pass through the legislative process and become law at the same time as the Home Rule Bill. But in the Lords it was amended to exclude the whole of Ulster from Home Rule for an unlimited period. Asquith, desperate, fell back on the idea of a conference; this was held at Buckingham Palace in July 1914 but failed to reach any accommodation. The next logical step seemed to be the setting up of an Ulster Provisional Government. By now the strain on the Irish Nationalists was beginning to tell. Redmond was threatened not only by Liberal backsliding but by Irish extremism. It was essential for him to assert his authority. He attempted to gain control of the Irish Volunteer movement, never so formidable as the Ulster Volunteers, but potentially formidable all the same. But Redmond's authority was challenged by a minority faction, and the movement eventually split between the majority National Volunteers and the minority Irish Volunteers, who became the 'irreconcilables' and in due course the nucleus of the Easter Rising of 1916. Nationalist gun-running at Howth led to military intervention and three deaths which further exacerbated the tense situation and left even less room for concession by the Nationalist leaders.

Deadlock now seemed complete. Asquith announced the indefinite postponement of the Amending Bill: the Home Rule Bill would go forward alone for the royal assent. But in any case the Irish crisis was now overwhelmed by the infinitely greater European crisis. Redmond's final bid to gain general British public acceptance of Home Rule was, without consulting his main advisers, to pledge Irish Nationalist support for the war. Redmond hoped that this magnificent gesture would get Home Rule pure and simple at last in the statute book; but he was disappointed. Asquith decided to combine it, along with Welsh disestablishment, with a Suspensory Act which delayed its operation until after the end of the war. And he further appeased the Unionists by stipulating that Home Rule would not become effective in any event until parliament had a further opportunity of considering any amending legislation relating to Ulster. The Nationalists were helpless. Bringing down the Liberal government would do them no good. Electoral trends indicated that the next general election to be held within the five-year period from 1910 provided for in the

1911 Parliament Act might go badly for the Liberals. This risk the Irish could not take. Redmond had no option but to make the best of it: his argument was that Home Rule would be guaranteed by the shedding of loyal Irish blood in the battlefields of France. But it was an argument that never gained a convincing hold on Irish nationalist opinion. Redmond's only hope now was that the war would be short and glorious and that British Liberalism would come through it unscathed. In every one of these respects he was to be fatally disappointed.

VI

From an insular British point of view war came out of the blue. Relations with Germany were better than they had been for a long time. Agreements were reached in June 1914 over the Portuguese colonies and the Baghdad Railway. The jubilant Radicals looked for an end to the *ententes* and their replacement by a grouping of the civilized and progressive Western forces of Britain, Germany and France against the Russians: the old Crimean concept in a new guise. Grey, on the other hand, could claim that the policy of the *ententes* was successful and was a policy to preserve peace rather than to foment war. When he went to Paris with George V in April 1914 he felt he could afford to parade British freedom of manoeuvre and refused to promise British support for Russia against Germany in the event of a German attack arising out of the Russo-German quarrel over German influence at Constantinople and Russian sensitivity about the Straits being controlled by a possibly hostile power. Grey's argument to the French was that it was 'possible' that British public opinion would condone British intervention on behalf of France in the event of a 'really aggressive and menacing attack made by Germany on France'; but that it would not support Russia in a like case. This put the French in a quandary: their support for Russia against Germany could not be construed as an 'aggressive and menacing attack' upon them by the Germans. The French were, after all, to be kept guessing up to the last moment.

The second Bosnian crisis was sparked off at the end of June.

The Archduke Francis Ferdinand, heir to his aged uncle Francis Joseph's throne, went to observe the annual Army manoeuvres which happened that year to be in Bosnia, accompanied by his wife. In Sarajevo on 28 June they were both assassinated by a young Bosnian Serb student named Gabriel Princip, a member of a Serb irredentist secret society.

The Austrians made no immediate decisive demonstration; and in Britain opinion was strongly condemnatory of the Serbs, already notorious for the atrocious murder of their last Obrenovich king in 1903. Ulster claimed all attention; and Joseph Chamberlain's death early in July further removed the events in Sarajevo from immediate general consciousness. But in Vienna and Budapest the calculations were that it was now or never. Conrad, the Army chief, demanded war. He had got complete assurances from his German counterpart, Moltke,[4] that Germany would follow Austria through thick and thin. Berchtold, the foreign minister, felt he could no longer afford the hesitations of Lexa in 1909. Nothing was to be gained by further procrastination, providing the Germans guaranteed support as they had done in 1909. Despite some hesitations by Bethmann-Hollweg, this the Germans eventually did on 5 July. Austria was to be given a blank cheque: if she decided to eliminate Serbia as a political factor Germany would accept the full consequences of such a decision. This indeed set the pattern in 1914: in no instance did a power reluctantly go to war because of alliance obligations. The alliances were consequences of predispositions to act in certain eventualities rather than causes of action. In Berlin also the calculation was that it was now or never. German military efficiency and organization, following the new Army Law of 1913, was at its peak. Austria-Hungary in existing circumstances would not get any stronger with the passing of the years. The Franco-Russian combination was steadily growing in power. The military arguments in Berlin were plausible and there was no civilian authority capable of standing up to them.

On 23 July Vienna startled the world with an ultimatum to Belgrade designed to make acceptance impossible. The Austrians could not prove Serbian official complicity with the murders of 28 June; but this was really beside the point. On 28

July the Austrians hastily declared war on Serbia to forestall the attempts at mediation proposed by Grey and the Russians, many of whom had no great desire to fight for Serbia unless really necessary, and not until after 1917 if at all possible. The Russians had already decided to take military measures against the Austrians in such an event. The French in turn gave assurances to Russia. There was no occasion for excuses as in 1909. They calculated that their independence was at stake, and they would fight for that, not for Serbia or the Straits. Nicholas II ordered Russian mobilization on 29 July. On 31 July the Germans demanded cessation of the Russian preparations and inquired at Paris as to what the French would do in the event of war between Germany and Russia. The Russians refused to halt their mobilization and the French replied that they would be guided by their own interests. The Germans also made a bid for British neutrality in return for an undertaking that Germany would not annex any French territory in Europe. The Germans declined a British request that they undertake to respect the neutrality of Belgium. The French and the Germans simultaneously began mobilization on 31 July. The Germans declared war on Russia on 1 August and on France on 3 August.

The Germans committed themselves to implement the war plan inherited from a former chief of staff, Schlieffen, which postulated war on two fronts against Russia and France. Schlieffen assumed that Germany's only hope of a successful conclusion to such a war would be a massive offensive against the French, wheeling through the Low Countries to outflank the French armies and round them up in a great victory of envelopment. Minimal forces would be left in the East to contain the much slower Russian mobilization and cooperate with the Austrian armies in Poland. The time-table allowed six weeks for a decisive result against the French and then six months against the Russians. Thus the essence of German grand strategy was to strike very quickly at the French by way of Belgium (Holland was spared this fate by a subsequent revision of the plan).

This strategy had important consequences as far as British public attitudes were concerned. First, it had all the appearance of a wanton German aggression against France over a dispute in which France was not a party such as Grey had stipulated for as an indispensable criterion of support in April 1914; second, it involved the wanton repudiation of the Public Law of Europe by violating the neutrality of Belgium. The basic materials thus existed for public approval of a policy of British intervention. The question was whether the government would give a lead to the public in this direction.

The advice the government was being given from the Foreign Office was unanimous and insistent. Britain must stand firmly and unmistakably by France and Russia and leave the Germans in no doubt that Britain would not remain neutral. Grey asked for a decision from the cabinet on 27 July: would they support France and Russia in a war against Germany and Austria? The cabinet was divided and made no decision. The anti-war forces rallied strongly. In the *Manchester Guardian* of 1 August, C. P. Scott denounced 'an organized conspiracy to drag us into the war'. He argued that the detestable and false principle of the balance of power demanded in any case a German victory against Russia; that Britain was under no unilateral obligation to go to war for the integrity of Belgium: such a war would be merely a right, not a binding duty. Nor was Britain bound in honour in any sense to go to the aid of the French: 'if we decide differently then we violate dozens of promises made to our own people, promises to seek peace, to protect the poor, to husband the resources of the country, to promote peaceful progress.'

Clearly this pressure for unconditional neutrality would be formidable. Lloyd George by now, moreover, was no longer the Lloyd George of Agadir: following on from his land campaign, he was building up for a big Liberal–Labour radical crusade for the impending elections. He had made trouble over the naval estimates in 1914 in quite the old style of 1908 and 1909. Grey still felt himself unable to give the French ambassador, Cambon, any formal assurances of support. Nicolson and Crowe threw all their weight into advocacy for intervention. Henry Wilson intrigued to get a decision to go to the aid of the French. After a cabinet on 1 August Grey informed Cambon that 'France must take her own decision at this moment without reckoning on any assistance that we are not now in a position to promise'. Cambon, prompted by Nicolson, made the obvious French point about the undefended French Atlantic coasts left under British naval protection as a result of the 1912 naval agreements. On 1 August, after having seen Cambon, Nicolson expostulated to Grey: 'You will render us a by-word among nations.' Here indeed was a crucially revealing moment in the development of the policy-influencing role of the Civil Service. At a cabinet on 2 August a compromise was reached: the 'peace party' (Morley, Harcourt, Lloyd George, Samuel, Burns, Pease, Simon, Runciman and two or three others) were mollified by an undertaking not to assure the French of support; on the other hand, Grey was authorized to assure the French that the Germans would not be permitted to attack the French northern or western coasts. The Navy, taking advantage of a concentration for the annual summer manoeuvres, was placed by Churchill and the First Sea Lord, Battenberg, on a 'preparatory and precautionary basis' on 28 July; by 31 July the major fleet squadrons were ready at their designated battle stations.

Further, the cabinet decided on 2 August to treat German violation of Belgian neutrality as a *casus belli*. This was the decisive turning point. It was made possible by Asquith's and Grey's success in converting Lloyd George, hitherto the mainstay of the non-interventionist faction. Belgium enabled a majority of the cabinet to fudge the 'balance of power' issue. Had the Germans reverted to their pre-Schlieffen strategic plan and turned first against the Russians in full cooperation with the Austrians and held back the French in Alsace-Lorraine, it is extremely doubtful that Britain could have gone to war. But from the German point of view the British were a marginal factor in the European equation and certainly not worth a reversal of grand strategy. German naval policy in 1914 did not involve the conception of an aggressive challenge to the British to decide naval supremacy: in fact war contradicted the point of German naval policy, and in five years of war to come the German High Seas Fleet left its harbours only twice to fight indecisive engagements. For the purpose of a war against Britain the Germans had to invent from scratch an entirely new naval policy, going back to the French *guerre de course* theories of the 1880s. Militarily, the Germans did not reckon on Britain as a serious factor. Nor, for that matter, did the French. In this, as it happened in August and September 1914, the Germans were wrong, for the two British corps turned out to be more useful than the French anticipated; but both the Germans and the French could be pardoned for their opinion. The British generals never themselves expected that they would be called upon to bear the burdens of such decisive responsibility; and they shared with the French generals the delusion that the Germans would be defeated by a great Napoleonic French thrust into the German heartland through Lorraine.

This was the other decisive assumption bearing on British action in July and August. The British themselves never expected to be more than a marginal factor in the continental war. Very few generals had the prescience of Henry Wilson that Britain would eventually have to accept conscription and become a fully-fledged continental-scale military power. This was unthinkable to the vast majority of politicians and public in August 1914. If they had been able to foresee it, and the costs of it, they certainly would have opposed intervention. Grey supposed that Britain would suffer most from a commercial recession. He told the Commons on 3 August in a speech advocating war for Belgium: 'For us with our powerful fleet . . . if we are engaged in war, we shall suffer but little more than we shall suffer even if we stand aside.' British marginality, in other words, secured maximum benefits at minimum costs. The admirals had agreed reluctantly and grudgingly to see to the transport of Haldane's Expeditionary Force to northern France; but this they, and the politicians and the public at large, still thought of as a minor preliminary operation to be got out of the way before the real war started, which they assumed would be a great Nelsonian Armageddon of the fleets in the North Sea.

Thus the British decision to accept war on 4 August, after the expiry of the ultimatum demanding German evacuation of Belgium, depended essentially on fudging the main issue of the balance of power and misconstruing totally the nature of the war on both land and sea. Even so, several cabinet ministers intended to resign, and in the end two, Morley, as keeper of the Gladstonian conscience, and Burns, actually did so.

On the foundations of such evasiveness and misconstruction, the majority of Liberals were more or less willing to endorse the policy of intervention. In terms of immediate political convenience, indeed, war had much to offer: evasiveness on the balance of power was an opportunity for evasiveness on Home Rule and getting out of the Ulster impasse. Moreover, if the war were short and glorious, the government would be immensely strengthened and in a condition to face new elections with a degree of confidence totally lacking before 4 August 1914. Certainly a Liberal government going to war in such a way and on the basis of such misconceptions was the only way the British could have gone to war as a generally united people: if a Unionist government had been in power, as a consequence, say, of Irish Nationalist intransigence, there is no doubt that there would have been a most serious rift in public opinion along the lines, though in a much more intense form, of dispute over the war in South Africa from 1900.

For national unanimity indeed the Unionists had Liberalism gratefully to thank. They too had cause to welcome war. It relieved them of the distasteful prospect of a unilateral Ulster declaration of independence. And they were pre-eminently the 'national' party, the party of assertion of British power to protect British interests. Here at last was the chance to do properly what had been so mismanaged in South Africa. The Unionist leaders urged Asquith on 1 August not to hesitate in supporting France and Russia. They were wholehearted balance of power advocates; they did not need Belgium as the Liberals did. The great difference between the two major parties was that the war would remain politically advantageous to Liberalism only if it proved indeed to be limited in scope and duration and ultimately successful. Liberalism was not up to coping with the consequences of the assumptions governing the decision to intervene in 1914 not being true. Unionism in general fully shared the misconceptions of 1914; but it was, by its nature, able to bear those consequences.

Initial British marginality at least preserved British military operations from the botch which all the other major belligerents got into as a result of their own peculiar misconceptions. The French launched their magnificent *élan vital* offensive in Lorraine and ended up in a shambles. The Austrians, falling over themselves in their eagerness to get at the Serbs in the south before the Russians could intervene in the north, were taken aback by the speed of the Russian mobilization and ended up botching up both campaigns, hanging on tenuously to Cracow and the Carpathian passes and calling for German assistance. The Russians more than counterbalanced their advantage over the Austrians in Poland by the catastrophe of their invasion of East Prussia, where a complete army was annihilated at Tannenberg. Above all, the Germans fumbled their immense western gamble. In the end Schlieffen's great enveloping manoeuvre proved beyond even their capacity. The French belatedly realized what was afoot in time and the British Expeditionary Force, initially of four rather than six infantry divisions, commanded by Sir John French and transported across with exemplary efficiency and dispatch, found itself usefully in the path of the German advance more by accident than design. The first shock of contact came on 23 August when the German 1st Army under Kluck on the right wing of the German manoeuvre brushed against the British II corps at Mons. The British had to join in the general French retreat. After a stubborn stand at Le Cateau on the 26th, which made the German advance recoil temporarily, the British fell back with the French to the Marne. The French were themselves able to outflank the German envelopment at the battle of the Marne, and the baffled Germans retired to positions along the Aisne where they dug themselves in. The French could not dislodge them, and the great entrenched stalemate of the Western Front began. By November, at the first battle of Ypres, the British forces also found themselves bogged down in static warfare. By now the capacity of Haldane's first-line Army was exhausted. It was clear also that the results of the first great collisions were indecisive. The problem of finding a new army to fight a new war thus presented itself to the puzzled public and the dismayed government.

On the naval side the British were baffled by the failure of the

Germans to behave according to expectation. There was no titanic clash of mighty fleets of dreadnoughts. Instead the British found themselves painfully surprised by torpedoes and mines. The Admiralty had to start hurriedly fortifying and securing an anchorage at Scapa Flow in which to store Sir John Jellicoe's precious Grand Fleet while it waited for the Germans to come out. These disconcerting failures of events to match expectations exposed painfully the neglect of the Navy to set up a proper general staff as the Army had done. This had to be hastily assembled. British naval strategy settled down to running a war of attrition at sea. The few German commerce raiders at large were destroyed. There was no threat to British sea communications. Instead the Admiralty set about throttling Germany's international trade. A blockade was established designed to prevent Germany getting supplies through Dutch or Scandinavian ports. The Admiralty interpreted the latest international convention on the law of blockade – the Declaration of London, 1909, which in any case Britain had never formally ratified – with an increasing disregard for legalistic scruples. Neutrals, especially the United States, always with the origins of the War of 1812 in mind, protested, to little avail. But the Admiralty would face its greatest problem in the war when the Germans seriously set about turning to a commerce war against the British.

Initial bafflement at the totally unexpected turn of naval events combined with the rampant general anti-German hysteria to force Asquith to make a scapegoat of Prince Louis of Battenberg, with whom Churchill got on well; and public feeling was appeased by the return to executive control of the Navy by the old sea dog Fisher, who got on well with very few people. The King, an old Beresford supporter, was intensely annoyed. Fisher in fact was now a menace, especially in combination with the headstrong Churchill. The qualities that had made him so incomparably an asset in 1904-10 were now wildly out of control. Fisher made an apt partner in this respect with Kitchener, another hero of the public whom Asquith appointed to succeed himself at the War Office on 5 August 1914. At a loss to cope with the ways and means of waging the new war that confronted Britain, Asquith transformed the Committee of Imperial Defence into a War Council. Asquith, Grey, Kitchener, Churchill and Lloyd George were the ministers who attended. Balfour was brought in as a gesture to the Unionists. Its secretary was the ubiquitous Maurice Hankey who had become secretary of the C.I.D. in 1912. It began immediately to search for a British war strategy.

VII

The fate of the government would depend on finding this war strategy. The final agony of the final phase of the Liberal impasse turns on an assessment of its chances in this search.

In its favour the government still retained general public and parliamentary confidence. The amount of dissent against the war in parliament was negligible. E. D. Morel founded the Union for Democratic Control in September 1914 to abolish secret diplomacy: his thesis was that democracies, being naturally pacific, would never go to war unless duped into it by the representatives of selfish social and economic interests. The U.D.C. attracted a good deal of support from among those who filled the ranks of the Foreign Policy Committee and the other groups critical of Grey's policy, especially in 1911. But as long as things went reasonably well and public confidence was not shaken, the U.D.C. would remain a coterie of radical intellectuals without popular impact. Morley gave no lead. He retired from public life. Keir Hardie no longer had the heart to fight. John Burns, like Morley, kept quiet. Many of Grey's former critics now felt it their patriotic duty to support the war once Britain was in it. C. P. Scott committed the *Manchester Guardian* to help towards victory and redoubled his efforts to find the twentieth-century equivalent of Gladstone, looking increasingly to Lloyd George. Ramsay MacDonald denounced the war but could not carry the Labour party with him, and resigned its leadership. The I.L.P. rallied to the dissenting thesis of Morel but the trade unions joined in the national patriotic concensus. On 24 August the T.U.C. chiefs offered full cooperation with the war effort, and Lloyd George, the government's specialist in industrial relations, set about the task of maximizing labour potential and industrial supply by bringing the unions officially into participation in the decision-making process: the small beginnings of the idea of a 'people's war'. Lloyd George took care to combat Labour suspicions of war 'profiteering' by unscrupulous industrialists; and his Defence of the Realm Act No. II, a fairly sweeping measure to control private industry, offended traditional Liberals by its implications of State control over private freedom. This indeed was increasingly to become the basic theme of British society at war.

The 'people' were in any case anxious to make it their war. A wave of anti-German hysteria flooded public life, expressive initially of frantic frustration at the failure of the victories to materialize. No rumours of German atrocities or manifestations of angels in the sky at Mons or vast Russian armies marching through Britain on their way to the front in France were too fantastic to be credulously received. Demagogic frauds like Horatio Bottomley preyed on this hysteria: Bottomley made a fortune in recruiting and propaganda tours exploiting the most shameless depths of xenophobia and chauvinistic sentimentality. The educated classes indulged themselves in such things as the cult of the heroic and beautiful Rupert Brooke, epitome of the Public School poet, who wrote heroic and beautiful sonnets about the morally cleansing virtues of war and who died of blood-poisoning before he could get to it.

But much the most impressive evidence of popular support for the war was the quite unprecedented and unsurpassed response to Kitchener's appeal for recruits. Kitchener was useless as an executive head of the War Office; but as a totem, or rather a poster, he was magnificent. His one great contribution to strategic thinking was to impress on his cabinet colleagues his conviction that the war would last a long time and that consequently a great New Army, of the order of seventy divisions of infantry (a million bayonets), would have to be raised. Asquith and his ministers ruled out conscription. They were determined not to let the war become an excuse for the erosion of fundamental Liberal values; and voluntary recruiting stood in this sacred category along with Free Trade. Kitchener set out to raise the New Army anyhow. In the end his campaign brought in nearly two million for the Territorial Army. It was an amazing feat both on his part and the public's. The one sour note was his mishandling of the delicate Irish situation. Sharing fully the prejudices of his caste, he welcomed the cooperation of the Ulster Volunteers but rejected the offers of the Irish Volunteers. This clumsiness compromised Redmond's prestige yet further and caused much disaffection and withdrawal of support for the war. But those side effects were not noticed in Britain amid the general applause for the creation of a mass army. It would be more difficult, indeed, to hit on a way of using it as successfully as it had been created.

The Unionists obviously would do nothing to impede the government's search for an effective way to wage the war. They were instinctively, after all, the 'national' party, the party of the South African war, the party of empire, the party of assertion of British interests. But their attitude to the government was profoundly ambiguous. Bitter memories of the Ulster crisis were still vivid. This resentment would well up if the government exposed any weaknesses. Unionists thought of themselves as the natural leaders of the nation at war. They resented the very fact of a Liberal government standing between them and the war. But on the other hand they well appreciated that Liberalism's commitment to war, however fudged, was crucial for the maintenance of national unity, so refreshingly different from the violent public rifts over the South African war. Still, given the first signs of serious failure on the part of the government, Unionism would inevitably tend to think of the desirability of a coalition government as more aptly representative of the nation's solidarity. In this way, in a supreme crisis of the State, the dream of the national efficiency movement of 1899, of Lloyd George in 1910, would be realized. Balfour had rejected these earlier projects because he would not sacrifice the historic identity of Toryism to any such expedient. But circumstances in the war might well be such that, far from involving a dilution of Toryism, a share in the direction of the war would give Toryism the means of fulfilling itself to an extent not provided either by Tariff Reform or Ulster. The delicate problem, in such a contingency, would be to reconcile a coalition ministry intended to express a national consensus with the distinct possibility that setting it up at the political expense of Liberalism might shatter that very consensus. Thus, while that risk remained, the government would be safe from Unionist attack.

The government's advantages included also the fact that within it there were talents of the highest order. Conspicuously, Churchill at the Admiralty greeted the war as the providential opportunity of his life and career. He was taken aback by the failure of the Germans to send out the High Seas Fleet; and he relieved his frustration by restless interference in the conduct of operations, demanding military commands from the astonished Asquith and personally taking charge of the defence of Antwerp. Churchill's was the loudest and most insistent voice in the War Council as it groped its way towards a strategy.

Again, as in 1908 and 1911, Lloyd George was the other cabinet force which, in combination with Churchill, had the power to give a decisive tilt to the course of policy. Not afflicted by Churchill's rashness and impulsiveness, Lloyd George was a more formidable and devious character. The war ruled out elections in 1915 and all his plans for a radical new departure were necessarily abandoned. Or rather, they were transformed by the new circumstances of war and put to different uses. The war also transformed the conditions in which Liberalism had to exist. 'Mainstream' issues like free trade were under constant and increasing pressure by the harsh force of circumstance; traditional Liberal values of peace, retrenchment and reform now meant nothing. While these issues and values still held sway in Liberal politics Lloyd George would remain sufficiently loyal; but in the conditions of war Lloyd George was liberated from the restraints of such loyalties. Again, the consequences of this liberation might well save the Liberal government from itself if the military aspect of things went well. If it did not, however, Lloyd George would unavoidably constitute a disruptive and dissolvent force in the texture of Liberal cohesiveness.

The vulnerability of Asquith's government lay essentially in its failure to establish a firm grip on the formulation of war policy. Under Asquith the War Council was a debating society, not a planning machine. The government was not weak so much because it tried to uphold traditional Liberal values like free trade and voluntary recruitment as such; it was weak because it regarded the war essentially in corresponding terms: it interfered as little as possible in the conduct of business by businessmen – Churchill in fact coined the slogan 'Business as usual' – and it assumed that the best thing would be to interfere as little as possible in the business of war and its conduct by the appropriate departments responsible and by the admirals and generals. These happened generally not to be of high calibre. Sir John French in France worried Balfour by his confidence based on no obviously convincing foundations. Yet Balfour felt 'ready to yield to his authority'. Kitchener at the War Office was treated with enormous deference until it was realized that behind the impressive façade lay a void. Kitchener had no idea of how to run a great modern war, and improvised in the same way in which he made his reputation in the Sudan. But his immense public reputation made it difficult to get rid of him. The same was true of Fisher: like Kitchener he kept his schemes jealously to himself and was unable to talk Churchill down in the War Council. Yet as a public hero his dismissal or resignation would rock the foundations of national confidence.

The basic data with which the War Council had to deal were, first, the stalemate on the Western front, which the French failed to break in attacks in Champagne in February and March 1915 and which the British failed to break in the battle of Neuve Chapelle in March and the second battle of Ypres in April. Secondly, there was the fact that majority opinion in Britain still regarded her main belligerent role in naval or amphibious terms. Britain would remain militarily auxiliary to the French; but would win the war against Germany by decisive interposition of force elsewhere than in France. Churchill and Fisher were elaborating grand schemes for a descent on Schleswig or the German Baltic Coast. The third datum was the sorry condition of the Russians as their military machine wore itself out in a series of desperate battles against the Germans and Austro-Hungarians in Poland. The fourth datum was the entry of Turkey into the war in November 1914 on the side of Germany and Austria.

Turkish intervention had the immediate effect of drawing

British attention to the Mediterranean theatre as a promising sphere of strategic possibilities. To a great extent tradition and habit determined this. British politicians, generals and admirals tended to feel far more at home in the Mediterranean and the Near East and Egypt than they did in the fields of Flanders. Moreover, war in this traditional theatre would necessarily be of an amphibious character. The admirals had no enthusiasm for arguments that Britain ought to devote her resources to building up a great military force in France. The logic of Kitchener's one great insight led in this direction; but his habits and affinities made him vulnerable to a Turkish campaign. Hankey favoured this as the central focus of the great new British strategic plan; and pointed especially to the Dardanelles and Constantinople. The Russians were appealing for a diversion against the Turks. Also the Italians needed encouragement to take the plunge into war against Austria.

Churchill gave the decisive push in this direction. He transferred his amphibious enthusiasm from the Baltic to the Mediterranean. He carried Fisher, grumbling and reluctant, with him; and the War Council, without adequate study, agreed in January 1915 that 'the Admiralty should prepare for a naval expedition in February to bombard and take the Gallipoli Peninsula, with Constantinople as its objective'.[5] By doing this, it was supposed, Russia could be relieved with supplies and munitions, and Germany somehow struck a mortal blow. Asquith, Grey and the others should have intervened at this point and inquired how the capture of Constantinople was to be effected by the Navy, what would it do to injure Germany, and also what supplies and munitions were available to succour the Russians. None of these questions was asked. The Russians, after all, had asked merely for a diversion to relieve Turkish pressure on them in the Caucasus; they did not ask the British to win the war by capturing Constantinople. In fact, they had already laid formal claim to the Straits as their prize of war, and the last thing they wanted was for the British to occupy them. When Fisher realized what the implications for the Navy were in trying to force the Dardanelles he turned violently against the scheme, but was persuaded by Kitchener not to make a scandal and overruled by

Asquith. Churchill rushed the project forward. In February the naval bombardments proved ineffectual. Losses by mines were heavy. It became clear that the Gallipoli peninsula could be secured only by military landings. A military force was hastily assembled under Sir Ian Hamilton, an officer of great charm and distinction but lacking both in ruthlessness and luck. The landings in April failed to take the peninsula. The heroism involved in them among the elements of the Australian and New Zealand Army Corps (ANZAC) marked the inauguration of an antipodean national mythology; they also marked the beginning of the end of the Liberal government.

This was the first, great, conspicuous botch of British war operations. It occurred contemporaneously with the rather less conspicuous failure by the British in France at second Ypres and in battles thereafter. To cover himself against criticism, Sir John French blamed failure on a shortage of shells. The 'shells scandal', as taken up especially by the Northcliffe press, tied up in a peculiar way with the rumblings of political machinations.

Shortage of shells, as dramatically revealed to the scandal of the public by Northcliffe's military expert, Colonel Repington, in *The Times*, made it clear that Kitchener's control over the war machine could not be allowed to continue. But as a national hero it was very difficult to shunt Kitchener aside. The generals would not tolerate him in a senior active military capacity. After exhausting all avenues of escape, Asquith saw that the expedient thing would be to retain Kitchener nominally at the War Office but to make sure that executive control of the vital areas of supply and organization should be in the hands of someone else. Lloyd George, the embodiment of the philosophy of State control of the war effort, the genius of labour-management cooperation, was the obvious candidate. The shells scandal, further, stirred up Unionist complaint and criticism about the way the Liberal government was running the war. The demand grew for dynamic action. Bonar Law was under pressure to take up the idea of a coalition. Lloyd George was convinced that some major change in the supreme direction of the war was essential. He was therefore receptive, rather in the spirit of 1910, to such an idea. Asquith hitherto had scouted this as unnecessary and undesirable. He had no confidence in the executive capacity of the Unionist leaders, especially Bonar Law, whom he despised and underrated. Yet with startling suddenness a coalition ministry came into being in May 1915.

Fisher's resignation as First Sea Lord on 15 May was the catalyst of change. He was convinced that Churchill and the Dardanelles adventure would destroy the Navy and destroy Britain. He made sure that Bonar Law was aware of his action and his motives. Law knew that once Fisher's resignation exploded in public he could no longer restrain his party from attacking the government. The renegade Churchill was a particular *bête noire* for the Unionists. Between them Lloyd George and Bonar Law concluded that a coalition was inevitable. There was no 'conspiracy'.[6] Asquith quickly accepted the logic of the situation. The Liberal government could no longer, in the circumstances, rightly or wrongly, retain public confidence. A coalition was the only way of preserving national unity, and, incidentally, Asquith's own position at the head of affairs.

Northcliffe's campaign on the shells issue drove Asquith further into the corner. Rather than challenge the Unionists to an open conflict in parliament, Asquith agreed to a coalition. This was constructed by 25 May. Asquith stayed on as prime minister. Grey stayed at the Foreign Office, now a department of secondary importance. Haldane, already under heavy public abuse as a 'pro-German', was ruthlessly dropped: Asquith could not bear even trying to explain. Birrell kept the Irish Office, which no one else wanted. Churchill was removed from the Admiralty, despite his shrill complaints, and dumped insultingly into the sinecure Duchy of Lancaster; he resigned shortly after and went off to command a battalion in France. His political career seemed to be finished. Arthur Henderson, the leader of pro-war Labour, was given the Education Office. Kitchener, adorned with the Order of the Garter, was kept on at the War Office as a continuing symbol of national patriotism; but Lloyd George, appointed to a newly created Ministry of Munitions, in fact took over direction of the essential sinews of war.

Liberals seemed to dominate the reconstructed cabinet: Unionists, apart from Balfour at the Admiralty, got the lesser departments – Law with Colonies, Walter Long with Local Government, Austen Chamberlain with India, Selborne with Agriculture, Curzon with the Privy Seal, Carson with the attorney-generalship and Lansdowne without portfolio. But in reality Lloyd George in any case had ceased to be anything regularly definable as a Liberal; and the coalition was formed at the political expense of the Liberal party. The Unionists did not need to take all the great offices to underline this point. Bonar Law deliberately restrained Tory appetites for fear of driving Liberalism into a sense of outraged betrayal.

Asquith assumed that he had saved his position by a tactical manoeuvre. However restless they might be, neither the Irish nor Labour would sustain a Unionist government in office. In this calculation Asquith reckoned without the fact that parliament, and majorities in parliament, would increasingly become marginal to the sort of war Lloyd George was preparing himself to lead. Asquith's only parliamentary chance now, in fact, would be to lead Liberalism in its natural bent, as Fox and Grey had done in the Revolutionary and Napoleonic Wars and as Campbell-Bannerman had done in 1900: to a demand for a compromise peace with Germany. In this way he could have kept secure the vital links with Labour, which was already drifting markedly in the U.D.C. direction. But as Loreburn pointed out, Asquith was a Liberal Leaguer; as such he was a prisoner of the war and, as it turned out, Lloyd George was his jailer. Thus the great Liberal bid to provide adequate political responses ended in hopeless impasse.

CHRONOLOGY

1865	General election: Liberal majority
	Death of Palmerston. Russell prime minister
1865–6	Second Russell (Liberal) ministry
	Transatlantic cables
1866	Resignation of Liberal government over franchise reform
1866–8	Third Derby (Conservative) ministry
1867	Second Reform Act: household suffrage in boroughs
1868	First Disraeli (Conservative) ministry
	General election: Liberal majority
1868–74	First Gladstone (Liberal) ministry
1869	Disestablishment of Irish Church
	Opening of Suez Canal
1870	Franco-Prussian war
	Irish Land Act: fixed tenure, fair rents, free trade
	Education Act: principle of elementary education for all
	Russian repudiation of Black Sea clause of Treaty of Paris (1856)
1871	Trade Union Act: legal status of unions regularized
1872	Ballot Act: secret voting
	Alabama settlement with U.S.A.
	Disraeli's Crystal Palace and Manchester speeches on Conservatism
1873	Liberal government defeated on Irish Universities question
1874	General election: Conservative majority
1874–80	Second Disraeli (Conservative) ministry
1875	Public Health Act: consolidation of sanitary legislation
	Artisans' Dwellings Act: government aid for housing
	Trade Union Act: legalizes peaceful picketing
	Purchase of Khedive of Egypt's Suez Canal shares
1876	Queen becomes Empress of India
	Turkish massacres in Bulgaria
	Gladstone's pamphlet on *Bulgarian Horrors*
	Telephone invented by A. G. Bell

1876   Principle of internal combustion engine

1876–7   Conference at Constantinople on Near Eastern question

1877   Annexation of Transvaal Republic

1877–8   Russo–Turkish war

1878   Treaty of San Stefano between Russia and Turkey

     Berlin Congress to settle Near Eastern crisis

1878–9   Afghan war

1879   Onset of agricultural depression. Evictions in Ireland

     Zulu war

     Gladstone's first Midlothian campaign

     Irish National Land League formed

     Edison's electric light; first electric tram cars

1880   General election: Liberal majority

1880–85   Second Gladstone (Liberal) ministry

1880   Revolt of Transvaal Afrikaners

1881   Pretoria Convention between Britain and Transvaal

     Second Gladstone Irish Land Act: principle of dual ownership

1882   'Kilmainham treaty' of cooperation between Gladstone and Parnell

     Murder of Lord F. Cavendish in Phoenix Park

     Occupation of Egypt

1883   Fabian Society founded

1884   Third Reform Act: household franchise extended to counties

     Social Democratic Federation founded

     London Convention on Anglo-Transvaal relations

     Berlin Conference on partition of Africa

     Parson's steam turbine engine

1885   Redistribution Act: modern pattern of parliamentary constituencies established

     Death of Gordon at Khartoum

1885–6   First Salisbury (Conservative) ministry

1885   General election: Liberal majority

     Linotype and monotype printing systems

1886   Third Gladstone (Liberal) ministry

     Irish Home Rule Bill; defection of Liberal Unionists from Liberal party; bill rejected in Commons

     Discovery of gold in Witwatersrand

     Indian National Congress founded

     General election: Unionist majority

1886–92 Second Salisbury (Conservative) ministry, with Liberal Unionist support

1887 Mediterranean Agreements with Italy and Austria
Queen's Golden Jubilee; Colonial Conference

1888 Local Government Act: County Councils established

1889 Naval Defence Act in response to French and Russian pressure
Dunlop pneumatic rubber tyre opens way for bicycle and automobile
London dock strike

1890 Fall of Parnell

1891 Liberal party adopts 'Newcastle Programme'

1892 General election: Liberal-Irish majority
Death of Tennyson

1892–4 Fourth Gladstone (Liberal) ministry

1893 Second Irish Home Rule Bill. Rejected by Lords
Independent Labour Party founded
Franco-Russian alliance

1894 Resignation of Gladstone: Rosebery prime minister

1894–5 Rosebery (Liberal) ministry

1894 Harcourt budget: new principle of redistributive taxation
Petrol-driven automobile

1895 General election: Unionist majority

1895– Third Salisbury (Unionist) ministry
1902 Marconi invents wireless telegraphy
Diesel engine
Beginnings of cinematography
Trial of Oscar Wilde

1896 Jameson Raid on Johannesburg; 'Kruger Telegram' from Emperor William of Germany
First issue of Harmsworth's *Daily Mail*

1897 Queen's Diamond Jubilee; Colonial Conference
Workmen's Compensation Act: first effective measure

1898 First German Navy Law
Kitchener's victory at Omdurman in Sudan; Madhist régime destroyed
Fashoda crisis between France and Britain

1899– Boer war between Britain and Afrikaner republics of
1902 Transvaal and Orange Free State

1900 Transvaal and Orange Free State annexed
Labour Representation Committee formed

1900 General election: Unionist majority
Second German Navy Law: bid to compete with Britain for naval primacy

1901 Death of Queen Victoria: Edward VII succeeds
Hay-Pauncefote Treaty with U.S.A.: British appeasement of new American power in Western hemisphere

1902 Anglo-Japanese alliance
Resignation of Salisbury: Balfour prime minister
Colonial Conference

1902–5 Balfour (Unionist) ministry
Taff Vale case: trade unions liable for damages
Education Act: State secondary education

1903 Balfour's reconstruction of Unionist cabinet
Chamberlain launches Tariff Reform campaign against free trade

1904–5 Russo-Japanese war

1904 Anglo-French *entente*

1905 Resignation of Balfour: Campbell-Bannerman prime minister
Franco-German crisis over Morocco

1905–8 Campbell-Bannerman (Liberal) ministry

1906 General election: Liberal 'landslide'
'Military conversations' between Britain and France; launching of *Dreadnought*
Responsible government granted to Transvaal

1907 Anglo-Russian *entente*
Expeditionary Army and Territorial Army formed

1908 Resignation of Campbell-Bannerman: Asquith prime minister

1908–15 First Asquith (Liberal) ministry
Old Age Pensions Act

1908–9 Bosnian crisis

1909 Lloyd George budget: principle of redistributive taxation extended
Budget rejected by Lords
Anglo-German naval scare
Blériot flies across channel

1910 General election (January): reduced Liberal majority dependent on Labour and Irish
Constitutional crisis over Lords' veto
Death of Edward VII: George V succeeds
General election (December): situation unchanged

1911	Parliament Act limits Lords' veto power
	National Insurance Act: sickness and unemployment insurance for certain trades
	Second Morocco crisis between Britain and Germany
	Balfour resigns as Unionist leader; Bonar Law succeeds
1911–14	Industrial unrest: transport, railway, docks and coal strikes
1912	Third Irish Home Rule Bill
	Welsh Disestablishment Bill
	Militant 'suffragette' campaign
1913	Irish Home Rule Bill twice passed by Commons and twice rejected by Lords; threat of civil war in Ireland
1914	Outbreak of First World War
	Irish Home Rule and Welsh Disestablishment Bills become law but suspended for duration of war
	British Expeditionary Force sent to France
	Stalemate on Western Front
1915	Decision to invade Dardanelles and occupy Constantinople
	Failure of Dardanelles campaign
	Asquith forms a coalition ministry with the Unionists
1915–16	Second Asquith (Coalition) ministry

BIOGRAPHICAL NOTES

ARCH, Joseph (1826–1919): son of Warwickshire agricultural labourer; formed first agricultural labourers' union 1872; Liberal M.P. 1885–6, 1892–1902; political career obscure; deeply proud of having Sandringham in his parliamentary constituency.

ARNOLD, Matthew (1822–88): poet and critic; son of Dr Thomas Arnold of Rugby; ed. Winchester and Balliol, Oxford; became H.M. Inspector of Schools and one of the great Victorian sages; urbane conservative social critic of philistine middle classes in *Culture and Anarchy* (1869).

ASQUITH, Herbert Henry (1852–1928): son of Yorkshire woollen spinner; ed. City of London School and Balliol, Oxford; barrister; Liberal M.P. 1886–1918, 1920–24; Home Secretary 1892–5; Chancellor of Exchequer, 1905–8; Prime Minister 1908–16; Earl of Oxford and Asquith, 1925; married second wife Margot Tennant 1894; called 'Last of the Romans'.

BAGEHOT, Walter (1826–77): journalist and economist; ed. Bristol and University College, London; son of shipowner and banker; son-in-law of owner of *The Economist*; editor of *The Economist* 1860–77; conservative upholder of Palmerstonian system in *The English Constitution* (1867).

BALFOUR, Arthur James (1848–1930): ed. Eton and Trinity, Cambridge; inherited great wealth; nephew of Lord Salisbury; Conservative M.P. 1874–1922; president Local Government Board 1885–6; Secretary for Scotland 1886–7; Chief Secretary for Ireland 1887–91; leader of Commons and First Lord of Treasury 1891–2, 1895–1902; Prime Minister 1902–5; resigned Conservative leadership 1911; First Lord of Admiralty 1915–16; Foreign Secretary 1916–19; Lord President 1919–22 and 1925–29; Earl of Balfour 1922; bachelor and philosopher; pro-American and pro-Zionist.

BARING, Evelyn (1841–1917): member of banking family; ed. Woolwich; soldier; private secretary to his cousin Lord Northbrook, Viceroy of India; British commissioner in Cairo 1876–9; member of Indian government 1879–83; agent and consul-general in Egypt 1883–1907; Lord Cromer 1892; Viscount 1899; Earl 1901; declined Campbell-Bannerman's offer of Foreign Office 1905; one of the great proconsuls.

BRIGHT, John (1811–89): son of Rochdale mill-owner; ed. four different schools; entered textile trade; Quaker; collaborated with Richard Cobden in agitation against the corn laws; Liberal M.P. 1843–89; president of Board of Trade 1868–70; Chancellor of Duchy of Lancaster 1873–4 and 1880–82; opposed Church of England, landed order, Crimean war, interventionist foreign and imperial policy, and Irish Home Rule; epitome of puritan bourgeois morality; Liberal elder statesman in later years.

BROADHURST, Henry (1840–1911): trade union leader; stonemason and son of stonemason; secretary of Labour Representation League 1873; secretary of T.U.C. parliamentary committee 1875; Liberal M.P. 1880–92, 1894–1906; Gladstonian sympathies; hostile to socialism and new unionism.

BURNS, John Elliot (1858–1943): son of engine fitter; left school at ten; engineering apprentice, London; joined Social Democratic Federation 1884; founded Battersea Labour League 1889; M.P. 1892–1918; 'first artisan to reach cabinet rank' as President of Local Government Board 1905–14; President of Board of Trade 1914; resigned in protest against war; moved from extreme left in 1880s to right-wing Lib-Lab position.

CAMPBELL-BANNERMAN, Henry (1839–1908): born Campbell; son of Glasgow wholesale draper; ed. Glasgow High School and University, and Trinity Cambridge; Liberal M.P. 1868–1908; added name of Bannerman 1872 on inheriting from uncle's will; financial secretary to War Office 1871–4; Secretary for Ireland 1884–5; Secretary for War 1886, 1892–5; knighted 1895; Liberal leader in Commons 1899; Prime Minister 1905–8.

CARDWELL, Edward (1813–86): son of Liverpool merchant; ed. Winchester and Balliol, Oxford; barrister; Conservative M.P. 1842–6; Peelite and Liberal M.P. 1847–74; President of Board of Trade 1852–5; Secretary for Ireland 1859–61; Secretary for Colonies 1864–6; Secretary for War 1868–74; Viscount 1874; author of major Army reforms.

CARSON, Edward Henry (1854–1935): Dubliner; son of civil engineer; ed. Portarlington School and Trinity College, Dublin; barrister; Irish Solicitor-General 1892; M.P. Dublin University 1892–1918; Solicitor-General for England 1900–5; leader of Ulster Unionist movement 1911–14; Attorney-General 1915–16; First Lord of Admiralty 1916–17; Belfast M.P. 1918–21; Lord of Appeal 1921–9.

CHAMBERLAIN, Joseph (1836–1914): Unitarian; son of boot and shoe manufacturer, ed. University College School, London; joined Birmingham screw-manufacturing firm; Chairman, National Education League 1870; Mayor of Birmingham 1873–5; reputation for municipal reform; M.P. for Birmingham 1876–1910; assumed leadership of the Radicals in the late 1870s and 1880s; inspiration of National Liberation Federation 1877; President of Board of Trade 1880–85; President of Local Government Board 1886; opposed Irish Home Rule and led Radical Unionists out of the Liberal party; leader of the Liberal Unionists in Commons 1892; Colonial Secretary 1895–1903; led Tariff Reform movement from 1903 until stroke forced retirement in 1906; the greatest imperialist among British statesmen.

CHAMBERLAIN, Joseph Austen (1863–1937): son of Joseph Chamberlain; ed. Rugby and Trinity, Cambridge; Liberal Unionist M.P. 1892–1937; minor office 1895–1903; Chancellor of Exchequer, 1903–5; cabinet office 1915–17, 1918–22; leader of Conservatives, 1921–2; Foreign Secretary 1925–9; 1st Lord of Admiralty 1931; a softer, more gentlemanly version of his father.

CHILDERS, Hugh Culling Eardley (1827–96): son of parson; ed. Cheam and Trinity, Cambridge; Australia 1851–6; Liberal M.P. 1860–92; cabinet office 1868–71, 1872–3, 1880–85, 1886; supported Gladstone on Home Rule; 'businesslike administrator'; one of the first important Liberal leaders to be converted to Home Rule.

CHURCHILL, Lord Randolph Henry Spencer (1849–94): younger son of 7th Duke of Marlborough; ed. Eton and Merton, Oxford; Conservative M.P. 1874–94; leading spirit of 'Fourth Party'

1880; Secretary for India 1885-6; Leader of the House and Chancellor of Exchequer 1886; resigned in unsuccessful effort to assert his 'Tory Democrat' views of the party's future.

CHURCHILL, Winston Leonard Spencer (1874-1965): son of above; ed. Harrow and Sandhurst; Unionist M.P. 1900-4; crossed to Liberals over free trade; Liberal M.P. 1904-22; returned thereafter to Conservatives; M.P. until 1964; twice Prime Minister; Colonial Under-Secretary 1906-8; President of Board of Trade 1908-10; Home Secretary 1910-11; 1st Lord of Admiralty 1911-15; Chancellor of Duchy of Lancaster 1915; with Lloyd George the most dynamic and energetic of the Liberal ministers before the 1914 war.

COBDEN, Richard (1804-65): son of small farmer; ed. at prototype of 'Dotheboys Hall'; clerk, commercial traveller, businessman in Manchester; Liberal M.P. 1841-65; became leader of the Anti-Corn Laws agitation and head of the 'Manchester School' of political and economic doctrine; failure in business; career sustained by public subscriptions; prophet of the universal beneficence of Free Trade.

CROSS, Richard Assheton (1823-1914): son of Lancashire lawyer; Rugby and Trinity, Cambridge; barrister; Conservative M.P. 1857-62 1868-86; Home Secretary 1874-80, 1885-6; Viscount 1886; Secretary for India 1886-92; Privy Seal 1895-1900; one of the 'new men' encouraged by Disraeli; associated with W. H. Smith.

CURZON, George Nathaniel (1859-1925): son of the Rev. Lord Scarsdale; ed. Eton and Balliol, Oxford; Conservative M.P. 1886-98; Irish peerage 1898; Viceroy of India 1898-1905; Earl 1911, Marquess 1921; cabinet office 1915-25; supposed himself the inevitable choice as prime minister 1923; proconsular imperialist, notorious for his pomposity and aristocratic hauteur.

DARWIN, Charles Robert (1809-82): grandson of naturalist Erasmus Darwin; ed. Shrewsbury, Edinburgh and Christ's, Cambridge; developed theory of evolution by natural selection 1844; published *Origin of Species* (1859), *Descent of Man* (1871); the central figure in a biological revolution of far-reaching implications.

DAVITT, Michael (1846-1906): son of Roman Catholic Irish peasant; Fenian 1865; founded Land League of Ireland 1879; several times Irish M.P. and several times imprisoned for sedition; revolutionary, land nationalizer, anti-clerical; pre-eminent representative of Irish 'folk' or democratic nationalism.

DERBY, Edward Stanley, 14th Earl of (1799–1869): son of 13th Earl ed. Eton and Christ Church, Oxford; Whig M.P. 1822–34; turned to Conservatives 1835; created Lord Stanley 1844; cabinet office under Grey and Peel; leader of protectionist Tories 1846; succeeded to earldom 1851; Prime Minister 1852, 1858–9, and 1866–8; collaborator with Disraeli on reform 1866 and 1867; called 'the Rupert of Debate'.

DERBY, Edward Stanley, 15th Earl of (1826–93): son of 14th Earl, known as Lord Stanley till 1869; ed. Rugby and Trinity, Cambridge; Conservative M.P. 1848–69; Indian Secretary 1858–9; Foreign Secretary 1866–8, 1874–8; joined Liberals 1880; Colonial Secretary 1882–5; Liberal Unionist 1886; declined the throne of Greece.

DEVONSHIRE, Spencer Compton Cavendish, Marquess of Hartington and 8th Duke of (1833–1908): son of 7th Duke; ed. privately and Trinity, Cambridge; Liberal M.P. 1857–91; Marquess of Hartington 1858; Secretary for War 1866; Postmaster General 1868–70; Chief Secretary for Ireland 1870–74; Liberal leader in Commons 1875; Secretary for India 1880–82; Secretary for War 1882–5; opposed Home Rule; succeeded as Duke 1891; President of Council 1895–1903; resigned on tariff reform issue; thrice declined premiership; the greatest Whig chieftain of his times.

DILKE, Charles Wentworth (1843–1911): son of baronet; ed. privately and Trinity Hall, Cambridge; barrister, Liberal M.P. 1868–86, 1892–1911; radical and republican opinions; Under Secretary at Foreign Office 1880–82; in cabinet as President of Local Government Board 1882–5; career blighted by divorce action; an important early exponent of the imperial idea.

DISRAELI, Benjamin (1804–81): son of Jewish man of letters; dandy and society novelist; Conservative M.P. 1837–76; Leader of the House and Chancellor of Exchequer 1852, 1858–9, 1866–8; Prime Minister 1868, 1874–80; Earl of Beaconsfield 1876; bitter critic of Peel and great rival to Peel's chief disciple, Gladstone; credited as founder of modern Conservative party.

EDWARD VII (1841–1910): eldest son of Queen Victoria and Prince Albert; Prince of Wales as Albert Edward until succeeding his mother to throne in 1901; the German Emperor William II was the son of his older sister Victoria, the Empress Frederick; a *bon vivant*, he lacked his mother's capacity for application; his francophile sympathies were important in the era of the *entente cordiale*; married Alexandra of Denmark, 1862.

FISHER, John Arbuthnot (1841–1920): son of Army officer; Navy 1854; captain 1874; admiral 1901; First Sea Lord 1904–10; great reformer and reorganizer; admiral of the fleet 1905; Baron 1909; First Sea Lord 1914–15; resigned over Dardanelles adventure; made the Navy fit to cope with war in 1914.

GEORGE V (1865–1936): second son of Edward VII; educated for Navy; came in line for throne on death of elder brother Duke of Clarence 1893; as Duke of York married his deceased brother's fiancée Mary, Princess of Teck, 1894; Prince of Wales 1901; succeeded to throne 1910; of rather simple tastes and habits; more 'constitutional' than his father or grandmother.

GLADSTONE, William Ewart (1809–98): son of Liverpool Scottish merchant; ed. Eton and Christ Church, Oxford; Tory M.P. 1832–46; Peelite 1847–59; joined Liberal ministry 1859; Liberal M.P. until 1895; Board of Trade 1843–5; Colonial Secretary 1845–6; Chancellor of the Exchequer 1852–5, 1859–66; Prime Minister 1868–74, 1880–85, 1886, 1892–4; searcher after great moral missions in politics; pious High Churchman; rescuer of prostitutes; called the 'Grand Old Man' and 'The People's William'.

GRANVILLE, Granville George Leveson-Gower, 2nd Earl (1815–91): son of 1st Earl; ed. Eton and Christ Church, Oxford; Whig M.P. 1836–46, when succeeded to peerage; minor office 1840–41, 1848–51; Lord President 1852–4, 1859–65; Duchy of Lancaster 1854–8; Colonial Secretary 1868–70; Foreign Secretary 1851–2, 1870–4, 1880–5; Liberal leader in Lords 1855–91; refused premiership 1859 and 1880; important as a confidant of Gladstone; Liberal leader in Lords from 1855; suave and amiable; known as 'Pussy'.

GREEN, Thomas Hill (1836–82): son of Anglican parson; ed. Rugby and Balliol, Oxford; philosopher; influential in the development of ideas of State action to create social conditions enabling true human freedom; the 'Mr Gray' of Mrs Humphry Ward's *Robert Elsmere*.

GREY, Edward (1862–1933): son of Northumberland squire and baronet; ed. Winchester and Balliol, Oxford; Liberal M.P. 1885–1916; Rosebery's Under-secretary at F.O. 1892–5; Foreign Secretary 1905–16; Viscount 1916; Roseberyite imperialist; architect of policy of *ententes* with France or Russia to balance German power; first Foreign Secretary to publish account of his policy; bird-watcher.

HALDANE, Richard Burdon (1856–1928): son of Scottish lawyer; ed. Edinburgh and Göttingen; philosopher and barrister; Liberal M.P. 1885–1911; Liberal imperialist; Secretary for War 1905–12; Lord Chancellor 1912–15, 1924; efficient administrator; ponderous intriguer.

HARCOURT, William George Granville Venables Vernon (1827–1904): grandson of Archbishop of York; ed. privately and Trinity, Cambridge; barrister; Liberal M.P. 1868–1904; Solicitor General, 1873–4; Home Secretary, 1880–85; Chancellor of Exchequer 1886, 1892–5; Liberal leader in Commons 1894–8; rumbustious, rather bullying aristocrat; strongly anti-imperialist and anti-ritualist. His son Lewis Harcourt (1863–1922) was in Liberal cabinets 1907–15.

HARDIE, James Keir (1856–1915): son of Lanarkshire ship's carpenter; miner; socialist journalism; Secretary of Scottish Miners' Federation 1886; Chairman of Scottish Labour Party 1888; Independent Labour M.P. 1892–5; Chairman I.L.P. 1893–1900, 1913–15; Labour M.P. 1900–15; greatest pioneer of political Labour movement.

HARDINGE, Charles (1858–1944): grandson of Field Marshal Lord Hardinge; ed. Harrow and Trinity, Cambridge; Foreign Office 1880; Permanent Under Secretary 1906–10, 1916–20; Viceroy of India 1910–16; played decisive part in tilting the Foreign Office in direction of accords with France and Russia.

HARMSWORTH, Alfred Charles William (1865–1922): son of impecunious barrister; popular journalism; *Answers* (1888); founded *Daily Mail* (1896); *Daily Mirror* (1903); saved *The Times* from extinction 1908; Baronet 1903; Baron, as Lord Northcliffe, 1905; supported Lloyd George 1915 and 1916; first modern British press magnate; Viscount 1917; 'the greatest man who ever strode down Fleet Street'; his brother and collaborator Harold Sidney (1868–1940) became Viscount Rothermere.

HICKS BEACH, Michael Edward (1837–1916): son of baronet; ed. Eton and Christ Church, Oxford; Conservative M.P. 1864–1906; minor office 1868; Irish Secretary 1874–6; Colonial Secretary 1871–80; Chancellor of Exchequer and Leader of House 1885–6; Irish Secretary 1886–7; President of Board of Trade 1888–92; Chancellor of Exchequer 1895–1902; Viscount St Aldwyn 1906; Earl 1915; known as 'Black Michael'; strong opponent of Tariff Reform.

HOBSON, John Atkinson (1858–1940): son of journalist; ed. Lincoln, Oxford; economist and publicist; influential in development of under consumptionist critique of capitalism; critic of imperialism; wrote extremely influential *Imperialism* (1902); pioneer of welfare state economics; Cobdenite and internationalist; preached from pulpit of South Place Ethical Society.

HUXLEY, Thomas Henry (1825–95): son of schoolmaster; medicine and natural science at London; became major exponent of claims of science in education and society; defended Darwin; pugnacious and effective controversialist; president of Royal Society 1883–5.

JAMES, Henry (1843–1916): born in New York; grandson of Irish immigrant who became a millionaire; Harvard and cosmopolitan education; settled in England and published first novel *Roderick Hudson* 1876; major novels include *The Portrait of a Lady* (1881) and *The Wings of the Dove* (1902); admired, studied and parodied as the 'master' of the theory and practice of the novel of form.

KIMBERLEY, John Wodehouse, 1st Earl of (1826–1902): ed. Eton and Christ Church, Oxford; succeeded grandfather as Lord Wodehouse, 1846; minor office under Aberdeen and Palmerston; Lord Lieutenant of Ireland 1864–6; Earl of Kimberley 1866; Lord Privy Seal 1868–70; Colonial Secretary 1870–74, 1880–82; Indian Secretary 1882–5, 1886, 1892–4. Foreign Secretary 1894–5; a Liberal pillar in the Lords and one of the few Liberal peers to stay with Gladstone over Home Rule.

KIPLING, Joseph Rudyard (1865–1936): born Bombay, India, son of art-teacher; cousin of Edward Burne-Jones the pre-Raphaelite painter and of Stanley Baldwin, the prime minister; ed. United Services College, Westward Ho!; made reputation with journalism and literature of British India; *Barrack-Room Ballads* (1892); *The Seven Seas* (1896) expressed commitment to imperialism; supported Chamberlain and Tariff Reform.

KITCHENER, Horatio Herbert (1850–1916): son of Army officer; ed. Woolwich; Army 1871; major-general 1896; defeated Dervishes and occupied Khartoum 1898; South Africa 1900–2; Viscount 1902; Commander-in-chief in India 1902–9; field-marshal 1909; Egypt 1911–14; earl, 1914; Secretary for War 1914–16; drowned en route to Russia.

KRUGER, Stephanus Johannes Paulus (1825–1904): son of Afrikaner farmer in Cape Colony; emigrated across the Vaal 1839; leading figure in Transvaal; President of Transvaal Republic 1882–1900; took refuge in Holland, 1900; a staunch Calvinist who regarded the Afrikaners as a Chosen People; devoted to securing and preserving the independence of the Transvaal from British control; 'political heir to the Great Trek'; symbol of Afrikanerdom.

LAW, Andrew Bonar (1858–1923): born in New Brunswick, Canada son of Ulster Presbyterian minister; ed. Glasgow High School; banking and iron; Unionist M.P. 1900–23; minor office 1902–5; succeeded Balfour as Unionist leader 1911; strong Tariff Reformer and staunch defender of Ulster against Home Rule; Colonial Secretary 1915–16; Chancellor of Exchequer 1916–18; Lord Privy Seal 1918–21; brought down Lloyd George in 1922; Prime Minister 1922–3; first colonial to become prime minister; looked to Joseph Chamberlain as his hero.

LLOYD GEORGE, David (1863–1945): son of Welsh dissenting schoolmaster; born Manchester; ed. in Church school; solicitor; Liberal M.P. 1890–1945; championed Welsh, radical and Nonconformist causes; President of Board of Trade 1905–8; Chancellor of Exchequer 1908–15; Minister of Munitions 1915–16; Prime Minister 1916–22; dynamic breaker of parties; known as 'the Welsh Wizard'.

MACDONALD, James Ramsay (1866–1937): born illegitimately of Morayshire farming stock; joined Social Democratic Federation 1885; Fabian Society 1886; unsuccessful I.L.P. candidate 1895; journalism; secretary of Labour Representation Committee 1900–12; Labour M.P. 1906–18, 1922–31; Chairman of I.L.P. 1906–9; Chairman, parliamentary Labour group 1911–14; opposed entry in war 1914; first Labour Prime Minister 1924; Prime Minister 1929–35; broke with Labour party on foundation of National Government 1931; Lord President 1935–7.

MARX, Karl (1818–83): born into middle-class Jewish Rhineland family; ed. Bonn and Berlin; revolutionary Socialist; Paris 1843–5; London 1849; first volume of *Das Kapital* 1867; among founders of first Socialist International, London, 1864; Friedrich Engels a collaborator and disciple; established Communist theory of inevitable historical evolution though class conflict towards classless society; inspiration of Hyndman and Social Democratic Federation 1884.

MILL, John Stuart (1806–73): son of James Mill, Bentham's disciple; subjected to utilitarian indoctrination by his father; became leading philosopher of the Liberal movement; regarded *On Liberty* (1859) as his most enduring achievement; Liberal M.P. 1865–8; exponent of equal rights for women; regarded by Carlyle and Fitzjames Stephen as lacking in masculine qualities of mind and character.

MILNER, Alfred (1854–1925): born in Germany; ed. Tubingen, London and Balliol, Oxford; barrister; social worker and civil servant; Liberal imperialist; service in Egypt, then 1897–1905 High Commissioner in South Africa; promoter of war with Transvaal to save South Africa for British Empire; member of Lloyd George's small War cabinet 1916–18; Colonial Secretary 1918–21; Viscount 1902; convinced 'race patriot' and critic of liberal internationalism.

MORANT, Robert Laurie (1863–1920): son of decorative artist; ed. Winchester and New Coll., Oxford; civil service; major figure behind Education Act of 1902; Chairman, National Health Insurance Commission, 1911–19; constructed Ministry of Health; prime example of important new generation of 'constructive' civil servants.

MORIER, Robert Burnett David (1826–93): son of a diplomat; ed. privately and Balliol, Oxford; diplomatic service 1851; minor posts at German courts 1853–76; Minister at Lisbon 1876–81; Madrid 1881–4; Ambassador at St Petersburg 1884–93; knighted 1882; cosmopolitan diplomat of conspicuous ability, pro-Russian, anti-German.

MORLEY, John (1838–1923): son of Blackburn surgeon; ed. Cheltenham and Lincoln, Oxford; journalist; successor to J. S. Mill as philosopher and conscience of Liberalism; Liberal M.P. 1883–1908; Chief Secretary of Ireland 1886 and 1892–5; identified with policy of Home Rule for Ireland; Secretary of State for India, 1905–10; Viscount 1908; Lord Privy Seal 1910–14; resigned in 1914 in opposition to the war; nicknamed 'Priscilla'; biographer of Cobden and Gladstone.

MORRIS, William (1834–96): son of a wealthy bill-broker in City; ed. Exeter, Oxford; associated with Rossetti, Burne-Jones, Madox Brown and Philip Webb in Pre-Raphaelite tradition; major successor to Ruskin as exponent of medievalism; convert to revolutionary socialism; poet, painter, designer, founder of Arts and Crafts movement.

PALMERSTON, Henry John Temple, 3rd Viscount (1784–1865): ed. Harrow and St John's, Cambridge; Tory M.P. 1807–82; Canningite and Whig M.P. 1828–65; minor Office 1809–28; Foreign Secretary 1830–34, 1835–41, 1846–51; Home Secretary 1852–5; Prime Minister 1855–8, 1859–65; John Bullish epitome of British self-confidence; known as 'Lord Cupid', 'Pam'.

PARNELL, Charles Stewart (1846–91): scion of Anglican baronetical and baronial Wicklow gentry; ed. Magdalene, Cambridge; Irish M.P. 1875–90; strong Irish nationalist; displaced moderate Isaac Butt as Irish leader in Commons 1878; leader of agitation for Irish Home Rule; forced Liberal appeasement from 1881; co-operation with Gladstone over Home Rule 1886–90; ruined by divorce action 1890; became romanticized hero of later nationalist generation.

PATER, Walter Horatio (1839–94): son of physician; ed. Queen's, Oxford; influenced by Ruskin and T. H. Green; aesthetician; Fellow of Brasenose 1856–94; *Studies in History of the Renaissance* (1873); *Marius the Epicurean* (1885); leading influence in the 'art for art's sake' movement.

REDMOND, John Edward (1856–1918): son of Irish Catholic gentry M.P.; ed. Trinity College, Dublin; Irish Nationalist M.P. 1881–1918; leader of Parnellite faction of Nationalist party; leader of reunited party 1900; hoped for Irish Home Rule within British imperial framework; crushed by Easter Rebellion of 1916.

RHODES, Cecil John (1853–1902): son of parson; ed. Bishops Stortford Grammar School; went to South Africa to benefit health 1870; interests in diamonds; attended Oriel, Oxford, returning to South Africa for long vacations 1873–8; back in South Africa created great diamond empire; M.P. Cape Legislature 1880–1902; creator of Rhodesia 1889; interests in Transvaal gold 1890; premier of Cape Colony 1890–96; champion of concept of British South Africa against Afrikaner separation led by Paul Kruger; one of the great prophets of imperialism; 'Anglo-Saxon' racialist.

RIPON, George Frederick Samuel Robinson, 1st Marquess of (1827–1909): son of 'Prosperity Robinson' (Prime Minister as Lord Goderich 1827); Liberal M.P. 1853–9; succeeded as Earl of Ripon and Earl de Grey 1859; minor office under Palmerston; Secretary for War 1863–6; Lord President 1868–73; Marquess 1871; convert to Roman Catholicism 1873; Viceroy of India 1880–84; 1st Lord of Admiralty 1886; Colonial Secretary 1892–5; Lord President 1905–8; a Liberal pillar in Lords.

ROBERTS, Frederick Sleigh (1832–1914): son of a general; ed. Sandhurst; Bengal Artillery 1851; V.C. Indian Mutiny 1858; Major-General 1878; successful campaigns in Afghanistan 1878–80; Baronet 1880; C. in C. India 1885–93; peerage 1893; Field Marshal 1895; C. in C. Ireland 1895–9; Supreme Command Boer War 1899–1900; Earl 1900; Commander-in-Chief of the Army 1900–15; advocate of national service 1905–14; highly popular personal embodiment of the spirit of the Army, known as 'Bobs'.

ROSEBERY, Archibald Philip Primrose, 5th Earl of (1847–1929): grandson of 4th Earl; ed. Eton and Christ Church, Oxford; succeeded to title 1868; minor office 1881–5; Liberal imperialist; Foreign Secretary 1886, 1892–4; Prime Minister 1894–5; Chairman London County Council 1889–90; resigned Liberal leadership 1896; advocate of imperialism, efficiency and non-party government; models Cromwell and Chatham; won Derby three times; 'wanted the palm without the dust.'

RUSKIN, John (1819–1900): only son of prosperous sherry merchant and pious evangelical mother; ed. at home and Christ Church, Oxford; *Modern Painters* (1843–60); *The Stones of Venice* (1851–3); *Unto this best* (1868); Whistler *v.* Ruskin libel action 1877; through his voluminous writings powerfully influenced younger artists and educated generations of social reformers; 'a violent Tory of the old school . . . the reddest also of the red'.

RUSSELL, Lord John, 1st Earl Russell (1792–1878): younger son of 6th Duke of Bedford; ed. Westminster and Edinburgh; Whig M.P. 1813–61; cabinet office 1831–4; Home Secretary and Leader of the House 1835–9; Colonial Secretary 1839; Prime Minister 1846–52, 1865–6; Foreign Secretary 1852–3; cabinet 1853–5; Foreign Secretary 1859–65; exponent of classical Whig doctrine; made his reputation by support of reform and the Italian *risorgimento*.

SALISBURY, Robert Arthur Talbot Gascoyne–Cecil, 3rd Marquess of (1830–1903): son of 2nd Marquess; ed. Eton and Christ Church, Oxford; Conservative M.P. 1853–68; journalism as Lord Robert Cecil; Viscount Cranborne 1865; succeeded as Marquess 1868; Secretary for India 1866–7; resigned on reform issue; Secretary for India 1874–8; Foreign Secretary 1878–80; Prime Minister 1885–6, 1886–92, 1895–1902; also Foreign Secretary (except for a few months in 1886, and from 1900 to 1902); presided over transformation of Conservative party from landed to business basis: uncle of Arthur Balfour; cautious, sceptical, a 'pessimistic utilitarian', with a strong bent for physical science.

SEELEY, John Robert (1834–95): son of publisher and evangelical publicist; ed. Christ's, Cambridge; Professor of Latin, U.C.L., 1863; published *Ecce Homo* (1865); Professor of Modern History, Cambridge, 1869–95; published *Life and Times of Stein* (1878) and *The Expansion of England* (1883); a pioneer intellectual force behind imperialism.

SMITH, William Henry (1825–91): born over father's newsagent shop in Strand; Methodist; developed newsagency and railway bookstall business; became Anglican; 'Liberal Conservative' M.P. 1868–91; 1st Lord of Admiralty 1877–80; War Office 1885 and 1886; Leader of the House 1886–91; represented the new bourgeois Conservatism; popularly known as 'Old Morality'.

SPENCER, Herbert (1820–1903): son of dissenting schoolmaster; largely self-educated; engineer on London–Birmingham Railway, 1837–46; friend of Darwin, Lewes, Huxley; *Social Statics* (1850); *Principles of Psychology* (1870–72); *Principles of Sociology* (1877–96); the philosopher of evolution and a founding father of sociology.

TENNYSON, Alfred (1809–92): son of parson; ed. Trinity, Cambridge; Poet Laureate 1850 in succession to Wordsworth; Baron 1884; pre-eminent poet of Victorian era, faithfully reflecting its doubts and certainties; in later years a disillusioned Liberal.

VICTORIA (1819–1901): only child of Edward, Duke of Kent, son of George III and younger brother of George IV and William IV; succeeded latter as Queen regnant 1837; married 1840 Albert of Saxe-Coburg-Gotha (d. 1861), her cousin; Empress of India 1877; rendered the monarchy acceptable to middle-class opinion; a staunch Protestant; disliked teetotalism and feminism; in youth her political loyalties Whig, but in old age anti-Liberal and especially anti-Gladstone; found Disraeli the most sympathetic of her prime ministers; largely lost her youthful popularity during her long, secluded widowhood, but regained it again in old age in the jubilees of 1887 and 1897; known as 'the Grandmother of Europe'.

WHISTLER, James McNeill (1834–1903): son of American army officer; ed. West Point; studied painting in Paris; lived mostly in London from 1860; importer of French aesthetic doctrine; Bohemian and wit; collided with Victorianism in the shape of Ruskin 1877–8.

WILDE, Oscar Fingal O'Flahertie Wills (1856–1900): son of Dublin physician; ed. Trinity College, Dublin and Magdalen, Oxford; early disciple of Pater and the 'aesthetic' movement; socialite and wit; famous for scintillating social comedies, especially *The Importance of Being Earnest* (1895); ruined 1895 by imprisonment for homosexuality; became symbol of the artist destroyed by bourgeois philistinism.

WOLSELEY, Garnet Joseph (1833–1913): son of Army officer; Army 1852; quartermaster-general 1880–82; occupied Egypt 1882; General and Baron 1882; Nile 1884–5; Viscount 1885; Commander-in-Chief in Ireland 1890–95; Commander-in-Chief 1895–9; Field-Marshal 1894; 'the very model of a modern major-general'; the major professional force behind making the Cardwell reforms a working reality.

FURTHER READING

There are two extremely valuable concise general bibliographies: Joseph L. Altholz, *Victorian England, 1837–1901* (1970), and G. R Elton, *Modern Historians on British History, 1485–1945. A Critical Bibliography 1945–1969* (1970). These include major articles as well as books.

The economic foundations are well laid by W. Ashworth, *An Economic History of England, 1870–1939* (1960), and S. G. Checkland, *The Rise of Industrial Society in England, 1815–1885* (1964). W. H. B. Court, *British Economic History, 1870–1914* (1965), is a useful collection of documents.

Good introductions to the social aspect are D. C. Marsh, *The Changing Social Structure of England and Wales, 1871–1951* (1958), and H. Perkin, *The Origins of Modern English Society, 1870–1880* (1969). E .C. Midwinter, *Victorian Social Reform* (1968) and M. E. Rose, *The Relief of Poverty, 1834–1914* (1972), are very serviceable short introductions.

For politics the most profitable introductory books are G. S. R. Kitson Clark, *The Making of Victorian England* (1962) and the excellent concise seminar study book by P. Adelman, *Gladstone, Disraeli and Later Victorian Politics* (1970). E. C. Black, *British Politics in the Nineteenth Century* (1970) is a useful collection of documents. Conservatism is well covered by Robert Blake, *The Conservative Party from Peel to Churchill* (1970), and the Labour party likewise by Royden Harrison, *Before the Socialists. Studies in Labour and Politics, 1861–1881* (1965) and H. Pelling, *The Origins of the Labour Party 1880–1900* (2nd edn, 1965), continued by F. Bealey and H. Pelling, *Labour and Politics 1900–1906* (1958). There is as yet no good general study of the Liberal party. The story has to be filled in by such authoritative works as D. Hamer, *Liberal Politics in the Age of Gladstone and Rosebery* (1972), P. F. Clarke, *Lancashire and the New Liberalism* (1971) and H. V. Emy, *Liberals, Radicals and Social Politics, 1892–1914* (1973). The classic study of the 1867–84 period is H. J. Hanham, *Elections and Party Management. Politics in the Time of Disraeli and Gladstone* (1959). Hanham also covers the constitutional side of politics in *The Nineteenth-Century Constitution, 1815–1914* (1969).

The general survey for foreign affairs is still R. W. Seton-Watson, *Britain in Europe, 1789–1914* (1937; 2nd edn, 1955). Three more recent general books are indispensable: A. J. P. Taylor, *The Trouble-makers. Dissent over Foreign Policy, 1792–1939* (1957), both entertaining and remunerative, and two collections of documents, J. B. Joll, *Britain and Europe: Pitt to Churchill, 1793–1940* (1950), and K. Bourne, *The Foreign Policy of Victorian England, 1830–1902* (1970).

Of the vexed issues of imperialism consult D. K. Fieldhouse, *The Theory of Capitalist Imperialism* (1967).

The most adequate general surveys of political thought are still Ernest Barker, *Political Thought in England from 1848 to 1914* (2nd edn, 1950) and Crane Brinton, *English Political Thought in the Nineteenth Century* (2nd edn, 1949).

On cultural history the best introductory guides are R. Williams, *Culture and Society, 1780–1950* (1958), J. Holloway, *The Victorian Sage* (1953) and M. S. Bradbury, *The Social Context of Modern English Literature* (1971).

NOTES

Introduction

1 P. Deane and W. H. Cole, *British Economic Growth 1688–1959* (1962), 282.

Chapter One

1 Palmerston, as a viscount of the Peerage of Ireland, could sit for a non-Irish constituency in the House of Commons: he was a member for Tiverton in Devon.

2 All statements of economic estimates are derived from Deane and Cole, *British Economic Growth 1688–1959* (1959).

3 Baxter's estimates are conveniently abstracted by H. Perkin, *The Origins of Modern English Society, 1780–1880* (1969), 420.

Chapter Three

1 D. C. Moore, 'Political Morality in Mid-Nineteenth Century England: Concepts, Norms, Violations', *Victorian Studies*, xxiii (1969), 29–30.

2 F. B. Smith, *The Making of the Second Reform Bill* (1966), 132.

3 Adullam was the cave where the opponents of Saul joined the exiled David: I Samuel xxii, 1–2.

4 Smith, *The Making of the Second Reform Bill*, 217.

5 E.g. Paul Smith, *Disraelian Conservatism and Social Reform* (1967).

6 Shaftesbury's son, Palmerston's nephew and secretary and biographer, Liberal M.P. 1874–85.

7 W. L. Guttsman, *The British Political Élite* (1963), 181.

Chapter Four

[1] Anglicans, 11 per cent; Roman Catholics, 78 per cent; Protestant dissenters (mainly Presbyterian), 9 per cent. Emigration reduced the Catholic proportion to 74 per cent by 1911.

[2] G. A. Craig, *The Battle of Königgrätz* (1964), 184.

[3] This was actually officially formulated as a basis of policy in the 'Stanhope Memorandum' of 1891 by E. Stanhope, Secretary for War 1887–92 in Salisbury's second cabinet.

[4] Scotland and Ireland had their own distinctive systems of elementary education. The Scottish system was still based essentially on the Act of 1696, providing for a school supported by the rates in every parish. Reform and extension involved no great problems. The case of Ireland was very different. Irish elementary education was based throughout the nineteenth century on the Act of 1831, which attempted to bypass denominational differences. In this it failed. By the end of the century only 2 per cent of Catholic children attended schools in which any of the teachers were non-Catholic. The Irish Catholic illiteracy rate was 16·4% in 1901: twice that of Anglicans and more than three times that of other Protestants.

[5] A French term coming at that time into currency in Britain.

[6] Anglican: 11,777 schools, 1,885,802 children; Wesleyan: 458 schools, 125,727 children; Roman Catholic: 1,045 schools, 255,036 children; other: 1,079 schools, 220,032 children.

Chapter Five

[1] These things are, of course, relative: Cross was educated at Rugby and Trinity, Cambridge. Ostensibly he was no more 'middle class' than Disraeli himself. The difference was that Cross took no pains to camouflage himself.

[2] Smith, *Disraelian Conservatism and Social Reform*, 199.

[3] H. Pelling, *Popular Politics and Society in Late Victorian Britain* (1968), especially 'The Working Class and The Origins of the Welfare State', puts the case for a very slow and late development of social reform consciousness among the working classes.

[4] S. B. Saul, *The Myth of the Great Depression, 1873–1896* (1969) lists conveniently the literature of the debate.

[5] This was about the average of the previous five years.

[6] P. W. Clayden, *England under Lord Beaconsfield* (1880), 539.

Chapter Six

1 His eccentricities included mild kleptomania. E. A. Freeman used always to refer to him (in Greek) as 'the Spoonstealer'.

2 M. MacColl, *Three Years of the Eastern Question* (1878), 38.

3 Constantinople, Istanbul.

4 Now Plovdiv.

5 Bulwer, a particular protégé of Palmerston, was ambassador at Constantinople from 1858 to 1865. Cr. Lord Dalling, 1871.

6 E.g., R. W. Seton Watson, *Disraeli, Gladstone and the Eastern Question, 1875–1880* (1935), 103.

7 'We don't want to fight;/But by Jingo, if we do,
We've got the men, we've got the ships,/We've got the money too'.

8 The Afrikander Bond was founded in 1879, with Hofmeyr in the Cape as its major influence, designed to eliminate the interference of the British government.

9 Income tax was 2*d*. in the £ at £100 exempt in 1874; from 1876–8 it was 3*d*. at £150 exempt; 1878–80 it was up to 5*d*.

10 A Liberal had in fact won it in 1868.

Chapter Seven

1 In 1880 Gladstone apologized for his own action in 1874, pleading special circumstances, and specifically repudiated any desire for novel procedures and hoped that in future the 'old method of the Constitution' would henceforth be adhered to. See H. J. Hanham, *The Nineteenth Century Constitution* (1969), 123–4.

2 Under-Secretary of State for Foreign Affairs, 1880; president of the local government board in the cabinet, 1882.

3 W. S. Gilbert, *The Pirates of Penzance*.

4 Captain Charles Boycott was Lord Erne's agent in County Mayo.

5 The generic name for Europeans in the Levant.

6 On this theme generally see R. Robinson and J. Gallagher, *Africa and the Victorians* (1963).

7 Robinson and Gallagher, *Africa and the Victorians*, 59.

8 D. M. Schreuder, *Gladstone and Kruger* (1969), 472 ff.

Chapter Eight

1 'Temperance' was the word applied generally to the movement trying by various means to reduce the consumption of alcoholic

drink. Strictly, 'temperance' involved the ideal of 'moderation' in liquor consumption as against the total abstinence or 'teetotal' section of the movement. There were, broadly, two main sides to it: the 'moral suasionists', who warned people off drink, and those who, led by the United Kingdom Alliance for the Suppression of Traffic in all Intoxicating Liquors (founded in Manchester in 1853), argued that the attack must be made at the production end rather than at the consumption end. Thus the Alliance was the most direct and dangerous enemy of the 'Trade'. The movement was most successful in its propaganda with children: the Band of Hope Union by 1889 had 16,000 societies throughout the U.K. with a membership of two million. About two-thirds of Nonconformist ministers and one-third of the Anglican clergy were pledged abstainers at the height of the temperance movement's prestige in the 1870s and 1880s. Despite its internal disputes it was a formidable and aggressive political interest.

² Acts passed in the 1860s to regulate prostitution in garrison and dockyard towns. An attempt to extend the system of compulsory licensing and medical inspection of prostitutes to the country at large provoked a counter-agitation to repeal the original Acts as condoning immorality, as being oppressive to prostitutes, and above all as conflicting with the principle of equal rights for women by giving legislative recognition to different standards of morality for men and women. Stansfeld abandoned his regular political career to lead this cause finally to success in 1886.

³ One Arthur Orton, a butcher's son from Wapping, claimed to be Roger Tichborne, who disappeared in South America in 1854, and thus rightful possessor of the wealthy Tichborne estates. The Dowager Lady Tichborne, who was French and who disliked her family-in-law, recognized Orton as her son. Two trials in the High Court between 1871 and 1874 made it a *cause célèbre*. Orton and his counsel, Dr Kenealy, became popular heroes. Kenealy, disbarred in 1874, was elected M.P. for Stoke-on-Trent, 1875–80. Orton was imprisoned for perjury, 1874–84. The case led many anxious Liberals to doubt the capacity of the working classes for sustained intelligent interest in serious public affairs.

⁴ Clayden, *England Under Lord Beaconsfield*, 542.

⁵ D. A. Hamer, *John Morley, Liberal Intellectual in Politics* (1968), 119 ff.

⁶ The Third Party being of course the Irish.

⁷ C. F. G. Masterman, 'Realities at Home' from *The Heart of the Empire* (1901).

8 He was first elected to parliament in 1832.

9 Sir Courtenay Ilbert (1841–1924), law member of Ripon's council in India, 1882–6, proposed in a Criminal Jurisdiction Bill to extend the criminal jurisdiction of Indian magistrates over Europeans in the Presidency towns to the country as a whole. A modified version of the bill was enacted in 1883. The outcry against the proposed concession in both India and Britain became a classical source of propaganda for the nascent Indian nationalist movement.

10 Liberals, 333; Conservatives, 251; Parnellites, 86.

11 This increasingly acrimonious relationship was dissolved in 1905.

12 By 1887 the League had over 500,000 members, by 1900 about 1,500,000. Queen Victoria had sent a wreath of primroses to Beaconsfield's funeral in 1881, with a note that they were his favourite flower.

Chapter Nine

1 ' "Locksley Hall" and the Jubilee', *Nineteenth Century*, xxi (1887).

2 For this latter argument, and a review of the general debate, see C. Wilson, 'Economy and Society in Late Victorian Britain', *Economic History Review*, Vol. 18 (1965). See also S. B. Saul, *The Myth of the Great Depression* (1969).

3 Consult, as well as Saul and Wilson cited above, R. S. Sayers, *A History of Economic Change in England, 1880–1939* (1967), S. B. Saul, *Technological Change: The United States and Britain in the 19th Century* (1970), and E. J. Hobsbawm, *Industry and Empire* (1968).

4 The best general introduction to the debate on this issue is D. K. Fieldhouse, *The Theory of Capitalist Imperialism* (1967).

5 Adult male literacy was 69 per cent in England and 89 per cent in Scotland in 1850; 96 per cent in England and 98 per cent in Scotland by 1900.

Chapter Ten

1 The aesthetic anti-hero of the Gilbert and Sullivan comic opera *Patience* (1881). D. G. Rossetti was the principal inspiration. The young Oscar Wilde was doing his best to live up to it.

2 This was an attempt to improve the Conservative Local Government Act of 1888 by setting up democratically elected authorities beneath the County Council level. Radicals had long yearned to re-establish the Anglo-Saxon hundredmote as the basis of a general re-establishment of Anglo-Saxon liberties.

Chapter Eleven

[1] Salisbury 1885–6, Rosebery 1886, Iddesleigh (Stafford Northcote) 1886–7, Salisbury 1887–92, Rosebery 1892–4, Kimberley 1894–5.

[2] One of Rosebery's first acts on becoming prime minister in 1894 was to knight Seeley.

[3] A member of a morganatic branch of the grand-ducal House of Hesse-Darmstadt, later notable for their successful matrimonial connections with the British royal House. One of them from this springboard even became Queen of Spain.

Chapter Twelve

[1] On this theme see J. Summerson, *Victorian Architecture* (1970).

Chapter Thirteen

[1] There were 173 science departments in elementary schools in 1891; 1,396 by 1895.

[2] By 1905–6 Britain was expending £115,000; Prussia, £588,000.

[3] In Wales most elementary schools were church schools, the spearhead of the policy of anglicization in the nineteenth century. Lloyd George himself was educated in one.

[4] Gerald Balfour, Salisbury's nephew and Balfour's brother, went to the Board of Trade. Salisbury's son-in-law Selborne went to the Admiralty. Salisbury's son Cranborne became Under-Secretary at the Foreign Office.

[5] In 1880, 1886 and 1887 (after Churchill's resignation).

Chapter Fourteen

[1] That is, of white population. The blacks would be witnesses of, not participants in, the transactions decisive for South Africa's future, whichever side won.

[2] G. H. L. LeMay, *British Supremacy in South Africa, 1899–1907* (1965), 35.

[3] Estimates after the war were that the Afrikaners put between 60,000 and 70,000 men in the field, including old men and boys and a considerable number of Cape Dutch.

⁴ Dust-coloured military field dress was introduced into the British service after the Egyptian campaign of 1882 to replace the traditional but inconvenient scarlet.

Chapter Fifteen

¹ Cotton exports were 51 per cent of British exports in 1830; 36 per cent in 1870; 24 per cent in 1910.

Chapter Sixteen

¹ E.g., P. Rowland, *The Last Liberal Governments. The Promised Land, 1905–1910* (1968), 234–5.

² B. B. Gilbert, *The Evolution of National Insurance in Great Britain. The Origins of the Welfare State* (1966), 156.

³ These efforts resulted in retaining under the British Crown the protectorates of Basutoland (Lesotho), Swaziland (formerly a Transvaal protectorate) and Bechuanaland (Botswana).

⁴ The rationale of this was that the Lords as a whole thereby would retreat from involvement in controversial political matters in the way they had retreated from their judicial functions, leaving their exercise to a specialized minority.

⁵ In England and Wales there was one constituency to every 74,500 of population; in Scotland a constituency to every 60,500 of population; in Ireland a constituency to every 40,000 of population.

Chapter Seventeen

¹ For a list of occasions of bad information, see G. Monger, *The End of Isolation* (1963), 307–8.

² J. A. Hobson, their principal intellectual inspiration, published a study of Cobden in 1919: *Richard Cobden, the International Man.*

³ To give an idea of comparative 'front line' infantry complements on a peace footing, the German pre-war military organization was based on 19 Prussian, 3 Bavarian, 2 Saxon and 1 Wurtemburg corps: 647 battalions. French strength was 21 corps, comprising (including colonial contingents) 578 battalions. The Austro-Hungarian Common Army of 16 corps comprised 467 battalions. The Russians disposed 1,016 battalions in 27 corps in Europe.

⁴ The beautiful Italianate villa of the Austrian ambassador at St Petersburg, Count Leopold Berchtold.

⁵ In 1910 Hardinge replaced Minto as Viceroy of India.

⁶ E. Halévy, *A History of the English People in the Nineteenth Century, VI, The Rule of Democracy* (1943), 7.

Chapter Eighteen

¹ The two parties were formally united in May 1912 as the Conservative and Unionist Party.

² This was an historical allusion to the Solemn League and Covenant drawn up by the Scots in 1638 to defend Presbyterianism.

³ Isaacs, Lloyd George and Elibank speculated in shares of the American Marconi Company which was associated with the English Marconi Company, which had a contract with the British government to provide a system of wireless telegraphic communications stipulated by the Imperial Conference of 1911. Godfrey Isaacs, Rufus's brother, was managing director of the English company.

⁴ Nephew of the great field-marshal of 1866 and 1870–71.

⁵ Much the fullest and most reliable account of the Gallipoli adventure is in M. Gilbert, *Winston S. Churchill* III (1971).

⁶ On this theme generally see C. Hazlehurst, *Politicians at War* III (1971).

INDEX

3509